Knowledge, Organization, and Management

"Max Boisot's key message has lost none of its topicality and importance: the form and communication of knowledge lie at the heart of human social organization. This book provides an excellent discussion of the challenges and opportunities involved—be they the cultural and institutional differences of systems or the complexity of today's (organizational) world."

Gilbert Probst, Managing Director, World Economic Forum, and Professor for Organizational Behavior and Management, University of Geneva, Switzerland

"For those of us who had the pleasure of knowing Max Boisot, he was one of the most creative and original of people. He had an extraordinary ability to understand how things were actually working and to create an image of how they could be changed. He not only had a powerful imagination, but also was deeply grounded in pragmatism. This book is a splendid tribute to a remarkable man. A real visionary."

Nicholas Stern, IG Patel Professor of Economics & Government at the London School of Economics, President of the British Academy, and ex-Chief Economist of the World Bank

"Max Boisot was a deep thinker whose interest in knowledge enabled him to make important contributions to many areas. In this volume, Child and Ihrig bring together Boisot's pathbreaking articles, and combine them with thoughtful appreciations by those who knew him best. The result is a worthy tribute to Boisot's legacy, and a wonderful way to introduce his thinking to a new generation of scholars."

Henry Chesbrough, Faculty Director, Garwood Center for Corporate Innovation, Haas School of Business, UC Berkeley, and Esade Business School, Ramon Llul University

"Boisot's deep insights are brilliantly unpacked and situated, both socially and epistemologically, in this superb collection. Given that nearly every economy is now being disrupted, his I-Space adds timely insights to how to move beyond simplistic analyses to ones that honor the embedded nature of the tacit."

John Seely Brown, Former Chief Scientist of Xerox Corp and Director of Xerox PARC

"Max Boisot's lucid explanations of the workings of the knowledge economy profoundly changed my perspective on strategy. He was years ahead of most of us in explaining why periods of maximum value are so fragile and why we need an entirely new logic for business—one that emphasizes sharing and speed—if our organizations are to be successful. In the knowledge economy, hoping to hide behind entry barriers is futile. As this excellent book demonstrates, Max showed us all an alternative."

Rita Gunther McGrath, Associate Professor, Columbia Business School

Max Boisot, Montpelier, 2010. Photograph by Dorota Boisot.

Knowledge, Organization, and Management

Building on the Work of Max Boisot

Edited by
John Child
and
Martin Ihrig

UNIVERSITY PRESS

Great Clarendon Street, Oxford, OX2 6DP,
United Kingdom

Oxford University Press is a department of the University of Oxford.
It furthers the University's objective of excellence in research, scholarship,
and education by publishing worldwide. Oxford is a registered trade mark of
Oxford University Press in the UK and in certain other countries

© Oxford University Press, 2013, except Chapter 2, 8, and 10

The moral rights of the authors have been asserted

First Edition published in 2013

Impression: 1

All rights reserved. No part of this publication may be reproduced, stored in
a retrieval system, or transmitted, in any form or by any means, without the
prior permission in writing of Oxford University Press, or as expressly permitted
by law, by licence or under terms agreed with the appropriate reprographics
rights organization. Enquiries concerning reproduction outside the scope of the
above should be sent to the Rights Department, Oxford University Press, at the
address above

You must not circulate this work in any other form
and you must impose this same condition on any acquirer

British Library Cataloguing in Publication Data

Data available

ISBN 978–0–19–966916–5

Printed in Great Britain by
CPI Group (UK) Ltd, Croydon, CR0 4YY

Links to third party websites are provided by Oxford in good faith and
for information only. Oxford disclaims any responsibility for the materials
contained in any third party website referenced in this work.

To all those like Max Boisot who willingly share knowledge rather than hoard it.

Foreword

Glimpsing an Unknowable Future

Stuart Kauffman

In a wonderful, mere ten days, I met Max and fell in love with his humanity and mind. As it happened, I was at CERN conspiring with Markus Nordberg to link efforts in studying the origin of life, an old passion, with CERN, focused on physics. I again, thank Markus.

Max, in a blizzard of wisdom and intuition, and I in a blizzard of confusion, explored new territory that lay between us. This territory is the subject of this Foreword. I believe Max would approve of what I write below, for he, more rapidly than any I have met, listened to my own thoughts and built upon them in ways that, we both felt, might expand his life work.

At root, as this book amply demonstrates, Max was profoundly interested in knowledge and its effective sharing. Perhaps the latest full formulation of his ideas are in his *I-Space*, augmented with real life and knowledge options, as discussed in the book co-authored by Markus Nordberg and Max. It is a superb book. I ventured, in the small blurb I felt honored to write for that book, that Markus and Max spoke not just of big science, but of a starting pattern of thinking about how a world civilization of our 30 civilizations might weave together fruitfully, leaving the ancient, hence near-sacred, roots of each intact, but allowing us to jointly co-create what we will become. The ways CERN is finding to co-discover in its efforts to explore an unknown, is deeply like what we face in the twenty-first century. We too face Mystery, a major theme Max and I discussed in our few, fine, days together.

I miss him.

The world seen as a statable complex combinatorial optimization problem

As Max and I probed this issue, we realized that we usually begin with a mistaken belief. We begin with the presumption that we know all the relevant variables bearing upon some problem. Moreover, we know either the single "success criterion" or the figure of merit, or in a more complex but well understood case, we have multiple success criteria, but do not know their relative importance.

Consider a single figure of merit. Then over a discrete or continuous space of behaviors, strategies, actions, we can think of the success of each of these, shown by the figure of merit, as a height. This yields a payoff, or fitness landscape over the strategy space. If it is fixed in time, this fitness landscape may be flat, may have a single, Fujiyama-like peak which is also therefore the global optimum, or may have many peaks of different heights. In fact, the number of peaks can be exponential in the dimensionality of the space, that is in the number of different strategies. In the latter case, finding the global optimum is exponentially hard: Pretty much the entire space must be searched to find the global optimum.

A large literature, growing out of "spin glasses" in physics, with their complex Potential Landscapes, where low energy is "good", and their cousin, NK fitness landscapes, exists. Search on these more or less rugged landscapes is quite well understood now by a variety of search techniques including simulated annealing, the genetic algorithm, and others. The "No Free Lunch" theorem asserts that, averaged over all possible fitness landscapes, no search procedure outperforms, on average, any other. In short, we need to know something about the landscape itself to search it wisely. This raises the new, still only partially explored issue of learning the landscape's structure as we search it.

In the more complex case of multiple incommensurate success criteria, the solution concept that is widely accepted is Global Pareto Optimality. A Pareto optimal point on a, say, continuous strategy space, is one in which no move can improve one fitness criterion without making another worse. Global Pareto optimal points are those that are both Pareto Optimal and maximize all the different success criteria simultaneously. Again a large literature exists on this topic.

Options

In Max Boisot's *I-Space* and the Boisot-Nordberg book about big science, the concept of options plays a major role. Small, competing yet collaborating work groups, in face of an overall goal, but, critically, facing unknown physics, seek to find good pathways. In this effort, options for future actions and search pathways plays a major role. This is very wise. But it is deeply hampered by an essential feature. Consider options on the stock market. Given the famous ITO equation, one can price options, which has driven us to complex financial instruments. But pricing options demands that we know the probability distribution of future events, as in the ITO calculus. In turn, this demands that we know the SAMPLE SPACE OF THE PROCESS.

Sometimes we do know the sample space of the process so can "sensibly" calculate the value of options, financial and real life.

But as Taleb and others point out, sometimes we do not know the sample space, or cannot learn it. For example, if the true sample space is given by a power law distribution with a slope less than minus 1, that distribution has neither a mean nor a variance. So no sampling will tell us the "real" sample process.

Can we always prestate the relevant variables?

I now come to one of the major points Max and I discussed with a mixture of awe and awareness for its potential implications: In the evolution of science, for example, CERN's work, and in the evolution of the biosphere, the econosphere and culture, we cannot, I urged upon Max, always prestate the variables that will BECOME relevant.

I give a simple example from economic evolution. When Turing invented the Turing machine, its invention enabled von Neuman to invent the digital mainframe computer. Thomas Watson Sr. of IBM thought there would be a market for three of these, invented to calculate shell trajectories in naval battles in WWII, in the Eniac. Watson was wrong. Now the wide sale of mainframe computers created a market that did not CAUSE but did ENABLE, i.e. make possible, the invention by Jobs and others of the personal computer. The wide sale of the personal computer created the market that did not cause, but enabled, the invention by many including Microsoft, of word processing. The wide sale of word processing enabled sharing of files. The sharing of files enabled CERN scientist to invent the beginnings of the World Wide Web. The Web, once in place, did not cause, but enabled, selling things on the Web, and Amazon and eBay emerged. The emergence of content on the Web enabled a market for web browsers and Yahoo and Google grew. With them, came Facebook and LinkedIn.

We have all lived much of this IT revolution. Do any of us think Turing could have foreseen Facebook or Google? No. More, these newly relevant features of contemporary economic and social life arose with no one's INTENT.

In short, in the evolution of the econosphere, we CANNOT PRESTATE THE VARIABLES WHICH WILL BECOME RELEVANT. This has very large implications that Max and I glimpsed. First, we do not know the sample space. Knowing the sample space of a process means that we know what CAN happen but do not know what WILL happen, like flipping a coin 10,000 times. We know all possible outcomes, but do not know if we will get 5460 heads. Knowing the sample space and using the binomial theorem, we can calculate the probabilities of 5460 heads.

But if we do not know the sample space, not only do we not know what WILL happen, we do not even know what CAN happen. Then REASON, the highest human virtue of the ancient Greeks and our beloved Enlightenment, cannot be a sufficient guide to living our lives forward, for we must act without knowing what CAN happen.

In turn, this means we cannot "price options", as Max would wish us to do in the case of CERN strategies for learning in the face of unknown physics Mystery. Who could calculate Einstein's probability of success inventing General Relativity?

The problem above is deep and even deeper. Since losing Max, my colleagues, Giuseppe Longo and Mael Montevil, French mathematicians at the Ecole Polytechnique, Paris, and I, have published, "No entailing laws, but enablement in the evolution of the biopsphere," online posted Physics ArXhiv Jan 11, 2012, and in press, GECCO conference, (1,2). We think we have shown that this is the end of the reductionist world view at the watershed of evolving life. No law, we claim, and you can read the above article should you wish, entails in a Newton-like or even Schrodinger-like way, the evolution of the biopshere or, a fortiori, the economy or culture. We arise beyond entailing law, and beyond knowing what CAN happen.

More, with no selection, the evolving biosphere creates its own possibilities for becoming. In parallel, the evolving econosphere, Turing to Facebook, creates, often with no intent or foresight, its own opportunities for evolving further.

But if this is so, then the knowledge CREATION and management and dissemination that was the life work of Max Boisot, needs unknown extension. Again, Max and I glimpsed all this in our magical ten days together, with croissant and cafe au lait at CERN. How I wish he were still with us.

For this means, for science, and for humanity evolving, that we co-create without the capacity to prestate in many cases, the opportunities, the Adjacent Possibles, into which we become. We must live "Well Discovered Lives," not knowing ahead of time what we will co-create with one another.

If the above is true, as I think it is, CERN is a "small" but critical example of how we live with and find our way in the face of Mystery, here is unknown physics where we cannot calculate the value of the options of which Max wrote.

But this is real life. We do live, all the time, not knowing what we will co-create. This suggests something like "wise enablement," perhaps indeed along the lines of *I-Space* and CERN as an early and now studied example, of how to do this well. So, too, the evolution of English Common Law, inventing its way around a framework of ancient precedent which serves as its skeleton for variations that allow it to evolve as the world invents itself ever anew.

Max loved the glimpses. The above is at most a glimpse. His life was dedicated to open exploration of how we may do all this well. Bless you Max Boisot.

Acknowledgements

This work was partially funded by the TEKES Foundation of my Finland Distinguished Professorship.

Acknowledgements

The process which led to the production of this book originated a few days after Max Boisot's untimely death in September 2011. The shock of Max's death gave rise to an outpouring of sorrow and appreciation of the man and his work, as witnessed by many communications both on-line and off-line. As Max's close colleagues and friends, both of us were stunned and shared this sense of deep loss. So when Chris Mabey sent us an email suggesting that "we might collect together some record of Max's achievements, memories of his life and personality," we quickly took up the idea of editing a collection of Max's papers accompanied by commentaries on his life and work.

The book would not have been possible without its various contributors who all responded to the opportunity to join it with an enthusiasm that itself is a tribute to the regard in which they held Max Boisot as a scholar, colleague, and friend. The writers of commentaries and reflections are acknowledged in the relevant headings, but we should like to thank them all here as well. Others also contributed to this book through the interviews they generously gave—Derong Chen, Barry Dornfeld, Yuan Lu, Chris Mabey, and Ian MacMillan. We also appreciate Stuart Kauffman's deeply insightful Foreword which he provided at a difficult time.

We have benefitted from the valuable advice and input offered by Liliana Petrella of EFMD, Anne Tsui, past-President of the Academy of Management, Graham Leicester of the International Futures Forum, and the anonymous reviewers of our book proposal. We were touched and inspired by the moving obituary that David Snowden wrote for Max in the Cognitive Edge Network blog.

David Musson of Oxford University Press has given unfailing support to the concept and then the materialization of this book from start to finish. Having published many of Max's books, David has a deep appreciation of his work as well as being one of Max's many personal friends. Emma Booth at OUP ensured the smooth passage of the book into production and made our lives much easier.

Special thanks also go to Wolfgang Güttel who co-organized two memorable and well-attended sessions on "Remembering Max Boisot" and "Building on the Work of Max Boisot" at the 2012 Colloquium of EGOS (The European

Acknowledgements

Group for Organizational Studies). These sessions brought together some of the contributors to this book, as well as other colleagues and friends of Max, and they helped to inform many points of relevance.

Following these two sessions, the EGOS board decided to establish an annual "EGOS Award in Honour of Max Boisot." This award is supported from the royalties accruing from this book. Max was a regular participant in EGOS Colloquia, and EGOS is therefore the ideal home for it. The award is intended to be both a memorial to Max Boisot's work and a means of encouraging further contributions to his field of scholarship. The topic for the award is the knowledge-based study of complex organizations and systems. Contributions in any of the main areas in which Max forged new understanding through a knowledge perspective are eligible for the award. Further information on the award is available on the EGOS website (www.egosnet.org). We are grateful for the considerable advice and support that members of the EGOS Board gave in the creation of the award.

As well as being compiled for Max, and for the readers who cannot fail to benefit from a greater appreciation of the man and his work, this book is also for Max's family, in particular Dorota Boisot. Despite facing the many burdens of grief and rebuilding a life, Dorota has in so many ways supported our efforts with encouragement and insights that have made all the difference.

John Child	Martin Ihrig
Universities of Birmingham and Plymouth	University of Pennsylvania

Permission Acknowledgements

Chapter 2: Originally published as Max Boisot and John Child (1996). "From Fiefs to Clans and Network Capitalism: Explaining China's Emerging Economic Order." *Administrative Science Quarterly*, 41 (4): 600–628. Reprinted with kind permission of SAGE Publications Inc.

Chapter 6: Originally published as Max Boisot (2002). "The Creation and Sharing of Knowledge." In C. W. Choo and N. Bontis (eds), *The Strategic Management of Intellectual Capital and Organizational Knowledge*, 65–77 © 2002 by Oxford University Press, Inc. By permission of Oxford University Press, USA.

Chapter 8: Originally published as Max Boisot (2011). "Generating Knowledge in a Connected World: The Case of the ATLAS Experiment at CERN", *Management Learning*, 42 (4): 447–457. Reprinted with kind permission of SAGE Publications Ltd.

Chapter 10: Originally published as Max Boisot and Michel Fiol (1987). "Chinese Boxes and Learning Cubes: Action Learning in a Cross-Cultural Context." *Journal of Management Development*, 6 (2): 8–18. Reprinted with kind permission of Emerald Insight.

Contents

List of Figures xxi
List of Tables xxiii
Contributors xxiv

I. Setting the Stage

1. Max Boisot and the Dynamic Evolution of Knowledge 3
   Martin Ihrig and John Child

II. Analyses of the Chinese System

2. From Fiefs to Clans and Network Capitalism: Explaining China's Emerging Economic Order 19
   Max Boisot and John Child

3. Analyses of the Chinese System 49
   John Child

III. Organizational Complexity

4. Extreme Outcomes, Connectivity, and Power Laws: Towards an Econophysics of Organization 61
   Max Boisot and Bill McKelvey

5. Reflecting on Max Boisot's *Ashby Space* Applied to Complexity Management 93
   Bill McKelvey

IV. The Strategic Management of Knowledge

6. The Creation and Sharing of Knowledge 109
   Max Boisot

7. The Strategic Management of Knowledge 129
   Martin Ihrig and Ian MacMillan

Contents

V. Knowledge in Big Science

8. Generating Knowledge in a Connected World: The Case of the ATLAS Experiment at CERN — 143
   Max Boisot

9. Knowledge in Big Science — 155
   Agustí Canals

VI. Innovations in Education

10. Chinese Boxes and Learning Cubes: Action Learning in a Cross-Cultural Context — 169
    Max Boisot and Michel Fiol

11. Innovations in Education — 181
    Dana Kaminstein and John Child

VII. Concluding Reflections

12. The *I-Space* as a Key to History and to Culture — 199
    Gordon Redding

13. The Three Phases of Max Boisot's Theorizing — 205
    John-Christopher Spender

14. Writing with Max Boisot — 213
    Marshall Meyer

15. Remembering Max Boisot: Recollections of a Gifted Intellect at Work — 221
    Ron Sanchez

16. *I-Space* and the Value of Basic Research — 229
    Markus Nordberg

17. Boisot and the God Particle — 237
    Marzio Nessi

18. Conclusion and Outlook — 241
    John Child and Martin Ihrig

    Bibliography — 249
    Index — 275

List of Figures

1.1	The Information-Space and the paradox of value	4
1.2	The Social Learning Cycle	5
1.3	Institutions and cultures in the *I-Space*	6
2.1	Institutions in the C-Space	22
2.2	Transactional environments created by information codification and diffusion	22
2.3	Chinese and Western paths to modernization	44
4.1	First, second, and third phases of complexity science	64
4.2	Stylized Pareto distribution on log-log scale	68
4.3	The Ashby Space	73
4.4	Three regimes in the Ashby Space	76
4.5	Three schema judgments in the Ashby Space	78
4.6	The pattern processing challenge	81
5.1	Example Pareto Distribution and PL distribution	101
5.2	Stylized Pareto distribution on log-log scales	102
6.1	The codification-diffusion-abstraction curve in the *I-Space*	122
6.2	The six steps of a social learning cycle	123
6.3	Maximum value (MV) in the *I-Space*	126
8.1	The Information-Space (*I-Space*)	145
8.2	Institutions and cultures in the *I-Space*	146
8.3	Ordered, complex, and chaotic regimes in the *I-Space*	147
8.4	The impact of ICTs in the *I-Space*	148
8.5	The ATLAS performance spidergraph	149
8.6	The organization of the ATLAS collaboration	150
8.7	Adhocracies and boundary objects	153
9.1	The agent-in-the-world (Boisot and Canals 2004)	158
9.2	Institutions and cultures in the *I-Space*	163
9.3	Cultures and institutional structures	163

List of Figures

10.1	The three dimensions of learning	172
10.2	The Learning Cube	172
10.3	The traditional Chinese view of technology transfer	175
10.4	The CEMP approach to technology transfer	175
11.1	Types of knowledge identified by the *I-Space*	183

List of Tables

2.1	Classification of Chinese enterprises	30
4.1	Empirical basis of scale-free causes of Power Laws	68
4.2	Relation of dots to links and to patterns	80
6.1	The six phases of the Social Learning Cycle	124
8.1	Cultures in the *I-Space*	146

Contributors

Agustí Canals is Associate Professor of Knowledge Management at the UOC in Barcelona, where he leads the KIMO Research Group on Knowledge and Information Management in Organizations. He is also Lecturer in Strategy at the ESADE Business School (Barcelona) and Senior Research Fellow at the *I-Space* Institute (Philadelphia, PA). He has a PhD in Management Sciences and MBA (ESADE Business School) and MSc in Physics (Universitat Autònoma de Barcelona). His current research interests are the strategic management of knowledge, big science organizations, knowledge networks and organizational complexity.

John Child is Emeritus Professor of Commerce at the University of Birmingham, UK and Professor of Management at the University of Plymouth. He is a Fellow of the Academy of Management, the Academy of International Business and the British Academy of Management. In 2006, he was elected a Fellow of the prestigious British Academy (FBA). Professor Child has published 21 books and approximately 150 articles primarily in the fields of international business and business organization. He has been editor-in-chief of Organization Studies and Senior Editor of Management and Organization Review.

Martin Ihrig is President of *I-Space Institute, LLC* (USA), an Adjunct Assistant Professor at *Wharton* and a Senior Fellow at the *University of Pennsylvania's Graduate School of Education* (USA), and a Visiting Professor at *Lappeenranta University of Technology* (Finland). He conducts research in and consults on the strategic and entrepreneurial management of knowledge (SEM-K) and directs the SEM-K research initiative at Wharton's *Snider Entrepreneurial Research Center*. In developing strategy tools for corporate and public-sector decision makers, Dr. Ihrig has worked with organizations such as *BAE Systems* (USA), *The Boeing Company* (USA), and *Vale* (Brazil). His research projects have been funded by *The Economic & Social Research Council* (UK), *The ATLAS Collaboration at CERN* (Switzerland), and *Tekes* (Finland).

Dana Kaminstein, primary affiliation is with the University of Pennsylvania. He is an Affiliated Faculty with the Organizational Dynamics Graduate Studies Program in the School of Arts, and also teaches in the Mid-Career Doctoral Program at the Graduate School of Education. He is a Fellow at the Aresty Institute, Wharton Executive Education, The Wharton School. Dr. Kaminstein also maintains a private consulting practice. His areas of expertise are: organizational diagnosis, groups and teams, and leadership development.

Contributors

Stuart Kauffman is a well-known theoretical biologist with interests in physics, economics, and philosophy. He has done fundamental work founding aspects of Complexity Theory, Systems Biology, aspects of the Origin of Life, rugged "fitness landscapes" and most recently work on quantum aspects of the mind brain system, with G. Longo on an end to reductionism at the watershed of evolving life. He has published over 250 papers, four books, is a MacArthur Fellow and Fellow of the Royal Society of Canada.

Ian C. MacMillan is the Dhirubhai Ambani Professor of Entrepreneurial Management at the Wharton School, University of Pennsylvania and the Academic Director of the Sol C. Snider Entrepreneurial Center. Formerly, he was Director of the Entrepreneurship center at NYU and taught at Columbia and Northwestern Universities and the University of South Africa. Prior to joining the academic world, MacMillan was a chemical engineer. He has also been a director of several companies in the travel, import/export and pharmaceutical industries, and has extensive international consulting experience. He has published articles in ASQ, AMJ, SMJ and HBR and books on new ventures, innovation, organizational politics and strategy formulation.

Bill McKelvey is UCLA Professor Emeritus of Complexity Science & Econophysics. His book, *Organizational Systematics* (1982) remains the definitive treatment of organizational taxonomy and evolution. He oversaw the building of the Anderson Complex (1983–1993). In 1997 he co-founded UCLA's Center for Human Complex Systems. He co-edited *Variations in Organization Science* (1999). He co-edited *SAGE Handbook of Complexity and Management* (2011); Editor of *Routledge Major Work: Complexity Concepts* (2012; 5-volumes). He has 70+ publications applying complexity science to organizations and management since 1997.

Marshall Meyer is the Tsai Wan-Tsai Professor in the Wharton School of the University of Pennsylvania, where he is also Professor of Management, Professor of Sociology, and Associate Member of the Center for East Asian Studies. His research interests include management in China, the measurement of organizational performance, organizational change, and organizational design. He holds both a PhD and an MA from the University of Chicago. He is widely published in leading journals and has written several books.

Marzio Nessi is Professor of Physics at the University of Geneva and CERN ATLAS Technical Director. He graduated from ETH Zurich, with a PhD in Particle Physics. He has been active in teaching and basic research at ETHZ and at Rice University with experiments at all major European and US laboratories. He is an expert in hadron physics, first as a member of the UA2 experiment, and then at the LHC collider, where he was among the founding fathers of the LHC-ATLAS project, which he lead as overall Project Manager since 1999.

Markus Nordberg is the Resources Coordinator of the ATLAS project at CERN, Switzerland, where his responsibilities include budget planning and resources allocation for the ATLAS project. He has also served as Visiting Senior Research Fellow at the Centrum voor Bedrijfseconomie, Faculty ESP-Solvay Business School, University of Brussels, and as a member of the Academy of Management, Strategic Management

Contributors

Society and the Association of Finnish Parliament Members and Scientists, TUTKAS. He has a degree both in Physics and in Business Administration.

Gordon Redding is Professor Emeritus, University of Hong Kong, and Adjunct Professor of Asian Business, INSEAD. He studied Economic Geography at Cambridge, spent a decade in UK industry, and then took a doctorate at Manchester Business School in organization theory. He then spent 24 years at the University of Hong Kong, founding and directing its business school, and researching the varied growth patterns of Asian business. Later Director of the Euro-Asia Centre at INSEAD, he has continued researching comparative capitalisms, and now runs a think-tank in Singapore.

Ron Sanchez is Professor of Management, Copenhagen Business School. He received his PhD in Technology Strategy from MIT. He has previously held appointments at the University of Illinois, University of Western Australia, and IMD, as well as visiting positions at National University of Singapore and other universities. His research interests include issues at the interfaces of strategy, organization, and technology. He has published in numerous journals in several disciplines, including Strategic Management Journal and Journal of Marketing. He is founding editor of Research in Competence-Based Management and co-author (with Aimé Heene) of the strategic management textbook "The New Strategic Management: Organization, Competition, and Competence."

John-Christopher Spender was trained as a nuclear engineer, worked for Rolls-Royce on UK nuclear submarines, later with IBM as large account team manager. PhD (Manchester Business School). Faculty at City U, UCLA, Glasgow, Rutgers. Retired 2003 as Dean of the School of Technology & Business at SUNY/FIT. Ongoing Visiting appointments in Sweden, Spain, France and UK. Also 2007–2008 Fulbright-Queen's Research Chair. Current research—managing under conditions of Knightian uncertainty, history of management education, strategy, and knowledge management.

Part I
Setting the Stage

1

Max Boisot and the Dynamic Evolution of Knowledge

Martin Ihrig and John Child

Introduction

Following Max Boisot's death in September 2011, several renowned scholars shared ideas as to how his contributions might be remembered and brought to a wider audience. They were also concerned to show how Boisot's work opens up new avenues for future inquiry. One idea that emerged was a book combining examples of his work with commentaries by those who worked closely with him.

The purpose of this book is to offer to a wider readership the remarkable contribution that Boisot made through his recognition that the form and communication of knowledge lie at the heart of human social organization. While Peter Drucker in the 1960s first drew attention to the fact that increasingly we are living in knowledge societies, Boisot provided a conceptual framework that enables us to appreciate the significance of that trend. His framework offers an understanding of how the ways we choose to express, communicate and share knowledge are intrinsic to how we relate to one another in organizations and societies. Boisot also recognized that knowledge is an asset that we can enhance both through well-conceived learning processes (exploration) and through the better coordination of existing information (exploitation) (March 1991). Better coordination, in the latter case, could come both from appreciating and reconciling the cultural nuances in how people structure and share information, as well as from utilizing modern information and communication technologies.

Boisot's doctoral thesis contained the first articulation of the codification-diffusion [C-D] framework, also known as the *C-Space* (Boisot 1987b), which was to form the basis for much of his subsequent work and later became elaborated into the three-dimensional Information Space, or *I-Space* (Boisot 1995a, 1998). The *I-Space* is a conceptual framework that facilitates the study of knowledge flows in diverse populations of "agents"—individuals, groups, firms, industries, alliances, governments, and nations. As one of Boisot's most fundamental innovations, it enabled him, and the many other researchers he inspired, to study and advance understanding of the emerging knowledge-based society and the implications of the information revolution. All chapters in this book use or touch upon the *I-Space* in one way or another. Therefore, let us briefly outline the *I-Space* framework and introduce it to readers who may not be familiar with it.

The Information-Space

The *I-Space* relates the degree to which knowledge is structured (i.e. its level of codification and abstraction) to the ease with which that knowledge can be diffused. Tacit, highly unstructured knowledge flows very slowly between agents and often only in face-to-face situations. Highly structured knowledge by contrast, which has been codified and abstracted, can diffuse rapidly and impersonally throughout a population, whether such diffusion is desired or not. As shown in Figure 1.1, knowledge is unstructured and undiffused at point A whereas at point B, it is both structured and diffused. Over time, knowledge that starts off at point A, gradually gets structured and diffused to end up at point B.[1]

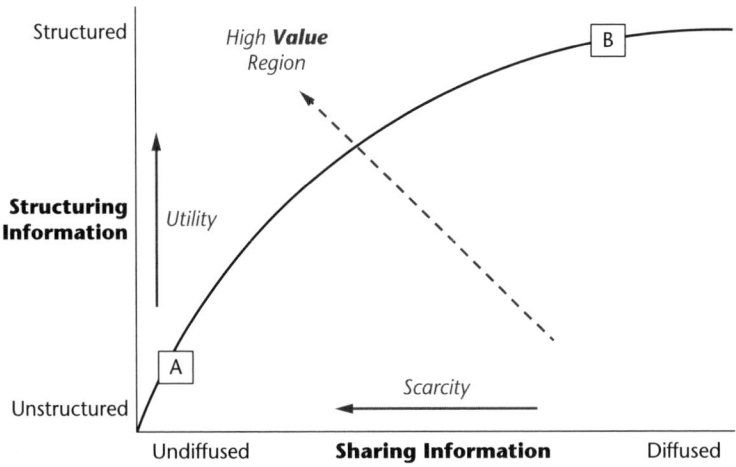

Figure 1.1. The Information-Space and the paradox of value

---

[1] This is a simplified, two-dimensional version of the *I-Space*. In the more elaborated, three-dimensional version, Boisot breaks down the *Structure* of knowledge into its dimensions of

Max Boisot and the Dynamic Evolution of Knowledge

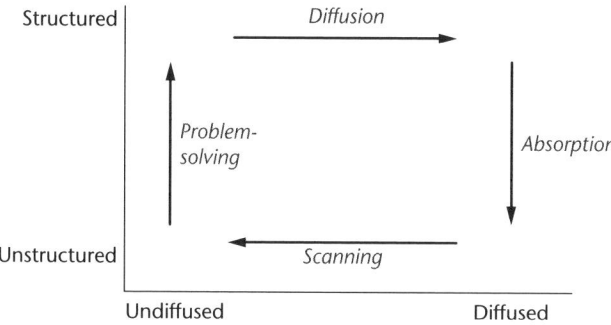

Figure 1.2. The Social Learning Cycle

As indicated in Figure 1.2, knowledge flows give rise to a four-step learning process within a population of agents in the *I-Space*, called the Social Learning Cycle or *SLC*. The *SLC* consists of four phases: *1.)* a *scanning* phase, in which novel tacit insights emerge in an undiffused form from the pool of generally available knowledge; *2.)* a *problem-solving* phase that articulates and structures the insights; *3.)* a *diffusion* phase in which the structured insights are picked up by a wider population; *4.)* an *absorption* phase in which, through a learning-by-doing process, the structured insights are gradually internalized by the members of that population and become part of their set of tacit, commonly-held beliefs.

An agent's stock of knowledge evolves over time, through deliberate acts of learning, or through transactions with other agents. But how can one extract value from the *SLC*? Economic value is a function of utility and scarcity. Both are at a maximum in the top left-hand corner of Figure 1.1. The structuring of knowledge increases its utility, but it also increases its diffusibility, which—once diffused—reduces its scarcity. This means that the point of greatest economic value is also the point at which a competitive advantage is most vulnerable. The value of knowledge goods, in contrast to that of physical goods, is inherently transient because it diffuses over time, and therefore requires a more dynamic treatment than the value of physical goods. An *I-Space* analysis enables the agent to decide how to manage the value of its knowledge assets by investing in their development and then extracting value, either by hoarding knowledge or by selectively sharing it with other agents.

Codification and *Abstraction*. For the purpose of this introduction, we will stick to the more simple representation. Chapter 6 reproduces an article in which Boisot explains in detail the *I-Space* in its three-dimensional form, defining codification and abstraction and also describing the distinction between data, information, and knowledge.

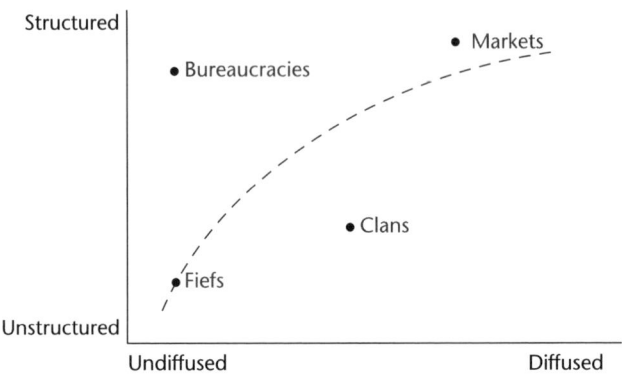

Figure 1.3. Institutions and cultures in the *I-Space*

The *I-Space* also permits the diagnosis of knowledge cultures and institutional structures that emerge in organizations and societies over time. Such cultures reflect the extent to which knowledge is distributed in a particular region of the *I-Space*, as well as the prevailing patterns of knowledge development and sharing. The different cultures embedded in an organization and/or a society profoundly influence knowledge evolution and utilization. Four cultural archetypes are depicted in Figure 1.3, each stemming from the pattern of repeated knowledge-based interactions between agents: Bureaucratic cultures try to keep knowledge structured and undiffused—their "files" of knowledge are typically confidential. Market cultures learn to operate with highly structured, highly diffused knowledge. Clan cultures try to keep their unstructured knowledge diffused within their in-group, but undiffused to others. Fief-based cultures keep their strategic knowledge closely held—unstructured and also undiffused. Organizations unaware of the different cultures that operate within their boundaries can miss opportunities to exploit knowledge strategically and may succumb to the pathologies that stem from their culture.

The *I-Space* and the *SLC* enable us to analyze the dynamic evolution of knowledge. Let us apply the framework and concepts to review Max Boisot's life and achievements and reflect on how his career path and the collaborations he formed helped to shape the development of his work.

Max Henri Boisot: An Organization Scholar and Management Visionary

Boisot's formation laid the foundations for his later achievements. Born in Maidenhead, UK, he had a cosmopolitan background and life, and when young travelled extensively. He was bi-lingual in English and French, and had good knowledge of other languages too. In many respects he was both very English, and completely un-English, and this certainly shaped his outlook and encouraged him to be open to new ideas and cultures. In terms of his formal education, his life-long quest for knowledge started at the boarding school he attended in Scotland: Gordonstoun, founded by the German educator Kurt Hahn. His experiences and the knowledge accumulated there most probably touched many different regions of the *I-Space*, both structured and unstructured, since for Hahn experiential education and outdoor adventure were integral to his educational philosophy. At university, Boisot certainly saw himself confronted with more structured knowledge. He studied architecture at the University of Cambridge and then had the rare distinction of being awarded two Master's degrees in the same year (1971) by MIT—one in city planning and the other in management.

He subsequently worked as a general manager (1971–72), founding partner of an architectural and planning firm (1972–75), and consultant (1975–78). His unusual ability as a theoretician to converse meaningfully with senior executives, and to make theory relevant to them, was honed by this early senior managerial experience. His academic career began with an appointment at the Euro-Asia Centre, INSEAD in 1979. This evoked an interest in East Asia which provided the substantive focus for the PhD he completed in record time at Imperial College London in 1982. His supervisor there was Dorothy Griffiths and the subject of his dissertation was the diffusion of technical knowledge in the chemical industry in Asia. Informed by sources such as Bernstein's research into the codes used by children from different social classes, Boisot developed a precursor to the *I-Space*: the *C-Space* model (*C* for culture). Thinking in terms of "spaces" and multiple dimensions came naturally to Boisot as a student of architecture. He had a habit of sketching ideas out on paper (often paper napkins in the coffee shops where he loved to work), and usually in diagrammatic form, as an aid to thought and clarification.

Professorial appointments followed between 1981–86 in Fujinomiya (Japan), Paris (France), and Hawaii (USA). In 1984, Boisot became Dean and Director of the China-EEC Management Programme (CEMP). This was a five-year program (the first in the PRC) financed by the EEC and run in the Training Centre for Economic Cadres of the State Economic Commission in Beijing, China. The program was conceived, negotiated and set up by Boisot on behalf of the EEC Commission between 1981 and 1984 when he was asked to take over its overall direction in Beijing. It later became the China-Europe Management Institute (CEMI) and has since evolved into the China-Europe International Business School (CEIBS), located in Shanghai, now number 24 in the FT Global MBA Rankings 2012. Boisot's time in Beijing allowed him to gather a wealth of first-hand experience about China, its society and culture. He was able to obtain unique new insights that he subsequently developed into important academic contributions in the form of journal articles.

Boisot decided not to renew his contract at the China-EEC Management Institute Beijing at the end of 1988. He resigned in June 1989 as Director of Executive Programs. Boisot then held various visiting appointments between 1989–90: at Aston University and the Ashridge Management College in the UK, at ESADE in Spain, and at the University of Hong Kong Business School in Hong Kong. In 1991 he found his academic home in Barcelona and became a Professor at ESADE Business School (University of Ramon Llull), where he stayed until 2002. During that time, he was in engaged in many interesting projects and collaborated with different institutions. He was associated with the Judge Institute of Management Studies at the University of Cambridge (1991–2011) and held visiting appointments at the Hong Kong University Business School (1993) and at Imperial College (1993). From 1994 to 1995 he successfully designed and initiated the Euro-Arab Management School for the European Union in Granada, Spain and served from 1995–96 as its Academic Coordinator for the Master of Management Development Program. He also began relationships that endured until his death: in 1996 he became a Senior Research Fellow at the Sol C. Snider Entrepreneurial Research Center at The Wharton School of the University of Pennsylvania; in 1998 an Associate and Academic Advisor at The Chinese Management Centre at Hong Kong University; and in 1999 an Associate Fellow at Templeton College, University of Oxford.

After he left ESADE in 2002, Boisot become a Professor at the Universitat Oberta de Catalunya in Barcelona and stayed there until 2005. During that time, in 2003, he also became a Visiting Professor at Birmingham Business School at the University of Birmingham in the UK. Before he was appointed to the Chair of Strategic Management there in 2006, he was an Adjunct Professor at INSEAD (2005–06) and a Visiting Professor at the Management School at Xi'an Jiaotong University in Xi'an, China (2005–06). He left Birmingham in 2009 to re-join ESADE, this time as a Visiting Professor. Finally, since 2007 he conducted research with the ATLAS Collaboration at CERN in Geneva, Switzerland.

An interesting characteristic that marked out Max Boisot was that he was an independent scholar in the very best senses of the term: both independent of mind and not affiliated full-time to any institution in a way that constrained his intellect or pulled him into unproductive activities. In many respects Boisot did not have a classic "academic career" in the sense that many people might understand the term, and his choice not to be a permanent member of an institution fostered the original and independent path of enquiry he followed.

In addition to his academic appointments and his work as a researcher, teacher, or administrator, Max Boisot was an experienced consultant. He acted as a consultant and external lecturer for international firms such as BP, Thomson CFS, Saint-Gobain, Valeo, Union des Banques Suisse, The Trustee Savings Bank, Olivetti, Courtaulds, A.T. Kearney, Shell, and IBM. He also helped the South African Railways (Spoornet) with a business transformation operation on behalf of the Wharton School and was working with BAE Systems to operationalize the Information-Space. At various times, Boisot also acted as consultant to the World Bank in China and Vietnam, to the UNDP in Albania, to the EC Commission in South East Asia, to the European Foundation for Management Development in Eastern Europe, to the C.I.S. in the Middle East, and to the French Ministry of Foreign Affairs in Iraq.

Max Boisot was a founder member of the International Futures Forum, a project based in Scotland committed to moving beyond Enlightenment frames of reference, knowledge and sense-making to think in terms of a "second Enlightenment." He was closely involved, for example, in the long term recovery and regeneration of Falkirk after large job losses at the local BP refinery (2002–2007); issues of democracy, leadership and governance in India (2007); reforming Scotland's education system (2010–11); exploring how to fund a creative ecosystem of the arts and culture in the UK (2008–10); and considering how a city like Glasgow can configure life resources to promote health and wellbeing (2011—drawing on his work with the ATLAS experiment at CERN).

Boisot's Mode of Knowledge Creation

Boisot was constantly on the move. He joked that his forwarding address was "care of British Airways." His professional and teaching interests included the interaction of corporate and national culture in business enterprises; identifying and managing the firm's knowledge resources; organizational learning, competence and innovation; business policy; and the changing nature of the business enterprise. He also offered a novel course on research philosophy and methods. His various appointments and collaborations enabled him to work on many fascinating projects throughout the world. Most importantly, he had a distinct skill of using all his encounters with different people and organizations to continuously produce new insights and develop new knowledge—he himself was a master in performing each and every step of the social learning cycle, continuously creating, developing, sharing, and exploiting knowledge.

Boisot's mode of creating and disseminating new knowledge is deeply admired by all who knew him and his work. It is instructive to reflect that the way he went about this process accords closely to the Social Learning

Cycle (*SLC*), which he saw as the process through which knowledge evolves dynamically within the *I-Space*. In its simplified form, the *SLC* consists of four stages (see Figure 1.2). *Scanning* is the first stage which is "identifying threats and opportunities in generally available but often fuzzy data" (Boisot 1998, 59). Scanning permits the discovery of new insights or unique ideas. Boisot constantly had new thoughts and generated hypotheses about phenomena he observed in the world. Here he was assisted by the huge scope of his reading. He preferred to ration the attention he gave reading reports on the narrow hypothesis testing so characteristic of academic journals in favor of concentrating on a broad spectrum of ideas and theories drawn from a wide reading of books not only in the social sciences, but also in biology, history, physics, philosophy and technology (he was indeed one of the last true polymaths (Snowden 2011)). His many airplane flights were not so much an opportunity to take a nap as to read another book. He built a huge carefully classified (codified) library at his Sitges home. His scanning activity went far beyond the norm, as did his ability to extract and absorb new insights from his reading.

But having great ideas and nascent knowledge was not enough, which brings us to the next stage of the learning cycle: *problem-solving*. For Boisot, problem-solving is "the process of giving structure and coherence to such insights—i.e. codifying them" (1998, 59). This includes the process of abstraction whereby newly codified insights are grouped together into their most essential features—i.e. conceptualized. This process enables them to be generalized to a wider range of situations. In this stage, Boisot converted knowledge that was embodied in a combination of his reading and experience to a more abstract symbolic form, often using the *C-* and *I-Space* frameworks as an aid. However, in moving towards abstraction, Boisot also made significant use of discourse with collaborators. Once Boisot had identified an opportunity for an interesting project, he would try to bring people and organizations together, set up a framework, and then start to research and develop. Typically his collaborators were less well read and less theoretically versed than he was. On the other hand they often brought specialized empirical knowledge and a questioning perspective to the process, which helped to put Boisot's abstractions to the test of validity. It is therefore no accident that Boisot wrote relatively few single-authored papers.

Based on his unique ideas, there were always many fascinating projects "in the hopper". His intellectual dedication went hand in hand with his entrepreneurial spirit—a combination which is very rarely found. The most important project for him in recent years was his research with the ATLAS Collaboration at CERN. The culmination of his work there was the book (his sixth) on the organization of learning in the ATLAS experiment at the LHC, published in the year he died. This summarized and structured the new insights and knowledge gained from the ATLAS experience.

The next stage in the simplified *SLC* is *diffusion*. Diffusion is the process of disseminating and sharing your knowledge with a wider audience. Boisot did this intensively. He regularly offered papers at conferences as well as being an inveterate international traveler between different universities and assignments. At one point he had seven different institutional affiliations. These networking activities developed a shared context for his work which in later years became formalized in social constructions such as the *I-Space* Institute and the research initiative at the Snider Entrepreneurial Research Center at the Wharton School and the workshops organized at the Academy of Management (AOM) Annual Meetings and the European Group for Organizational Studies (EGOS) Colloquia, whose 2011 conference he attended in Gothenburg shortly before his death. Boisot had a special skill in synthesizing streams of knowledge and putting them into words everyone could understand. The unanimity among the contributors to this book is that it was a great pleasure to work with him, because he didn't presuppose one would know all the theories he related to, but explained in simple words where he was coming from.

Boisot generously shared his knowledge and while doing so, made others feel good. This is why his collaborators and colleagues so thoroughly enjoyed working with him and that is how he will be remembered. The reflections they offer in Part VII of this book testify to this. Many people and organizations hoard their knowledge. Boisot truly lived what he was writing about in his academic work, namely that in an information-based economy hoarding is an ultimately self-destructive approach and sharing knowledge and continuously further developing and creating new knowledge is the way to competitive success.

A further stage of the *SLC—absorption—*consists of "applying the newly codified insights to different situations" (1998, 61). Boisot believed that he had discovered the basis for a general analysis of information which, as such, could and should be applied to a wide range of different situations. The variety of situations to which he applied his ideas, usually through collaboration, is indicated by the scope of this book and the wide spread of journals in which he published. In intellectually stimulating and rewarding discussions, he would share with his collaborators the concepts he had read about and apply them to whatever they were currently working on. While Boisot was an incredible source of knowledge, it was not the possession of that knowledge per se that was so special; rather it was how he processed and put it to use. The desire to progress the absorption of Boisot's work is one of the prime motivations for this book. As we argue in the Concluding chapter, this stage is by no means complete either in terms of its potential impact on managerial and educational practice, or in terms of the program of further research that deserves to be inspired by Boisot's insights.

The Structure of this Book

This book commemorates Max Boisot's life and work. But it also aims to disseminate his work and to indicate its potential for informing further inquiry into many significant issues. Its unifying theme is Boisot's treatment of knowledge and the relevance of his conceptual analysis for practice in ways that he himself demonstrated so powerfully. With a knowledge-based lens, Boisot studied agents (people, organizations, society) and revealed patterns in the way they process information-bearing data. This is the thematic unity of his work which it is our purpose to honor and articulate. The various chapters describe how Boisot's thinking and ideas can help make sense of many important phenomena in a distinctive way. Although divided into sections representing the principal areas of Boisot's achievement, the book can be regarded as a holistic entity that gains life and significance from this thematic unity.

The book organizes Boisot's work into five categories and has a number of leading scholars in the field comment on his contributions, put them into perspective, and highlight their implications for both academia and practice. It thereby brings together in one book—for the first time ever—the breadth and depth of Boisot's work. The book provides much more than just a selection of Boisot's papers by including multiple reflective essays on the key themes in his work.

It is structured into the following five core sections that cover the main areas in which Boisot forged new understanding:

1. Analyses of the Chinese System
2. Organizational Complexity
3. The Strategic Management of Knowledge
4. Knowledge in Big Science
5. Innovations in Education

Every section features one key paper that Boisot had written or co-authored, accompanied by a commentary. Each section has been the responsibility of one or two people who had published with Boisot in the thematic area and who have also written the reflective commentary on the theme.

Analyses of the Chinese System. Boisot had a long and continuing fascination with China as a distinctive cultural and institutional system clearly destined to become a great power. From 1987 until the year of his death he produced a series of papers which applied his information-based framework to the challenge of making sense of China's economic reform and the business systems emerging from it. The analysis he and his collaborators developed over time provides a highly insightful understanding of the distinctiveness and complexity of the Chinese system. Boisot and Child (1988) maintained that the extent of information codification has an important bearing on the governance options available either at the level of the firm or at the broader institutional level. Postulating an "iron law of fiefs", they noted bureaucratic failure in China and argued, unconventionally for the time, that this was likely to give way to a regime based on fiefs rather than markets due to a cultural preference for relatively uncodified relationships and transactions. A subsequent article reprinted in this book—Boisot and Child (1996a)— expanded and updated this argument, concluding that under China's reform program decentralization of the state command bureaucracy was giving rise to a distinctive institutional form, that of "network capitalism." This form was seen to arise from a combination of limited information codification in China combined with communal property rights and organization of economic transactions. China's path to modernization through network capitalism contrasted with the Western path of modernization through the development of markets based on high levels of information codification. A recent article (Boisot, Child, and Redding 2011) again addressed the question of whether under globalization there is likely to be a convergence towards a market order. Taking China as their case study, the authors identified three emergent business systems—the state sector, local corporates and the private sector. In terms of Boisot's *I-Space* framework, activities and transactions in the state sector are governed by a "bureaucratic" order and are characterized by structured but undiffused information. Under the pressure of competition, however, these are tending to move towards a market regime. Local corporates are characterized by relatively unstructured and only partially diffused activities governed by local and personalized organizational networks of a "clan" nature. Firms in the private sector tend to be governed as fiefs, albeit transacting inputs and outputs through markets. The article concluded that although China's economy as a whole is being pulled towards greater structuring and diffusion of transaction-related information, this does not mean that it will adopt a market order as its dominant institutional framework.

Organizational Complexity. The seeds of Boisot's interest in complexity science are scattered here and there in his 1998 *Knowledge Assets* book about the *I-Space*, which was awarded the Ansoff Prize for the best book on strategy in 2000. His complexity perspective began to blossom in his 1999 article with John Child, which takes a complexity view of China's economic development (Boisot and Child 1999). This posits two modes of coping with external complexity—either attempting to reduce or absorb it—and argues that the latter approach was characteristic of Chinese organizations operating in the less structured regions of the *I-Space*. Boisot and Bill McKelvey began their series of publications two years after the 9/11 disaster. The "siloized" US agencies—CIA, FBI, and the military—are found unable to "connect the dots" of early indications that Islamic militants were planning to fly aircraft into buildings. In their first paper together (2003), they reach back to Ross Ashby's 1956 development of his *Law of Requisite Variety*, which they later update to the *Law of Requisite Complexity*. Ashby mentions the equivalent of twelve dots, which give rise to some 74 quintillion possible patterns. Boisot's *I-Space* morphs into the *"Ashby Space,"* which allows Boisot and McKelvey to consider the implications of how governments and firms can best respond to surrounding contextual complexity; it is the core feature of all of their subsequent publications. Their *requisite complexity* perspective bridges between Modernism and Postmodernism: Modernist thinking overly simplifies a firm's response to contextual complexity; postmodernism fails to find the meaningful patterns that allow efficacious adaptive responses. In a paper awarded the Academy of Management's *"Best Paper"* status (included in this book), they further develop the "complexity response region" of their Ashby Space. In subsequent publications Boisot and McKelvey move from complexity science to econophysics by shifting cognitive representations of managers' real-world and follow-on creation of response schemas from Gaussian to Paretian realities. They shift requisite complexity schema-development from research presuming normal distributions to research based on Pareto, power-law, and rank/frequency distributions (Boisot and McKelvey 2010; Boisot and McKelvey 2011a; Boisot and McKelvey 2011b, 2009). They show how the variety perceived to be requisite is sensitive to the type of ontological assumptions that are made and examine how this affects managers' social information processing strategies and schema formation. An organization science based on researching scale-free dynamics and fractal structures is outlined.

The Strategic Management of Knowledge. Boisot recognized early on in his career that in many industries and economies knowledge was replacing natural resources as the key source of wealth generation. However, notwithstanding the proclamations of knowledge management practitioners, the effective management of knowledge remained elusive. Boisot never tired of pointing out that nearly 2500 years after Plato first explored the concept of knowledge, there is still no clear consensus on what it actually consists of. We still lack a robust and agreed upon theoretical base from which to manage this new source of wealth strategically. Hence, Boisot's goal was to push the envelope in the strategic management of knowledge. He was passionate about conducting research that improved our understanding of how knowledge is generated, diffused, internalized and managed by individuals and organizations under both collaborative and competitive learning conditions. "The Creation and Sharing of Knowledge" (reprinted in this book) illustrates Boisot's approach to the effective management of knowledge resources (Boisot 2002). It starts to explore the particular link Boisot made to strategy. Boisot worked with academic, corporate, and public sector partners to further our understanding of the strategic management of knowledge. The strategy-related research that Boisot and his partners conducted at the Snider Entrepreneurial Research Center at the Wharton School of the University of Pennsylvania was aimed at transforming what was still a collection of loosely-coupled practices into a full-fledged, theoretically grounded professional discipline. Boisot's thesis was that in the information age, the competitive success of innovating businesses depends on having the right conceptual framework and decision making tools to allow firms to manage their portfolios of knowledge assets as opposed to physical assets. To develop those tools, Boisot, together with Ian MacMillan and Martin Ihrig, started a small research and development venture in 2006, called the *I-Space Institute* (Boisot, MacMillan, and Han 2008). The goal was to develop, test, and exploit the *I-Space* as a conceptual and applications framework and to build *strategic knowledge management tools* that have the potential to assist corporate decision makers to navigate the knowledge economy. In recent years, Boisot focused his efforts in two areas: *mapping* critical knowledge assets, cultural and institutional structures, and learning paths; and *simulating* strategic knowledge management processes, in particular knowledge flows and knowledge-based agent interactions.

Knowledge in Big Science. In the last years of his life, an important part of Boisot's research was devoted to the study of the organizational and strategic aspects of big science projects. He could not find a better test bed of his ideas on information and knowledge and their role in complex social systems than the ATLAS Collaboration at CERN. After all, science has been historically the first social system that specialized in turning data into information useful to generate knowledge. Much of Boisot's earlier work could be applied in this context and contributed to the understanding of big science projects like ATLAS. There are some fundamental questions about the nature of knowledge and its differentiation from the concepts of data and information. From his original insights on these issues (Boisot and Canals 2004), Boisot derived interesting implications for organizations and the economic view of knowledge assets. Boisot spent a lot of time studying various aspects of big science projects, which culminated in the article "Generating Knowledge in a Connected World: The Case of the ATLAS Experiment at CERN" (Boisot 2011), reproduced in this book, and his latest book "Collisions and Collaboration" (Boisot, Nordberg, Yami, and Nicquevert 2011). Issues ranged from learning, culture or leadership to new management research models or e-science. Boisot was working on some fascinating ideas in the last months of his research about big science and some possible avenues for further research. Among them, we find the problem of coordination in a complex big science project, and the transfer of knowledge in an open innovation context.

Innovations in Education. The *I-Space* adds dimensionality, breadth, width, and volume to our understanding of the learning process. Most learning models are two dimensional and linear. The *I-Space* and the Social Learning Cycle bring recent developments in complexity science to bear on how learning develops and occurs. In addition, the Social Learning Cycle helps us to better understand and practice innovative learning methods because it models complex interactions and cultural differences. Although Boisot's writing on education is sparse (in this book we reproduce Boisot and Fiol 1987), all his writing can be seen as letters from a master teacher who is exploring and developing ideas and knowledge, to his colleagues and students. Furthermore, those of us who had the privilege to design programs and teach with Boisot know that all his waking moments were devoted to learning and diffusing knowledge. He clearly appreciated that learning is not a passive experience, but an active, alert, engaged process. One of the most important sources of information about his innovative approach to education are of course colleagues who worked and taught with Boisot in China, the Euro-Arab Business School, EU, ESADE, Birmingham, and Wharton. Boisot's innovative education vision, which was only partially realized, touched on different categories of management education innovations: 1.) philosophical innovations, 2.) design innovations, 3.) methodological/instructional innovations, 4.) technological innovations, 5.) innovations related to the transfer of knowledge, and 6.) innovations related to the reception of knowledge. Some of the innovative educational ideas that Boisot tried and envisioned can help to revitalize the current graduate and management educational arena. Boisot realized that current educational practice is often Byzantine in its administration and lifeless in its application. Partly through his own *joie de vivre* and his enthusiasm for ideas and knowledge, Boisot systematically experimented with innovative educational ideas. Although many of these ideas are not captured in his writing, Dana Kaminstein and John Child have collected more of them through interviews and reminiscences.

To give other former collaborators of Boisot an opportunity to express their views on his work and on the experience of collaborating with him, the final part of the book contains a number of relatively short reflective essays. These are of a more personalized nature than other contributions to the book. They reflect how the people who worked with Boisot regarded him as a human being as well as an outstanding innovator. In total, there are eighteen chapters: an introduction and a conclusion by the editors; five papers of Boisot's for each of the thematic sections and five overviews by the section leads; and six short reflections. It is the combination of Boisot's articles and the essays by prominent scholars that make this book distinctive.

Part II
Analyses of the Chinese System

2

From Fiefs to Clans and Network Capitalism: Explaining China's Emerging Economic Order

*Max Boisot and John Child**

China has sustained a rapid rate of economic growth since the inauguration of its economic reform in 1979, with only short-lived interruptions. This success contrasts favorably with most other developing countries (*The Economist* 1995b) and prompts enquiry into the kind of economic organization that is facilitating such an impressive performance. China's growth has been stimulated by two main developments. The first is a shift in industrial ownership and property rights, with the state playing a diminishing role. The second is the increasing part played by market transactions, including a growing integration with the world economy. These developments would appear prima facie to be moving China's economic system toward market capitalism. China has distinctive political, institutional, and cultural characteristics, however, and it is recognized that such factors can give rise to different modes of economic organization (Hamilton and Biggart 1988; Whitley 1994). Two broad questions therefore arise. The first is what kind of economic order is emerging in China, an answer to which is complicated by the country's size

---

* Originally published as Max Boisot and John Child (1996a). "From Fiefs to Clans and Network Capitalism: Explaining China's Emerging Economic Order." *Administrative Science Quarterly*, 41 (4): 600–628. Reprinted with kind permission of SAGE Publications Inc. Earlier versions of this paper were presented to the Conference on "Management Issues for China in the 1990s," St. John's College, Cambridge, March 1994 and to the 12th EGOS Colloquium, Istanbul, July 1995. The authors are grateful for comments received from participants and for comments by two anonymous *ASO* reviewers, the associate editor, and Dr. Yuan Lu. The alphabetical ordering of the author's names denotes equal contribution to and responsibility for the paper.

and heterogeneity and by the uneven spread of its economic reform (Tu 1993; Ungar and Chan 1995). The second is how far China's emerging economic order can be analyzed in conventional Western terms. The ability of Western neoclassical economic theory to account for the nature and success of other Asian business systems has already been put in doubt (e.g. Biggart and Hamilton, 1992).

These broad questions subsume a number of more specific issues that this paper addresses. The first concerns the type of business system now operating in China. If, as Nee (1992) suggested, there is a newer system of marketized transactions in addition to state-dominated nonmarket firms, does this merit special attention as the Chinese economic system of the future (cf. Qian and Xu, 1993)? Second, do the arrangements through which the marketized sector operates conform to the Western model? Third, and notwithstanding protestations by the Chinese leadership to the contrary, is the economic order that is emerging in China from the dismantling of the socialist system a capitalist one—as understood by Western observers and as judged by the criteria of ownership and property rights—or does it require its own specific designation? Fourth, if a distinctive economic system is emerging in China, what part does government play in its operation and does this require an elaboration of our conventional theories about the role of the state in economic life? Answers to these questions would be of considerable moment for Western academics and business people. A good understanding of Chinese economic organization would bear on Western discussions of modernization, many of which assume that this requires the building of market, property rights, and other institutional systems of essentially the same kind that supported earlier instances of industrialization. Such answers would also carry useful implications for foreign investors and business people. Better knowledge of the Chinese business system would help foreign companies enter the system and point to where power and decision making are located within it.

In this paper, we argue that China is treading a path toward modernization that differs from Western experience and that the essence of this can be analyzed in institutional terms. We then tentatively identify the distinctive characteristics of China's emerging economic order, by reference to China's business system and markets, capitalism, and government within that system. The paper as a whole should be read as a prolegomenon to the research that its subject richly deserves, its purpose at this stage being to elaborate relevant questions rather than to offer adequate answers.

In theoretical terms, the paper extends the markets and hierarchies debate initiated by Williamson (1975) in a new direction. As it evolved, the markets and hierarchies formulation established a unidimensional continuum, with market coordination at one end and hierarchical coordination at the other.

Clan or federal forms of governance (Ouchi, 1980; Butler, 1983) and relational contracting (Williamson, 1985) could then be located at notional points along this continuum—not quite markets but not quite hierarchies either. Boisot (1986b) questioned the ability of a unidimensional markets and hierarchies continuum to capture adequately the transactional options available in different cultural and institutional settings. Using a conceptual framework that he labeled the culture space or "C-Space," which relates the diffusion of transactionally relevant knowledge within a given population to how far it has been codified, he showed that the clan forms of governance, together with a form of governance that he labeled "fiefs," could not be convincingly depicted as mere staging posts between markets and hierarchies. We use the C-Space framework here to illustrate the special and challenging characteristics of China's modernization.

Use of the C-Space to contrast European and Chinese modernization

The Chinese authorities have always explicitly conceptualized their economic reform as a program of modernization or, to be more precise, the "Four Modernizations" of agriculture, industry, science and technology, and defense. What has happened under the reform does not, however, appear to accord with the European experience of modernization. Prior to developing a market order, Europe went through an absolutist phase in which emergent nation states created strong centralizing bureaucracies that codified a rational-legal approach to government administration (Elias 1939; Anderson 1974). Only with the advent of a liberal ideology in the 18th and 19th centuries did decentralization to a market order gradually take place (Kumar 1978).

Analysis of the contrast between China and Europe is facilitated by reference to the C-Space (Boisot 1986b, 1987a), a conceptual framework that relates the extent to which transactionally relevant information can be diffused, and hence shared, within a target population to how far it has been codified. Codification, the selection and compression of data into stable structures (Shannon 1948), is a matter of degree: If Zen masters trade in the kind of tacit knowledge that is hard to codify and that can only be imparted slowly and face to face to a limited number of disciples, bond traders, by contrast, deal in well-codified prices that can be diffused worldwide in seconds by electronic means. As shown in Figure 2.1, the codification and diffusion of information create a transactional environment that conditions the institutional possibilities to be found in different regions of the C-Space and endows them with some quite specific features, which are listed in Figure 2.2.

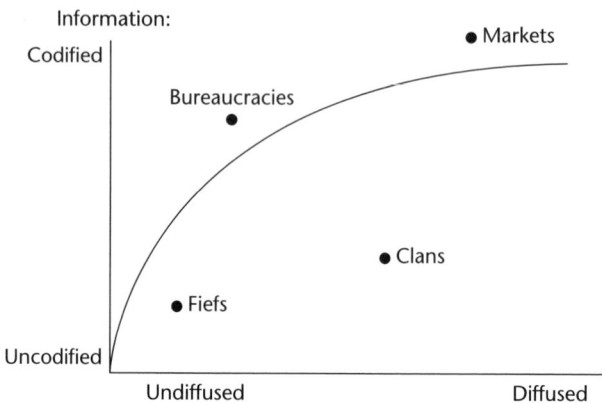

Figure 2.1. Institutions in the C-Space

Information	Undiffused	Diffused
Codified	**BUREAUCRACIES** Diffusion of information: Centrally controlled Relationships: Impersonal Goals: Hierarchically imposed Coordination: Hierarchical Numbers: Medium Uncertainty: High	**MARKETS** Diffusion of information: Virtually unlimited Relationships: Impersonal Goals: Freeiy chosen by agent Coordination: Self-regulation Numbers: Very large Uncertainty: Low
Uncodified	**FIEFS** Diffusion of information: Very restricted Relationships: Personal Goals: Hierarchically imposed Coordination: Hierarchical Numbers: Small Uncertainty: High	**CLANS** Diffusion of information: Limited Relationships: Personal Goals: By negotiation Coordination: By mutual adjustment Numbers: Medium Uncertainty: High

Figure 2.2. Transactional environments created by information codification and diffusion

An institutional order can be thought of as the center of gravity of a scatter of transactions in the C-Space and a change of institutional order as a shift in the center of gravity. In practice—and certainly in pluralist regimes—the scatter is likely to be quite wide. An institutional order in this analysis—such as the "markets" category in Figure 2.2—is therefore an ideal type that is useful for pointing up analytical distinctions. It is not intended to depict the implausible situation in which all transactions are confined exclusively to one of the four categories. In reality, all the institutional forms depicted in Figure 2.1 are likely to find a niche within a given institutional order, even if one of these forms predominates. Thus it is acknowledged that market transacting in the West can involve elements of personal trust (cf. Zucker 1986; Portes 1994) and that Western bureaucracies rely to a degree on informal processes and on-going personal relationships (e.g. Blau 1955; Dalton 1959). The argument, rather, is that the Western market system is characterized by impersonal economic relationships, large-numbers transacting, relatively decentralized self-regulating economic units, a plurality of goals, and the other constituents of the ideal type. Much Western analysis has accepted this characterization, and the question we shall be addressing is whether it can be applied to China and, if not, what kind of alternative characterization would be appropriate for that country.

In the C-Space, the European experience of modernization entailed, first, a shift in the transactional center of gravity from an institutional order based on feudal fiefs to one based on bureaucracies and, second, from there a decentralization toward markets. The move required both an ability and a willingness to codify. The very act of selection entailed by codification, however, leads to the suppression, or even the rejection, of data not selected and, hence, to the sacrifice of contextual data. Transactional coverage—the ability to subsume a large number of particular cases under a general coding scheme—is achieved at the expense of transactional nuance and richness. The depersonalization associated with codified transactions merely reflects the difficulty of maintaining a dense network of interpersonal obligations as small-numbers transacting gives way to large-numbers transacting. What Williamson (1975) termed "atmosphere" is lost as exchange loses its "embeddedness" (Granovetter 1985). The move toward greater codification thus corresponds to what Hall (1976) termed a shift from high context to low context or to what Habermas (1970) called a shift from "lifeworld" to "system." It stimulates and facilitates but does not guarantee decentralization and the development to large-scale markets. Indeed, the centralized bureaucratic state typically restricted the evolution of markets by operating monopolies under its own direct control. In such a state, prevailing belief systems and institutional norms favor the hoarding rather than the sharing of information. Applied to problems of modernization, the C-Space indicates how a greater propensity to codify transactions can usher in a bureaucratic order like that aspired to by the 16th-century European absolutist states. Whether, and to what extent, codified transactions are subsequently decentralized is a function of how effectively power holders can, or wish to, resist the forces of diffusion set in motion by the very act of codification itself.

A bureaucratic order, however, could only stabilize on the basis of a rational-legal approach to the problems of statecraft and institution building. In Western countries, it was the development of systems of universalistically applied laws that provided the framework within which a market system could develop. Thus it is argued that the evolution of property rights was a necessary condition for sustained economic growth in the Western world (North and Thomas 1973; *The Economist* 1994b). Using the codification/diffusion framework as an analytical tool, Boisot and Child (1988) argued that China would have been inhibited in decentralizing from bureaucracies to markets, had it wanted to, because it had not actually built up a stable codified bureaucratic order from which to decentralize. A preference for interpersonal accommodation—an orientation to particular individuals and relationships rather than to impersonal rules—coupled with the irrationalities of the post-1949 command economy, was always undermining the country's attempt to develop into bureaucracies and pulling China toward its traditional mode of social organization (Gernet 1982). The process is self-reinforcing in that the absence of a rational-legal institutional framework fails to engender confidence in a wider system of bureaucratic or market transacting outside networks based on personal power, commitment, and trust. Boisot and Child labeled this tendency the "iron law of fiefs."

In the countries of Central Eastern Europe, especially Czechoslovakia, Hungary, the Baltic States, and (to a lesser extent) Poland, rational-legal state bureaucracies predated the advent of Marxism-Leninism. When Marxism-Leninism was imposed upon these countries, with its erosion of legality and economic rationality, it still had to contend with the countervailing effects of the institutional order that had been in place. This undoubtedly helps to account for their rapid transformation toward Western institutions since 1989. In China, however, the bureaucracy that the communists inherited in 1949 was "patrimonial" (Weber 1964) and feudal in its operations. It was in the hands of an unspecialized class of literati that, although dirigiste, interventionist, and particularistic in its orientation, was more concerned with the formality of bureaucratic codes than with their rational-legal content or effects. Its survival owed much to the fact that the simple and cellular preindustrial society it had presided over was comparatively undemanding of coordination and rationality (Balazs 1968). The modernizing Chinese assumed that Marxism-Leninism would show the way to the attainment of a codified rational-legal order. Stalin's forced collectivization of the Soviet Union in the 1930s and the latter's subsequent ability to confront an armed Germany's industrial might in the Second World War had suggested that, with the right policies, socialism in one country was indeed a live option. Without the countervailance of a legal-rational bureaucracy, however, Marxism-Leninism in China operated through the fieflike traditional mode of social organization. This was reinforced by a Chinese cultural and cognitive bias against abstraction (Bond and Hwang 1986).

Abstraction is a prerequisite for the creation of robust codifications and the construction of a rational-legal order. If codification seeks to economize on data processing by assigning the data of experience to categories, abstraction seeks to economize on the number of categories used in the act of codifying (Boisot 1995a). It involves a move away from treating each specific exchange concretely sui generis and toward the use of general principles that apply predictably and systematically to every case. The central role of law in modern societies illustrates the importance of abstraction to the notion of modernization. The modernization hypothesis assumes that there is a shift from particularism to universalism and from substantive to procedural rationality. Thus the ability to move toward higher levels of codification, and to stay there, requires a greater disposition for abstract thought than Chinese culture has shown up until now. Remove abstraction from efforts at codification and one obtains little more than ritual and mock bureaucracies (Gouldner 1954), low in institutional stability. Sooner or later under these conditions, transacting gravitates back toward the lower regions of the C-Space. Japan held a similar disposition toward concrete particularisms when it started modernizing in the last third of the 19th century, but this disposition was attenuated rather than reinforced by the development model that it borrowed at the time. In contrast to the Marxist-Leninist model adopted by China after 1949, the Western liberal model that guided Japan's efforts was conducive to the emergence—at least to some extent—of rational-legal economic order (Sansom 1931).

What appears to be happening in many parts of China's economic sphere is that the system continues to reproduce a model of organization specific to the relations between the governmental authorities and the enterprises within their hegemony. The authorities concerned are industrial ministries, provincial governments, and (more often) local governments. Interorganizational relations between governmental bodies and the enterprises within their purview, relations that in other industrial economies would be conducted at arm's length through markets, are managed through personal interactions. The impersonal abstract order associated with a decentralization to markets has yet to replace the much more concrete personalized order that delegation within a patrimonial system can allow. The institutional model currently in use thus fails the test of abstraction implicitly posed by the modernization thesis. Instead, people "make out" through interpersonal accommodation and negotiation that is specific to each relationship and to each situation and, in so doing, they continue to sustain the iron law of fiefs.

The Chinese authorities themselves experience this law without being able to articulate it or incorporate it in their policies. They implicitly adopt the unidimensional perspective of the markets and hierarchies approach—albeit at a macroeconomic level—when they explain the economic reforms they have undertaken since 1978, in institutional terms, as a restructuring of the system from bureaucratic to market governance. According to the Chinese, the shift away from bureaucracy has taken two forms. The first form is a delegation of administrative power within the state bureaucracy from the central government to provincial and city governments. For example, responsibility for large state-owned enterprises was transferred from central to provincial governments, while for medium-sized state-owned enterprises it was transferred from provincial to city or county governments. Powers to enter into foreign trade relations and to approve the establishment of smaller joint ventures have also been delegated. The second form is a decentralization of economic power from the state bureaucracy to firms: state-owned enterprises, collective enterprises, and private businesses. State-owned firms have been given a measure of managerial discretion over what they produce, over securing inputs, over marketing outputs, and over organizational and personnel policies (Child 1994). Moreover, there has been a considerable expansion in the share of industrial output accounted for by non-state firms, which are not formally so dependent on higher governmental authorities (Qian and Xu 1993).

Although economic reform measures were enacted at an ever-accelerating pace throughout the 1980s and the early 1990s, decentralization measures have encountered problems on the ground. The state has lacked both the appropriate economic and institutional concepts and the "low-context" (Hall 1976) culture that would allow such measures to usher in a workable market order. The situation has not appreciably changed in the 1990s. The institutions that characterize a rational-legal system—an effective central bank, macroeconomic levers, enforceable and consistent laws—remain absent, all official rhetoric to the contrary notwithstanding. The freeing up of the financial system, for example, has led to the emergence of a sizeable secondary credit sector in which lending takes place through direct relationships between firms and other bodies at very high interest rates; this sector is beyond the control of the monetary and regulatory authorities (CEA 1993). China's growth has been barely controllable, with a continuing tendency to overheat, and the only tools available to central policy makers for bringing the economy under control remain the microeconomic ones designed for a command economy in which firms come under direct administrative authority (*The Economist* 1995a). To function at all they require direct interpersonal encounters between state actors and myriad economic agents in highly particularistic circumstances. Under the economic reform, governmental encounters with economic agents have shifted significantly to the local level and the center has lost much control over the provinces and municipalities. This is evidenced by the share of tax revenue accruing to the central government, which, according to the World Bank, amounted to 34 percent of gross domestic product (GDP) at the beginning of the reform process 15 years ago and shrank to 19 percent by 1994 (*The Economist* 1994a).

If, according to Western experience, modernization requires institutional changes moving transactions first toward bureaucracies and then toward markets, China cannot be said to be modernizing effectively. Yet if China is not modernizing effectively, how does one account for its spectacular performance on the criterion of growth—an average of 9 percent per annum in the 1980s and in double figures since 1992?

One answer would be that modernization does not reduce to growth. As Schumpeter once quipped (1978, 64, note 1), "Add successively as many mail coaches as you please, you will never get a railway thereby." Rather, just as total factor productivity identifies those elements of growth that cannot be attributed to any single factor but are rather the product of how the factors are organized at both macro and micro levels (cf. Porter 1990), we might consider that modernization speaks about how growth is organized, about its quality, and about the institutional choices that drive the process. This means the question can now be reformulated: How can China be achieving such rapid rates of growth while retaining an institutional order so heavily invested in the lower, uncodified regions of Figure 2.1?

Two explanations suggest themselves. The first is that with a per capita income of $US300 or so in 1980 (in 1980 dollars), the country started its reforms from a very low base (World Bank 1985). Most of its growth is the result to bringing into play factors that had hitherto been underutilized, rather than of any effort to reorganize them. According to this explanation, reorganization has a part to play, but it hardly drives the process. Many countries that undergo economic take-off indeed start from a low base, and in the case of China this must certainly count as part of the explanation for its spectacular growth rate in the 1980s. For the 1990s, however, the explanation begins to lose some of its force. The World Bank's "World Development Report" has recently taken to estimating GDP per head for various countries on a purchasing-power parity basis to take into account international differences in prices. Using such calculations, China's GDP per head was $US1680 in 1991 and possibly $US2000 in 1994, figures that place it among middle-income countries. From such a perspective, the low base vanishes, as do the arguments that it was used to support. At this income level, many economies have already acquired the rudiments of a rational-legal bureaucracy as well as those of efficient market institutions—hence their claim to be modernizing.

A second explanation is that the iron law of fiefs only applies to the state sector, victim of the continuing irrationalities of the planned economy. It is argued that transactions in the non-state sector are becoming codified, as they should, according to the conventional argument (Fischer 1993). The significance of the non-state sector in China today is undeniable; it now accounts for around 50 percent of industrial output (Qian and Xu 1993), while the state sector has been "hollowing" itself out through subcontracting to non-state firms and/or through forming joint ventures both with non-state firms and foreign partners. Yet the non-state sector is, by and large, made up of small, undercapitalized collective or family businesses. They operate discreetly, sometimes clandestinely, and where they do so most successfully it is because they are beyond the reach of the state central bureaucracy. They do not, however, escape the exactions of local bureaucracies with which they must reach some accommodation if they are to survive (Nee 1992). Here the relationship remains essentially feudal, with the local bureaucracy offering protection in return for loyalty from the private and collective enterprises that come under its jurisdiction.

The infrastructure available at the local level does not necessarily energize such enterprises; it can also impede them. The phenomenal growth of official corruption in recent years bears eloquent testimony to this problem. The implementation of company and contractual law enacted by the central government is very much at the discretion of local authorities and often comes down to a matter of individual application. These considerations indicate that the non-state sector in China is not pushing toward the codified areas of our framework. Rather, it is having once more to fend off, or at least manage, the personalized impositions of ostensibly formal governmental organization as it had to in late-imperial times (Mann 1987). Bruun's (1993, chap. 5) ethnographical account of private household businesses in contemporary Chengdu richly illustrates this phenomenon.

We are thus left with a country representing over a fifth of the world's population that is achieving an unprecedented level of economic performance through a relatively uncodified system of ownership and transacting. Whatever efforts at codification have taken place—and there have been some—have tended to be in response to external rather than internal demands and to be concentrated in areas that affect inward foreign direct investment (Potter 1995; Carver 1996). In effect, China's rapid growth and development over the last 15 years challenges our concepts of modernization initially as an institutionalization toward greater codification (cf. Durkheim 1933; Tönnies 1955; Habermas 1970) followed by a decentralization toward a market order. We either have to imagine a country as being capable of growing at 13 percent per annum without modernizing—theoretically conceivable at least—or we have to reconceptualize the process of modernization itself to take account of the way it is being achieved in China.

Casual empiricism refutes the first option—a visit to any of China's cities or to the villages of its coastal regions overwhelmingly confirms that something we can call modernization is taking place. We are then left with the need to rethink the concept of modernization itself and to extend it beyond its Western conception. This opens up the possibility that China is not even trying to move further up the transactional framework toward a more codified rational-legal order as a precursor to a less troublesome decentralization—that it is not attempting to build a Western type of economic order. If China's rapid development is being pursued through its own model of economic and social organization, can more be said about the distinctive features of this model? We attempt this, in terms of China's business system and markets, capitalism, and government within that system.

Some features of China's emerging economic order

What kind of business system?

China has always had a significant amount of small-scale commercial and industrial activity outside the centrally planned command economy, but since 1979 the industrial system has become considerably more diversified (Hussain 1990, 1992). An outstanding feature of China's economic reform has been the steady and substantial growth in the share of the non-state sector in the national total (Qian and Xu 1993). Today, there is a free market for most consumer goods, while the market remains supplementary to planning only in the production and supply of some industrial goods and materials, especially those considered to be of strategic significance. Moreover, several different forms of industrial property rights have now emerged alongside a diversification in the forms of enterprise ownership and of relationships with the organs of government, including different types of contracts for the management of state-owned enterprises. We therefore need to use a framework for analysis within which the spread of markets and changing structure of property rights in China can be taken into account.

One available framework is that developed by Whitley (1991, 1992, 1994) for comparing business systems. He argued that business systems vary internationally in terms of three main sets of characteristics: (1) the nature of firms as economic actors, especially their autonomy, (2) the way relations between firms are structured to form markets, and (3) the logic that governs managerial systems of coordination and control within the firms. He applied his analysis of these three constituents to "market economies" in which "control over economic resources is decentralized to private owners" (1994, 155). While

29

reference to the three constituents can potentially identify differences between Chinese economic sectors, the way he posited a necessary conjunction of market transactions and capitalist ownership appears to be less appropriate.

Nee (1992) has identified three categories of Chinese enterprise according to the predominant mode through which their transactions are coordinated and the rights over industrial property they embody. He called the three types the "non-marketized firm," the "marketized firm," and the "private firm." Table 2.1 builds on Nee's classification but also adds certain refinements.

Non-marketized firms, which are also state-owned enterprises, form part of a now greatly diminished centralized structure of economic transactions in which state agencies control the circulation of goods and services through their redistributive mechanisms; to a large extent they also redistribute income between the firms. They predominate in heavy industries such as petroleum, chemicals, power, iron, and steel. Those goods for which the state still sets fixed plan prices come within this category. Within this sector, personalized relations between senior enterprise managers and higher state officials remain of considerable consequence, especially for the allocation of major investment funds (Lu and Child 1996).

The marketized firm, according to Nee, falls outside the bounds of central planning, though it may rely to some extent on local government to secure access to resources allocated through the plan. He regards the collectively owned enterprise as the stereotypical marketized firm, and the economic contribution of collective enterprises has grown considerably under the reform. It is necessary, however, to make some distinctions that Nee has overlooked, within both the state-owned and collective categories. First, many state enterprises now engage fully in market transactions and report to local government authorities (see Child 1994, for examples). They are therefore distinguished in Table 2.1 as "marketized state enterprises." Second, collectively owned enterprise is a very broad category. It includes quite large urban manufacturing enterprises that may in reality have a rather similar relationship with local government to that of a marketized state enterprise and are to that extent state-dependent. Thus the assumed conjunction

Table 2.1. Classification of Chinese enterprises

Mode of coordination	State	Ownership/property rights collective	Private
Non-market	Non-marketized state enterprise	—	—
Market	Marketized state enterprise*	Collective enterprise*	Private enterprise

* Later in the text of this article, these two categories are subsumed into the "marketized non-private" sector.

between market relations and capitalist (or at least non-state) ownership, made by both Nee and Whitley and drawn from the Western model, does not necessarily apply to China.

The category of collectively owned enterprise also includes small collectives running facilities such as restaurants that are largely free from regulation. Many collective enterprises, especially the smaller ones located in townships and villages (the so-called township-village enterprises, or TVEs), operate entirely in the market and with considerable freedom from government control. Their markets are not efficient neoclassical markets of the kind depicted in Figure 2.1, however, since they remain for the most part small, local, and hierarchically ordered. They retain formal links with local authorities and may enjoy some preferences over access to resources such as working capital. Otherwise they come close to Nee's third, private-firm category. Foreign-funded firms also enjoy a private status, albeit usually with state-owned partners, and operate in the market. These distinctions point to the presence of three main sectors within China's economic order: (1) a non-marketized state-owned sector, (2) a marketized non-private sector, and (3) a (marketized) private sector. The application of Whitley's (1994) criterion characteristics helps to make these distinctions more specific and in so doing demonstrates the plurality of China's present economic order.

The first sector, comprising non-marketized state-owned enterprises, remains at least as much an administrative as a business system. Despite the formal decentralization of decision making to their managements under the responsibility system (Chen 1995), state enterprises in this category continue to depend on vertical ties to higher-level agencies that transfer to them materials and capital resources according to central plans. They can only produce for the market once they have satisfied the requirements of the plan, and in many cases the prices of both inputs and outputs under the plan are fixed administratively. Their performance is judged more in the light of plan fulfillment than of hard budget criteria. One-third of state enterprises are overtly loss-making, while another third have so-called hidden (unpaid) debts; these firms rely on subsidies to keep them afloat. This undermines the decentralization of responsibility to enterprises as economic actors since it is not clear under a non-market system who should bear the responsibility for losses, and under soft budget constraints it is effectively government that does so.

By contrast, the marketized non-private sector in China can be said to be a business system because it constitutes a mode of organizing market transactions, even though this organization relies a great deal on local government intervention. Comprising larger collective firms and many state enterprises responsible to local authorities, this sector bears some resemblance to Whitley's state-dependent type of business system. Firms in this sector do not enjoy the same degree of formal autonomy as do private firms, although their effective freedom of economic action is usually greater because of the support they enjoy from local institutional intermediaries such as banks. The growth and profitability of marketized non-private firms have a larger and more direct impact on the income of local government than do those of either private firms or non-marketized state firms (Nee 1992, 11). This encourages local authorities to assist the former by providing them with valuable networks and assistance in gaining access to capital, raw materials, and labor.

In this way, local agencies of the state fill many of the roles that in other business systems are played by private intermediary institutions. The isolation of firms in this sector from supporting institutions, at least those within the local economy, is therefore relatively low. The localized nature of state-dependency for firms in this sector supports the development of their personal interorganizational connections, which are of greater importance than appears to be the norm for this type of business system, as described by Whitley (Child 1994). These connections are often arranged by local officials, and they may be a continuation of arrangements previously made under the planning system, as Solinger (1989) has illustrated through her study of relational contracting in Wuhan. The localized and informal decentralization of economic power to the marketized non-private sector in China would place it in the clan rather than the market region of Figure 2.1—in effect, a decentralization in the lower region of the C-Space.

The characteristics of the Chinese marketized private sector have several similarities to those of Whitley's "centrifugal" business system, which he illustrates by the example of the non-mainland Chinese family business. Within this system, economic power is decentralized to firms, only to a limited extent, however, partly because there is a lack of stable institutional procedures (especially laws) governing economic relations. Nor can firms in this sector expect much support from intermediaries like the Chinese banks which, having hitherto remained as government agencies, continue to offer loans as much on the basis of political as economic criteria, favoring state and larger collectively owned firms.[1] These firms operate under hard budget constraints and have to be self-reliant; as a result, they remain small and undercapitalized. Many private firms in China attempt to compensate for these disadvantages by seeking close ties with local government, but they cannot take support from that quarter for granted. They often have to pay a "management fee" to the local authority for assistance in securing access to resources and political protection, or they have to register as collective enterprises to

---

[1] Similar considerations tend to govern the allocation of materials in short supply. The situation regarding finance will probably change as, for example, foreign banks are permitted to play a more active role in the Chinese economy.

obtain greater support (Kraus 1991; Nee 1992). This mode of compensation parallels a characteristic of the centrifugal business system posited by Whitley, namely, that in the absence of stable institutional procedures and well-developed private intermediaries, the managers of firms have to use personal connections. A difference is that the key personal connections in China lie with local government officials rather than with other firms.

While there are some similarities between the private sector in China and Whitley's centrifugal type of business system, they nevertheless diverge in two main respects. The first is that private companies in China are normally still small-scale organizations, unlike some centrifugal firms. Thus the diversity of their operations is limited, and they achieve a relatively high level of internal integration under the close personal control of their owners. The second is that, because the ownership of property in China does not furnish unambiguous legal property rights, such rights continue to depend importantly on the sanction of local governments and their officials. Even the private sector in China thus continues to be shaped partly by governmental institutions.

The nature of market arrangements

The development of marketized sectors within the Chinese economy indicates that a growing proportion of economic transactions has become subject to market forces. Byrd's (1991a) analysis indicates that this is the case even with the distribution of industrial goods by state-owned enterprises, in which central allocation previously played an important role. The special characteristic of market transactions in China lies, however, not so much in their spread but in their mode of organization.

Many business transactions in China appear to be settled through negotiation within a system of networked relations based on interpersonal reciprocal obligations (*guanxi*), with local government being a major player as resource provider, facilitator, and tax collector (see Pye 1995). These transactional arrangements, "weak" in Western terms (Granovetter 1985), appear to have considerable latent strengths. Thus the institutionalized use of negotiation between enterprises and local authorities appears to introduce flexibility into regional property rights and to allow for the reconstitution of transactions to meet new opportunities and changing circumstances. Solinger (1989) indicated how, in Wuhan, the withdrawal of the planning system based on quotas and local government-directed input and output transactions gave rise to relational contracting in which many of the former business relationships were maintained. She pointed to the advantages these long-established relationships could provide in an economic environment in which uncertainties persisted about the honoring of trading agreements, the assurance of quality in goods exchanged, the provision of working capital, and so forth. These transactions were founded on longstanding economic relationships between key individuals within the organizations concerned. The assurances that underpinned the transactions derived from mutual trust.

The description offered by Solinger appears to be broadly consistent with Nee's (1992) analysis of local quasi-market networks in which local government agencies play a facilitating role and benefit from the tax revenues that derive from the stimulation that dynamic networks provide to local economic growth. The development of both internal and external subcontracting, particularly by larger enterprises, serves to extend such networks. External subcontracting encourages the growth of close personal relations between managers and technical staff of the collaborating firms, particularly when technical quality specifications and delivery schedules need to be tightly controlled (Child 1994, chap. 7).

It has also become quite common for Chinese enterprises to form alliances and mergers to provide horizontal and vertical integration (Su 1994). These alliances contribute to the development of quasi-market networks within China and appear to constitute a growing trend. In cases known firsthand to the writers, the initial moves in establishing these alliances were made by the enterprise director approaching persons from his home town in other units who were acquainted with him personally. Later on, endorsement from the relevant government ministry became necessary to ensure the support of local government departments and encourage coordination between them. Once in operation, integration between the constituent units of these alliances appears to depend heavily on close personal relations among senior managers and, to some extent, the interlocking of roles between the units.

Richardson (1972) came close to recognizing the phenomenon of relational transacting in his discussion of cooperative interfirm relationships, and Williamson (1985) has brought it into his perspective. While these contributions diverge importantly from neoclassical market analysis, they still regard relational transacting as falling within the domain of codified transactions at an intermediate point between hierarchy and market. The Chinese system of networked transactions, however, is relatively uncodified, and it is based on trust and longstanding personal connections. It does not therefore fit with Western analyses, nor is there reason to suppose that the Chinese system is merely in transition to a Western model; quite the contrary. For instance, the rapid spread in China today of modern technology for personal communications (such as mobile phones) is actually reinforcing the system by removing some of the constraints on the diffusion of personalized transacting previously imposed by low levels of codification. It facilitates the extension of economic fiefs into clan-type networks that achieve a measure of market coverage through relatively uncodified, personal means.

Do the "new" networking arrangements in China derive their distinct character from drawing on pre-1949 modes of economic transacting and the institutional supports for these? The issue here is whether we are now seeing in Chinese economic organization the reemergence of traditional social structures and behavior patterns or, rather, the establishment of new forms (cf. Siu 1989). There is some reason to expect a degree of continuity with pre-communist society, because it is recognized that social institutions and traditions are deeply embedded and extremely persistent (Granovetter 1985; Powell and DiMaggio 1991). The imperial era was characterized in many parts of China by both a highly organized market system and well-established practices for the conduct of business (Faure 1994). Thus Wong and Perdue (1992, 143–4) commented on the "mounting evidence of active, integrated markets" in Qing China, while Rawski and Li (1992) noted the active intervention of the Qing government in the grain market to stabilize prices and avert catastrophes. Skinner (1964; 1965a, b) has analyzed the hierarchical ordering of market structures in pre-communist China and the extent to which this subsumed a conjunction of administrative and market units, especially at prefectural level and above. Cohen (1993, 156) remarked that "China was notable for the cultural, social, political, and economic interpenetration of city and countryside" during the later imperial era, which provided the organizational infrastructure for business and trade. Although the markets referred to were unlikely to be efficient in the neoclassical sense of the term and hence would not be assigned to the market region of the C-Space, the previously established institutional system appears prima facie to provide precedents for the market-oriented, administratively supported system of networked transacting that has developed recently in China's non-state-dependent sector.

A new form of capitalism?[2]

There is a major debate in Western economics about the relevance of property rights to economic performance. Economic reform in the different socialist countries since the 1970s has intensified this debate, on which the Chinese case should offer an important comment. Arguably the seminal text in the modern debate is that of North and Thomas (1973, 157), who maintained that the key factor explaining the "rise of the Western world" was the evolution of "a set of property rights that provided the incentives necessary for sustained growth;" they attributed economic failure, including that of "much of Latin America, Asia and Africa in our times," to "inefficient property rights." A large literature has emerged, arguing on both theoretical and practical grounds that,

---

[2] This section has been informed by comments from our colleague Peter Nolan.

with certain exceptions, state ownership of industrial assets is incompatible with efficient operation. This argument has shaped the policy advice received by developing countries, often as a condition of further aid from the Bretton Woods organizations (Cook and Kirkpatrick 1988). Most recently, it has informed the advice given to the reforming communist countries: "The hallmark of market capitalism is that private capital has wide autonomy to enter or leave industries by creating or closing enterprises and it has substantial control over the management of the enterprises it owns" (EBRD 1993, 113).

China's rapid growth, and that of a wide spectrum of East Asian countries, calls these broad judgments into question. The case of China prompts the realization that "property rights" can be a complex mixture that does not constitute a simple binary set of possibilities—"state" versus "private." In China, a bundle of property rights is exercised by different bodies, and de factor property rights tend to emerge from continuing processes of negotiation between central, regional, community, and private interests. Moreover, the rights relate to such diverse matters as the appointment of senior enterprise managers, allocation of profits, investment funding, and formation of interfirm relationships. These rights, in the context of different categories of firms, are articulated through a variety of institutional structures, some of which are more strongly oriented toward the interests of the community than those of either the individual or the state. In this respect, again, the contrast between China's economic development and that of the West is consistent with the view that different institutional frameworks are capable of generating economic development in different societies.

While the Chinese have explained the post-1978 economic reforms as a move from a bureaucratic to a market-led system of industrial coordination, they have been at pains not to present this as a move toward capitalism and private property rights. Chinese economists and political theorists have therefore been concerned to distinguish the two dimensions in Table 2.1. They have repeatedly claimed that a market economy does not equate with a capitalist one, just as a planned economy does not necessarily amount to a socialist one (Gong 1992; Jiang 1993; Wang 1993). Markets and hierarchies, in this perspective, are just tools—mechanisms for coordinating transactions—that with suitable adjustments can each be placed equally effectively at the service of a socialist or a capitalist order.[3] Even a Western writer like Solinger (1993), who from a close vantage point suggested that China is developing a form of capitalism, nevertheless argued that this will not be based on Western institutions but will depend very much on adaptation by a state that continues to

---

[3] Experience with privatization in Western economies, however, suggests that whether a firm has public or private ownership does influence its behavior toward the market, particularly whether it pursues the goal of profit seeking to the exclusion of other goals.

regulate property rights. Faure (1994, 57) commented: "I am not saying that China, by discarding Marxism, is necessarily becoming capitalist. It is not clear to me that such words as socialism or capitalism are applicable to this emerging society in any absolute sense."

Whether these writers' claims are correct or not, their disassociation of marketization from private ownership reflects a distinctive feature of China's economic development that appears to be socially embedded. Up to 1949, industrial property rights in China were granted more or less under license from the state, and the continued approval of local officials was required (Jiang 1992). Faure (1994) indicated how firms in the early stages of Chinese industrialization in late-imperial times usually depended on the patronage of senior government officials. Similarly, the property rights enjoyed by "state-owned" enterprises today are in practice negotiated with higher authorities, whether these concern specific resource commitments (Child and Lu 1996) or the implementation of responsibility contracts in general (Chen 1995). In the rapidly growing non-state sector, the ownership of collectives has not been clearly defined, and local government retains an important supportive and supervisory role in their operation (Nee 1992).

While state enterprises in China are officially owned by "the whole people," government being the de facto representative of their owners, the intention of the economic reformers has been to separate public administration from business management by decentralizing powers of enterprise decision making to the latter through the Contract Responsibility System (CRS) (Byrd, 1991b). As Chen (1995) has shown, the property rights enjoyed by the managers of state enterprises under the CRS are established through their negotiation with administering authorities rather than on the basis of codification, with the result that the rights of their official owners are becoming increasingly attenuated. The lively current discussion on the possibility of introducing stockholding systems to state enterprises points to a further impending redefinition of their ownership. The nature of such redefinition is uncertain, since it will depend on the determination of which groups are entitled to own stock and the percentage of enterprise assets that are allocated to stockholders. It is therefore quite difficult at this moment to comment on the prospects that the state sector will be privatized and whether, in this respect, there will be a move toward a capitalism of the Western variety. If there is, it is quite likely that the institutional basis on which ownership rights are defined will not accord to the highly formal and legalized Western pattern.

Whereas the reform of state enterprises has been from the top down, township-village enterprises (TVEs) have emerged and proliferated from the bottom up. The consequence is that their ownership status is very ill-defined. Weitzman and Xu (1993) argued that TVEs do not have any owners in the spirit of Western property rights theory. Nominally, TVEs are collectively owned enterprises, with community members being the owners. These collective owners do not, however, have shares in a formal sense and are permitted to participate in the TVE on the basis of their residency, a right that is mandated by the community government. The community government is the de facto executive owner of the TVEs and is reported, normally, to control them. The TVE is therefore not a private capitalist firm in disguise, and there are legal restrictions to prevent it from converting into one. So, while TVEs are highly successful non-state enterprises, with a growth rate of total factor productivity about ten times that of state enterprises and accounting for about 38 percent of China's industrial output by 1991, they do not represent a shift toward capitalism in the Western sense. TVEs and other Chinese enterprises today may behave like Western capitalist firms, and indulge in an increasingly entrepreneurial pursuit of market opportunities, but this does not necessarily mean that their constitution is of the Western capitalistic variety.

This failure to match the Western model generates ambiguity in the minds of some writers. Bolton (1995, 8), for example, questioned whether "TVEs can be expected to be a stable institutional arrangement which could form a long term alternative to private ownership of firms." An alternative reaction would be to suggest that if TVEs have emerged from and retain their roots within a traditional system of community cooperation and transacting, then they are founded on a sound institutional bedrock. Further investigation into this question will require close attention to the property rights and transactional arrangements pertaining to TVEs and other collectives in particular communities. It is not clear, for instance, how much variance there is in such arrangements between different local areas. Overall, it seems appropriate to break away from the legally based Western notion of property rights that emanates from ownership and, instead, adopt a concept more appropriate to China that allows for the possibility that (1) such rights may be granted upon administrative sufferance and (2) that their terms can be subject to a continuing process of renegotiation. In that case, the significant research question is not so much who owns Chinese business assets as who controls and regulates them and through what social process, a question that Berle and Means (1932) asked of the large American corporation six decades ago.

Another feature of growing importance in the Chinese economy, in which government agencies are often active partners, is the development of various forms of hybrid firms (cf. Borys and Jemison 1989; Su 1994). These organize business activities across ownership forms and systems and include Sino-foreign joint ventures, Sino-Sino joint ventures, and partnerships between state, collective, and private ownership forms. Su concluded from his research in Xiamen that hybrid firms have provided an extremely important dynamic for economic growth and development at the micro level. They also contribute importantly to the formation of business networks that, among other things, stimulate innovation through information exchange and innovation. They are often formed and operate on a basis of personal trust rather than formal contract.

There is a juxtaposition in China of (1) an emergent form of what at best can be termed "quasi-capitalism," incorporating important aspects of governmental patronage, and (2) marketization. This will, according to conventional Western thinking, inevitably generate certain fundamental tensions, and it remains to be seen how significant these are. One such tension stems from the temptation of government officials to introduce non-economically rational criteria into resource allocation by firms (cf. Child and Lu 1996). Another derives from the increasingly local focus of industrial governance, which may in several ways inhibit the flow of investment funds to their nationally most beneficial uses, such as through pressures to retain surplus funds within the locality or the discouragement of outside investors because of the risks they perceive to stem from local interpretations of the law and the distortions introduced by local corruption. As Faure (1994, 87) stated, "The present danger in the development of a market in China lies in the very real possibility that with the devolution of state power, local authorities may take away what the state would concede. It is as yet unclear if the state can effectively curb the emergence of patronage networks built upon the personal influence of members of the officialdom."

The role of government

It has been said that China is a nation searching for a country. Huge size and topographical barriers have contributed to an historical problematic in China concerning the relations between the state—the central overall authority that organizes and symbolizes a country—and the nation. The contrast between the Western and Chinese models of the state's economic role are illuminated by the differences among the concepts of a "nation-state," "the nation and the state," and "the nation or the state." The first concept assumes that there is a positive valence between government and society, with the state being the codification of the nation through the constitutional and legal system. This approximates the Western model. The "nation and the state" points to a situation in which the population accords legitimacy to the central authority while seeking to keep it at arm's length. The saying that "Heaven is high and the Emperor is far" has traditionally met with approval in China, signifying that the state does not codify the nation that prefers to conduct its transactions according to customary uncodified norms. The third concept, "the state or the nation," envisages a sharp distinction between government and people, in which the state may be oppressive and fail to secure popular legitimacy. It may be conjectured that in the former Soviet Union and in China by 1976, the situation was one of "the state or the nation" and that this contributed importantly to the failure of the planning system.

The post-1949 communist regime saw the most far-reaching attempts in China's history to bring economic and social life under the central control of the state. The first was via the central planning system that was established in the 1950s but which never attained the detailed coverage of the Soviet system. The second was via the ideologically sustained mass mobilizations of the Great Leap Forward and the Cultural Revolution, which while ostensibly encouraging local initiatives were nevertheless centrally orchestrated. By the late 1970s, it was realized that both systems of central state control or initiative had failed to provide for sustained economic development: China had not been able to sustain a satisfactory position in the "bureaucracies" region of Figure 2.1 (economic regulation via a central planning bureaucracy), while the attempt to have the state exercise direct central initiative and control through traditional fieflike social formations proved disastrous.

Since 1979, there has been a steady decentralization of economic initiative to provincial, municipal, and even more local tiers of government, a shrinking of the state-owned component of the industrial economy, a consistent decline in the proportion of capital investment controlled directly by central government, a shrinking share of tax revenue accruing to central government, and an official aspiration to concentrate central government intervention on tuning the economy as a whole through fiscal and monetary instruments (Naughton 1987; *The Economist* 1994a). Together with the encouragement of market transacting, this may at first sight appear to be a redefinition of the state's economic role toward the Western model, which would be an erroneous interpretation. For it does not mean that government in China now takes a hands-off stance towards business. Rather, the system that is now emerging involves a sharper differentiation between the role of central and regional authorities, the latter comprising layers of government down from province, city, county, and township to village. Various bureaux and commissions operate at each level within this tiered system, each having its own goals for the economy. The resulting vertical and horizontal cleavages within the system give rise to multiple power centers with which enterprises have to deal, depending on their scale, legal status, and sector (Wank 1995).

Government officials at the different levels and in the various units have been enjoined to support profitable economic developments, and their departments often take a stake in these. Economic decentralization has meant that only large state-owned enterprises, normally located in strategic industrial sectors, retain a direct responsibility to central ministries. For other enterprises, it has led to a closer interdependence between local governments and enterprises led by managers or entrepreneurs who are part of the same community. Local governments and associations may even sometimes ally with the enterprise managements under their purview to resist the encroachment of the central state over matters such as investment approval and taxation (Ungar and Chan 1995). Wank (1995) noted that such local alliances can reduce the need for enterprises to look to the central authorities for resources and that these authorities are often critical of them. He concluded from an in-depth study of private and cooperative enterprises in Xiamen that "entrepreneurial connections with the bureaucracy create clientelist networks that are neither market relationships nor formal command-economy relationships.... They are patron-client relations between actors who control asymmetrical resources and forge alliances for mutual benefit. The alliances... are embedded in personal ties between entrepreneurs and officials who know and trust each other" (1995, 69–70).

The new system bears some similarities to that which evolved during the early stages of Chinese industrialization in late-imperial times. This was a system of state patronage in which officials took an active role in promoting and supervising private enterprises, especially the more significant ones. The rapid growth of the economy after 1895 brought about a decentralization and broadening of bureaucratic involvement in industry in collaboration with local networks of gentry families (Faure 1994). During the period of Nationalist government, many so-called "national capitalist firms" were owned and controlled by politically dominant families (Coble, 1980). The Chinese tradition was therefore one of close alliance between government officials and communities in industrial governance.

The combination in contemporary China of decentralization from central authorities with the bottom-up dynamic provided by township and village enterprises leads to a perspective on the role that government can play in facilitating business networks at the local level that is quite different from Western experience. Tu (1993, xi) observed that the collusion of state and entrepreneur made for a peculiar economic strength:

> The interdependence of economy and polity is such that the state plays a vitally important role at all levels in removing structural impediments to development and building necessary infrastructures for manufacturing industry, commerce, and trade. The mixed pattern is certainly not a socialist planned economy, nor is it a Western capitalist system. The so-called township village enterprise is a new animal, a species in economic development that has yet to be properly defined.

Bruun (1993) argued that the state and the family (or community)—fundamental institutions in China—present a dichotomy that has historically been in mutual tension. We are suggesting, by contrast, that the significant feature of the emerging Chinese system lies in the ways government and community or family work together within a system of relatively uncodified relationships that derives legitimacy from embedded social practice rather than from formalized ownership and property rights. In some forms, government and family work constitute a fieflike relationship, as with some large enterprises that report directly to a ministry or with business ventures that have been started by the children of senior party members or by the People's Liberation Army. In other forms, like many township or village collective enterprises, government and community organizations work together with firms in a more extensive clan-like network. In both instances, there is an evident contrast with the Western market capitalism model in which government codifies the rules and monitors adherence to them from outside the transactional arena. In China, government operates from within the transactional arena. The distinction between the inside and the outside remains itself uncodified and hence subject to arbitrary interpretation by power holders.

This is not to claim that the economic role of the state is unproblematic in China; far from it. A major problem is that the emerging "new" economy of non-state enterprises does not remove the continuing headache of state-owned firms, among which it was recently estimated that as many as 80 percent are loss-making (private communication from a senior Chinese economist in 1994). One of the most difficult problems facing the current reform of state enterprises away from the contract responsibility system toward a modern corporate system lies in determining who has the right to select their boards of directors. If this is the state as owner, then it is hard to see how any reform will be effected. If this is not the state, then who else has the right, since there are no other owners? Collective and private firms avoid this dilemma insofar as tangible social units constitute their de facto ownership, whereas the ownership of a state-owned enterprise is intangible.

The question also arises as to whether or not local government enjoys the legitimacy to run economic networks. There can be tensions between government controls and the aspirations of firms (Ungar and Chan 1995). Within local communities, private businesses can feel exploited by local officials and to be the victims of growing corruption, as Bruun (1993) found in Chengdu. If local authorities do develop this legitimacy, will the emerging system be similar to Gellner's (1981) notion of a segmented society, in which there is a collection of local systems in competition with each other but coordinated by government at the next level up? The notion of a segmented society posits a clear functional role for government within an economic system that is vertically as well as horizontally networked. The parallel with Skinner's description of hierarchically ordered markets in pre-communist times is intriguing. The challenge of hierarchical ordering will always be particularly acute for China simply because of its huge size, topographical barriers, and tendency for interregional economic imbalance. It is important always to recall that in

China government straddles several hierarchical levels, and the resolution of the relationship between these levels in economic governance is inherently problematic.

The Western concept of the state in the process of modernization has envisaged it as the legislator of rules for economic behavior and of procedures for resolving disputes under these rules. In the liberal interpretation, the state acts on behalf of the majority in society through the democratic process, and, in the Marxist interpretation, it acts on behalf of the dominant capitalist class (Gran 1994). The state is not assumed to be the natural body either to own or directly to manage industrial organizations. Studies of East-Asian societies other than China have already called for the amendment of this theory about the role of government in modernization (Hamilton and Biggart 1988; Whitley 1992). The state has, for example, played a far more directive role in the industrialization of countries such as Japan and South Korea. China adds an interesting dimension, with its tiered system of governmental involvement creating an interdependence of economy and polity down to the bedrock of local communities. As Tu (1993) observed, this mixed pattern is neither a socialist planned economy, nor a Western capitalist system. It requires an elaboration, if not amendment, of conventional theories about the role of the state in economic life, including further development of those that do adopt a comparative institutions perspective.

Conclusion

It has been argued that even a superficial examination of the emerging Chinese economic system calls for a reappraisal of the universal validity of conventional Western assumptions about modernization. That analysis has largely confined itself to the codified reaches of the codification-diffusion framework presented earlier. Application of the framework suggests that we can derive a conceptual language from Western economic and social analysis that is useful for elucidating the Chinese case but that Western assumptions about the variables identified by the concepts will not apply, either in terms of the configurations of variables (at one point in time) or movement along the variables over time. The Chinese system, in particular its underlying logic and its gestalt, will be different. This difference, as it emerges from our discussion, is summarized by Figure 2.3 and can be simply stated: The Western path to modernization, involving first an increase in codification toward rational-legal administrative systems (i.e., bureaucracies) and then a decentralization toward a market order, created the institutions of modern "market capitalism." Such a path, at least when codification has been achieved, is consistent with the unidimensional markets and hierarchies perspective. The Chinese

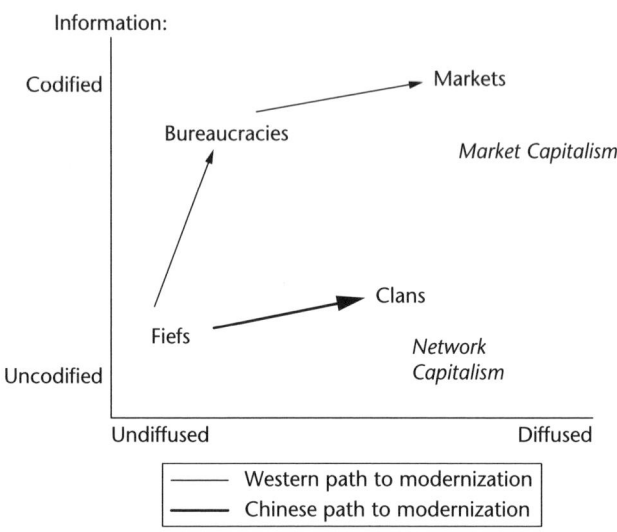

Figure 2.3. Chinese and Western paths to modernization

path to modernization since 1949, by contrast, involved first an abortive move up the codification scale (state planning), punctuated by wild oscillations toward mass mobilization, and then, after a reversion into fiefs, a subsequent decentralization, coupling with traditional systems in the lower reaches of the C-Space. In the absence of effective codification, and given traditional Chinese social organization, such decentralization leads not to markets but to clans and permits the more local and personalized institutional order, which, following other observers of Asian economic institutions (Biggart and Hamilton 1992; Gerlach and Lincoln 1992; Berg 1994), we shall label "network capitalism."

Three main sectors have been distinguished within China's emerging economic order. These are the non-marketized state-owned sector, the marketized non-private sector, and the marketized private sector. They vary in the extent to which their constituent enterprises engage in market transactions and enjoy autonomy from the state in the exercise of property rights. They share, however, a high level of engagement in transactional networks based on relational contracting and interfirm alliances that involve governmental agencies in approving, supporting, and sometimes initiating roles. China's emerging economic order is constituted by a combination of communal property rights and transactions in which contingent risks are managed in these networks informally on the basis of accepted social practice rather than by reliance on formal laws of contract. The security of property rights, which, according to the Western tradition is guaranteed by the rule of law in democratic societies, in China derives primarily from a relatively uncodified process of legitimization within the community as a socioeconomic network. The security of Chinese rights to employ economic assets in the fulfillment of transactional obligations is supported by the intervention of officials at the various levels of government to safeguard what is a politically and socially acceptable use of those rights. In terms of our analytical framework, China appears to show how a clan-based system of transactions can function successfully based on a communal definition of property rights, rather than these being defined externally and from above through a legal system that identifies property rights based on individual ownership. China thus demonstrates that a modernizing economic order is able to operate in the less codified domain of the C-Space.

Despite this limited reliance on codification, there is an increase in the diffusion of economic transactions within China's economy. A shift from fieflike to clan-based transactions within China's economic order is evidenced by several developments. The first is the growing share of economic activity accounted for by non-state-owned enterprises. State-owned enterprises are more beholden than other Chinese firms to specific governmental authorities in which custody of their ownership is vested, such as ministries and economic commissions. The structure of control over state-owned enterprises, and in some cases their input-output transactional networks, tends to be narrower in scope and to retain more fieflike characteristics. Control over non-state enterprises is less specific, and their patterns of resource dependency lead them into a wider network of external organizations from which they transact factor inputs and dispose of their outputs. Second, an increasing number of enterprises are widening the scope of their transactions, and securing greater economic independence from higher governmental bodies, through the formation of joint ventures with foreign firms investing in China. These linkages with foreign firms extend their networks beyond the scope of localized fiefs. Third, more Chinese enterprises are forming alliances between themselves, chiefly to provide horizontal integration and to enlarge the scope of their transactions within the Chinese economy as a whole.

Networked relationships have for a long time played a significant role in Western economic life, a fact that became obscured by the hegemony of the atomistic market model of classical and neoclassical economics (Berg 1994; Powell and Smith-Doerr 1994). There has also been a rapid growth of various forms of economic networking in recent years, such that it has been described as the characteristic organizational form of the "new competition" (Nohria and Eccles 1992). It is therefore not the presence of networking that is distinctive about China's emerging economic order but, rather, the depth and nature of its social embeddedness. Regarding the former, we have cited evidence of continuities between contemporary and historic networking, with agents of the state playing an integral role in both. Redding (1990, 95) has noted how living "in a collectivist and group-dominated society" is a cultural tradition for the Chinese. The roots of networking as an institutionalized practice are ancient and extensively developed in China. The fundamental contrasts in the institutional constitution of property rights and transactional safeguards between Western (especially Anglo-Saxon) societies and China also imply that the nature of the social processes sustaining networking in China are also quite different from those in Western countries.

Biggart and Hamilton (1992) noted that economists have long had difficulty applying the Western neoclassical model of markets and firms to Asia, with its developed interfirm networks (Goto 1982; Aoki 1984, 1990). They point out that a model of Asian capitalism is long overdue. The analysis of the Chinese economic reforms in the C-Space contributes both to the institutional interpretation of Asian capitalism and offers an indication of where China stands with respect to it. The analysis yields two related propositions:

> **Proposition 1:** The markets and hierarchies perspective, when applied to the modernization process, assumes that policy options are located along a single dimension with the state (bureaucracies) at one extremity and autonomous firms (markets) at the other. This perspective assumes, therefore, that decentralization involves a transition from bureaucracies to markets. A C-Space analysis indicates that it is also possible to decentralize at a lower level of codification than is implied by the markets and hierarchies perspective. In that case, the move will be from fiefs to clans.

> **Proposition 2:** China offers an instance of such a decentralization and, in so doing, it is moving not toward a market order, as it claims, but toward a form of economic organization that can be labeled network capitalism and that to a large degree appears to be characteristic of East Asian societies.

Taken together, these two propositions extend the institutional options available for the modernization process beyond those offered in the markets and hierarchies framework. They do so in a way that challenges both the widely held assumption that capitalism is a unitary market-oriented phenomenon (cf. Braudel 1979) and the popular belief that institutional and economic development invariably lead to a convergence with a unitary capitalist order.

Applied to the Chinese case, a further and more detailed investigation of these propositions would benefit from a focus on selected local economies and their linkages to the wider national and international economy. A local focus is justified by the emergence of the non-state sector, to which many state enterprises are becoming increasingly tied through sub-contracting and alliances (Su 1994). It is the sector from which much of the bottom-up momentum of the reform has derived and within which new business networks are emerging with local government support. Questions of ownership, financing, trading, and regulation need to be investigated as components of a wider regional commercial system, and with regard to its historical antecedents, and this comprehensive perspective can only be practically accomplished on a local basis. Some localities should furnish records relevant to a reconstruction of the pre-1949 economic system, and it should be possible to question those influential in establishing the new system as to their design templates and the normative framework that informed them (cf. Jiang 1992).

Western capitalism in its mature form has directed its codifying efforts toward increasing efficiency and managing risk. It has striven toward order and predictability through both the codification of law outside enterprises and the codification (formalization) of management structures and systems within them. This is a path that an increasing number of Western writers are now urging corporations to abandon in favor of modes of organizing that are more consistent with the concept of networking, such as subcontracting and temporary alliances (e.g. Kanter 1983; Hastings 1993; Miles and Snow 1994). Peters (1992) has called this the "necessary disorganization for the nineties." While this emerging thinking might be more accurately described as the search for the self-learning and self-reconstituting organization, the significant point is that networking is increasingly being seen as a necessary way of achieving this end.

The Chinese system of network capitalism works through the implicit and fluid dynamic of relationships. On the one hand, this is a process that consumes much time and energy. On the other hand, it is suited to handling complexity and uncertainty. Networks offer greater capacities for generating and transmitting new information, and when they are sustained by trust-based relationships they offer a cushion against the possibility of failure that is a concomitant of uncertainty. We have argued that, in this last respect, the networks of the emergent Chinese capitalism are qualitatively different from those within the Western market system, for the latter continue to be based on legal contract and ownership rights rather than on long-term trust relationships. If Peters (1992) is correct in seeing Western capitalism as exhibiting conditions of increasing impermanence and fickleness, with businesses joining in more and more temporary alliances, then it clearly is not developing toward the long-term clan-like relationships of Chinese network capitalism. Rather, Western networking is likely to be characterized by short-term expediency that will increase rather than cope with uncertainty and in which there may well be an increasing resort to litigation to deal with disputes arising from broken business marriages. These differences between the emerging Chinese and Western economic orders point clearly to the influence of the institutional systems in which they are respectively embedded.

For those transacting directly with the Chinese system, useful practical insights would arise from investigating the issues addressed in this paper. Light should be thrown on entry points into Chinese economic networks, and this would have direct implications for European companies' market entry and marketing policies with respect to China. It would be useful to compare foreign companies that have achieved differing levels of success in their China market policies. One might expect to find differences between overseas Chinese and Western companies. Westerners may well believe that their best policy is to enact their Chinese business environment via formal dealings with the state, whereas Chinese investors may well enact their environment via the invisible, "weak" network. Research in progress at Cambridge University on Sino-foreign joint ventures confirms that overseas Chinese investors are more likely to establish business relationships through friendship ties or other informal contacts than are Western investors. Further investigation into local economic systems would also help to throw light on the question of where the key decision makers are located within what appear to be quite fluid and dynamic systems. This is of obvious potential importance to foreign firms seeking to secure a commitment to actions that will further their business operations. This returns us to the main point of the analysis presented in this paper. The social rules of business in China are not those to which Westerners have become accustomed or which conform to their stereotype of "socialist" economy. What they find when engaging with China is a system that in its transformation is giving rise to a distinctive institutional form—network capitalism.

3

Analyses of the Chinese System

John Child

Max Boisot had a long and continuing fascination with China as a distinctive cultural and institutional system clearly destined to become a great power. He regarded the Chinese economic reform initiated at the end of 1978 as the world's largest and most ambitious program of economic and social change. It was a significant intellectual challenge to conceptualize and understand this change. In his endeavors to provide this understanding, Boisot cautioned against interpreting China's reform in terms of a simple shift from a centrally-managed socialist system to a decentralized market-based one, and against assuming that China was moving toward adopting a Western-style capitalist order. Instead, he and his collaborators argued that the origins and likely trajectory of China's reform required analysis in terms of a more complex conceptual framework that recognized several contrasting cultural and institutional configurations and allowed for various paths to modernization.

As section VI of this book relates, Boisot was commissioned by the European Community in 1981 to work out a plan for a new management education program to be run in China. In his 1983 report, he pointed out that Western approaches to management had developed in their own social and economic environment and that careful consideration would have to be given to how far such approaches were applicable and adaptable to China. He was therefore aware from the outset of the need to analyze the Chinese system in its own right rather than in terms of Western models, and he appreciated the conceptual challenge this presented. This issue continues in the debate as to whether Western theories can be adapted to a study of management and organization in China rather than requiring a unique China-specific theory (Barney and Zhang 2009). From 1986 until the year of his death in 2011 Boisot and his co-authors published 21 papers and book chapters on China. The most influential of these writings applied his information-based framework to the challenge of making sense of China's economic reform and the business systems emerging from it.

The analysis Boisot and his collaborators developed over time provides a highly insightful understanding of the distinctiveness and complexity of the Chinese system. It was essentially based on the "Culture Space" (C-Space), later elaborated into the "Information Space" (I-Space). As Boisot pointed out (1983, 1986b, 1987a), Kroeber and Kluckhohn (1952) after examining several hundred definitions of culture came to the conclusion that the term described the ways that people structure and share information. The C-Space, defined by the two dimensions of information codification and information diffusion, identified four transactional or organizational modes. These were (1) the bureaucratic (in which transactions are based on codified knowledge the diffusion of which is largely restricted to the focal organization or system); (2) the market (with transactions based on codified knowledge that is widely diffused among market players); (3) the feudal or "fief" (with highly personalized transactions using uncodified and undiffused knowledge) and (4) the clan (in which transactions are also based on uncodified knowledge which is more widely diffused among the members of a network).[1] In his 1986 *Organization Studies* article, Boisot applied this framework tellingly to the contrast between reform in China and in the then Soviet Union. He made the crucial observation that China operated at a lower level of codification:

> The Chinese have been altogether less imprisoned by rules, regulations, definitions, and so on, than have the Soviets. In short, Chinese culture operates at a lower level of codification. This gives them an ideological flexibility and a possibility of changing the system that is not available to their Soviet counterparts (p. 153).

The 1988 article with John Child in *Administrative Science Quarterly* (Boisot and Child, 1988) referred to the four quadrants of the C-Space to argue two key related points. First, that discussions of economic system reform in socialist countries were too limited in basing their argument on a postulated dichotomy between bureaucratic and market transaction-governance systems—Williamson's (1975) "hierarchies" and "markets." Even official Chinese documents were adopting this dichotomy in describing the Chinese economic reform as entailing a move from administrative to market coordination. Second, rather than the dynamic of the Chinese reforms pushing toward markets as an alternative to bureaucratic state planning, there were signs that patrimonial values were reasserting themselves and pushing towards

---

[1] In his early writings, Boisot called this fourth transactional mode the "federation,," later adopting Ouchi's term "clan." See Boisot (1981, 1986b) and Ouchi (1980).

Analyses of the Chinese System

fiefs as the dominant transactional mode. At this relatively early stage in China's economic reform modest moves towards market governance were evident in both the commercial and light industrial sectors. However, much of Chinese industry remained subject to bureaucratic administration but this was neither comprehensive nor rigorous, certainly by comparison with Soviet practice. So while China had not adopted a market system to any great extent, it was also demonstrating signs of bureaucratic failure. Instead, what were ostensibly bureaucracies were actually dependent on impacted and uncodified information distributed within fiefs. These operated within the state bureaucracy as clusters of hierarchical relations in which authority rested heavily on personal loyalty.

The explanation offered for this bureaucratic failure was partly the deeply rooted cultural preference in China for personalized hierarchical relations, and partly the country's incomplete modernization. China at the time still lacked both the codification skills required to handle the large transactional volumes entailed by bureaucratic and market governance and the legal and information infrastructure that could take it beyond localized particularistic negotiations. In other words, the shift towards the codified universalistic norms required for an efficient market system was neither consistent with traditional Chinese culture nor supported by a "modern" institutional system. The article's thesis was that the Williamson model required "extension to take into account other transaction-governance possibilities that may be more consistent with the social preferences emanating from a traditional culture and that are also easier to support with the limited infrastructure of an economically less developed nation" (p. 507). It advanced an "iron law of fiefs" applicable to those bureaucratic failures which result from the absence of a transactional system that can sustain a high degree of codification and hence an adequate level of formal rationality. The iron law of fiefs clearly applies to many other developing economies as well.

The article reprinted here—Boisot and Child (1996a)—expanded and updated the analysis of the 1988 paper. It concluded that under China's reform program decentralization of the state command bureaucracy was giving rise to a distinctive institutional form, that of "network capitalism." This form was seen to arise from a combination of limited information codification in China combined with communal property rights and organization of economic transactions. China's path to modernization through network capitalism contrasted with the Western path of modernization through the development of markets based on high levels of information codification.

Through applying the C-Space framework, the universal validity of conventional Western assumptions about the path to modernization could be questioned:

> The Western path to modernization, involving first an increase in codification toward rational-legal administrative systems (i.e. bureaucracies) and then a decentralization toward a market order, created the institutions of modern "market capitalism." Such a path, at least when codification has been achieved, is consistent with the unidimensional markets and hierarchies perspective. The Chinese path to modernization since 1949 by contrast, involved first an abortive move up the codification scale (state planning), punctuated by wild oscillations toward mass mobilization, and then, after a reversion into fiefs, a subsequent decentralization, coupling with traditional systems in the lower reaches of the C-Space. In the absence of effective codification, and given traditional Chinese social organization, such decentralization leads not to markets but to clans and permits the more local and personalized social order, which following other observers of Asian economic institutions... we shall label "network capitalism" (pp. 621–2).

This analysis extended the institutional options available to support modernization beyond those offered in the markets and hierarchies framework. China's modernization suggested that it is possible to decentralize at a lower level of codification than is implied by the markets and hierarchies perspective. Later papers (Boisot and Child 2007; Boisot, Child, and Redding 2011) recognized that modern information and communication technologies (ICTs) facilitate this latter alternative by lowering the costs of transacting through less codified clan-like structures within populations that are larger and located across great distances than before. This conceptual extension of modernization possibilities helped to inform the then emerging challenge to the widely held assumption that there is one form of capitalism based on similar institutional foundations (e.g. Whitley 1999; Hall and Soskice 2001). It also questioned the belief, which had become even more popular following the transitions from socialism in Eastern Europe, that institutional and economic development inevitably leads to a convergence between national economic systems onto a unitary capitalist order.

In fact, China was (and still is) a complex mixed economy that cannot be neatly placed into a single category. Nee (1992) had pointed out that China's emerging economic order was not internally homogenous but consisted of three main sectors: the non-marketized state-owned sector, the marketized non-private sector and the marketized private sector. These sectors varied "in the extent to which their constituent enterprises engage in market transactions and enjoy autonomy from the state in the exercise of property rights" (Boisot and Child 1996a, 622). This mixed picture arose because the Chinese leadership wanted to adopt only a limited number of market institutions and to allow market forces to operate in certain sectors such as consumer goods but not in others. Some parts of the economy had therefore become located in the market region of the C-Space. Boisot and Child suggested that what the leadership did not want was for an institutionally fully fledged capitalist system to supersede those aspects of the previous economic order that it wished to retain. These included socialist features such as the state ownership of strategic enterprises, bureaucratic features such as an influence on enterprise governance through administrative controls and enterprise Party organs, and feudal features in respect of the allegiance of key enterprises to central ministries and of local enterprises to local governments. This was economic reform "with Chinese characteristics."

Although networked relationships had for a long time played a significant role in Western economic life and were returning to favor as firms disaggregated themselves to cope with competitive pressures, the distinctive feature of networking in China's emerging economic order lay in "the depth and nature of its social embeddedness" (Boisot and Child 1996a, 623). It had deep historical roots as a cultural tradition that had grown up under conditions of very considerable uncertainty engendered by a combination of natural disasters and arbitrary rule. The Chinese system of network capitalism works through the implicit and fluid dynamic of trust-based relationships. That trust is heavily based on familial or community membership and is hard for others to gain, but it is highly valued and respected. Network capitalism is "suited to handling complexity and uncertainty. Networks offer greater capacities for generating and transmitting new information, and when they are sustained by trust-based relationships they offer a cushion against the possibility of failure that is a concomitant of uncertainty" (p. 625).

In their next main article, Boisot and Child (1999) contrasted this capacity to "absorb" complexity and its associated uncertainties with an alternative approach more usually associated with Western practice which is to "reduce" complexity though a combination of imposing codified structures and systems. Whereas Western organizations and institutions generally operate with codified information, communication and formal roles, their Chinese equivalents tend to operate with less codification. The Chinese approach based on clan-like networks has an advantage in handling and responding to cognitive complexity in which the interpretation of subtle uncodified information is required. However, it does this by keeping down the numbers of interacting persons (reducing "relational complexity"), albeit, as already mentioned, that modern ICT technologies have now considerably reduced this limitation. The Western approach relies on the establishment of codified structures and systems that are in principle able to disseminate explicit information very widely, hence facilitating the management of global businesses. This approach may, however, face serious disadvantages in coping with more tacit uncodified information. The difference in the two approaches suggests a trade-off between the complexity or scope of relationships that can be handled and the complexity of the substantive content that can be transacted through such relations. "A market order can handle relational complexity of a high order by codifying and abstracting the content of transactions into prices and quantities. Clans, on the other hand, can handle greater cognitive complexity, but only by keeping the numbers down. We have suggested that Western and Chinese societies reflect this contrast" (Boisot and Child 1999, 250).[2]

Boisot's last published article on the Chinese system, co-authored with John Child and Gordon Redding (Boisot, Child, and Redding 2011), returned to the question of whether under globalization there is likely to be a convergence towards a market order. Taking China as its case study, this article brought together and built on the insights contained in previous work. These were the use of the *I-Space* framework to identify the structuring and diffusion of information as two key dimensions for identifying distinct sectors and organizational types; the recognition that China's evolving economy comprised three main sectors; and the part played by ICTs in widening the possibilities for transacting information and messages that are not in a codified and abstract form. The authors also resurrected the cultural emphasis of Boisot's early work by employing the concept of semantic field. This refers to a coherence between different forces operating in the *I-Space*, such as a particular configuration of knowledge structuring and diffusion. Actors are said to share a culture to the extent that their semantic fields overlap and they occupy the same finite provinces of meaning. Different institutions will be associated with their own semantic fields though sufficiently strong clusters of institutions may exercise an attraction beyond their semantic fields.

The *I-Space* framework and these insights were used for a critical examination of the belief that ICTs facilitate globalization, seen as the movement towards the integration and convergence toward a market order of what are nationally distinctive economic, political, institutional, organizational and cultural features. The authors developed their argument at two levels of analysis—the Chinese system as a whole and the business systems operating within it. They argued that, overall, there is a drift within the *I-Space* toward a greater diffusion of information without necessarily a significant increase in the structuring of information or institutions. Three contextual factors account for this shift. First, as the big questions of political economy come to be resolved by experimentation rather than bureaucratic or ideological dogma, so alternatives such as private firms offer more flexible, less structured models which apply fief or clan forms of organization to address market challenges. Second, the new ICTs are rapidly changing China's information environment,

---

[2] By the time that this article was written, Boisot had elaborated the C-Space framework into the *I-Space* through incorporating into the notion of informational "structure" a distinction between the codification and abstraction of information. Codification involves the assignment of data to categories, whereas abstraction involves a reduction in the number of categories to which data need to be assigned for a phenomenon to be understood. See Boisot (1995a, 1998).

increasing both the diffusion of information and the capacity to bear informal personalized communications through means such as video-conferencing and social networking. Third, the changes brought about by China's accession to the WTO in 2001 increase its international interactions with other business systems and hence exert a pull towards the greater diffusion of information and communication. However, this shift does not necessarily imply a move to a market order as the dominant institutional framework for China, or indeed other non-western economies, because alternative clan-like arrangements can meet the challenge of combining decentralization with the maintenance of order. The historical example of the South Korean chaebol is cited to illustrate this point.

The diversity of business systems within China also speaks against the assumption of convergence onto a single market order. The authors identified three main business systems within China—the state sector, local corporates and the private sector. In terms of Boisot's *I-Space* framework, activities and transactions in the state sector are governed by a "bureaucratic" order and are characterized by structured but undiffused information. Under the pressure of competition, however, state-owned enterprises are tending to move towards a market regime. The dominant rationales within their semantic field are national development, control of state assets, and efficiency. The local corporate system is characterized by relatively unstructured and only partially diffused activities governed by local and personalized organizational networks of a "clan" nature. These networks generally have a strong presence of local government and Party interests. The dominant rationales within their semantic field are territorially-based competition, local opportunism, alliances, efficiency and professionalism. Firms in the private sector tend to be governed as fiefs, albeit transacting many of their inputs and outputs through markets. The dominant rationales within the semantic field of private firms are private wealth, secrecy, control, entrepreneurship and personalism.

The conclusion is reached, based on the case of China, that ICTs have an enabling rather than a determining effect with regard to the cultural, institutional and organizational characteristics of business systems. Moreover, while national economic systems may be converging in respect of a particular component of an economic system, such as market transacting, this does not mean that there is a convergence on the overall configuration of institutional structures. It has become clear that so-called capitalist systems vary in their specific institutional structures and dynamics; China with its mixture of capitalist and socialist features adds to the variety. China therefore continues to provoke questions such as "what kind of business system?," "what form of capitalism?" and "what kind of market arrangements?" (Boisot and Child 1996b).

In addition to the core fundamental issue of how to analyze China's economic and social transformation, Boisot also contributed to certain more specific aspects of Chinese business management and strategy. One was managerial work. His article with Guo Liang Xing (Boisot and Xing 1992) drew on Xing's close observation of the activities of six enterprise directors, each for a period of six weeks in 1987. This provided an opportunity to apply the C-Space framework to analyzing the nature of managerial work in the early days of the Chinese enterprise reform. Among questions raised by the article is whether the ostensible intention of the reform to allow enterprises to move towards the market quadrant of the C-Space was being matched by a growing capacity of enterprise directors to scan their environments in order to make rational market-informed decisions and develop an entrepreneurial capability.

The evidence of this study showed that the Chinese managers' scanning of the external environment was very weak, and that they lacked the supporting problem-solving routines that would enable them to remove the bounds to making economically rational decisions. They faced considerable complexity which they lacked the tools to reduce and which instead they had to try to absorb. Despite the managers' jobs being constrained by tight rules and technical regulations, the evidence indicated that they lacked a reliable framework of codification within which they could delegate with confidence. The profile of their activities indicated that they engaged heavily in personalized, hierarchical and negotiated relationships which are more characteristic of the fief quadrant of the C-Space. They had to face continuing problems of bounded rationality, and needed to spend considerable time in upward personal interaction with superiors, with the result that they were overloaded. This situation clearly did not encourage the entrepreneurial orientation that the reform was supposed to develop.

Part of the problem facing Chinese enterprise directors back in 1987 lay in the then incomplete development of institutional arrangements that would grant them autonomy from various hierarchical superiors in governmental supervisory agencies. Escaping the transaction costs imposed by institutional restrictions is identified by Boisot and Meyer (2008) as one incentive for Chinese firms to internationalize. In contrast to the more conventional explanations for the rapid increase in Chinese outward foreign direct investment, they argue that China's economic reforms have further increased the fragmentation of the Chinese economy thus raising domestic transactions costs such as those of transacting across internal provincial boundaries. These costs of domestic transacting arise because of institutional provisions such as discriminatory tolls and local taxes, and inconsistent provincial regulations governing commerce. It is particularly difficult for smaller Chinese firms to bear these costs. Consequently, Boisot and Meyer argue, the internationalization of Chinese firms, especially SMEs, can be understood as an exit strategy *from* the domestic market rather than as the pursuit of an entry strategy *into* foreign markets motivated by the attractors of asset acquisition or asset exploitation that are identified in conventional analysis. They comment that for Chinese firms "it costs far less to do business with the nearest country than with the furthest province" (p. 357). The lowering of tariff and other barriers to international trade that has been a key element in globalization makes exit to a foreign market an increasingly feasible option. Boisot and Meyer's analysis points to strategic market exit as being of equal interest to that of strategic market entry.

What overall conclusion can be drawn from this brief review of Max Boisot's contributions to the analysis of the Chinese system and his application of insights into that system to the development of theory more generally? Clearly he was among the first of a now large number of scholars who have taken an interest in China and the remarkable changes that have taken place there since the late 1970s. More particularly, he was in the favorable position of being able to apply a clear analytical framework to the interpretation of evidence that he could gather on the spot himself, through his collaborators and through his students in the China-Europe Management Institute (CEMI) which he directed from 1984 to 1988. Max's application of the C-Space (subsequently *I-Space*) framework provided the basis for a precise yet parsimonious insight into the Chinese system and how it contrasted with the more familiar ones of the West. It is probably no exaggeration to say that this framework was, and is perhaps still, the most powerful available for capturing the cultural and institutional essence of the Chinese system. He used firsthand evidence from China to illustrate and elaborate the details of his framework, though it is fair to say that he did not use such evidence inductively to develop his theory.

Max Boisot's passionate belief in his root paradigm was the source of great strength and enabled him to make many outstanding contributions. However, as just intimated, it also had some limitations, one of which was apparent in his work on China. Max generally treated information as a cultural phenomenon, regarding the way it was articulated and shared reflecting cultural norms. He called his original framework the "culture" space. When he depicted institutional or organizational arrangements in terms of different configurations of informational dimensions, he was implicitly regarding them as cultural constructions. This tended to overlook another factor that influences the shaping of institutions and organizations, namely power. I came away from many conversations with him on this issue with the impression that Max certainly appreciated the connection between power and information, but that he preferred to put the issue to one side because it would unduly detract from the elegance of his framework. Yet three of the quadrants of the C-Space are structures of asymmetric power, the exception being markets in their "perfect" form in which every player has the same information and the same market power. In reality, very few markets are perfectly structured in this way and certain players have power by being able to manipulate market information.

The retention of considerable power in the hands of government is unquestionably a key characteristic of contemporary China, which has deep historical roots (Redding and Witt 2007). The Chinese system as a whole is based on the ultimate centralization of power within it, focused on the one-party state. This explains why the so-called "strategic" sectors of industry are kept under close state control and why only part of China's business system has moved under the Reform to the market segment of the *I-Space*. The Chinese authorities also face a dilemma over the rapid spread of internet use in the country. While, as Max recognized, the internet can lower the costs and broaden the scope of transacting through the less codified clan-like structures that the Chinese generally prefer, the unrestricted diffusion of information through the internet may also engender opposition to the regime. A fear of this happening explains why the Chinese authorities are so insistent on control and censorship of the internet and its use. While Max was correct in his technical appraisal that ICTs enable a greater diffusion of information at a given level of structuring, he did not address the question of whether the Chinese authorities would permit this to happen. The tendency of Chinese organizations to favor interactions and transactions within fief or clan-like boundaries can be attributed not only to cultural preferences but also to the fact that this renders them more readily subject to control through, for example, the inclusion of party officials within the fief and clan structures and/or the holding of their local leaders to account.

Part III
Organizational Complexity

4

Extreme Outcomes, Connectivity, and Power Laws: Towards an Econophysics of Organization

Max Boisot and Bill McKelvey

Introduction

In a world characterized by turbulence and uncertainty, managers are often required to respond in adaptive ways to the threats and opportunities presented by extreme, discontinuous, and hence rare outcomes—negative ones such as the Asian financial meltdown, 9/11, Enron, Hurricane Katrina, and most recently the 2011 earthquake and tsunami in Japan and Hurricane Sandy in 2012 in the U.S. but also positive ones such as the emergence of the Internet, Google, Apple, and the sudden lifting of millions out of poverty in China and India. Organization science, however, earns its spurs as a science by studying nicely behaved linear trends characterized by predictable averages—take a sample of 25 database studies published in the *Organization Science* journal and you will get the point. The challenge posed by extreme outcomes, to be sure, is acknowledged at the narrative level in books such as Perrow's *Normal Accidents* (1984) and Vaughan's *The Challenger Launch Decision* (1996), but they remain beyond the reach of any fruitful theorizing or research by the discipline at large. While popular management books tend to attract their readers by focusing on rare extremes—of success, of failure, of leadership, etc.—academics attempt to analyze and interpret these in terms of averages and variances around the averages, publishing their findings in journals little read by practitioners. Do the dramatic effects achieved by "selecting on the dependent variable" by popular books necessarily lead to irrational responses by practitioners? More provocatively, by relating everything that they study to normal distributions, means, and variances, do academics really achieve a greater level of rationality in their analyses than practitioners?

In dealing with extreme outcomes, the choice facing organizational scholars appears rather stark. They are often either saying something that practitioners want to hear but do so by via narratives in which dramatic effects are achieved at the expense of academic rigor. Or, they maintain their academic integrity by sacrificing practitioner relevance. In fact, the social sciences as a whole have found it difficult to deal with extreme outcomes. These are all classified as major discontinuities that can neither be foreseen nor readily interpreted when they occur. Such "samples of one" (Campbell 1975; March, Sproull, and Tamuz 1991) have been dealt with in the humanities as instances of "idiographic science," ones that, like history, yield some measure of retrospective understanding (*verstehen*) but little by way of prediction (Dilthey 1883/1988). Social sciences such as economics, by contrast, aspire to being "nomothetic." They seek out law-like regularities discernable in social processes and aim to achieve some degree of predictability (Friedman 1953), even in the absence of any clear understanding of how such regularities emerge.

The strategy adopted by organization science in its search for law-like regularities—dating back to Kaplan (1964) and even Popper (1935)—helps to explain why it is often useless when most needed. It seeks inspiration from intellectual traditions established in the disciplines it looks up to—physics, sociology, economics, etc. (White 1963; Lewin 1951; Mirowski 1989). These tend to share a Gaussian perspective of the world, one built on assumptions of independent and identically distributed outcomes (*i.i.d.*)—i.e. on *atomism*. This privileges stability over instability, structure over process, objects over fields, and being over becoming (Prigogine 1980). Extreme outcomes, however, do not fit comfortably into the Gaussian perspective (McKelvey and Andriani 2005; Andriani and McKelvey 2007). Yet these outcomes cannot just be treated as "outliers" which, being located beyond the range of the normal distribution, can reasonably be ignored on a day-to-day basis as "errors in the data." In fact, they make the "front page" when they happen. To accommodate them one needs to complement a Gaussian ontology with one based on a new set of assumptions that admit of tension, connectivity, complexity, and Pareto distributions (West and Deering 1995; Barabási 2002; Newman 2005; Andriani and McKelvey 2007, 2009, 2011a, b, c; McKelvey and Andriani 2010)—call this a *Paretian* ontology.

We focus on the conceptual challenges that anomalies and extreme outcomes pose for organization science. At present, these remain under-theorized and are therefore dealt with descriptively—through case studies and other forms of narrative discourse. We believe that organization science now needs to go beyond narratives about extremes. In the work of Lewin—field theory (1951), Starbuck—math (1965), and Hage—axioms (1965), organization science drew from physics, albeit the old physics. In the past three decades a new type of physics has emerged to address problems of complexity (Gell-Mann 1988, 2002; West and Deering 1995; Bak 1996; Newman 2005). *Econophysics* is the name given to the application of this new physics to economic problems (Mantegna and Stanley 2000; Sinha et al. 2011). New physics is less reductionist than the old physics. By embracing complexity, it effectively moves towards rather than away from the kinds of problems that the social sciences have been grappling with (Morin 1992). Furthermore, it incorporates *biological* concepts of organization, ones in which organization becomes an attribute of the elements of a group or aggregation in interaction (Kauffman 1993)—an emergent property of the aggregation's internal connectivity (Holland 1998)—rather than some self-contained and isolatable entity that has been designed *ex ante* (Boisot and Cohen 2000). Such connectivity is the manifestation of either physical laws or memory at work in the system. Econophysics is currently especially focused on financial economics and stock markets (West and Deering 1995; Mantegna and Stanley 2000; Sornette 2003; McCauley 2004; Vasconcelos 2004; Chakrabarti, Chakraborti, and Chatterjee 2006; Chatterjee and Chakrabarti 2006).

Our paper draws on a different method of understanding and dealing with complex phenomena than organization science has traditionally felt comfortable with. Throughout, we will continually connect back to Nobel Laureate Murray Gell-Mann's (2002) distinction between the *old simplicity* of reductionism, equations, linearity, and predictions of *old* physics and the *new simplicity* of insignificant initiating events (what we will call *"butterfly-events"*), nonlinearity, similar causal dynamics at multiple levels, power laws (PLs), and scale-free theories (SFTs). We will shift our cognitive representations of the real-world and our follow-on response schema from *old* to *new simplicity*-based research. We follow Gell-Mann's (2002) tripartite classification of incoming real-world stimuli into Gaussian regularities studied in normal science, scale-free regularities stemming from the tiny initiating (butterfly) events of chaos theory, and residual noise. Complexity science studies them all.

In the second section we introduce the growing influence of econophysics in separating the Gaussian and Paretian worlds. In the third section, we frame the challenge of organizational schema formation and adaptation within these ontologies in terms of Ashby's *Law of Requisite Variety* (1956). We show how the variety perceived to be requisite is sensitive to the type of ontological assumptions that are made and examine how this affects an agent's social information processing—schema formation—strategies. In the fourth section, we develop some implications for organization science. A conclusion follows.

From Gauss to the Paretian world of extremes

The growing influence of complexity science and econophysics

Complexity science has emerged in three phases. The first appeared in Europe, led by Nobel Laureate Ilya Prigogine (1955, 1980; Prigogine and Stengers 1984). He built on Bénard's (1901) study of emergent structures in fluids. Because these serve to dissipate energy imposing on a system from outside, he labeled them "dissipative structures". In a tea kettle, for example, the "rolling boil" familiar to chefs is a shift <u>from</u> molecules dissipating heat by vibrating faster in place <u>to</u> molecules circulating around the pot, thereby speeding up heat transfer. This *phase transition*—which occurs at the so-called "*1st critical value*" of imposed energy (what McKelvey, 2001, calls "adaptive tension")—defines what we may call "*the edge of order*"—see Figure 4.1. This phase is predominantly physics and math intensive (Prigogine 1955; Haken 1977; Nicolis and Prigogine 1989; Mainzer 2004/2007). It underlies our focus on the role of adaptive tension.

At the left in Figure 4.1 we see the edge of order. The *1st critical value* creates a bifurcation point: below the 1st critical value order persists; above the 1st critical value we see the phase transition into the region of emergent new order. Moving more to the right, we then see the *2nd critical value* and the bifurcation between the system moving into the region of chaos as opposed to remaining in the region of emergence. Whereas the region of chaos looks sort of ordered going from left to right, looking oppositely from right to left, we see the chaotic outcome of a system responding to a series of random bifurcation points. Figure 4.1 also shows the one aspect where chaos theory (Guastello

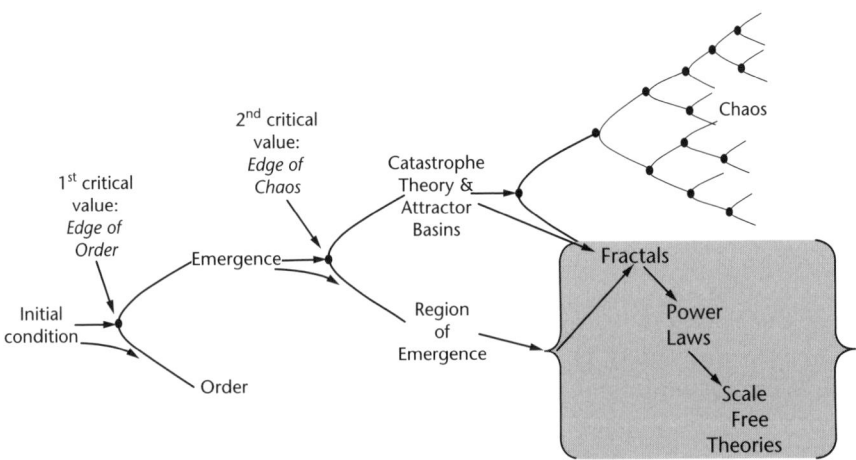

Figure 4.1. First, second, and third phases of complexity science

1995) and complexity theory overlap, which is shown at the lower-right as the region of fractals, PLs, and SFTs.

The second phase was initiated by Nobel Laureates Murray Gell-Mann and Philip Anderson along with Stuart Kauffman (1969, 1993), John Holland (1988, 1995), and Brian Arthur (1990, 1994), at the Santa Fe Institute. It is oriented more toward biology and the social sciences. Their focus is on heterogeneous agents in *"complex adaptive systems"* interacting at what was early on called *"the edge of chaos"*. This occurs at the *"2nd critical value"* of imposed energy—the tension is so high that multi directional, maladaptive, and chaotic responses result. Their approach favors primarily agent-based computational modeling rather than math modeling. In between the *"edges"* of order and chaos is the region of emergent complexity or what Kauffman (1993) terms the *"melting"* zone of maximum adaptive capability. Per Bak (1996) argued that to survive, organisms have to have a capability of staying within the melting zone, maintaining themselves in a state of "self-organized criticality" (defined in Table 4.1). The signature elements within the melting zone are self-organization, emergence and nonlinearity. *Self-organization* begins when three elements are present: (1) heterogeneous agents; (2) connections among them; and (3) motives to connect (which are usually the result of exogenous or endogenous sources of adaptive tension—such as mating, improved fitness, performance, individual objectives and motivations, and learning. Remove any one element and nothing happens. Self-organization results in *emergence*, that is, new order of some kind. For more background see Andriani and McKelvey (2007, 2009).

The third phase began at a conference in Kolcata, India where Eugene Stanley coined the label *"econophysics"* in 1995 (Sinha et al. 2011). Besides being a group of physicists who applied their math and empirical skills to the vast amounts of free economic data (and especially stock-market data after the beginning of the Great Recession in late 2007), they applied a statistical physics totally different from Ludwig Boltzmann's invention of statistical mechanics in 1877 (to allow exact physics to persist, even though random Brownian motion had been discovered by Robert Brown in 1827). Whereas econometrics (e.g. Greene 2011) adopted Boltzmann's statistics, econophysicists start their statistical physics from Pareto (1897). We offer two quotes from the beginning of two exemplary works:

> It is convenient to assume that the disturbances are normally distributed. (p. 17) The issue of sample selection arises when the observed data are not drawn randomly from the population of interest. Failure to account for this nonrandom sampling produces a model that describes only the nonrandom subsample, not the larger population. (**Greene 2011, 801**)

For Greene the *law of large numbers* comes to the rescue—the larger population will be normally distributed.

The Italian social economist Pareto [1897] investigated the statistical character of the wealth of individuals in a stable economy by modeling them using the [rank/frequency] distribution $F \sim N^{-\beta}$, where F is the number of people having income N and ß is an exponent that [is constant]. Pareto noticed that his result was quite general and applicable to nations "as different as those of England, of Ireland, of Germany, of the Italian cities, and even of Peru". (**Mantegna and Stanley 2000, 2**)

Mantegna and Stanley then focus their application of statistical physics in their book, *Introduction to Econophysics*, on rank/frequency skew distributions such as Pareto, Lévy, and power laws.

Econophysics focuses on the *outcomes* of self-organization and emergence, that is, new order. Econophysics brings PLs (Zipf 1949; Stanley et al. 1996; Mantegna and Stanley 2000; Newman 2005), scalability (Gell-Mann 1988, 2002; Brock 2000), and SFTs (Zipf 1949; Newman 2005; Andriani and McKelvey 2009) into prominence. According to Holland (2002) we recognize emergent phenomena in multi-level hierarchies, due to intra- and inter-level causal processes, and appearing as nonlinearities. Nonlinearity incorporates two key outcomes: the *butterfly effect* and *scalability*. Scale-free causes are Holland's "*levers*". Holland (2002, 29) says: "Almost all *CAS* [complex adaptive systems] exhibit *lever point* phenomena, where 'inexpensive' inputs cause major directed effects in the *CAS* dynamics". These triggers, what we call "butterfly events/effects," extend across multiple levels.[1] A butterfly-effect is a nonlinear outcome occurring when a single event out of myriad very small random ones gets amplified to generate an extreme effect.

Norway's coast, for example, appears jagged no matter what kind of measure is used: miles, kilometers, meters, or centimeters. Such self-similarity is called "*scalability*"—phenomena appear the same, no matter what the scale of measurement. A cauliflower offers a different kind of example. Cut off a "floret;" cut a smaller floret from the first; then an even smaller one; and another even smaller still, and so on. Each subcomponent is smaller than the former, but each exhibits the same shape, structure, and causal dynamics. The cauliflower gets this way because of its adaptive, biological basis of survival—it is governed by Galileo's square-cube law of surface-to-volume ratio (defined in Table 4.1). The Norway effect, by contrast, is caused by physical erosion. Both offer real-life examples of *Fractal Geometry* (Mandelbrot 1983).[2]

---

[1] Our term, butterfly effect, simply recognizes E. Lorenz's famous phrase which is the title of one of his presentations, "Predictability: Does the flap of a butterfly's wings in Brazil set off a tornado in Texas?" Presented at the 1972 meeting of the *American Association for the Advancement of Science*. Washington, DC.

[2] Fractals are defined as shapes that can be subdivided into parts, each of which is (at least approximately) a reduced-size copy of the whole (Mandelbrot 1983). The same mathematical equation—or adaptive causal dynamic in biology—creates "self-similar" parts at each level of a fractal structure.

Fractals typically appear as Pareto distributions that, if plotted on double-log X- and Y-axes, also appear as PL distributions.[3]

Organizations also exhibit scalability, fractal structures, extremes, and "long-tailed" Pareto distributions (Stanley et al. 1996; Axtell 2001; Andriani and McKelvey 2009). In 2005, Walmart's profits were some 30 billion dollars larger than those of thousands of small "Ma & Pa" stores; the assets of GE, Microsoft, and Exxon-Mobile are hundreds of billions of dollars larger than those of small individual proprietors; the largest organizations employ hundreds of thousands more people than small stores and they may sell millions more products than the smallest of these. Because of these extremes and the possibility of changes in the extremes, a Pareto distribution will show an unstable mean and a (nearly) infinite variance; therefore, it has no "average" that can meaningfully represent the typical features of the distribution and no finite variance upon which to base confidence intervals (Moss 2002); Axtell (2008) says that a "typical firm" doesn't exist! The mean, median, and mode are different. Absent a stable mean and finite variances, extracting information from the distribution to give a probabilistic assessment of individual outcomes becomes much more difficult, and hence misleading.

Coasts, cauliflowers, firms and other PL phenomena are fractal structures calling for *SFTs* because the same causal dynamics apply at whatever level they are examined. Fractals result from scale-free causes; they are explained via SFTs. Such theories point to a single generative cause to explain the dynamics at each of however many levels that are being studied. SFTs yield what Gell-Mann (1988, 3) refers to as "deep simplicity." What the philosophy of science calls explanatory power (Lakatos 1978, Glymour 1980)—fewer theories explain more phenomena—traditionally has rested on the idea that lower-level dynamics can explain and predict higher-level phenomena and simplicity comes in the form of (usually) linear mathematical equations (Gell-Mann 2002), i.e. reductionism. SFTs point to the same causes operating at multiple levels—simplicity here consists of one theory explaining dynamics at multiple levels. Andriani and McKelvey (2009) apply fifteen of these SFTs to organizations. In Table 4.1 we identify seven of them. Scale-free causes typically produce Pareto distributions. Andriani and McKelvey (2011c) apply ten SFTs to explain ten more detailed managerial examples.

As stylized in Figure 4.2, if a well-formed Pareto distribution is plotted using double-log X- and Y-axes, it will appear as a negatively sloped straight line—its PL "signature." PLs appear to be ubiquitous—they apply to word usage, papers published, book sales, and web hits (Newman 2005). Cities follow a PL distribution when ranked by population (Auerbach 1913; Krugman 1996; Batty

---

[3] Power law distributions appear as rank/size expressions such as $F \sim N^{-\beta}$, where F is frequency and N is rank (the variables), with β, the exponent, is constant.

Table 4.1. Empirical basis of scale-free causes of Power Laws*

Rules	Explanation
Spontaneous order creation	*Heterogeneous agents* seeking out other agents to learn from so as to improve fitness generate networks; such that some networks become groups, some groups form larger groups and hierarchies.
Phase transitions	*Turbulent flows*: Exogenous energy impositions cause autocatalytic interaction effects at a specific energy level—the 1st critical value—such that new interaction groupings form.
Preferential attachment	*Nodes*: Given newly arriving agents into a system, larger nodes with an enhanced propensity to attract agents will become disproportionately even larger.
Least effort	*Language and change*: Word frequency is a function of ease of usage by both speaker and listener; this law now found to apply to language, firms, and economies in transition.
Square/Cube Law	*Cauliflowers*: In organisms, surfaces absorbing energy grow by the square but the organism grows by the cube, resulting in an imbalance; fractals emerge to bring surface/volume back into balance.
Connection costs	*Growth unit connectivity*: As cell fission occurs by the square, connectivity increases by $n(n-1)/2$, producing an imbalance between the gains from fission vs. the cost of maintaining connectivity; consequently organisms form modules or cells so as to reduce the cost of connectivity.
Self-organized criticality	*Sandpiles, forests*: Under constant tension of some kind (gravity, ecological balance), some systems reach a critical state where they maintain stasis by preservative behaviors—such as sand avalanches, forest fires, changing heartbeat rates—which vary in size of effect according to a power law.

* Paraphrased from Andriani and McKelvey (2009); they list a total of fifteen.

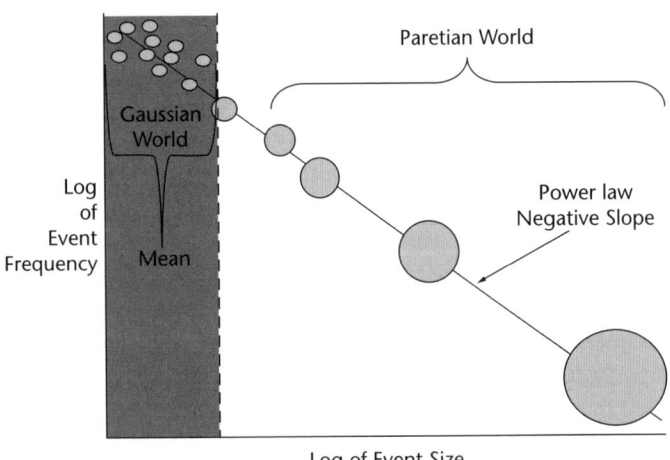

Figure 4.2. Stylized Pareto distribution on log-log scale

2005; McKelvey, forthcoming). Using a Compustat sample of all manufacturing organizations, Stanley et al. (1996) find that firms' rates of growth exhibit a PL distribution. Axtell (2001) finds firm size is Pareto, i.e. PL, distributed—that is, one very large firm in one long tail of the Pareto distribution and hundreds of very small firms in the opposite tail. PL distributions characterize economic fluctuations (Gabaix 2009), growth rates of countries (Lee et al. 1998), structure of the Internet (Albert, Jeong, and Barabási 2000; Adamic and Huberman 2002), size and duration of recessions (Ormerod and Mounfield 2001), financial markets (Sornette and Zhou 2006), director interlocks (Battison and Catanzaro 2004), entrepreneurial innovation (Poole et al. 2000), firm's bankruptcies (Fujiwara 2004), alliance networks (Gay and Dousset 2005), firm growth rates (Fujiwara et al. 2004), stock market returns and volatilities (Kang and Yoon 2007), macroeconomic disasters (Barro and Jin 2011), M&A waves (Park, Moral, and Madhavan 2010), performance of entrepreneurial start-up companies (Crawford 2012) and individuals' performance in organizations (O'Boyle and Aguinis 2012). Barabási and Albert (1999) mention some early studies of rank/frequency Pareto-distributed *social networks* (e.g. Lawrence and Giles 1998; Watts and Strogatz 1998); many other studies of social network PL phenomena follow (e.g. Battison and Catanzaro 2004; Souma et al. 2006; Santiago and Benito 2008). Andriani and McKelvey (2007, 2009) list over 140 kinds of PLs that range in application from atoms to galaxies, from DNA to species, and from networks to wars. McKelvey and Salmador Sanchez (2011) list ~70 more just in financial economic and stock-market phenomena.

Moving organization science thinking from Gaussian to Paretian worlds

In Figure 4.2 we graphically separate Gaussian from Paretian ontologies, using the stylized PL. At the upper-left, using a Gaussian ontology, researchers collect samples of the many *i.i.d.* events; they aim to generate statistically significant law-like results based on stable means and well-defined confidence intervals. Their results ignore scale-free causal processes that amplify to become extreme events of potential interest to practitioners. At the lower-right, we depict the extreme outcome of the underlying Pareto distribution—the result of nonlinear emergent scalability and fractal dynamics.

What is a probability distribution? A summary description of a state space of possible outcomes. A probability measure that satisfies the probability axioms can be assigned to each outcome so as to legitimately give rise to a truth claim. Different conditions give rise to different types of distributions. Here we briefly compare the conditions required for a Gaussian or normal distribution with those required for a Paretian or PL distribution.

THE "NORMAL" WORLD OF GAUSS

A Gaussian world is populated by outcomes and stable objects that are disconnected from each other and hence independently distributed—they are *additive-independent*. Human bodies are good examples; a sample of the very largest adults weighs roughly four times as much as a sample of the smallest adults; a crowd of a thousand people weighs about 10 times more than a crowd of 100 people and can collectively lift about 10 times as much; double the size of the crowd and, on average, it can lift twice as much; most people are at, or close to, the mean. This is the world inhabited by most of neoclassical economics (Greene 2011), and mainstream sociology (Snijders and Bosker 1999). It is the world that—barring the works of Perrow (1984), Arthur (1990, 1994), Lichtenstein (2000), Starbuck (n.d.), and a few others—organization science has aspired to occupy.

The Gaussian, or "normal," distribution—the standard bell-shaped curve—generated by additive-independent data points, is characterized by its mean and variance (Greene 2011). The assumption of normality ensures that the mean and the variance of the distribution constitute sufficient statistics; the confidence intervals are stable and conveniently compressed toward the mean, thereby making it easier for researchers to claim statistical significance; the payoff to the claim comes from publications and promotions. For most purposes, a Gaussian world is a predictable one in which the future, within limits, can be inferred from the past through an inductive process based on the repeatability of normally distributed outcomes judged to be similar in some respect. In a Gaussian world, extreme outcomes are so different from the typical and so rare that they don't significantly influence either the mean or the variance. Hence, ignoring them is considered to be a safe strategy—in current statistical practice underlying almost all published quantitative analyses, outliers are deleted (winsorized), ignored or somehow linearized (e.g. converted to lognormal distributions) so that their effects are minimized (Greene 2011). Under assumptions of normality, extreme outcomes do not shape managerial expectations; nor do they drive organizational adaptation.

THE "LONG-TAILED" WORLD OF PARETO

If we now perform a "gestalt switch" (Kuhn 1962) and shift our attention from aggregates of atomized individual agents[4] to the many different ways these may interact with each other, we discover that in many cases assumptions of independence and additivity should be replaced by assumptions of connectivity, multiplicativity, interaction, and positive feedback. These dynamics give rise to Pareto (PL) distributions that have "long tails," infinite variance, unstable means, and unstable confidence intervals. Three Mile Island, the

---

[4] "Agent" is a generalized term used in modern science and computational modeling that can refer to atoms, molecules, biomolecules, cells, organisms, species, people, process elements, groups, organizations, societies, etc.

1997 Asian Financial Crisis, 9/11, the Internet, Google's share price, Apple's spectacular growth after inventing the iPhone, the sudden emergence of China on the world stage, etc., all indicate that we are far from living in a "normal" organizational/business world. In fact, the most interesting action and the highest costs and returns reside in the tails rather than the means of the distribution (Kirchgaessner and Kelleher 2005). To take an entrepreneurial example, in the movie industry, almost all the profits come from the blockbusters—i.e. extreme outcomes—with the vast majority of the movies contributing next to nothing to profitability (De Vany 2004). And even in the upper left hand corner of Figure 4.2, Anderson (2006) describes how Internet sales allow Amazon and other retailers to exploit the microdiversity contained in the variance of what appears to be a Gaussian distribution—and hence usually treated as noise[5]—and sell a few customized items at a premium in a large number of product niches.[6] He compares this with drug companies selling an identical drug to millions within a single market segment. In such cases, normal distribution statistics conceal rather than reveal the opportunities or the threats. In a Paretian world, using the mean as a descriptive convenience to capture the nature of a phenomenon without attending to its underlying structure, and then relying on measures of variance to build confidence intervals with which to assess its likelihood, becomes either misleading or openly wrong. And, of course, so does systematically excluding outliers because they cannot be captured by a normal distribution.

In sum, organizations and organization science exhibit a natural bias towards Gaussian thinking and the world of stable and finite objects that it generates. What price do they pay for this bias? In the next section we shall argue that they sacrifice a capacity to adapt to the range of phenomena that they are called upon to respond to.

Ashby's Law of Requisite Variety

What adaptation challenges do Pareto distributions present? We first frame the challenge of adaptation in general terms using Ross Ashby's *Law of Requisite Variety* (1956), discussing it in both Gaussian and Paretian terms.

---

[5] What Anderson (2006) refers to as the "long tail" should not be confused with "long tails" or "fat tails" in discussions of power law distributions. Anderson is in fact referring to that part of any distribution that deals with small, highly frequent events, which tend to be treated as noise and hence ignored.

[6] Recent confirmatory research has been carried out by Brynjolfsson, Hu, and Smith (2006).

A cognitive interpretation of Ashby's Law

Biological behavior, like that of certain artifacts, is driven by informational as much as by mechanical action (Boisot 1995a). This insight gave rise in the 1940s to the science of cybernetics, the science of control and communication in animals and machines (Wiener 1948). Ashby, one of the founders of this science, was interested in the range or variety of situations that an animal or a machine could respond and adapt to. His *Law* states that *"only variety can destroy variety"* (Ashby 1956, 207): the range of responses that a living system[7] must be able to marshal in its attempt to adapt to the world must match the range of situations—threats and opportunities—that it confronts. In some cases, the response might be wholly behavioral and often outside a system's cognitive control—as in the case of a hormonal response or a reflex. In other cases—say those requiring a fight-or-flight decision—the response might be a blend of behavior and cognition that is contingent on the system successfully classifying a stimulus as foreshadowing, say, the presence of a foe. It will then respond to *representations* of its environment that are constructed out of such classification activity rather than to its environment directly (Plotkin 1993). Gell-Mann (2002, 16–17) sees representations as "schema"—descriptions of real world *"regularities"* that form the basis for predictions and responses in living systems. In science they may appear as equations; in culture as laws, customs, and memes; and in management as strategies and practices. What advantage do better schema confer?

Not everything in a living system's environment is relevant or meaningful for it, however. If it is not to waste its energy responding to every will-o-the-wisp, a system must distinguish schema based on meaningful information (signals about real-world regularities judged important) from noise (meaningless signals). Note that what constitutes information or noise for a system is partly a function of the organism's own expectations, judgments, and sensory abilities about what is important (Gell-Mann 2002)—as well as of its motivations—and hence, of its models of the world. Valid and timely representations (schema) economize on the organism's scarce energy resources (Zipf 1949; Ball 2004; Vermeij 2004).

We can illustrate this interpretation of Ashby's law by means of a simple diagram that we label the *Ashby Space* (Figure 4.3). On the vertical axis we place the real-world stimuli that impinge on an organism. These range in their variety from low to high. A low-variety stimulus might be an image of the moon; a high-variety stimulus might be the trajectory of an insect in a swarm. On the horizontal axis, we place the system's response schema to the stimuli.

---

[7] Although Ashby talked of "systems" *tout court*, we shall be dealing with "living systems," we use the term as Miller (1978) does to cover systems made up of bio-organisms and ecologies, people, groups, and organizations.

Extreme Outcomes, Connectivity, and Power Laws

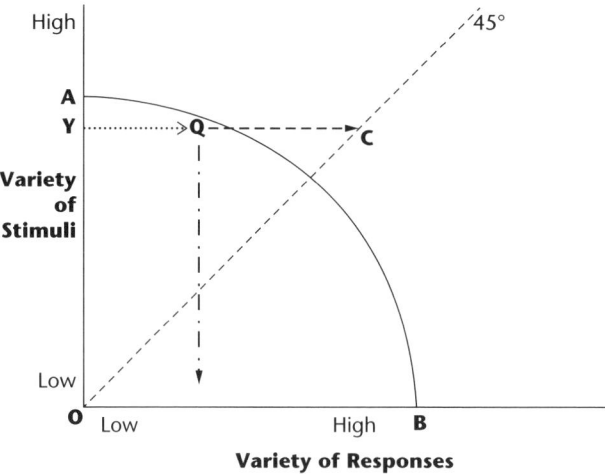

Figure 4.3. The Ashby Space

These also range in variety from low to high. A low-variety response to the stimulus presented by the moon would simply be to stare at it, meditate, and otherwise do nothing. A high-variety response to the insect swarm, by contrast, might be to chase after each individual insect flying past. The first type of response saves energy; the second wastes it. The diagonal in the diagram indicates the set of points at which variety can be considered "requisite," that is, where the variety of a system's response matches that of incoming stimuli in an efficiently adaptive way.[8]

Ashby stressed the need to reduce the flow of some forms of variety from the external environment to certain essential processes in a living system. This was the role of regulation, and, as Ashby pointed out, the amount of regulation that can be achieved is bounded by the amount of information that can be transmitted and processed by the system (Ashby 1956). The variety that it then has to respond to depends in part on the system's internal schema development and transmission capacities and in part on the operation of tunable filters—controlled by the system's cognitive apparatus—used by the system to separate out regularities from noise (Clark 1997). The more intelligent a system, the higher will be the cognitive component in its response relative to the purely behavioral one. Cognitive and behavioral actions both complement and substitute for each other. There is, thus, a trade-off between the behavioral and the cognitive resources that a living system will have to marshal in response to external stimuli. Birds mostly act according to

---

[8] Since efficient matching of stimulus and response occurs at every organizational level, it falls within the domain of Zipf's (1949) *"Least Effort"* scale-free theory in Table 4.1.

genetically derived behavioral instincts; monkeys show both behavioral and cognitive responses; humans exhibit higher cognitive skills.

The diagonal locates those points for which the variety of the stimulus and the variety of the system's response schema to the stimulus are evenly matched. This matching can only be considered adaptive, however, if it occurs inside the region of the diagram labeled OAB, which defines the energy budget available to the living system. To the right of this region, the variety developed by a system to adapt is too high, causing it to expend too much of its energy budget and, thus, eventually leading to its physical disintegration. Above this region, the data processing resources required to register incoming stimuli, to interpret them, and to formulate adaptive responses exceeds the system's data processing capacities of the system, eventually leading to errors and adaptive failure. Cognitive and physical disintegration, however, are not mutually exclusive alternatives: the first will sooner or later lead to the second. Even within the budget area OAB, at any point above the diagonal, the system is still under-adapting—cognitively or behaviorally—relative to what is required. Likewise, at any point below the diagonal it is using up its response budget wastefully or ineffectively relative to what is required (Thaler 1992). The challenge for an adaptive system, then, is to locate itself at some point on the diagonal within the budget area OAB. An intelligent system can use its data processing and transmission capacities to convert a high-variety stimulus into a low-variety one, or vice versa. It does this by *interpreting* the stimulus, by distinguishing which part of the variety associated with it is information bearing and which part is noise. In doing so, it moves either down or up the vertical dimension of the Ashby Space.

Consider a system located at point Q in Figure 4.3, corresponding to some prior activity level X along OB, which registers a stimulus at point Y along the vertical scale, for example. It could respond to the high variety associated with point Y directly in a purely "mindless" behaviorist fashion by simply moving horizontally to the right until it hits the diagonal at C—no cognitive simplification of the stimulus; just a behavioral response to it. But in doing so, the system would move outside its budget area OAB, and would rapidly deplete its energy resources. Call this a *headless chicken strategy*. Alternatively, the system could respond in a purely cognitive fashion by moving vertically down the diagram until it approaches the horizontal axis. In this case, the system treats *all* incoming stimuli as already known regularities and noise and thus is not in need of any new behavioral response. This is the response of the "been-there-done-that" person who overconfidently feels no need to actually *do* anything different. Call this a *routinizing strategy*. Yet, since any downward movement calls for an interpretation, classification, and simplification of the incoming stimuli, whether this second response is adaptive or not will depend on how well the resulting schema match the most problematic real-world regularities confronting the system.

In the real world, then, intelligent adaptive systems are best off locating on the diagonal in the Ashby Space, somewhere between O and the point at which the diagonal intersects the budget curve AB. That is, they first need to *interpret* the stimuli impinging upon them—a cognitive move either up or down the vertical scale in the diagram that attempts to extract relevant information about regularities from the noisy incoming signals that register as data with them. They then they need to develop relevant schema and respond with some *action* to the regularities so extracted—a behavioral move horizontally across the diagram towards the right that is only adaptive if it stops when it meets the diagonal and does so before it hits the budget limit AB. A cognitive move up the Ashby Space expands the range and variety of stimuli that a living system will need to process before responding—in Gell-Mann's terms, schema become more complex; it constitutes an exploratory learning process. By contrast, a cognitive move down the Ashby Space draws on prior learning to reduce both the range and variety of stimuli and simplify the schemata required—an exploitative learning process (Holland 1975; March 1991). Clearly, the further down towards O a system can move before having to turn right and respond with a physical (behavioral) action, the more easily it can secure a quiet life for itself. Conversely, the further up the vertical scale toward A the rightward move occurs, the more turbulent life becomes for the system and the more energy it has to expend in order to adapt.

The trajectory of a living system through the Ashby Space reflects its "intelligence"—its capacity to discern meaningful regularities and develop adaptive schema. Given the limited number of stimuli that a bird can "make sense" of, the trade-off between energy and data processing favors drawing predominantly on its energy resources. The variety of stimuli that a human being can respond to adaptively, by contrast, is much greater so that the trade-off favors drawing predominantly on its data-processing resources. A living system's trajectory through the space also tells us something about its physiology. Not only are there physiological limits to what can count as a stimulus, and hence as data, for a given type of system—a frog, for instance, can only detect and process peripheral movement (Lettvin et al. 1959)—but there are also cognitive limits on the system's capacity to process the data. Thus, it confronts a problem of bounded rationality (Simon 1986). Above the budget line the variety of stimuli may be such that a system cannot even register them. Yet, for living systems in general, and for human beings in particular, the budget area OAB is constantly being expanded outward from the origin by means of artifacts (Clark 1997), cultural transmission (Gregory 1981; Boyd and Richerson 1985) and through collective organizational action (Corning 2003). These simultaneously increase a system's energy and data-processing resources, and the complexity of its schema, while expanding its *life-world* (Schutz 1972)—the world within which it feels capable of adapting.

Gauss and Pareto in the Ashby space—three ontological regimes

Is there, then, any limit to the expansion by human beings of their data-processing and schema-building resources—i.e. to the expansion in the Ashby Space of the budget area OAB? Computational theory teaches us that problems whose size grows much faster than their inputs may require what effectively amounts to an infinite amount of data processing for their solution (Chaitin 1974; Sipser 1997). From the computational perspective, an intelligent organism grappling with such vast computational-size problems will experience input stimuli as being unfathomable. If we now assume that problem-input size correlates with stimulus variety for an intelligent organism such as a human being (Grünwald, Myung, and Pitt 2005), we can locate threats and opportunities of varying input sizes on the OA axis of Figure 4.3 to give us three distinct *ontological regimes* that confront the organism: the Chaotic, the Complex, and the Ordered. We show these in Figure 4.4. We also have expanded discussions of the Ashby Space in Boisot and McKelvey (2010, 2011a).

In his discussion of the phenomena giving rise to the three regimes, Gell-Mann (2002) distinguishes between two fundamentally different *"underlying generative mechanisms"* (Bhaskar 1975):

> *Reductionist Regularities:* The reductionist causal mechanisms (more broadly, processes) of normal science, which are predictable and easily represented by equations—the data and information much preferred in classical physics and neoclassical economics (Gell-Mann, p.19).

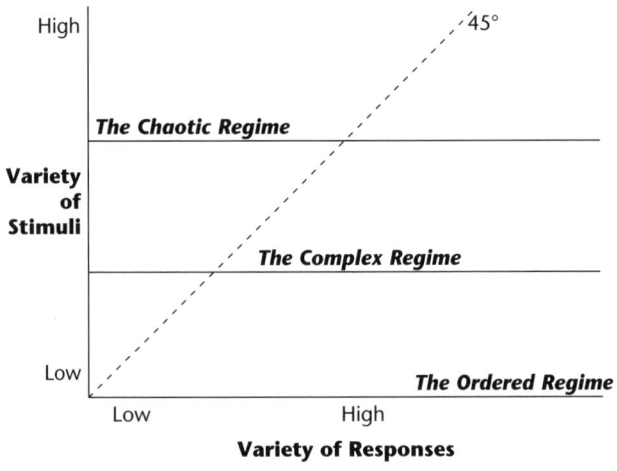

Figure 4.4. Three regimes in the Ashby Space

These are the point attractors of chaos theory—defined by natural trends toward equilibrium and energy conservation.

> *Scale-free Regularities:* Outcomes over time that result from an accumulation of random tiny-initiating-events that have lasting effects, are amplified and propagated by positive feedback effects over time, and may become *"frozen accidents"* (Gell-Mann, p.20).

These are the strange attractors of chaos theory, i.e. never repeating, fostering indeterminacy, or offering a different kind of regularity.

The first process generates the regularities that characterize the Ordered Regime. These may be confidently described and allow predictions, which then become the basis of schemata and prescriptive solutions. The second process generates Gell-Mann's tiny-initiating-events and accidents frozen in time. We refer to these as *"butterfly-events"*. They correspond to the bifurcation points of chaos theory (Gleick 1987). The butterfly-events of chaotic histories are never repeated, usually are random, are not predictable, but they occasionally can produce dramatic nonlinear outcomes—specifically, extreme outcomes. Consequently, descriptions of these systems are at best problematic and beyond the reach of the explanatory/scientific traditions of normal science.

Stimuli appearing in the *chaotic regime* at the top of the diagram are hard to extract useful information from and may be experienced as being computationally intractable, not just because of the size problem but because they are also experienced as chaotic. Unless luck intervenes, an intelligent organism unaware of chaos dynamics can typically make no sense of these stimuli within an adaptive time frame by drawing on any conventional representation. Stimuli appearing in the *ordered regime* at the bottom of the diagram, by contrast, are mostly linear in nature and are experienced as relatively unproblematic by an intelligent organism—the stuff of normal experience and normal science. Here we see linear regularities, trends toward equilibrium and white noise. The ordered regime is the natural home of normal distributions and of Gaussian thinking.

Stimuli appearing in the *complex regime* of Figure 4.4 are experienced as a blend of Gell-Mann's two processes—a partly law-like and partly an unpredictable mix of butterfly-events that may evolve into occasional accidents frozen in time (plus noise of course). Schema development in this regime is challenging to be sure, but computationally tractable once methods for separating out what are now two different kinds of regularities from the noise. It is the butterfly-effect phenomena characteristic of this regime that call for Paretian thinking.

The larger the proportion of phenomena that a human being can classify unproblematically as ordered, the more she/he will be able to economize on scarce data-processing and energetic resources, holding these in reserve for the most challenging phenomena—i.e. in responding, she/he will attempt to minimize the distance that it has to travel to the right in Figure 4.3. Humans thus have a historically validated interest in steering phenomena downward in the Figure towards the ordered regime if they possibly can, in order to "keep their powder dry"—this is the origin of the Gaussian bias identified in the first section. But they can overdo it. If too many of their "interpreted" experiences end up in the ordered regime—i.e. if they all "make sense" and can be taken for granted—humans lose their sense of the essentially contingent nature of things and maladapt or fossilize.

Clearly, the first step in schema development with respect to some impinging real-world phenomenon is to identify the ontology appropriate for dealing with it. We outline three possibilities in Figure 4.5. If, for example, a system interprets a phenomenon as being ordered, it will find itself on a Gaussian trajectory, that of the cognitively-routinizing strategy. This is the least-cost trajectory within the budget area OAB—the data-information-schema-development process underlying the regularities is well understood. If, by contrast, the system views the phenomenon as chaotic, it will find itself on a purely behavioral trajectory that we have labeled the headless chicken strategy—the methods of scalability, PLs, and SFTs are cognitively unknown and latent regularities are unapparent. On this trajectory the system cannot make sense of anything and so responds mindlessly, expending so much undirected energy that it can end up outside its budget area, where it eventually disintegrates.

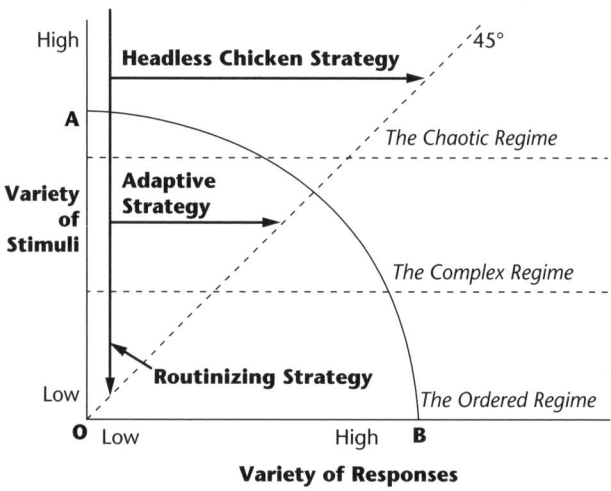

Figure 4.5. Three schema judgments in the Ashby Space

If the system takes the phenomenon to be complex—i.e. neither so ordered that it can mobilize a least-cost response, nor so chaotic that it can mobilize no meaningful schema at all—it is on a Paretian trajectory, one defined both by butterfly-events, frozen accidents, and nonlinearities as well as those attributes that characterize the ordered regime. Here an adaptive response is feasible but more expensive than on a Gaussian trajectory since schema development combines both law-like *and* butterfly-events. However, it can now more successfully move up the diagonal and still remain within its budget frontier.

A key point is that if a system represents phenomena with schema based on the wrong ontological assumption, it will be unable to make sense of them and thus runs the risk of finding itself saddled with the headless chicken response as a default option. To repeat, living systems need to conserve their energy. Moving down the Ashby Space is one way of achieving this, but assuming an ordered ontology from the outset is risky since, if the assumption turns out to be wrong, adaptive failure follows.

Which ontology a system operates within in may depend on the level of adaptive tension it is exposed to. Sometimes, increasing adaptive tension increases the level of connectivity between hitherto unconnected phenomena, thus transforming what would ordinarily appear to be a Gaussian ontology into a Paretian one—which is to say, the butterfly-effects propagate and spiral up more easily through a system because the tension serves to amplify the small initiating events and tighten their connectivity so as to produce a nonlinear outcome. To illustrate: Imagine a net—e.g. a fishing net—just lying crumpled up in a pile. Cut the net between any two nodes and the rest of the net will remain undisturbed. The effects of the cut will remain strictly local. Now stretch the net taut. If it is taut enough, a single cut could begin a tear in the net that would quickly spread from end to end. A similar dynamic underlies the power blackouts that occasionally afflict the power grids when the utilities unexpectedly lose one overloaded station, which triggers a cascade of further shut downs throughout the power grid. Under tension, what starts off as a tiny butterfly-event, rapidly propagates through the network of connections to produce a broader butterfly-effect—a possible extreme outcome. An adaptive strategy in the complexity regime of the Ashby Space, thus, needs an epistemology appropriate to the Paretian ontology that it is called upon to deal with. What kind of data processing challenges might such an epistemology present?

Information processing in the Ashby space

In developing schema to represent the regularities judged important in real-world stimuli, we extract information from data—that is, we "join dots" to build intelligible patterns (Boisot and Canals 2004). The dots correspond to data points. Whatever links we establish between the dots—whether systematically through correlations or through other means—together constitute the information that we extract from them. Finally, the different patterns that we can extract and stabilize from linked dots make up the knowledge—i.e. the interpretations—that we can claim to have with respect to the phenomena generating the dots (Boisot and McKelvey 2006a). Now in defining variety, Ashby pointed to the following series: "*c, b, c, a, c, c, a, b, c, b, b, a.*" He observed that *a*, *b*, and *c* repeat, meaning that there are only three distinct *elements*—three kinds of variety or three degrees of freedom (Ashby 1956, 124–5). In the language of patterns, however, this is variety at the level of "dots" alone. Suppose, instead, that we define variety in terms of the number of *patterns* that can be derived from a given number of dots. Then, using the formula in Table 4.2, we see that 12 dots allow approximately 4,700 quadrillion possible patterns—a truly vast amount of variety to be processed! Even supposing most of these are not worth paying attention to, billions are left, and one still doesn't necessarily know, up front, which ones represent important regularities and which represent noise. Which ones should we select? Which ones should we then stabilize? How might such combinatorial possibilities deliver relevant schema?

Processing *dots*—i.e. data—is appropriate to what we label the routinizing strategy. Processing *patterns*, on the other hand—i.e. knowledge—better serves what we call the Pareto-adaptive strategy. Processing dots means processing data, a low-level cognitive activity. By contrast, processing patterns—pattern recognition—is a high-level cognitive activity, one that involves selecting relevant patterns from among myriad possibilities (Churchland 1993; Thelen and Smith 1994). If we view organizations through a schema-building information lens, then we see that data-processing organizations based upon Gaussian principles tend to be hierarchical in nature, generating data at the base, linking data items to each other in the middle reaches of an organizational hierarchy, and leaving the pattern-recognition-and-processing tasks to senior managers located at the top of the organizational pyramid (Anthony 1965; Galbraith 1973). This is a sequential process of upward filtering that works well in a stable and routinizable world when the relevant patterns are

Table 4.2. Relation of dots to links and to patterns

Number of dots: N	Number of possible links: $L = N(N-1)/2$	Number of possible patterns: $P = 2^L$
$N = 4$	$L = 6$	$P = 64$
$N = 10$	$L = 45$	$P = 35$ trillion
$N = 12$	$L = 66$	$P = 73.8$ quintillion

well-known or easily discovered regularities. Figure 4.6 depicts this data-processing strategy as a pyramid, *A*, that acts in a top-down fashion as an informed selection device. Its approach to learning is exploitative (Holland 1975; March 1991). Linear programming and optimization models work well here, as do reductive mathematical equations in general (Gell-Mann 2002).

But, when the pool of relevant patterns is large, novel (stemming from butterfly-events and frozen accidents), and nonlinear (the processes underlying extreme outcomes that are hard to recognize), then the pattern-processing task does not lend itself to the hierarchical approach. Here the organizational task appears as an inverted pyramid, *B*, in which a limited amount of data at the base (e.g. twelve dots) generates an unimaginable number of candidate patterns (e.g. quintillions) for processing, and potentially overwhelming complexity. Given this, how to build schema based on relevant regularities? In contrast to Gaussian data-processing strategies, we no longer have the luxury of treating all the patterns at the top of the inverted pyramid as validly reducible to a few predictive schema—equations and prescriptions. There are no law-like regularities reducible to equations that would allow us to distinguish meaningful patterns from noise. These patterns, each of which contains potentially relevant information, call for an approach to learning that is exploratory (Holland 1975; March 1991)—i.e. some method allowing us to discover regularities that stem from frozen accidents, connectivity and adaptive tension, and that lurk behind nonlinearities.

Figure 4.6 highlights the nature of the problem by presenting data-processing strategies and pattern-processing tasks as two intersecting pyramids. Whereas processing the huge number of patterns in the inverted pyramid, *B*, requires the bulk of an organization's data-processing resources be toward the top, under the hierarchical data processing regime of pyramid *A* they are mostly at the bottom. This could be one possible explanation for the cognitive inertia that is known to afflict large hierarchical organizations that face

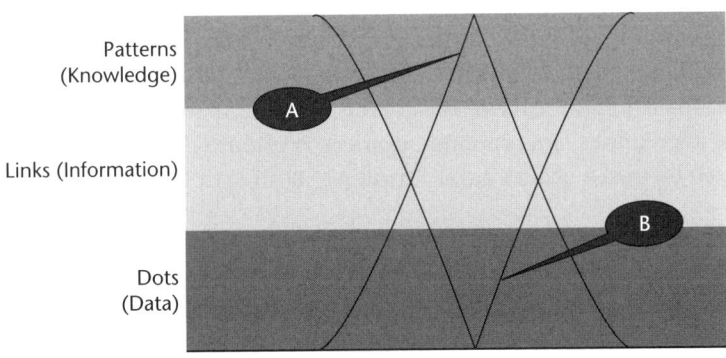

Figure 4.6. The pattern processing challenge

adaptive tensions and stress [see for example the *"groupthink"* literature started by Janis (1972) and the *"threat-rigidity"* research begun by Staw, Sandelands, and Dutton (1981)].

One response to processing huge numbers of patterns is abductive reasoning. According to Peirce, "abduction... consists of examining a mass of facts and in allowing these facts to suggest a theory" (1933, 205). Abduction is a "logic of discovery," an "inference to the best explanation" (Aliseda 2006; Thagard 2006) that uses *all* available data to generate coherent patterns. Abduction rests upon context-dependent intuitions (Hoffman 1996). It complements induction and deduction, both of which can connect the dots—i.e. establish linkages between data points—but on their own, can never establish patterns; abductive reasoning is well suited to the inferential challenges posed by Pareto distributions. If it were simply a question of the "size" of the pattern-processing problem, traditional approaches to inference would still be applicable. But Gell-Mann's identification of scalable regularities as separate from traditional "law-like" regularities (as well as the separation of both from noise) gives us new leverage on the problem, allowing us to adopt the middle Pareto-adaptive strategy located between chaos and order.

Yet, how does "Paretian" *scalable abduction* differ from "Gaussian" abduction? By exploiting the scale-free character of extreme outcomes. Applied to phenomena signified by PL distributions, it offers an inferential process aimed at uncovering multilevel system dynamics stemming from underlying scale-free causal processes. Though different from traditional reductionism—where parts explain the whole—Paretian abduction builds from understanding scale-free causes based on Gell-Mann's "middle level" causal generating mechanisms/processes—the same cause appears at multiple levels in a system.[9] In other words, a scale-free cause spiraling up to an extreme outcome has to exist at multiple levels of the rank/frequency hierarchy. Reductionism is a one-level explanation; scalable abduction "explains" by uncovering a SFT (and underlying causal-generating process) operating across multiple levels.

To sum up, if Gaussian abduction takes extreme outcomes to be outliers—too different from other outcomes in the sample to be accepted as a meaningful probability and thus to form part of the distribution that one is called to respond to—Paretian scalable abduction, by recognizing Gell-Mann's "other" class of regularities, incorporates outliers (exploding butterfly-events often generated by frozen accidents) as forming a significant part of the distribution.

---

[9] More specifically, one identifies scale-free dynamics by studying the many lower-level "tiny" events, some of which become butterfly-events that propagate across multiple levels and sometimes explode into the larger events and "frozen accidents" out in the Pareto tail. Once these regularities are discovered, one may extrapolate out to less frequent (more extreme) events that come with much stronger consequences. Given the negatively sloping PL straight line, and extreme statistics, this can be done with considerable accuracy (Baum and McKelvey 2006).

In effect, even if one cannot compute means and standard deviations and statistical significance—the unstable means and potentially infinite variances in rank/frequency distributions prevent it—PLs signify the existence of scale-free phenomena and make them worthy of our consideration. What are the implications of this kind of reasoning for organization science?

Research implications for organization science

Existing research methods fit both the Ordered and the Chaotic Regimes. In the Ordered Regime, Gaussian science offers the highly refined quantitative methods presented in textbooks such as Greene's (2011). In the Chaotic Regime we encounter rich, ethnographic or historical case studies, Yin (1998), but these lack the scientific legitimacy of quantitative methods. Our focus on the intervening Complexity Regime and on the Paretian ontology characterizing it is novel, stemming as it does from the recent emergence of econophysics as an intellectual field. We now discuss some of the implications of a Pareto-based organization science.

Toward an organization science of rank/frequency Pareto distributions

Consider two quintessential examples of normal distributions: (1) Most Americans are very close to the average height of 5 feet 6.8 inches; the extremes of 2' 5" and 7' 9" (in China) are within half a magnitude; and (2) The average political poll taken to represent "average" opinion in the U.S. has a sample of some 1200 people; the error variance around the mean response to a particular question is ± 3%. A rank/frequency Pareto distribution—stylized in Figure 4.2—looks quite different. Consider, by way of an example, Ma & Pa stores versus giant retailers:

> **First**, located in the upper-left region of Figure 4.2 we have the 17 million tiny Ma & Pa stores in the US (by the official census definition, they have Ma & Pa as owners and no paid employees). These stores show sales of less than $1 million each year, have little in the way of assets, cater to very local customers, show little if any growth year-on-year and are independent of each other. They are typically taken to be *i.i.d.* and treated in a Gaussian fashion.
>
> **Second**, at the lower right we have Walmart, now the world's largest retail firm. It employs two million plus workers, makes billions of dollars in profits, owns further billions of dollars in assets, sells thousands of products, and is increasingly global in its reach. It is now the second largest employer in the US, after the "Military."
>
> **Third**, in between Ma & Pa stores and Walmart we find many thousands of small to large firms. The "average" of these firms has almost nothing in common with

either the Ma & Pa stores or with Walmart. While the *modal* firm looks mostly like a Ma & Pa store, the average firm—whether viewed in terms of number of employees, assets, gross sales, or profits—looks and behaves neither like a Ma & Pa store nor like Walmart. The *median* looks neither like all the little stores nor has the financial and political power of Walmart.

Fourth, deleting the five largest firms located on the lower right of Figure 4.2 as outliers, could significantly change the average but wouldn't change the mode. Deleting a million stores located on the upper left of the Figure would only minutely change the mode or the average. From the foregoing we see that the characteristics of the two tails and those of the middle are vastly different. Simply put, getting rid of outliers simply deletes the very best (profits) or the very worst (losses) members of the retail rank/frequency distribution, thereby offering not so useful results for practitioners. Defined as rates of growth or failure, we see that Stanley et al. (1996) show both growth and failure are to PL distributed across their sample of some 4000 Compustat-listed firms.

Fifth, instead of a meaningful mean in the middle of the Pareto distribution, we have four very different phenomena to deal with:

Type 1. Some variables will, indeed, remain similar in their effect from one tail to the other—for example how subordinates deal with superiors, feelings of relative deprivation, tendencies toward groupthink, etc. Researching these variables offers lessons that retain their validity across the entire distribution. Many Gaussian processes are nested inside Paretian ones.

Type 2. The effects of some variables will be unique to each tail—cloaking good science with Gaussian statistics based on these kinds of variables will then be misleading. Small stores are frequently on a first name basis with regular customers; giant firms have financial and political clout that is unavailable to small store owners. Here, variables that are operational at one end of the distribution have nothing to offer to the other end.

Type 3. Some variables will turn out to be scalable, and, with slight modifications, will apply to firms located at the mean as much as to the giants located on the lower right. The founding technology and HR strategies of firms like Intel, HP, 3M, Microsoft, Walmart, Apple and the like, for example, have scaled up from their small beginnings to their current giant size. These variables are critically important to understand why firms grow—or don't. Scalability is what gets firms from the left or middle of Figure 4.2 out more toward the right.

Type 4. Anderson's book, *The Long Tail* (2006), discusses a modern marketing trend based on the reality that many customers located on the upper-left hand region of Figure 4.2 have unique tastes, live in small unique micro-niches, and now may be catered to in a customized fashion using Internet-based strategies and technologies—as done by Amazon and eBay, and Google. This ability to extract useful information from variances even in the upper left of Figure 4.2 further undermines the usefulness of averages and of Gaussian approaches in this region. Tesco's Fresh & Easy stores are explicitly designed to cater to their immediate neighborhood, as opposed to chains like McDonalds or 7Eleven that aim to be the same everywhere.

Sixth, each of the foregoing four classifications calls for a different scientific methodology:

Type 1. Gaussian statistics work just fine here.

Type 2. Gaussian statistics work on samples of stores and other small firms at the upper left of the diagram. New methods, however, will be needed to improve the scientific legitimacy and quality of truth-claims of research focused on the lower-right extremes. Gaussian statistics can also apply to "vertical slices" offering larger samples in between the ends of the two long tails (the many small firms at one and the giant at the other). For example, one could draw a sample from all firms of a specified size (by # of employees, gross sales, total assets, etc.) and then use control variables to distinguish among firms of the same size but in different industries.

Type 3. Studying scalable variables and causes calls for new theorizing along the lines of what we briefly describe in Table 4.1, as well as new ontologies, epistemologies, methodologies, and statistical support for truth claims. Here, agent-based modeling, abductive reasoning, and hermeneutic methods all seem particularly well suited to providing a more sophisticated basis for truth claims than current case study methods. Andriani and McKelvey (2011a) introduce the idea of "power-law science" applied specifically to rank/frequency distributions.

Type 4. Using gene-sequencing techniques, medical science shows a growing ability to define genetic profiles that are unique to individuals, and to "micro-design" uniquely suitable drugs in response (*The Economist* 2007). Here, as elsewhere, a *"science of the unique"* is emerging that contrasts with the science of the Gaussian average that most sciences focus on at present. Organization science needs to respond both theoretically and practically to rank/frequency and micro-design needs and opportunities.

Seventh, scalability effects are especially sensitive to the presence of adaptive tensions and the amount of connectivity within a given system. Complexity theory holds that tension leads to connectivity and that connectivity, in turn, leads to the generation of multiplicativity, interactivity, positive feedback and other scale-free causes and, then, to scalable outcomes. But, connectivities can also lead to the spread and growth of tension effects—as is the case with power-grid collapses and viral epidemics, etc.

We now discuss in further detail some aspects of the foregoing differences between Gauss- and Pareto-based organization science.

Connectivity

When dealing with outcomes of relevance to organizations, organization science tends to confine itself to the left-hand side of Figure 4.2, focusing on outcomes that have frequencies that are high enough to meet statistical sampling requirements and mostly similar enough in size not to violate the statistical requirements for similarity between members of the same sample.

Extreme outcomes occurring on the right-hand side of Figure 4.2 have been handled outside this frame through the use of case studies and scenarios (Perrow 1984; Weick 1993; Sheffi 2005). Given its analytical tractability, academics have been drawn to the left-hand side of the diagram. Yet given their need for relevance and for coping with extremes, practicing managers have been drawn to "stories" and lessons originating on the right. Many of these describe downsides, i.e. extreme outcomes that are judged to be highly negative by one or more players. Yet many extreme outcomes also have upsides—for at least some of the players. Entrepreneurs, for example, exploit Schumpeter's (1934) "gales of creative destruction," and Christensen's (1997) disruptive technologies to create as well as to destroy.

In practice, little integration occurs between the right and left segments of Figure 4.2. Outcomes located on the right in Figure 4.2 are treated as outliers by those focused on the Gaussian approach. The modal set of really small firms located on the left in the Figure are seldom relevant or uninteresting to managers worried about practical relevance and how to reach the *"stochastic frontier"* (i.e. well out beyond the average) (Lieberman and Dhawan 2005). We can best understand the dilemma by placing ourselves at some point midway along the PL slope in Figure 4.2. Looking upward and to the left increases the sample size, decreases the average size and complexity of outcomes under study, encourages simplification and reductionist thinking toward Gell-Mann's Type 1 "law-like" regularities, and makes them amenable to normal statistical methods. Looking downward and to the right, by contrast, decreases the sample size, increases the size, complexity, and importance of single outcomes and, thus, calls for an approach to complexity based on Gell-Mann's "deep simplicity" (1988), which he now calls scalability (2002).

What is the relevance of the above for organization science? If we choose to view organizations through a network lens, we can argue that organization science studies the regularities that govern the interactions linking different nodes together—that is, organization science studies the structure and the dynamics of the connectivities in a system, which studies increasingly show are scalable rank/frequency distributions (Gay and Dousset 2005; Newman, Barabási, and Watts 2006; Boisot and Lu 2007; Chmiel et al. 2007). The fact that nodes can represent whole organizations located within a network of organizations such as industries or alliances as readily as individuals or departments within a single organization, suggests that many of the regularities that are studied by organization science will be scalable (Barabási and Albert 1999; Battiston and Cantanzaro 2004; Souma et al. 2006; Song, Jiang, and Zhou 2009). And since the degree of connectivity that characterizes a system is a variable that reflects the level of adaptive tension being experienced by the system, it follows that organization science must engage with the PL distribution of Figure 4.2 as a whole without privileging one particular region of the distribution at the expense of another. Thus the rare, indeed, extreme, outcomes associated with extensive connectivities are as legitimate objects of study as the more frequent normally distributed outcomes produced by unconnected outcomes.

A Pareto distribution, in effect, tells us that "organization" is a matter of degree. What we conventionally call "organizations" are the outcomes of a process—Weick (1979) calls this "organizing"—through which different levels of connectivity get established over time by means of transactions. Such connectivities can either get established in an ad hoc incremental and evolutionary fashion or more systematically through design. A PL distribution of firm sizes, such as Axtell's (2001), essentially describes the extent of the tight coupling achieved by nodes to deliver "formal" organizations of different sizes, such as firms.

The problem of managerial coordination consists of picking and then maintaining the appropriate degree of connectivity between different nodes in a system so as to deliver value-adding outputs at varying levels of complexity. Making McDonalds hamburgers, for example, requires tightly coordinating the actions of a few people in each of the thousands of tiny independent stores spread all over the world and producing their output in small volumes. Or, trying to discover the Higgs boson—claimed to be the most ambitious experiment in high-energy physics ever undertaken—calls simultaneously for tight and loose coordination of two-to-three thousand physicists from over thirty countries and as many technicians in the underground test site (Bressan 2005).

Butterfly-levers

At first glance, we need to achieve a trade-off between the *ex-ante* costs of predicting and the *ex-post* costs of responding in adaptive ways to high impact, low frequency outcomes. This requires a trade-off at a second level, between:

1. An ability to make sense, *ex post*, of the extreme outcome.
2. An ability to respond adaptively to what has been made sense of *ex post*.

The opportunity or threat posed by an extreme outcome first appears as a small butterfly-event to which heterogeneous agents, initially endowed with zero-order connectivity, respond by searching for and connecting to other agents (Kauffman 1993; Batty 2005). Through such interactions, and providing that they can overcome any tendencies to passive dependence (Argyris 1957) or to "groupthink" (Janis 1972), the agents' sensing processes can reach beyond the individual atomized Gaussian outcome to apprehend the connected dynamics of an extreme Paretian one. As the pool of agents enlarges to straddle multilevel hierarchies, the probability of finding the butterfly-levers and emergent dissipative structures is enhanced. Agents, now joining to act as a complex adaptive system, learn enough about the outcome to avoid both the incoherence of the chaotic regime as well as the one-sided simplicity of the ordered regime in the Ashby Space. We know from basic complexity-science agent-based computational models that interacting heterogeneous agents are best able to correctly sense elements essential to adaptation (Kauffman 1993; Mitchell 1996, 2009; Prietula, Carley, and Gasser 1998; Gilbert and Troitzsch 1999; Ferber 1999; Johnson 2000; Miller and Page 2007; North and Macal 2007). As currently conceived, however, such computational agents are guided by "simple rules" based on "lean" ontologies. The "intelligent" agents populating our Ashby Space, by contrast, are guided by "rich" ontologies and complex representations of their environment. Human agents make sense of their worlds first and foremost by applying an ontology appropriate to the underlying structure of the phenomena that they encounter and must respond to. The ability of collectivities of heterogeneous human agents to discover things and make sound decisions is now well established. Surowiecki (2004) and Page (2007) give convincing evidence that such collectivities outdo experts in successfully responding to small, strange, and uncertain data. They show that when it comes to puzzle-solving, diverse agents beat experts much of the time. Escoffier and McKelvey's (2013) research shows that random moviegoers across the US offer crowd-wisdom-based ratings of the quality of movie trailers (i.e. they hadn't yet seen the full-length movies) that predicted the actual opening-weekend box-office receipts of eight movies. With a correlation at 0.79, their prediction was higher than that of professional movie critics who had actually seen the movie (correlation at 0.51).

Emergent scalability dynamics

How can scale-free butterfly-levers facilitate the generation of extreme responses? In addressing this question, the social sciences in general, and organization science in particular, may enjoy options that may not always be available to the natural sciences. For example, there are some 16,000 small quakes (from 1 to 4 on the Richter scale) in California every year. This adds up to over 2 million small "average" quakes since the last great quake of 1857. Though they are still trying (Sornette 2002), geologists have just about given up attempting to use small quakes to predict large ones (Main 1997). Their problem is that small quakes a few miles underground, and major quakes starting up to 400 miles underground, are hard to study. In organizations, however, the small butterfly-events that foreshadow extreme outcomes are still at a scale that makes them accessible to direct human observation and interpretation. This, we believe, gives people in organizations a better chance of detecting the scale-free causes of butterfly-events and then acting either to forestall them before they metamorphose into extreme outcomes, where these are expected to be negative, or to exploit them (as "levers") as they get amplified, where they are expected to be positive. Weick et al. (Weick, Sutcliffe, and Obstfeld 1999; Weick and Sutcliffe 2001) call this *"mindfulness,"* but they don't offer any specific theories about scalability that would help people zero in on the relevant tiny initiating events more quickly.

Given that one's ontological perspective often limits what one looks for and what one then sees—i.e. *"You don't see what you aren't looking for"* (McKelvey and Andriani 2010)—the key idea here is to switch from a Gaussian ontology that looks for regularities at one accessible level and then responds to an "average" of these, to a Paretian ontology that seeks out scale-free regularities, some of the causes of which we list in Table 4.1.[10] This switch involves shifting one's focus from the left side of Figure 4.2 to the whole of the PL distribution—i.e. going from left to right—in search of those leverageable regularities that straddle multiple levels of a rank/frequency hierarchy. Operating these at just one level delivers little to an organization. The lever-effect has to spread across multiple levels if it is to generate an extreme response. The presence of adaptive tension in the system provokes PHASE TRANSITIONS that initiate self-organizing processes and the emergence of new order across these multiple levels. A lack of tension at any given level, however, undermines the motivation of agents at that level to undertake the self-organizing activities leading to emergence. And absent emergence, a barrier is then created to the SPONTANEOUS CREATION of those adaptive responses that become a source of new order (Kauffman 1993; Holland 2002).

What does it take for an organization to operationalize Simon's (1962) architecture of complexity? Simon calls for "nearly decomposable" modules. In an emergent hierarchy, agency becomes nested in groups of individuals and organizational subunits. While creating more subunits increases organizational CONNECTION COSTS, without such connections to initiate scale-free dynamic, self-organization and emergence will weaken. The challenge of managerial coordination is one of balancing the advantages of many specialized nearly decomposable modules against the cost of keeping them connected. Scale-free dynamics often bring an organization to a state that Bak (1996) labels SELF-ORGANIZED CRITICALITY (SOC). Like small and large avalanches in the tiny single-sand-grain movements to large avalanches in the sandpiles that Bak uses to illustrate the SOC concept, organizations can either make many small moves to balance out the costs and benefits of connecting, or they can undertake major reorganizations; readily illustrated in Park, Moral, and Madhavan (2010): avalanches appear as M&A waves when applied to firms. Since the tension between the agents' need for autonomy and their need for

---

[10] They are signified in the following text by small capitals.

connections exists at all levels, the conditions for Bak's (1996) self-organized criticality also appear at all levels—i.e. the process becomes scale-free.

Much will depend on what effort is required, by which agent, at what level—and for what payoff. While Zipf (1929, 1949) is most famous for his PRINCIPLE OF LEAST EFFORT linking PLs to the study of language, he also applied the principle to various kinds of economic phenomena (communities, economic power, social status, income, marriage licenses, newspapers, corporate assets, etc.), including cities, more recently further studied by Krugman (1996), Batty (2005) and McKelvey (forthcoming). Least-effort theory as also been applied to high-growth firms (Ishikawa 2006) and to transition economies (Podobnik et al. 2006). Recent research suggests that the least-effort principle—together with the PLs that signify its presence—underpins the multi-scale entrepreneurial dynamics (or lack thereof) that we often observe (Crawford 2012). If the left hand side of Figure 4.2 supports Gaussian ontologies and *managerial* behaviors, the right hand side supports Paretian ontologies and *entrepreneurial* behaviors. To secure the extreme positive entrepreneurial outcomes achieved by the likes of Microsoft, Amazon, e-Bay, Silicon Valley or Google, the principle of least effort must operate across as well as within levels.

Conclusion

We begin by defining key elements underlying power laws (PLs). Then, drawing on Ashby's (1956) *Law of Requisite Variety*, we separate the Ashby response space into *Chaotic, Ordered,* and *Complex Regimes*. Next, we argue that practitioner-relevant research in the Complexity Regime space calls for a *"PL Science"* and offer six ways in which management inquiry could become more PL oriented. Organizing and management become *elements* of *connected* network processes, some of which yield adaptive structures and some of which do not. They all produce rank/frequency (more or less) PL distributions instead of "normal" Gaussian distributions. Our theoretical approach has the effect of *naturalizing* management inquiry, bringing it closer to recent trends in physics and biology—shades of econophysics (Mandelbrot 1983; Iannaccone and Khokha 1995; Mantegna and Stanley 2000; McCauley 2004; Chakrabarti, Chakraborti, and Chatterjee 2006; Sinha et al. 2011)—and making it less dependent on the "things" of engineering from which it sprang and more akin to connectivity and networks (see for example West and Deering 1995; Barabási 2002; Newman, Barabási, and Watts 2006; Andriani and McKelvey 2009, 2011c; McKelvey and Salmador Sanchez 2011).

Physics operates at the highest level of generality achievable in the natural sciences. Econophysics, as the name implies, involves the application of physics nonlinear methods to economic phenomena. By focusing on the "long tails" of Pareto distributions, econophysics increasingly uncovers phenomena that are best characterized by PL "signatures," and best explained by SFTs. A negatively sloping PL signature emerges when Pareto distributions are plotted on double-log paper. Scale-free processes result from causal dynamics that cross multiple levels of analysis—from atoms to galaxies; from DNA basepairs to species extinctions; from small stores to giant corporations. These applications can readily be extended into the organizational realm (Andriani and McKelvey 2007, 2009, 2011a, b, c; McKelvey and Andriani 2010).

Organization science, however, has yet to follow. It lacks an adequate conceptualization of extreme outcomes, and so, unsurprisingly, has proved unable to incorporate them into its current theorizing. In this chapter, therefore, we draw from econophysics to introduce a more penetrating treatment of PLs, extreme outcomes, and SFT into organization science. We believe that an *econophysics of management* will ultimately add much more practitioner value to organization-science research than is currently the case.

While most of orthodox economics is obviously attuned to the normal distribution of autonomous *i.i.d.* data points, so then is most of organization science, particularly that part of it which is under the sway of econometric analyses and statistics (Greene 2011). The result is an excessive focus on the stability and structural aspects of organizations, on those aspects that are robust against changing conditions, and that lend themselves to the prepensive "design" approach. Faced with the phenomenon of increasing connectivity (Wasserman and Faust 1994), social scientists are beginning to study the nonlinear PL dynamics of network evolution (Lawrence and Giles 1998; Watts and Strogatz 1998; Barabási and Albert 1999; Barabási 2002; Ravasz and Barabási 2003; Watts 2003; Gay and Dousset 2005; Newman, Barabási, and Watts 2006; Souma et al. 2006; Chmiel et al. 2007; Mislove et al. 2007; Saito, Watanabe, and Iwamura 2007; Santiago and Benito 2008; Song, Jiang, and Zhou 2009; Gerow and Keane 2011).

The advent of the information economy, however, is changing both the nature of organizations and management information systems (Benbya and McKelvey 2006, 2011a, b, 2012; Merali and McKelvey 2006). Organizations are becoming more flexible, more changeable, and their boundaries are becoming more blurred. They are becoming less object-like and more like extensible networks unconstrained by boundaries. This requires a new type of theorizing in which the shift initiated by Weick (1979) over three decades ago—from *organizations* as things to *organizing* as a process—is taken to its logical conclusion. "*Organizing*" now becomes a *dimension* of network processes some of which yield stable structures and some of which do not. Such theorizing will have the effect of naturalizing organization science, bringing it closer to recent physics and biology and making it less dependent on the engineering traditions from which it sprang (e.g. Chu, Strand, and Jelland

2003; Newman, Barabási, and Watts 2006; Andriani and McKelvey 2007, 2009, 2011 a, b, c; Boisot and McKelvey 2010, 2011a; and Allen, Maguire, and McKelvey 2011).

The forces of globalization are more densely connecting the various economies around the world by new information and communication technologies. The result is a faster pace of innovation and change. In such circumstances, to confine ourselves to a Gaussian orientation that screens out the rank/frequency and PL dynamics of emergent interactive complexities now challenging us is a tradition that we can no longer afford. The options available in the Ashby Space suggest that, to be adaptive, responses increasingly need to be both more varied and more rapid than those associated with the routinizing strategy, i.e. the one built on Gaussian assumptions.

5

Reflecting on Max Boisot's *Ashby Space* Applied to Complexity Management

Bill McKelvey

Max Boisot spent the first 15 years of his career as a professional architect and co-owner of an architectural firm. Architects design buildings, which are containers of space. *Space!* It is hardly surprising, then, that Max's 1995 book is titled *Information Space* (Boisot et al.'s 2007 book also has "Space" in its title). Also not so surprising, then, that my publications with Max very quickly began to focus on different applications of what Max called the "*Ashby Space*." What brought us together was Ross Ashby's "*Law of Requisite Variety.*"

In his classic work, *An Introduction to Cybernetics*, Ashby (1956) said: "When a constraint exists advantage can usually be taken of it.... Every law of nature is a constraint.... Science looks for laws.... Constraints are exceedingly common in the world around us.... A world without constraints would be totally chaotic.... That something is predictable implies that there exists a constraint.... Learning is worthwhile only when the environment shows constraint" (pp. 130–4). He also noted that order (organization) exists between two entities, *A* and *B*, only if the link is "conditioned" by a third entity, *C* (1962, 255). If *C* symbolizes the "environment," which is external to the relation between *A* and *B*, environmental constraints are what cause order (Ashby 1956). This, then, gives rise to his famous *Law of Requisite Variety*: "ONLY VARIETY CAN DESTROY VARIETY" (p. 207; his capitals). It holds that for a biological or social entity to be efficaciously adaptive, the variety of its internal order must match the variety of the environmental constraints.

If Ashby were writing now he would surely update his Law, as follows:

Only variety can destroy variety
Only degrees of freedom can destroy degrees of freedom
Only internal complexity can destroy external complexity

This rephrasing rests on the widely held view that complexity is a function of degrees of freedom.

The **first** lesson from Ashby is that for strategists to find emerging patterns in what appear to be chaotic environments, they need to uncover the contextual constraints and resources. The **second** lesson is that internal complexity needs to match the complexity of the environmental context. A **third**, related lesson comes from Allen (2001). Since it is impossible to know in advance which of a firm's degrees of freedom will actually be relevant to a particular environment, Allen proposes his *Law of Excess Variety*. A firm can't simply create internal variety to *match* the environment. It has to create *excess* variety. It follows that a pattern-finding social network within a firm has to be more complex than the complexity of its imposing competitive environment!

In defining variety, Ashby (1956, 124–25) pointed to the following series: "*c, b, c, a, c, c, a, b, c, b, b, a.*" He observed that *a*, *b*, and *c* repeat, meaning that there are only three "*distinct* elements"—three kinds of variety or three degrees of freedom. In the language of patterns, however, this is variety at the level of "dots." Suppose, instead, we define variety in terms of the number of patterns instead of the number of dots. Then, using the formulae from Table 4.2, we see that four dots lead to six possible links; they also generate 64 possible patterns (see Table 4.2 in Boisot and McKelvey [this volume]). With ten dots one gets 45 possible links and approximately 35 trillion possible patterns. Ashby's twelve "variety" dots produce 66 possible links and approximately 4,700 quadrillion possible patterns! Even supposing 99% of these are not worth paying attention to, trillions are left, and one still doesn't know, up front, which ones are trivial and which are not. Needless to say, finding which patterns are worth focusing on is an *information-processing problem—the core of Max's insights and contributions over the years.*

The *Ashby Space* dates back to our first presentation: (McKelvey and Boisot 2003), and subsequently appears in all of our publications; it also appears in our Academy of Management *"Best Paper Proceedings"* paper (Boisot and McKelvey 2007; this volume). In Boisot and McKelvey (this volume), in Figure 4.3, the vertical axis measures the variety of external stimuli that register with an agent; the horizontal axis measures the variety of responses generated by that agent. The diagonal indicates where the variety of responses matches that of incoming stimuli and is therefore adaptive. Above the diagonal, the variety of the responses fails to match that of incoming stimuli; below it, the variety of responses is excessive relative to what is adaptive and wastes energy resources. In Figure 4.4 we partition the vertical axis of the *Ashby Space* into different Regimes: *Chaotic*, *Complex*, and *Ordered*. In the chaotic regime, incoming stimuli exhibit no obviously discernible regularities; in the complex regime, they exhibit some, even if these still have to be teased out; in the ordered regime, one can subordinate all the variety encountered in incoming stimuli to some ordering principle—e.g. algorithmic compression—as when, for example, the sequence: a,b,a,b,a,b,a,b,a,b,a,b,a,b,a,b,a,b, can be reduced to 10(a,b).

Foresight: We presented our first co-authored work at the INSEAD Conference on *Expanding Perspectives on Strategy Processes* (August 2003), titled "Redefining Strategic Foresight: *'Fast'* and *'Far'* Sight via Complexity Science." It was published in 2009—our only paper with myself as first author. Whereas I had presented the *Fast* and *Far* Sight idea at an earlier conference up in Strathclyde, Scotland, it was only after Max joined me that Ashby's (1956) *Law of Requisite Variety* was updated to the *Law of Requisite Complexity* in this paper. It's about adaptive knowing:

> The only thing that gives an organization a competitive edge—the only thing that is sustainable—is what it knows, how it uses what it knows, and how fast it can know something new! (Prusak 1996, 6)

The "Foresight" paper defines the competitive circumstances within which we study processes leading to strategic foresight. Good strategy is no longer just picking the right industry; it is being at the right place in the industry—at the cutting edge of industry evolution—new technology, new markets, new moves by competitors. For firms in high-velocity environments (Eisenhardt 1989), emphasis needs to shift from the competitive dynamics of industry selection and interfirm competition to intrafirm rates of change (McKelvey 1997). As high-velocity product life cycles and hyper-competition have increased (D'Aveni 1994), speed of knowledge appreciation has become a central attribute of competitive advantage (Leonard-Barton 1995), as has organizational learning (Barney 1991; Argote 1999). Seeing industry trends (Hamel and Prahalad 1994) and staying ahead of value migration (Slywotsky 1996) are also valued. Porter (1996) emphasizes staying ahead of the efficiency curve. Dynamic ill-structured environments and learning opportunities become the basis of competitive advantage if firms can be *early* in their industry to unravel the evolving conditions (Stacey 1995).

Starting from scientific realism's transcendental causality (Bhaskar 1975), our theory about the strategy-finding process stresses the use of (1) *Farsight—pattern-processing* to simplify and focus information about a firm's *environmental context* so as to get a grip on *where to look*, and (2) *Fast*sight—*emergent complexity* to create and energize the kinds of social networks within a target firm so as to improve its external seeing ability and get a grip on *who looks* and *how quickly*. We use complexity science as the analytical engine to unravel both *far-* and *fast*sight dynamics.

This pattern-search, *far*sight procedure, however, requires a well functioning social network "seeing" device to deal with the *"who looks* and *how fast"* questions. In a recursive fashion, analyses about where a firm stands with respect to the broader adaptive tensions provide information that can be used to both motivate and steer phase transitions, coevolutionary events, and social networks' self-organizing behaviours. In short, *far*sight delineation of adaptive tensions motivates self-organization by social networks—improving their *fast*sight capability. *Fast*sight development by social networks, in turn, leads to better *far*sight seeing ability. Why? Broad trends decompose into higher frequency event horizons as one drops down levels of analysis (Simon 1999) and the events come closer to having impact on a firm. *Fast*sight becomes a crucial element of *far*sight as broad, seemingly slow moving patterns resolve into higher speed dynamics. Bottom line? Supra-forces and sub-forces coevolve to improve strategic *far*- and *fast*sight. Needless to say, reliance on a single visionary CEO (Bennis and O'Toole 2000) is prone to failure (Marion and Uhl-Bien 2001; Uhl-Bien, Marion, and McKelvey 2007).

Creating the needed cellular networks (Miles et al. 1999) in firms to pursue the *fast*sight path is not easy. McKelvey (2004, 2010) presents complexity-based "simple rules" (they are not really so simple—"action disciplines" is more accurate) essential to enabling emergent social networks. Boisot (1998) discusses essential organizational conditions for knowledge development. We also present the so-called "i^2 by k, v, t array", which offers a plan for pattern processing under conditions where one can expect vast numbers of possible patterns. We also develop our pattern processing approach in more depth elsewhere (Boisot and McKelvey 2006a, b; see below), focusing more on the speed problem.

We conclude by stressing the recursive nature of developing *far*- and *fast*-sight. Improving the one improves the other. Following Ashby, our use of complexity science shows that CEOs need to focus on environmentally imposed adaptive tensions that, then, may be used to initiate, motivate, and maintain their cellular networks in the *fast*sight mode. The presence of well working cellular networks leads to faster pattern processing, which leads to more efficacious *far*sight. Neither can work without the other. The bottom line is that complexity science offers a strategy-finding process *away* from foresight, vision, and witch doctoring or, put more bluntly, the hope of finding modern versions of the *Oracle at Delphi*. It takes internal complexity to develop strategies suitable for strategic success in a complex external environment.

Counter-terrorism & Whistle-blowing: Max's first creation and application of the *Ashby Space* appears in our work titled "Counter-Terrorism as Global Neighborhood Watch: A Socio/Computational Approach for Getting Patterns From Dots aimed at Counter-terrorism." It was first presented at the *Department of Justice Conference on Neighborhood Watch* (August 2005) and then at the 47th *Annual Conference of the International Military Testing Association*

(November 2005). It was also written up in a U.S. magazine titled *Government Executive* (Harris 2005) as "Global Neighborhood Watch." It appears in print as Chapters 3 and 4 in a book edited by Suder (2006). This paper offered Max an obvious way of connecting his prior works on information space and processing to the major issue of the time.

Chapter 3: Recently some emergent *nonlinear events* of historical proportions occurred: three of which were Al-Qa'ida's September 11 attack on the World Trade Center, the collapse of Enron, and the disintegration of NASA's space shuttle, Columbia. At the FBI there was a failure to *"fill in the dots,"* that is, failure to discover the early predictive patterns in a timely fashion. The failure was the result of spatial dispersion, hierarchy, and jurisdictional disputes. At Enron the problem stemmed from illegal activities, "don't ask; don't tell" managerial attitudes, and self-serving "reinterpretations" of accounting rules, coupled with conflict of interest between the CPA firm's and Enron's accountants. At NASA, budget cuts, flight schedules, and a lackadaisical organizational culture meant that top-management's responses were even slower than the steady accumulation of evidence pointing to the Columbia shuttle's vulnerability. In each case the rate at which the information pointing to an emergent problem progressed was higher than the rate at which top managers (of the FBI and NASA) or auditors or government regulators (of Enron) could appreciate the emerging patterns and take action. Similar historical failures come to mind: Pearl Harbour, the Cuban Missile Crisis and the Challenger shuttle explosion—all showing the same foresight failure to detect emerging patterns—in a timely fashion.

All of the foregoing triggered disasters. Failure to find patterns because of space, hierarchy, and information processing speed effects is also endemic to most firms. As noted earlier, Ashby (1956) put it in terms of building internal *requisite variety* to match environmental variety in a timely fashion. For March and Simon (1958) the issue was framed in terms of bounded rationality. Williamson (1975) blames asymmetric information and opportunism. McKelvey (1997) talks about the problem in terms of rate dynamics. Boisot (1998) talked about it in terms of abstraction and codification in the *I-Space*. Fine (1998) discusses competitive advantage in terms of "clock speed."

Emergent complexity events progress at different speeds. Firms don't need to reach for the moon; they just need to find instructive patterns faster than their competitors. More generally, firms need to uncover patterns at a rate faster than the rate at which the emergence process is unfolding. But, there are potentially hundreds or thousands of dots. Not all can be targets of attention and not all possible patterns are important. Yet the vast number of dots, the geometric increase in patterns, and the need for speedy pattern finding combined to create the foregoing failures.

Getting ahead of various kinds of danger comparable to the build-up of terrorist cells—in timely fashion—is demonstrably difficult, as is evident in the FBI's response to pre-9/11 events. It may very well be beyond the capability of a *human* organizational hierarchy, absent some kind of distributed information processing capability coupled with hi-speed computational help. In this work we, first, describe the threat of dangerous emergent events progressing at speeds beyond the pattern processing capabilities of most human hierarchies. We then turn to Ashby's *Law of Requisite Variety* and complexity science to outline an approach for:

1. Reducing the problem imposed by many quadrillions of possible patterns.
2. Changing organizational bureaucracies from modes of hierarchical command-and-control dating back to the Fordist Industrial Era to a Knowledge Era style featuring distributed intelligence (McKelvey 2001, 2008).

We argue that these two redesign approaches are recursive; the functioning of each is speeded up by improved performance by the other. Before concluding the chapter we return to the problem posed by hierarchies and silo effects.

As far back as 1945, in a classic paper entitled "The Use of Knowledge in Society," Friedrich Hayek showed how socially distributed processing could help citizens and organizations cope with a complex and fast-moving, nonlinear world. Such parallel processing strategies, he argued, were to be found in markets. In matters of intelligence, however, government agencies continue to operate exclusively through archaic Fordist organizations (MI-6, CIA, FBI, etc.) The proposed solution of the 9/11 Commission—to create a new intelligence Tsar—simply builds onto this traditional organizing strategy. It is really quite wrong-headed. By making the silo taller they actually risk making the pattern-processing problem even worse! The complexity of the security challenge suggests that these traditional approaches now need to be complemented by modern socio/computational data processing methods that integrate silicon- and carbon-based agents in novel ways.

Chapter 4: We then propose a solution that integrates new hi-speed computational processes with new organizational ones. Together, they suggest that significant organizational and cultural challenges loom if intelligence agencies are ever to efficaciously anticipate and counteract terrorism.

To deal with both pattern finding and rate problems, we suggest two not unrelated approaches. First, we focus on ways to simplify the potentially infinite patterns comprising external variety. We need to find patterns that are indicative of unfolding emergent events *before* the events actually become obvious—that is, before the 9/11 attack or before Enron's collapse. Consequently, instead of a few "knowns" in a sea of unknowns (the famous "dots" that weren't filled in), our proposed socio/computational approach uses state-of-the-art computational methods coupled with the use of contextual tensions, different vantage perspectives, and corroboration over time to simplify external pattern proliferation in timely fashion. In this way we reduce Ashby's external complexity.

Second, we focus on creating, activating, and speeding up the formation of internal complexity. To do this we develop a *socio/computational semi-autonomic human connectionist network* consisting of two elements: (1) a distributed intelligence spread across a large number of heterogeneous human agents using state-of-the-art detectors and mobile phones, and (2) the combination of a neural network computational model (Anthony and Bartlett 1999) and a structural-equation model (Kaplan 2000) located in a central intelligence organization.

Dealing with dangerous emergence events—possibly worldwide—when speed is what counts can only happen when the following are in place:

1. Widely dispersed and highly mobile human operatives in- and outside official intelligence Agencies offering "distributed" pattern processing and corroboration activities—i.e. "intelligence" distributed across thousands of Operatives (neurons) acting within a connectionist (synaptic) brain-like network.

2. Operatives all equipped with portable detectors, beepers, mobile phones, phone photos, and short-text-messaging. Only with these resources can Agencies move methodically and quickly from possible to probable knowledge via plausible knowledge.

3. A centralized socio-computational technology that:
   a) Can quickly reduce trillions of candidate patterns down to an actionable few. These then serve as inputs to parallel processors in the form of successively updated training patterns. We suggest structural equation (with block) modelling as a preferred method.
   b) Uses neural net parallel processing, driven by increasingly accurate training patterns, to focus searches through corroborated open-source information for relevant dot-links existing in the world as input data—especially those that foreshadow some imminent security threat.

We frame our argument mostly in terms of terrorism. But any firm needing rapid information processing—about new technology, consumer tastes, or competitor moves—could take advantage of our proposed method. Using our "global neighbourhood watch" methods also serves as an excellent platform for stimulating and then responding to any kind need to both encourage and process whistle-blowing.

Best Paper on Extremes & Econophysics: This work won us a *"Best Paper"* award at the 2007 Academy of Management Conference; it appears in an altered form in our *Journal of Management Inquiry* publication of 2011 (appeared two months before Max died). What is our point? This paper is a natural extension of Max's long-time interest in cognitive representations of extant phenomena, agents' development of adaptive response schema, ontological assumptions, and knowledge creation. It gave Max a chance to really expand the vague notions of complex information processing schema appearing in his 1998 book into more substantive representations of possible, plausible, and probable schema. An updated version of this paper appears in this Memorial volume.

Complexity Science Bridge: In this work, the complexity section of the *Ashby Space* gets used in a totally different way. Drawing on Ashby's *Law*, we separate the Ashby response space into *Chaotic*, *Ordered*, and *Complex Regimes*. Modernism equates to the highly ordered and simplified (lower) part of the *Ashby Space*. Postmodernism, where *"anything goes"* (Feyerabend 1975), equates to the upper "chaos" part of the *Ashby Space*—truth-claims can go in any and all directions. This idea dates back to a talk I gave in 1998, titled: " 'Good' Science from Postmodernist Ontology: Realism, Complexity Theory, and Emergent Dissipative Structures." Given Max's long interest in the clash of Modernism versus Postmodernism, it was easy for us to come together on this topic. This paper was written up, not presented anywhere, but published in the *Academy of Management Review* (2010). In this work Max comes full circle from his earlier interests in Modernist and Postmodernist approaches to schema formation in the sciences—especially physical versus social science—by putting them into the *Ashby Space* and thence relating them to complex information-processing dynamics. Discovering complexity science as the bridge between Modernism and Postmodernism is Max at his best.

The study of social systems such as organizations has long been caught between two conflicting bases of legitimacy: On the one hand, we have *Positivism*—a set of procedures for creating valid knowledge expressing a *Modernist* outlook that originated in the 18th century *Enlightenment* project. It presumes a real, relatively stable, and objectively-given world, populated by phenomena that can be rationally known and rationally analyzed by independent observers. Such phenomena can be decomposed into observation protocols resting on sense data and predictively related to each other through stable laws integrated via a mathematical syntax (Benacerraf and Putnam 1964; Lakatos 1976). Positivism promotes the modernist agenda: the understanding, manipulation and control of predominantly physical phenomena for beneficial social ends. In contemporary social sciences, neoclassical economics remains positivism's foremost exemplar (Colander 2006; Friedman 1953; Lawson 1997; Mirowski 1989).

On the other hand, the *Postmodernist* movement emerged in the late 1960s to challenge the basic tenets of modernism and its epistemological ally, positivism. Whereas in modernism the focus is on a phenomenal world directly and unproblematically observed and described by a disinterested actor who remains external to what is being observed, the postmodernist strategy problematizes the relationship of actors to observed phenomena by having language mediate it. Thus, instead of a single direct relationship between an external world W and an observer O, we now have two relationships: (1) between an external world W and a descriptive language, L; and (2) between L and an observer, O. Language is a *human* resource that places the relationship between W and O in a social context where divergent interests (Habermas 1972) and social power (Foucault 1969) come into play. These shape language and linguistic usage, and by implication, the regions of the phenomenal world to which they give access.

We offer a third alternative that draws on several well-known complexity principles to integrate the ordered world of modernists and the more "chaotic" world of postmodernists. We posit that the conjunction of *adaptive tension*—the gap between the variety internally available to a system and that which confronts it externally (McKelvey 2001, 2008)—connectivity, and interdependency in social phenomena reflect these principles and challenge the dominant assumption that social events are independent of each other and identically distributed (*i.i.d.*) so as to yield a normal distribution. Such a "Gaussian" default assumption underpins an *atomistic ontology*, one that takes the world as constituted by a collection of objects. Many events connected under tension, however, are often distributed according to a power law as illustrated in Figure 5.1, which shows a Pareto distribution on the left and its equivalent power-law distribution on the right. A power-law distribution is a Pareto distribution depicted on a log-log scale. Other (less extreme) skew distributions, reflecting the different ways that phenomena interact, are also

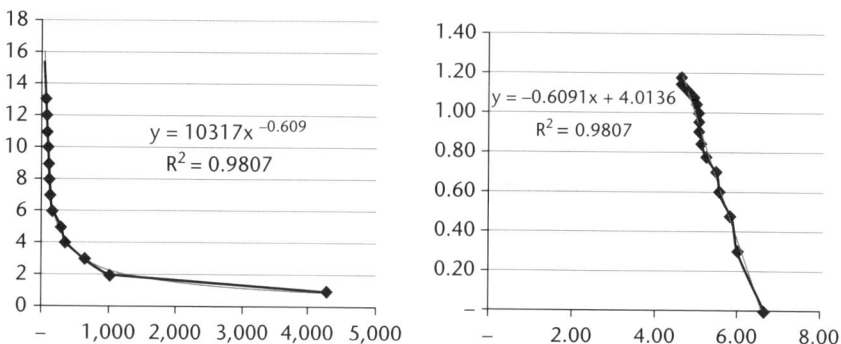

Figure 5.1. Example Pareto Distribution (on the left) and PL distribution (on the right). The R^2s show the goodness of fit of the market capitalizations of the largest American retail stores to the Pareto curve and the PL inverse-sloping straight line.

Source: Glaser (2012).

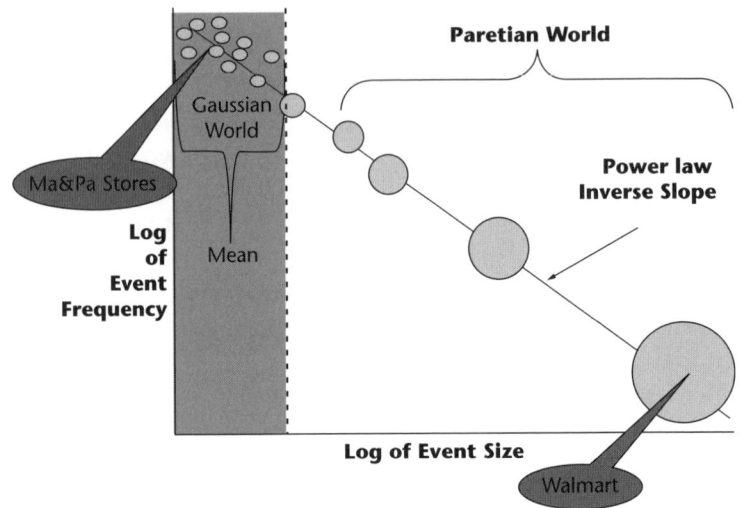

Figure 5.2. Stylized Pareto distribution on log-log scales

possible. Here we focus on rank/frequency power laws. In Figure 5.2 we show a stylized representation of the myriad small outcomes—such as the approximately 16,000 Californian quakes that go unnoticed each year, or the 17 million Ma & Pa stores that didn't grow like Walmart—that econometricians usually treat as *i.i.d.* and summarize with a normal distribution.[1] Toward the lower-right in the figure, by contrast, we see the increasingly high-ranked, very rare, *extreme* outcomes that defy prediction, e.g. earthquakes, floods, bankruptcies, stock-market crashes, giant firms (Microsoft, Walmart, Apple, etc.) and giant cities.

By accommodating the dynamics of tension and connectivity, an epistemology based on complexity science offers management and organizational researchers a more encompassing legitimacy than either modernist or postmodernist epistemologies on their own, one that is well aligned with emerging concepts of organizational complexity (*Organization Science*, Vol. 10, 1999; Maguire et al. 2006; Allen, Maguire, and McKelvey 2011). If "effective organizational complexity" lies between Order and Chaos, then by implication, so does the "effective legitimacy" of management research. This location implies a methodological expansion out from the world of stable, normally distributed entities towards the more kaleidoscopic and problematic world captured by power-law distributions.

---

[1] "Robustness" techniques (Greene 2002) translate skew distributions into normal ones, i.e. by making the X-axis a log scale so as to produce a log-normal distribution.

Our's is a plea for a new direction in organization and management research and information processing, and more broadly in the social sciences. The paradigmatic competition between modernism and postmodernism has not been fruitful. Natural scientists and neo-classical economists continue to espouse a modernist stance, and many social scientists that of postmodernism (Kelso and Engstrøm 2006; Mirowski 1989; Ormerod 1994, 1998; Colander 2006). Consequently, the legitimacy of management research's would-be truth-claims remains stuck in an epistemological information quagmire. The complexity perspective suggests that where prediction is problematic, *anticipation* offers usefully adaptive information, and hence becomes a legitimate goal for scientific endeavours. Thus, while the criteria of demarcation that separate science from non-science need not be abandoned—as advocated by Feyerabend (1975) and some other postmodernists—they need to be rather more accommodating than those promulgated by modernists.

Our publication in the *Journal of Management Inquiry* (2011) is an outgrowth and updating of our 2007 *Best Paper*—it includes some power-law (PL) analyses of cityscapes not available in 2007. In this work we further develop the complexity segment of Max's *Ashby Space*. We begin by defining key elements underlying power laws. Then we argue that the "complexity" segment of the *Ashby Space* calls for a *"PL Science"* and offer six ways in which management inquiry could become more PL oriented. Organizing and managing become activities within *connected* network processes, some of which yield adaptive structures and some of which do not. We also offer preliminary evidence that PLs can, indeed, indicate adaptive strength or unevenness in economic processes. Our theoretical approach has the effect of *naturalizing* management inquiry, bringing it closer to recent trends in physics and biology—shades of econophysics (McCauley 2004)—and making it less dependent on the "things" of physics and biology from which it sprang and more akin to information connectivities among agents and within networks (e.g., West and Deering 1995; Newman et al. 2006).

Management inquiry, however, has yet to take up the PL challenge! It lacks an adequate conceptualization of extreme outcomes, and so, unsurprisingly, is unable to incorporate them into its current theorizing. We, therefore, draw from complexity science and PL science to introduce a more penetrating treatment of PLs, extreme outcomes, and scale-free theory into management inquiry. We believe that a *PL science of management* will ultimately connect the concept of organization used in the social sciences with those used in the kindred fields of biology and ecology (Boisot and Cohen 2000). Solé et al. (2001) point out that biosystems are predatory fractals. McKelvey, Lichtenstein and Andriani (2013) apply fractality ideas to business systems.

Max's last publication with myself appears in the *Handbook of Complexity and Management* (Allen, Maguire, and McKelvey 2011). In this chapter, we build from our updating of Ashby's Law to the *"Law of Requisite Complexity"* (McKelvey and Boisot 2003). The latter holds that, to be efficaciously adaptive, the internal complexity of a system must match the external complexity impinging upon it.

Our *Ashby Space* depicts organizations as investing in adaptation in two ways: (1) simplify the complexity of incoming stimuli so as to reduce the cost of responding; (2) invest more resources in the response than is strictly necessary so as to ensure some degree of adaptation. The risks associated with the first approach are those of oversimplification—i.e., novel stimuli merely get assimilated to familiar ones and hence mis-classified. The risks associated with the second are that unnecessarily complex responses deplete resources before adaptation occurs. To explore the trade-off a system faces between stimulus simplification and response complexification, we introduce complexity theories into the *Ashby Space*, so as to help researchers and practitioners to frame the challenges of adaptively useful information processing in resource-efficient ways. We first briefly review key aspects of general systems theories, early organization theories, and complexity theories. We then draw on Ashby's *Law* to create the *Ashby Space* and illustrate its use by applying it to the 2007 liquidity crisis creating the Great Recession.

By integrating Ashby's perspective on the nature of efficacious adaptation with our growing understanding of complexity phenomena, the *Ashby Space* offers scholars and practitioners a conceptual framework for thinking through some of the more pressing information processing problems that confront the globalizing world. What, for example, are the challenges of adapting to nonlinear changes in the climate? Or, of adapting to the emergence of asymmetric threats? What are the scalable opportunities that we can associate with the spread of the Internet or of mobile phones? The above challenges will not be successfully addressed in the ordered regime of the *Ashby Space*. We must learn to wander out into the Complex Regime without falling into the chaotic one.

Upon reflection, we see that: (1) The *Foresight* chapter uses our updating of Ashby's Law to the *Law of Requisite Complexity* to set up complex information processing as management's tool to quickly and effectively adapt to impinging environmental threats. (2) The two *Counter-terrorism* chapters set up the *Ashby Space* to depict the use of socio/computational semi-autonomous methods to take advantage of and speed up the processing of emergent information from "in the neighbourhood" observers. (3) The *econophysics Best Paper* goes outside the box of conventional thinking in organization and management theorizing to substantiate the importance of Pareto and power-law distributions of information-based agent connectivities, the study of what's out in the long tails, and why extreme outcomes are much more relevant to practitioner success than what is at the "average" by highly revered conventional "normal distribution" research. (4) The *Bridge* article in *AMR* uses the Ashby Space and complexity science to bridge the gulf between over-simplified information processing and consequent theorizing building from physics and math and the chaotic consequences of the *"anything goes"* mantra of postmodernist constructivism. Neither the simplistic assumptions required making math-applied-to-human-behaviour valid nor the chaos of constructivism offer useful truth-based information-based insights to practitioners. (5) The need for *management inquiry*—theory and research—to pick up on the challenge of power-law science as a means of more accurately diagnosing how well industries and firms—as rank/frequency phenomena—are adapting to the impinging forces in their competitive environments. And (6) how to best manage scalability dynamics resulting from un-planned or hoped for agent self-organization and emergent behaviours, structures, and information processes that can lead to unwanted negative or hoped for extreme outcomes.

Part IV
The Strategic Management of Knowledge

6

The Creation and Sharing of Knowledge*

Max Boisot

Historical background

Most of the challenges posed by the effective management of knowledge resources are not particularly new. They have, in effect, been with us since the scientific revolution of the 17th century, if not before. The learned societies of the 17th century, the Académia dei Lincei in Rome (founded in 1603), the Royal Society in London (founded in 1660), and the Académie des Sciences in Paris (founded in 1666), were all concerned with the routinization of discovery and were all set up to promote the dissemination of useful knowledge (Shapin and Schaffer 1985). The European scientists of the day were grappling with the same sort of issues that confront knowledge management today: how to generate knowledge that is both valid and hopefully useful, how to share it, and how to keep in touch with each other as well as up to date (Sprat 1662).

In the 18th century, encyclopedias provided one way of storing and providing access to newly created knowledge. The nascent scientific community provided another. The key to the effective growth and management of scientific knowledge was thus as much social and institutional as it was technological. Technology, to be sure, was a trigger: the scientific revolution would not have been possible without the development of printing, the substitution of vernacular languages for Latin, and the subsequent spread of literacy (Goody 1987). Yet the emergence of learned societies with their corresponding secretaries, their frequent meetings, and their periodical journals were as

---

* Originally published as Max Boisot (2002). "The Creation and Sharing of Knowledge." In C. W. Choo and N. Bontis (eds), *The Strategic Management of Intellectual Capital and Organizational Knowledge*, 65–77 © 2002 by Oxford University Press, Inc. By permission of Oxford University Press, USA.

much the product of values and new habits of thought as they were of new means of communication (Shapin and Schaffer 1985, Foucault 1972).

If new knowledge could be first elicited and then made use of, then one obvious beneficiary would be the state. In mercantilist times, knowledge was perceived to contribute to the creation of national wealth and hence to the creation of a strong and competitive state. Unsurprisingly, therefore, the state attempted to foster the generation of new knowledge within its borders. Even in a later and somewhat more liberal age, the state retained—indeed, it deepened—its involvement in knowledge generation. The U.S. Congress, for example, was given the duty by the country's constitution "to promote the science of useful arts, by securing, for limited times, to authors and inventors, the exclusive right to their respective writings and discoveries." Was this granting of exclusive rights to the creators of new knowledge also intended to promote its sharing? In a roundabout way, yes, since it was only in return for a public disclosure of what would otherwise be privately held knowledge that a limited monopoly on its use was granted to its possessor.

Before the end of the 19th century, technological knowledge was neither generated nor disseminated in the same way as scientific knowledge. In the latter case, the scientific community would reward the creation of valid and useful knowledge by publicly acknowledging its source when use was being made of it. In this way, its creator was offered the esteem and recognition of his—or, more rarely, her—peers (Hagstrom 1965). In the former case, a broader community would reward the valid creation of technological knowledge by using it and, if it was suitably protected, paying for it. Thus, whereas the scientific community was engaged in what we might call "gift" exchanges, the technological community was engaged in trade.

It was not until the last three decades of the 19th century that a number of business enterprises—particularly those operating in the newly emerging chemical and electrical industries—began to concern themselves with the systematic creation and exploitation of knowledge for commercial purposes. It was at this time that the modern research laboratory first made its appearance (Chandler 1962, 1977). Research and development (R&D) activities systematically applied knowledge management principles inside one or two highly specialized departments within an organization. They greatly accelerated the pace of innovation and effectively helped to usher in the second industrial revolution (Landes 1969).

In sum, knowledge management has been around for some time—it is hardly a new kid on the block! Nevertheless, it is fair to say that it was only in the 1990s that managers in a large number of firms began to address issues that scientists have been grappling with for well over 300 years. What distinguishes corporate interest in knowledge management at the end of the 20th century from what has gone before, perhaps, is that the kind of knowledge

The Creation and Sharing of Knowledge

that is of interest today is as likely to arise *outside* the R&D laboratory as *inside* it. Indeed, it now emerges from the whole range of a firm's activities. Yet, instead of asking why firms have suddenly become interested in this area, one might reasonably ask, What kept them?

The present

I offer three possible reasons for the interest in knowledge management at the end of the 20th century:

1. Firms can only afford to concern themselves with what is observable and measurable, and in many cases—if not most—knowledge is neither. It often resides deep in people's heads, and it can be quite discontinuous in its effects. If firms have only recently become interested in managing their knowledge resources, it is because data capturing, processing, storage, and transmission costs have now dropped to the point where large quantities of data that were once beyond reach are now readily accessible. Whether knowledge—as opposed to data—has itself become any more accessible as a result of such falling costs is still a matter of controversy, the claims of some proponents of intellectual capital notwithstanding.

2. The rapid evolution of information and communications technologies has led to the "dematerialization" of economic activity—the substitution of data and information for physical resources—in many areas. Automobiles, for example, are getting lighter every year and are becoming "information rich" (Boisot 1998, Ayres 1994). And computers themselves are being miniaturized even as their data processing power continues to multiply. As we rejoice at the convenience and the energy savings made possible by this dematerialization, we suddenly find ourselves having to deal with ever larger quantities of data. In some cases, we become literally overwhelmed by the stuff, and overload threatens. The only way to deal with data overload is to extract useful information from it faster and more efficiently than before—that is, to increase the rate at which we metabolize data (Boisot 1995a). Knowledge management might help us to achieve this increase.

3. Underpinning the recent interest in knowledge management is a belated recognition that while information may be substituted for energy in many fields, one cannot manage a knowledge resource as if it were a physical resource. Although some economists are now adopting a different approach, they have traditionally viewed knowledge with a certain schizophrenia, treating it at their convenience either as being

completely appropriable—and hence behaving in economic terms like a tradeable physical good—or as being a public good whose supply is infinitely elastic and whose consumption is not subject to crowding. Yet, as anyone involved in its creation will know, knowledge evolves over time and can move either in the direction of full appropriability or in the direction of free availability (Shapiro and Varian 1999). It is at its most interesting—and, unfortunately, at its most analytically intractable—when it is located somewhere between these two poles.

Outstanding issues

Despite its growing appeal to practitioners, knowledge management faces three unresolved problems. The first is epistemological in nature: What exactly is it that is being managed? There are those who will count as knowledge only that which can be codified and durably stored. Here the focus is on knowledge as an objectively validated product to be inventoried (Dretske 1981). Then there are those who see knowledge as a largely tacit and more subjective phenomenon whose validation is problematic and that is not readily amenable to storing (Polanyi 1958). The first group would take Boyle's law as its exemplar of knowledge, whereas the second might well take Cézanne's painting of the *Mont Saint-Victoire*. Their different perspectives on what constitutes knowledge are not necessarily incompatible, but they have not as yet been reconciled in any way that commands wide assent.

The second problem concerns knowing as a social phenomenon: Is it, and can it ever be, a social phenomenon? The issue is not merely a philosophical quibble. It poses a problem of agency. If organizations do turn out to have something approximating "group minds" to direct their collective actions, then treating them as if they had individual personalities may end up being more than just a convenient legal fiction (Weick 1995). It also gives corporate culture a much larger role in the way that we conceptualize knowledge management than it has received hitherto. Cultures vary in their orientation to knowledge (Douglas 1973). Some are naturally inclined to hoard it; others, to share it. Much, of course, will depend on the nature of the knowledge that they deal with.

Power raises a third problem. From a purely societal perspective, knowledge is at its most useful when it is leveraged and shared. And public policy has often explicitly pursued leveraging and sharing as desirable policy goals. Yet it is also a commonplace that knowledge is power, and never more so than when it is retained rather than shared (Foucault 1972, Crozier 1964). Of course, it is often the case that some knowledge first needs to be shared if whatever the knowledge that is then retained is to constitute a source of power. The most obvious illustration of this point is advertising. Here, some product information must be given away in order to stimulate a purchase. But when the good that is for sale is itself an information good, how much information should be shared and how much should be retained? In other words, at what point is one beginning to give away what one is actually trying to sell?

Lack of space prevents me from dealing with these problems in any detail in this chapter. In what follows, however, I present a three-dimensional conceptual framework, the information-space, or *I-Space*, that helps to address them (Boisot 1995a, 1998). I first briefly deal with the epistemological issues that confront knowledge management. We need to understand, for instance, what knowledge is and how it differs from data and information. In this section, I introduce the first two dimensions of the *I-Space*, those of codification and abstraction. Then I examine some of the characteristics of knowledge flows that distinguish them from flows of physical resources. The focus in this section is on one of the issues that was being addressed at the very beginning of the scientific revolution: how new knowledge is generated. Next I address the issue of how such knowledge is shared, a second major concern of the period. In so doing, I introduce the third dimension of the *I-Space*. The questions raised by knowledge sharing are still with us today—albeit, with the emergence of the Internet, they have taken on a radically new form. I assess the managerial implications of the analysis.

What is knowledge?

How does knowledge differ from data and information? The three terms are often used interchangeably in casual conversation, and this can lead to sloppy thinking on the subject of knowledge. One approach is to think of data as being located in the world and of knowledge as being located in agents, with information taking on a mediating role between them. Data can be viewed as a discernible difference between different energy states *only some of which* have information value for agents. Bateson (1972) defined this information as "the difference that makes a difference" to someone. Where data is thus informative, it will modify an agent's expectations and dispositions to act in particular ways—that is, what we call its knowledge base. Note that for our purpose an agent does not have to be a human being. It could be an animal, a machine, or an organization made up of other agents. All that we require for it to be "knowledgeable" is that its internal dispositions to act can be modified upon receipt of data that has some information value (Arrow 1984, Popper 1972, Latour and Woolgar 1986).

What follows from the distinctions we have drawn between data, information, and knowledge? First, if we accept them, then we must recognize that, in reality, it is never knowledge as such that flows between agents, but data. Some measure of resonance can be achieved between the knowledge states of two agents that are sharing the same data—we can call this "getting on the same wavelength." But because of differences in their prior experiences as well as differences in the way that they will process the data, two agents can never achieve identical dispositions to act and hence identical knowledge states. Thus, when I talk about "knowledge sharing" I will actually be referring to some degree of resonance being achieved between the knowledge states of two or more agents following some sharing of data among them.

Second, we must accept that if knowledge is dispositional and hence rooted in agency, then it is not a single "thing" with easily traced contours. As the cognitive neurosciences have now established, it is more like a set of complex activation patterns that can vary greatly from agent to agent, or from moment to moment within a single agent (Churchland 1989). Thus, how easily knowledge can be "shared," in the sense that the activation patterns of different agents can be made to resonate, will vary from case to case as a function of its complexity. If we both see the same cat, for example, there will be some overlap in the patterns of neurons that are activated in our respective brains. But significant differences will also occur, for example, if I had some bad prior experiences with cats that you did not.

Variations in activation patterns have many sources which we cannot discuss here. But one important source is the fact that some types of knowledge can be more easily articulated than other types: the data that transmits it can thus flow more readily. People are concerned with saving time and resources required to articulate and transmit knowledge. They are thus more likely to share knowledge that is clear and unambiguous than knowledge of a more tacit and elusive nature (Nonaka and Takeuchi 1995). It will be easier to transmit a list of stock market figures by fax, for example, than to faithfully describe a Jackson Pollock painting in detail over the telephone. We can better understand this by looking at the data processing requirements associated with the articulation and transmission of knowledge. The articulation of knowledge, in effect, calls for two kinds of cognitive efforts: abstraction and codification.

Abstraction either invokes or creates the minimum number of cognitive categories through which an agent makes sense of events. The fewer the categories an agent needs, the more abstract becomes its apprehension of events. Conversely, the larger the number of categories it requires, the more concrete its apprehension of events. Thus, for example, a problem in particle physics has a more abstract character than a business problem that has to address myriad concrete realities. It draws upon fewer categories even if the relationships between these can be quite complex. Selecting the relevant categories for abstraction, however, requires an understanding of the problem's underlying structure—that is, some prior knowledge of context.

Codification, by contrast, refines the categories that the agent invokes or creates so that it can use them efficiently and in discriminating ways. The fewer data an agent has to process to distinguish between categories, the more codified the categories that it has to draw upon. If, for example, the black and white surfaces on a wall are separated by a thin straight line, an agent will have no difficulty establishing whether a given point lies within the black or the white region. If, on the other hand, the black surface gradually fades into the white surface, then many points will lie in a gray zone that will be hard to readily assign to either the black or the white category. In this case, the agent will have to engage in further data processing in order to make an accurate assignment.

Abstraction and codification are mutually reinforcing. They make up two of the three dimensions of the conceptual framework of the *I-Space*. The agent that is able to economize on its data processing resources through successive acts of codification and abstraction will be able to transact with other agents more economically and hence more extensively than will the agent that cannot. Phenomena that an agent can identify and describe parsimoniously can be readily referred to and discussed with others. Furthermore, knowledge that is well structured (codified and abstract) lends itself to appropriation and trading more readily than does knowledge that is not.

A problem arises, however, when much of the knowledge that is of potential value to other agents is of a more tacit nature and hence not readily amenable to trading. Much of an organization's technological know-how, for example, may be of this kind. It is the fruit of a slow accumulation of idiosyncratic experience, and it resides in the heads or the behaviors of employees, working singly or in groups. Such knowledge poses a problem of property rights. Because it is tacit, it cannot be clearly delimited or transferred to others in a controlled way. How can ownership claims to such knowledge be made good, then? Who, in effect, owns it?

In the days of the individual craftsman, such a question would have found a ready answer. Craftsmen invested in the acquisition of such knowledge and actually possessed it—that is, they carried it around in their heads. Therefore, since, as the saying goes, possession is nine-tenths of the law, it was clear that the craftsmen owned it. The craftsmen may, as Marx believed, have become alienated from the products of their labor, but they could not so easily be alienated from their knowledge unless they chose to be.

Yet, except for a few residual trades, the days of the individual craftsman are now pretty much over. Most new knowledge today is generated in groups and is therefore the possession of a group—in the R&D laboratory, in the engineering department, in the boardroom, and so on. The individual members of such groups may come and go, and when they go, they take part of the group's knowledge with them—one reason why some technologies are most effectively transferred through the movement of individuals. Are such individuals violating a group's property rights in knowledge when they take part of it with them? Here, the situation is complicated by the fact that the generation of much new knowledge is nonlinear in its effects—that is, small inputs of individual know-how can produce disproportionately large outputs of new knowledge—and often more so for new knowledge created by a group than for new knowledge created by an individual. The resulting whole is then worth more—and often much more—than the sum of the parts contributed by individuals. Thus, knowledge creation, in contrast to the creation of most purely physical goods, is sometimes subject to increasing returns (Arthur 1994).

One view holds that, in the commercial case, these increasing returns belong to the firm employing such groups, which acts as a residual claimant. The firm, after all, brings individuals together, pays them, and generally creates the conditions under which group knowledge can emerge. Where such emergence is value adding, therefore, the firm has a claim on its fruits. The intellectual capital school goes further since it implicitly assumes that, in addition to having a residual claim to the emergent knowledge of groups and teams within the firm, the knowledge possessed by individual employees constitutes part of the firm's intellectual capital base and can therefore also be owned by the firm. It further assumes, however, that such knowledge can be subjected to firm-specific accounting measures, implying that it can be *possessed* by the firm as well as *owned* by it (Edvinsson 1997).

From an intellectual capital perspective, knowledge management is about the capture, storage, and retrieval of knowledge located either in the heads of employees, in the heads of outside collaborators, or in documents. Capture, storage, and retrieval are brought about through a firm's *structural capital*, defined by Edvinsson (1997) as "the embodiment, empowerment, and supportive infrastructure of human capital." Structural capital is also where the value added by the nonlinearities of the knowledge creation process is assumed to reside. Inputs to the knowledge creation process are provided by human capital, and the firm, acting as a residual claimant, captures the surplus. What we have here, in effect, is a new variant of the firm as *entrepreneur*. The firm is cast as the entrepreneurial purchaser and organizer of productive factors, and the value that it manages to extract over and above the cost of those factors constitutes a return on its organizing efforts. Yet it is not clear that the nonlinearities associated with creating new knowledge arise solely from bringing people together. If, for example, an intense group discussion at the workplace triggers a brilliant idea in the head of one participating individual, does the idea necessarily belong to the employer if it remains unstated? If so, given that possession is nine-tenths of the law, how will the employer make good its ownership claim?

Yet even where structural capital can be considered a source of nonlinearities, does it necessarily follow that knowledge emerging within groups of organizational employees—such as communities of practice—belongs to the organization that employs them? Such a question has implications for the way that we look at competences and capabilities within firms. These are typically viewed as integrated streams of knowledge that are value adding yet hard to imitate or transfer (Prahalad and Hamel 1990). But is the integration of knowledge streams carried out by the firm as a whole? Or, rather, by groups within the firm? Or, indeed, by networks that cross organizational boundaries? Where the integration of streams of knowledge is tacit—a defining characteristic of a core competence, according to many scholars—then it cannot be traded by the firm (Foss and Knudsen 1996). But this is just another way of saying that it is likely to remain the possession of the group or groups that exercise the competence and that operate either within one firm or across firms. The organization might find it easier to exercise its ownership claim in the case of group knowledge than in the case of individual employees—the latter are more likely to come and go than are whole groups. Yet much of the group's tacit knowledge may still remain beyond the reach of ownership claims made by the firm. In short, it is by no means clear that the firm is either the sole or the natural residual claimant to such knowledge.

Knowledge management practices do take the firm to be the natural residual claimant to knowledge created within its boundaries. These practices aim to help a firm appropriate an individual or group's knowledge, tacit or otherwise, by having it systematically articulated and stored. In the case of tacit knowledge—and arguably, the most valuable components of an individual's knowledge is tacit in nature—they face two challenges.

The first challenge is that the process of articulating tacit knowledge can never be complete. As the philosopher Michael Polanyi put it, we always know more than we can say (Polanyi 1958). By their very nature, abstraction and codification are highly selective processes. Only a small part of a tacit knowledge base can ever be subject to articulation and structuring if genuine data processing economies are to be achieved. Thus, much tacit knowledge inevitably stays with its possessors whatever efforts at codifying and abstracting it has been subjected to—and much of this tacit knowledge will be valuable.

The second challenge is that the more tacit knowledge is articulated, the more readily diffusible it becomes. Although the articulation of knowledge makes it easier for a firm to exercise ownership claims over it, the process also allows knowledge to leak across organizational boundaries, often before such claims can be made good. This second challenge is discussed further below.

Learning and the generation of new knowledge

Knowledge, as I have argued, can be viewed as a stock of expectations or dispositions to act in particular ways conditional on the receipt of external information. From this perspective, learning amounts to a change of levels in such stocks. When learning adds to the range of contingencies over which one can entertain expectations (i.e. we learn to pay attention to events that we had hitherto ignored), the knowledge level goes up. Today, for example, we attend to and learn about many more environmental variables than we did, say, four decades ago. As a result, we now *know* more about the environment than we did then. When learning reduces the range (i.e. we decide that certain things can safely be ignored), the knowledge level goes down. Much folk learning about medicinal plants, for example, disappears when primitive societies are integrated into advanced civilizations. Learning can thus involve acquiring new knowledge or dropping old knowledge. When these two activities go on simultaneously, they serve to refine our stock of knowledge and adapt it to our changing needs.

Clearly, while learning is generally beneficial, we should not therefore assume that it only increases our knowledge stocks; it must also selectively decrease it as well. Unless we are able to metabolize our knowledge by eliminating those parts that are no longer useful, we risk information overload—that is, we would develop a disposition to respond to everything, and each piece of incoming data gets treated as potentially informative. In short, we would lose our capacity to be selective.

Social learning occurs when changes in the stocks of knowledge held by one or more agents in a given population trigger coordinate changes in the stocks of knowledge that are held by other agents in the population. The changes, of course, will not necessarily be all in the same direction for all agents, for it is how incoming information interacts with the existing stocks of knowledge held by different agents that determines the direction of the changes. Some agents, for example, will simply have their range of awareness expanded by the incoming information, while others will also experience a need to unlearn certain things if they are to make good use of it. The way that different agents internalize incoming information through adjustments to their existing stocks of knowledge, and the different meanings and interpretations that they attach to it, constitutes a source of further opportunities for generating new knowledge or discarding old knowledge—that is, for learning. The discussion below examines the process through which learning opportunities emerge and how they contribute to the generation of new knowledge. The following section looks at how newly created knowledge is shared and then internalized.

Learning opportunities

Spotting an opportunity or a threat involves seeing potentially fruitful patterns in the data of experience. Although many people may possess the same data, they will not interpret it in the same way. And the less codified and abstract the data, the more scope there is for extracting idiosyncratic patterns out of it. In cases where the data enjoys many degrees of freedom, individual agents will be free to project whatever they want to see in it—just as they do in the inkblot test. Thus, in many cases, particularly those where the data is fuzzy and ambiguous, spotting a particular opportunity or threat will often turn out to be a singular event, something that goes on in the heads of, at most, a few agents.

Extracting novel patterns from data is a creative activity. It typically requires imagination and independent thought. Imagination allows one to see what is tentative and possible as well as what is probable and obvious. New insights often reside in the gap between these two poles (Klein 1998). Independent thought involves a willingness to resist the pressures of those who see only what is probable and obvious and feel threatened by alternative possibilities (Janis 1982). These pressures will vary from culture to culture—corporate or otherwise—but they will always intensify where novelty is perceived to be destructive of existing arrangements as well as creative.

Knowledge generation

Once a possible new pattern has been identified, it needs to be stabilized and tested for robustness if it is to yield useful information. If it is idiosyncratic, fuzzy, and ambiguous—and as discussed above, this will be more likely in the case of concrete and uncodified data than in the case of well-codified and abstract data that readily lends itself to categorization—the pattern will have to be refined and worked up into something coherent.

We can treat this process of pattern elaboration as a problem-solving activity, one that involves teasing out whatever latent structures and forms that reside in the pattern and testing them against competing alternatives. In effect, over several iterations of generating alternative structures and forms, testing the evolving pattern against these, and selecting the best fit, the pattern is gradually being made more articulate and usable, that is to say, more codified and more abstract.

Emerging patterns correspond to provisional hypotheses that undergo testing and elaboration. As they compete with each other, many more hypotheses are discarded than are retained (Popper 1972). They are then lost to view. Clearly, then, the process of generating new knowledge involves forgetting as well as learning. Thus, although we frame the process as one of knowledge creation, it should be clear, following the above discussions, that knowledge destruction—the discarding of old knowledge—is a constituent part of the picture. Yet whatever is discarded, the process of forgetting it will always be partial. Many discarded hypotheses will maintain a tacit and twilight existence in the minds of those who entertained them, sometimes to be retrieved and reworked at a later stage. Do they therefore count as knowledge? This remains a controversial question. Having been discarded such hypotheses do not form part of any formal and public body of knowledge, one that has been successfully refined and tested in accordance with some socially acceptable validation criteria. Yet to the extent that they are unconsciously retained and shape one or more persons' expectations and dispositions, they must count as knowledge of sorts—albeit a more personal and subjective kind of knowledge.

Social knowing

Until the arrival of information and communication technologies (ICTs) that could handle the more personal and tacit kinds of knowledge discussed above, the prevailing assumption was that only well-codified and abstract knowledge that had been socially validated was a fit candidate for dissemination. After all, science gained credibility and respect as an institution only after it had successfully filtered out the dubious claims of charlatans and fraudsters—and it required three centuries to set up the appropriate safeguards (Butterfield 1931). From a scientific perspective, therefore, the only kind of knowledge worth having has tended to be the well-codified and abstract kind that has undergone rigorous public testing and is open to critical scrutiny and challenge.

The tradition of openness in science stands in sharp contrast to the tradition of secrecy in technology. In the latter case, the value of tacit and as-yet-undiffused knowledge, ignored as it is by official science, is much more readily recognized and prized (Rosenberg and Mowery 1989). After all, most valid and useful knowledge is wrought, directly or indirectly, from what is often initially dubious knowledge. Disdain and discard the dubious stuff and you lose the raw material out of which the valid stuff will eventually emerge. In the technological tradition, therefore, tacit and personal knowledge is treated as a rich uncle to be respected and courted rather than as a poor relation to be kept in the shadows. It is valued and not readily shared with outsiders.

Yet if it is to be put to some social use, all knowledge except personal knowledge needs to be shared to some minimal extent. For this reason, we take the diffusion of knowledge through a population of agents as the third dimension of the *I-Space*. It is not enough to diffuse knowledge, however. Such knowledge also needs to be internalized by recipients if it is to become knowledge to them in the sense that it comes to form part of their dispositional repertoire. I discuss knowledge sharing and internalization next.

Knowledge sharing

As discussed above, the tacit knowledge prized by the technological tradition is intrinsically hard to share. This is partly because uncodified and concrete knowledge is costly to communicate and does not easily diffuse. Yet even where ICTs have lowered the costs of sharing it—and in recent years they have done so dramatically—one still confronts the cognitive limitations of the human mind. Human attention is in limited supply (Simon 1982). Recall from the discussion above that it is never knowledge as such that flows between agents, but rather data from which information has to be extracted and internalized. Only when information has been successfully internalized and forms part of an agent's repertoire of expectations and behaviors can it properly be called knowledge. All that knowledge sharing can really mean, therefore, is that some degree of resonance has been achieved between the repertoires of two or more agents. At best, ICTs can increase the quantity of *data* that flows between agents—sometimes massively so. But agents are still required to sift through the data in order to extract useful information from it. Beyond a certain volume of data, however, either the agent's extraction processes become increasingly random and arbitrary—it cannot see the wood for the trees—or the agent blows a fuse.

Knowledge needs some minimum degree of articulation (i.e. codification and abstraction) before it can be shared. How much articulation will depend on how extensively it needs to be shared. The tacit knowledge held by a Zen master, for example, need only be communicated to a few disciples in face-to-face situations. Even so, it can take years for a disciple to "get the message." The more codified and abstract type of knowledge held by a bond trader, by contrast—prices, quantities, and contract conditions—can be diffused worldwide by electronic means in a matter of seconds. The way that abstraction and codification affect the diffusibility of knowledge is depicted in Figure 6.1.

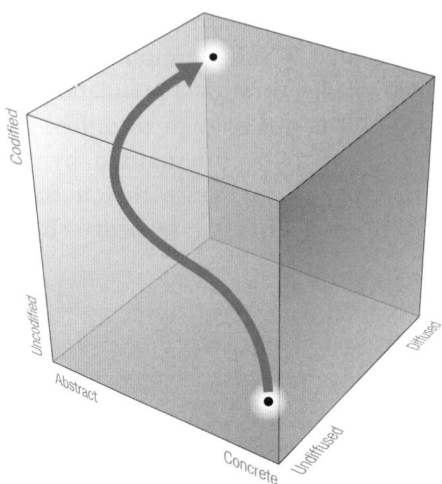

Figure 6.1. The codification-diffusion-abstraction curve in the *I-Space*

Knowledge internalization

But if articulating knowledge facilitates its diffusion and generally increases its availability, this by no means guarantees that it will be picked up, used, and subsequently internalized. If agents do not share the same codes, or if they operate with different conceptual schemes, then much readily available and diffused data will not register with anyone.

The absorption of external knowledge and information is a process whereby an agent's internal schemas assimilate external data and adapt to them (Piaget 1967). It is a process of interpretation and sensemaking in which new information is integrated with an existing knowledge base (Weick 1995). Three things are worth noting about this process. First, since, for reasons of differences in personal circumstances and biography, no two agents possess identical mental schemas, they will therefore assimilate and accommodate new knowledge in different ways. Thus, while the external data that different agents receive may be identical, what actually gets absorbed by each as knowledge will differ, even if only slightly, from case to case. Second, the absorption of new data goes hand-in-hand with a learning-by-doing or learning-by-using process that in the *I-Space*—and following Williamson (1975)—we call "impacting." What is initially received from outside may well be well codified and abstract. But as it gets used and gradually internalized, layers of uncodified and concrete experience gradually build over it, layers that are then much harder to share with others. Freshman physics students, for example, will all be exposed to the same set of basic equations, but the way each of them will internalize them will depend on the unique and often idiosyncratic

The Creation and Sharing of Knowledge

circumstances in which they may be required to put them into practice. Absorption and impacting are thus sources of variety. Finally, the successful integration of new data with the agent's existing knowledge base requires some positive fit between the two. If there is any incompatibility between them, then either the new knowledge will get distorted or rejected, or the existing knowledge base will need to be further modified—with some elements possibly being discarded—in order to achieve consistency between existing and new material.

Knowledge absorption and impacting, then, are personal and idiosyncratic processes. These processes effectively challenge any idea that knowledge is a "thing" that invariably maintains its identity as it is shared among agents. In the case of simple factual knowledge, maintaining a "thinglike" appearance may not be too difficult to achieve. For complex knowledge structures, however, it will be much more challenging.

Differences in the way that new knowledge is absorbed and impacted by agents have sometimes been downplayed in knowledge management, particularly where it is driven by information technology. This is understandable since such differences are difficult to handle. Yet it is often in differences of interpretation and sense-making, or in the difficulties of integrating new knowledge with an agent's existing and idiosyncratic knowledge base, that opportunities for identifying new patterns—and hence for generating new knowledge—in fact reside. Knowledge absorption and impacting, if properly understood and exploited, can thus help to initiate a social learning process that is cyclical in nature. A six-step social learning cycle is depicted in Figure 6.2. and briefly summarized in Table 6.1.

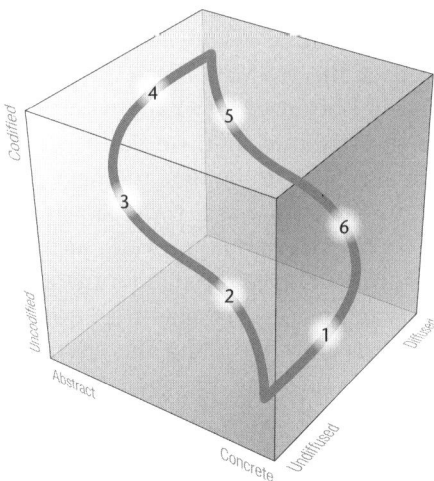

Figure 6.2. The six steps of a social learning cycle. See Table 6.1 for details of the steps.

Table 6.1. The six phases of the Social Learning Cycle

1. Scanning: identifying threats and opportunities in generally available but often fuzzy data—i.e. weak signals. Scanning patterns such data into unique or idiosyncratic insights that then become the possession of individuals or small groups. Scanning may be very rapid when the data is well codified and abstract, and very slow and random when the data is uncodified and context specific.
2. Problem Solving: the process of giving structure and coherence to such insights—i.e. codifying them. In this phase they are given a definite shape and much of the uncertainty initially associated with them is eliminated. Problem solving initiated in the uncodified region of *I-Space* is often both risky and conflict laden.
3. Abstraction: generalizing the application of newly codified insights to a wider range of situations. This involves reducing them to their most essential features—i.e. conceptualizing them. Problem solving and abstraction often work in tandem.
4. Diffusion: sharing the newly created insights with a target population. The diffusion of well-codified and abstract data to a large population will be technically less problematic than that of data which is uncodified and context specific. Only a sharing of context among agents can speed up the diffusion of uncodified data; the probability of achieving a shared context is inversely proportional to population size.
5. Absorption: applying the new codified insights to different situations in a learning-by-doing or a learning-by-using fashion. Over time, such codified insights acquire a penumbra of uncodified knowledge that helps to guide their application in particular circumstances.
6. Impacting: the embedding of abstract knowledge in concrete practices. This embedding can take place in artifacts, technical or organizational rules, or behavioral practices. Absorption and impact often work in tandem.

Managerial implications

As suggested by the above discussion of opportunity spotting and knowledge generation, sharing, and absorption, information goods differ in important respects from physical goods and cannot be managed in the same way. Understanding how they differ is an important prerequisite to developing an effective knowledge management system. One important difference between them concerns the way that each is valued. This section examines some of the difficulties encountered in valuing information and knowledge goods: How do the production and distribution of knowledge differ from those of physical resources? Here I approach the production issue via the distribution one.

Physical resources are characterized by what physicists call "locality." Simply stated, if they are here, then they are not there. Furthermore, if they are here one minute, then they are also likely to be here the next. Knowledge shares this characteristic of locality only insofar as it is tied down to a physical substrate that itself has locality. Stone, for example, provides such a substrate, one reason why it has been a material of choice throughout the ages for the purposes of commemorating events and places. Yet even the knowledge carried by stone reaches us—via the retina—only by riding the electromagnetic waves. And when it does so, it leaves its substrate, thereby acquiring a certain measure of nonlocality. In ancient times, of course, knowledge could not ride electromagnetic waves very far, so it tended to stay mainly local. Today, such local knowledge can be captured through digital photography and transmitted worldwide in seconds. It can thus be here, there, and everywhere at the same time.

What are the consequences? When knowledge is tied down to a physical substrate, it partakes of the natural scarcity of that substrate, a scarcity imparted by locality in time and space. When knowledge can be prized loose from its substrate, however, it ceases to be scarce. Thus, to illustrate, an oil field is a knowledge-bearing structure that cannot be photocopied. Oil is therefore a naturally scarce commodity. Yet the chemical formula for benzene can indeed be photocopied and ubiquitously distributed. Having once been extracted from the oil, it no longer enjoys a scarcity status. In dealing with the latter kind of knowledge, we face a *paradox of value* that is peculiar to knowledge goods and that affects their production.

The paradox of value

Extracting chemical information from oil is a costly and uncertain business. It requires extensive investments of time and effort, and results are not guaranteed. Yet whatever the costs incurred in first producing such information, the marginal costs of reproducing it are virtually nil—the cost of a photocopy. As just pointed out, the oil itself may be naturally scarce; the information extracted from it is not. Under such circumstances it may be hard to secure an adequate return on the extraction efforts.

Individuals create new knowledge for many reasons, not all of which are economic. Firms, by contrast, create new knowledge primarily in order to extract value from it, whether directly or indirectly. Economists see the value of a good as being a function of both its utility and its scarcity. The articulation of a knowledge good adds to its utility, so knowledge is at its most useful when it has been codified and made abstract. It can then be defined, made robust, standardized, and manipulated in value-adding ways. Such, for example, is the nature of chemical formulas. Yet it is precisely when a knowledge good has been so articulated that it is also most easily prized loose from its physical substrate. It then can be replicated and travel rapidly and extensively in a compressed form, thus losing its scarcity. Knowledge goods, therefore, in contrast to physical goods, behave paradoxically with respect to value. The more we aim to increase their utility by making them more codified and abstract, the more difficult it is to maintain their scarcity. In the case of purely physical goods, utility and scarcity are typically independent of each other. In the case of information goods, they are inversely related. Since utility and scarcity jointly determine the economic value of a good, we must conclude that, in contrast to a physical object, knowledge is inherently unstable in value.

The paradoxical nature of information goods with respect to value is depicted in Figure 6.3. The arrow points to the region of maximum value in *I-Space*, where the utility of an information good is at its maximum because of

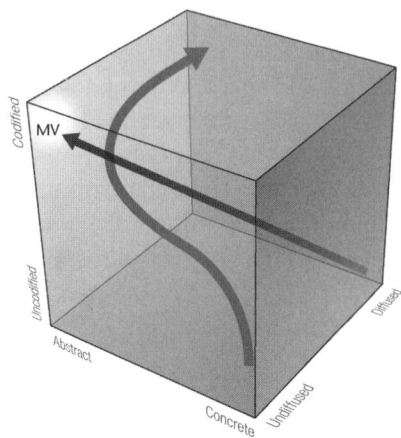

Figure 6.3. Maximum value (MV) in the *I-Space*

its high degree of abstraction and codification, and where it achieves maximum degree of scarcity. It is also clear from the diffusion curve that it is also the region in which scarcity is most difficult to maintain given the inherent diffusibility of well-structured information.

Patents, copyrights, secrecy clauses, and the like, all indicate that at a practical and intuitive level we understand the paradox of value very well. These devices grant a temporary monopoly on the use of a newly created knowledge good in order to encourage investment in its codification and abstraction—that is, investment in its production. Thus, the scarcity of a knowledge good is achieved artificially, by institutional means. If the good had the locality of physical goods, then it would be naturally scarce. There would be no need to maintain its scarcity artificially in this way.

The inherent diffusibility of well-articulated knowledge goods is what distinguishes them from physical goods, thus giving rise to the paradox of value. The paradox points to a challenge for the field of knowledge management. It suggests that we lack a workable theory of production and distribution for the information age. That is to say, we do not, as yet, have a political economy of information. We dichotomize knowledge, treating it one moment as if it is a physical good and hence appropriable, the next as a public good whose consumption does not reduce its supply.

Progress, to be sure, is being made. We do at least recognize that knowledge can evolve over time from one kind of thing to another. Yet we still tend to see the process as unidirectional: first we create new knowledge and try to keep it scarce; then as we articulate it, it loses its scarcity. This remains compatible with the idea that there is an equilibrium price for knowledge—its market price—that is reached when it is readily available to all who want it. Yet if, as I have argued above, knowledge is cyclical in the transformations that it undergoes, this equilibrium view is untenable. While in the knowledge generation phase it may become more codified and abstract, in the knowledge absorption phase it changes from codified and abstract to uncodified and concrete once more. It can then become idiosyncratic and local, thus reacquiring scarcity. As I have already shown, knowledge is not a thing in the way that physical objects are things, and it cannot be treated in the same way.

If the value of knowledge goods is inherently more unstable and transient than that of purely physical goods, then their production and exchange will require new theorizing. Without an adequate theory to guide us, we will find it difficult to devise efficient governance arrangements to facilitate and guide the process. In effect, managing a firm's knowledge resources presents new theoretical and practical challenges at three levels: governance, strategy and organization, and the operational level. Much of the literature on knowledge management has focused on the last of these. The first two are arguably more important. I conclude this section by briefly looking at challenges posed at each of the three levels.

Governance

The knowledge-based firm differs from the more traditional industrial firm in its governance requirements. In the latter, preserving shareholder value has meant fencing in the firm's asset base—for the most part physical in nature—and patrolling the firm's boundaries. The paradox of value makes this a dubious approach for the knowledge-based firm. Given the inherent diffusibility of useful knowledge, one may well end up fencing in an empty space, one from which the assets leaked out some time ago. Here, therefore, permanent firm boundaries matter much less. Rather, a dynamic stance is required, one that allows the firm to temporarily exploit a much more fluid and mobile class of assets: knowledge. These will, of course, pose new challenges of property rights. Is a knowledge worker who generates genuinely new knowledge, for example, to be treated as an employee of the firm or as an equity investor in the firm? If such an employee contributes to the firm's stock of intellectual capital, should he or she be considered on a par with external investors in the firm?

Strategy and organization

If firm boundaries matter less, then the critical strategic and organizational skills shift from maximizing value creation behind well-protected and stable boundaries to rapidly extracting value from kaleidoscopic networks, both internal and external (Kogut 2000). It is not that the boundaries have disappeared; rather, they are now constantly being reconfigured by social learning processes that redistribute opportunity spotting, knowledge generation, knowledge sharing, and knowledge absorption within a community of players. Communities do not necessarily reduce to hierarchical forms of organizational boundaries. How do we manage and extract value from the fleeting networking and exchange processes through which new knowledge enters and leaves the knowledge-based firm?

Operational level

How might a firm improve the numberless micro-interactions that take place between its own agents or between these and outsiders? And how might such improvements prepare the ground for opportunity spotting and knowledge generation, sharing, and absorption that make up a learning cycle? What transactional infrastructures and human resource systems need to be developed to discourage opportunistic behavior either by a firm's knowledge workers or, indeed, by the firm itself toward its knowledge workers?

Conclusion

Effective networking is built on reciprocity. A critical skill for the knowledge-based firm will thus be to know what to share and what to hold on to. Recognizing when knowledge should be actively diffused to outsiders rather than hoarded, when it can be used to extend the firm's organizational reach beyond its boundaries, will become an important source of competitive advantage. Building the capabilities of the networks a firm participates in, through a judicious sharing of its knowledge, strengthens its own competitive position within the network. Confining its internal focus to core strengths prevents it from overstretching what will always be limited cognitive resources.

In the information economy, a firm can sometimes come to know too much for its own good. It needs to avoid getting trapped by its own hard-won competencies while the world moves on (Leonard-Barton 1995), and it thus needs to unlearn as much and as fast as it learns. Knowledge has to be metabolized, and, as with any kind of metabolic processes, gluttony leads to indigestion—a challenge to the "more connecting and more collecting" perspective that is often promoted by knowledge management practitioners. Surprising as it may seem to some, managing the firm's knowledge resources does not necessarily mean maximizing them.

7

The Strategic Management of Knowledge

Martin Ihrig and Ian MacMillan

Introduction

Early on in his career Max Boisot recognized that in many industries and economies knowledge was replacing natural resources as the key source of wealth generation. However, notwithstanding the proclamations of knowledge management practitioners, the effective management of knowledge remained elusive. Max never tired of pointing out that nearly 2500 years after Plato first explored the concept of knowledge, there is still no clear consensus on what it actually comprises. We still lack a generally agreed and robust theoretical base upon which to strategically manage this source of wealth.

All the chapters in this book deal in some way or another with Max's treatment of knowledge, and he published four books on the topic (Boisot 1987b; Boisot 1995a, 1998; Boisot, MacMillan, and Han 2008). This chapter will focus on and explore the particular link he made to strategy. It will recount the strategy-related research that Max conducted in the six years before we lost him and briefly introduce the projects he was working on at the Snider Entrepreneurial Research Center at the Wharton School of the University of Pennsylvania, a research site he called home for more than ten years. This chapter draws on our personal experience working with Max over many years, published work by Max where referenced, and also unpublished manuscripts we had been working on before Max so suddenly left us.

Max was passionate about conducting research that improved our understanding of how knowledge is generated, diffused, internalized and managed by individuals and organizations under both collaborative and competitive learning conditions. The preceding chapter, "The Creation and Sharing of Knowledge," illustrates Boisot's approach to the effective management of knowledge resources (Boisot 2002). It describes the properties of knowledge, and explains learning and the generation of new knowledge through the Information Space (*I-Space*) via the Social Learning Cycle (*SLC*). It highlights managerial implications, explaining the challenges with extracting value from knowledge.

Max's *I-Space* (Boisot 1995a, 1998)—a further development of his *C-Space* (Boisot 1987b)—is a conceptual framework that has helped many people, academics and practitioners alike, to study knowledge flows in diverse populations of agents—individuals, groups, firms, industries, alliances, governments, and nations. Max worked with academic, corporate, and public sector partners to advance their understanding of how to manage knowledge resources effectively, and with the insights gleaned therefrom, intended to transform what was still a collection of loosely coupled practices into a full-fledged, theoretically grounded professional discipline.

Max's thesis was that in the information age, competitive success of innovating businesses depends on having the right conceptual framework and decision making tools to allow firms to manage their portfolios of knowledge assets as opposed to physical assets. To develop those tools and to push the envelope in the *strategic* management of knowledge, Max, together with MacMillan and Ihrig, started a small research and development venture in 2006, called the *I-Space Institute* (Boisot et al. 2008). The goal was to develop, test, and exploit the *I-Space* as a conceptual and applications framework and to build *strategic knowledge management tools* that had the potential to assist corporate decision makers to navigate the knowledge economy.

In the years since 2006, Max and the team focused on two areas: *mapping* critical knowledge assets, cultural and organizational structures, and associated learning paths; and *simulating* strategic knowledge management processes, in particular knowledge flows derived from knowledge-based agent interactions.

What is strategic about knowledge management?

In 2007, we decided to organize a professional development workshop (PDW) for the Academy of Management Conference (AOM) 2008 in Anaheim, CA. The goal was to present our view on the link between knowledge and strategy and facilitate a discussion with leading scholars in the field. The questions we wanted to address were as follows:

1. What would *strategic* knowledge management look like and what would it take to create it?
2. How might the strategic perspective differentiate it from current conceptions of knowledge management?

3. What would be the implications of such a differentiation for our current conceptions of strategic management?

We were aware that coming up with insightful and detailed answers to such questions would require more than a workshop. Max believed that they would only emerge over time as "the fruit of a process in which ideas and practices co-evolve in the marketplace." He felt that what a workshop could do, however, was "to sensitize those players that will contribute to this co-evolutionary process as to what the issues are so that they can respond to them more effectively when they arise." The approach, therefore, had to be exploratory and reflective, incorporating a variety of perspectives from which to look at the issues.[1]

Max's perspective was that knowledge management constituted a loosely coupled set of practices rather than an intellectual discipline, and that it was experiencing some difficulty in selling itself as much more than an information-tabulating exercise or an effort to avoid duplication of knowledge generation. He believed that knowledge management would only become a full-fledged domain of enquiry, with its own body of concepts guiding the future development of practice, when knowledge-based theories of organizations and firms from the strategy field demonstrably both informed, and became informed by, knowledge management practices.

The emergence of the knowledge economy has given rise to two complementary theoretical perspectives on strategy:

1. The *resource-based* view (RBV) of the firm takes the possession of unique non-replicable resources as constituting a source of competitive advantage for a firm. In much of the RBV literature, knowledge constitutes the key resource possessed by a firm—whether such knowledge is embodied in the minds of its employees, its rules, its routines, or its equipment.

2. The *knowledge-based* theory (KBT) of the firm takes the possession of such knowledge as constituting not only a source of competitive advantage for a firm, but also the justification for having a firm. Where knowledge is unique and hard to articulate, it cannot be the object of arm's length market contracting. For this reason, transactions that have such

---

[1] As an aside, the success of the initial PDW encouraged us to continue to organize workshops at AOM on a yearly basis, up to the year Max died. The four topics were: 1. What is Strategic about Knowledge Management? (AOM 2008); 2. The Energy Challenge: A Strategic Management of Knowledge Perspective (AOM 2009); 3. The Passion that Binds: Coordinating Knowledge Flows in Big Science (AOM 2010); 4. What Could Modern Management Learn from Big Science? An East-West Perspective on Trust (AOM 2011). For the European Group of Organizational Studies (EGOS) conference, we organized two "sub-themes": 1. The Strategic Management of Organizational Knowledge: Creation versus Control (EGOS 2009) and 2. Managing without Managers in Complex, Knowledge-based Organizations (EGOS 2011).

knowledge either as their focus or as a support have to be brought within the boundaries of the firm.

The KBT and the RBV thus come together when unique non-replicable resources turn out to be knowledge-based.

The rapid development and spread of knowledge management (KM) has reflected a general familiarity with the two perspectives. Yet neither the theory-based discourse on knowledge that interests strategists nor the practice-based discourse that characterizes much KM and attracts practitioners seemed to connect much. The prevailing view in the knowledge management community was (and for the most part still is) that knowledge management should act to *support* a firm's strategy. Yet, what if, using a strategic-management-of-knowledge perspective, knowledge management were to *drive* a firm's strategy?

Such a question lead to others: How does one know when a firm has an effective knowledge-based strategy? Is it when its primary asset is intellectual capital? And if so, how does one know that this is the case?

In a strategic-management-of-knowledge perspective, we proposed that knowledge management processes should drive a firm's strategy through the following activities:

1. Identifying the knowledge domains that are critical to a firm's operations.
2. Identifying how these domains are related to each other.
3. Assessing the firm's competence and skills in those knowledge domains—i.e. its ability to integrate streams of knowledge within and across such domains.
4. Assessing the firm's competitive position in those knowledge domains—both the firm's relative coverage of the domains as well as its relative integration skills.
5. Exploring the possible future evolution of these knowledge domains and the integration challenges that such an evolution will pose for firms operating in these domains.
6. Identifying the firm's strategic options given this evolution and the firm's current competitive position.
7. Assembling and pursuing a knowledge development strategy and associated plan to create knowledge based advantages that would deliver corporate competitiveness.

Knowledge management has mostly been *product-push*, a situation in which IT providers and consultants push "solutions" whether or not there is a problem. It is primarily driven by the possibilities offered by IT for gaining more efficient and speedier access to a firm's existing stock of knowledge. When

The Strategic Management of Knowledge

KM's focus shifts from stocks to flows of knowledge within and across firms, it engages with the firm's learning and change processes and often becomes the responsibility of its HR or its management development function. None of this is without value since, clearly, firms have difficulty managing their knowledge base. However, Max believed in a *demand-pull* approach to knowledge management that would seek to develop sophisticated tools in support of the strategic management of knowledge—i.e. in support of the strategic activities listed above.

What would a knowledge-based strategy look like?

If strategy can be viewed as the allocation of scarce resources to alternative ends under conditions of rivalry, Max posited that knowledge-based strategy can be thought of as the allocation of scarce resources to different types and configurations of knowledge assets in pursuit of competitive advantage. But what is a knowledge asset and what would make it strategic? How does allocating resources to a knowledge asset differ from allocating resources to plant, machinery or brands?

As we pointed out earlier, the nature of knowledge itself has been debated by philosophers ever since Plato, and although Max claimed that we are no nearer to agreeing on what it is, his work has given us important and original frameworks that make this "esoteric" topic more tractable. In the context of this chapter, two papers are particularly noteworthy: his paper with Agustí Canals on the differences between data, information, and knowledge (Boisot and Canals 2004), which clearly defines what knowledge is; and his article with MacMillan on the two distinct yet complementary epistemological paths to knowledge development (Boisot and MacMillan 2004), which highlights the differences between managerial and entrepreneurial mind-sets.

Max put forward a few basic features of knowledge that helped us move forward in defining the link between knowledge and strategy. In line with the pragmatists (Dewey 1998; James 1907; Peirce 1992), he took knowledge to be a set of beliefs that, if strongly held, take the form of a commitment to action and if weakly held take the form of options to act. A belief need not be strongly held to be actionable. Max explained that, for example, if I strongly believe that a stock's price is about to rise I can buy the stock, whereas if I weakly believe that the stock's price is about to rise, I can buy an option.

Max then suggested the following two definitions: To the extent that these beliefs, strong or weak, contribute to the survival and prosperity of intelligent agents (whether these are individuals or organized aggregations of these—firms, states, etc.), they can be considered knowledge *assets*. And to the extent that these beliefs contribute to the survival and prosperity of intelligent agents under conditions of rivalry, they can be considered *strategic* knowledge assets.

The problem is that most of the beliefs that contribute to our survival and prosperity are held implicitly, may therefore be hard to identify, and some may be hard to articulate. Such knowledge assets might be possessed, but not legally owned—unless the possessor can secure intellectual property rights by making them more easily communicable. Articulating them in order to establish intellectual property rights in them—as required, for example, by patenting or copyright—may actually erode the capacity to possess them. For this reason, compared with the property rights protection that can be granted for physical goods, IPR protection remains fragile. Based on this observation, Max pointed out four challenges that effective knowledge-based strategies face:

1. IPR protection is not solid and the rivalry is getting more intense (the music business, for instance). Legal systems do not have global reach, allowing firms to play off one legal system against another. Pharmaceutical products, for example, receive less IPR protection in India than in the UK.

2. With the globalization of markets, the cost of protecting IPRs is increasing, often placing them beyond the reach of small and medium-sized firms. It is costly to police knowledge in every jurisdiction; many firms do not bother.

3. Many, if not most of a firm's strategic knowledge assets, such as the tacit skills accumulated over the years in the heads of certain key employees—star scientists, master craftsmen, etc.—cannot be directly owned by the firm and hence subjected to IPR protection.

4. Firms find it hard to specify which of their knowledge assets are strategic. Most firms at best are aware of their patent positions. But they are often ignorant of what kind of knowledge underpins their core competences and have little idea of how to go about either protecting or exploiting these.

Knowledge management has tried to make some inroads with respect to the last of these challenges. Unfortunately, as mentioned above, too much of it has become a case of technology push. In response to the mantra "if only we knew what we know," some of the knowledge management tools on offer attempt to bring it all to the surface. All of it! Even if this were successful, it would lead to cognitive overload. Max argued that much of what passes for knowledge capture is thus little more than "noise masquerading as information."

The framework that helps address the issues and which firms can use to find a knowledge-based strategy is of course the *I-Space*. In Max's experience, as well as offering a useful framework for the strategic management of knowledge assets, the *I-Space* provided a language that allowed managers to discuss knowledge-based strategy in ways that they otherwise found hard to articulate.

In a knowledge-based economy, conventional strategy concepts still apply, but they are being applied to something much less tangible and much more elusive than "what you can drop on your foot"—i.e. a physical object. Max was adamant that you cannot approach the knowledge economy without some adaptation of the usual strategy tools. His concepts complemented rather than challenged current knowledge management practices. These tend to target the firm's knowledge base as a whole and are regarded as the province of the human resources and the IT departments. His own focus was more selective; it targeted that *subset* of a firm's knowledge base that is *strategically* relevant. For example, executives from *Alstom*, the French engineering company that designed and manufactured the French high-speed train—the TGV—used the *I-Space* to map the critical technologies of the high-speed train and their interdependencies in order to identify which ones could be released to a strategic client in the context of a technology transfer project and which ones the company should "hoard," in his terms. *BP* used the *I-Space* to explore some of the cultural and institutional challenges that confronted it when dealing with host governments and local suppliers in developing its oil assets in the Caspian Sea. BP discovered that certain critical intersections between its corporate culture and that of its local stakeholders would need special care if it was to maintain the integrity of its operations in the region. *Siemens* has developed a strong reputation in the area of knowledge management. It has used the *I-Space* as the conceptual framework that underpins its knowledge management systems and processes (Davenport and Probst 2002, 27). The *Defence Science and Technology Laboratories*, the research arm of the UK's *Ministry of Defence*, has used the *I-Space* as a framework for training a network of knowledge and information officers throughout its laboratories. *Deutsche Post* used the *I-Space* to explore and anticipate the significant challenges posed to the organization's German corporate culture and practices with its acquisition of a US company, DHL. Working with Wharton students Max mapped the cultures of the protagonists in the AOL–Time-Warner merger and was able to anticipate the market value destroying mêlées that arose from tensions emanating from clashes of these cultures.

As a result of this experience, use of the *I-Space* framework has given rise to the creation of two major types of intervention tools: for *mapping* critical knowledge assets and for *simulating* strategic knowledge management processes. These two applications of the *I-Space*, that have been built in recent years to help firms deploy the conceptual framework in their pursuit of finding a knowledge-based strategy, are briefly explained next.

Mapping knowledge assets in the *I-Space*

In the penultimate chapter of his award-winning 1998 book, Max talks about "Applying the *I-Space*" to test its practicability and recounts the "tale of two companies" he had worked with in identifying their knowledge-based competences (Boisot 1998). Here, as well as in his 1998 article with Dorothy Griffiths and Veronica Moles (Griffiths, Boisot, and Moles 1998), where he also describes the workshops conducted with the chemical firm *Courtaulds* and *BP*'s oil exploration business, he uses his "reduced form of the *I-Space*"—his C-Space, which goes way back to his dissertation on the diffusion of technical knowledge in the chemical industry in Asia. While Max had been working on ideas for knowledge mapping for a long time, it was during his time at Wharton's Snider Entrepreneurial Research Center that he and the *I-Space* team refined a methodology that would allow firms to capture the critical knowledge assets held by individuals, groups, or organizations and to map and analyze these in the *I-Space*.

The idea behind mapping is as follows. The *I-Space* allows us to represent an agent's knowledge as a portfolio of knowledge assets, as a network of nodes and their links to other nodes. So agents' knowledge can be represented in network form, which is scalable, since any node can be further broken down into a sub-network. Firms work with many different network representations of their knowledge—exploded parts diagrams, process charts, organizational charts. Each captures different aspects of their knowledge, and in each case the different elements of the network can be mapped in the *I-Space* as a plot of how much the knowledge has been structured and how many agents, either within the organization or outside it—have access to it.

Once we can map the different elements of a knowledge network in the *I-Space*, we can begin to consider its dynamic behaviour. And in a fast-moving knowledge-based society, it is the dynamic behaviour of knowledge networks that is a source of opportunities. The resulting portfolio of knowledge assets is both similar to and different from a more traditional strategy portfolio. Like many strategy matrices—Boston Consulting Group's, Arthur D. Little's etc.—the vertical axis of the *I-Space* captures opportunities whereas the horizontal axis captures competitive position. However, unlike a conventional strategy portfolio, the *I-Space* maps knowledge assets as linked together to form a complex adaptive system (CAS). In such a system, moving a single, heavily connected knowledge asset through the *I-Space* can trigger system-wide effects and allow strategists to analyse the strategic implications of company-planned or anticipated competitive shifts in the network structure. The movements of the knowledge portfolio elements through the Social Learning Cycle are subject to the paradox of value: nodes and their linkages increase in value as they become more structured, but also more susceptible and vulnerable to dynamic appropriation by other agents.

Max was convinced that mapping and analysing portfolios of strategic knowledge assets would offer a better understanding of an agent's current and emerging core competences and the economic value associated with them (Boisot and Griffiths 1999). By exploring their learning strategies (Boisot 1995b), individuals, groups and organizations could gain valuable insights into the strategic uses to which their knowledge assets could be put.

In 2009 the opportunity emerged to set up a major research project to test and further develop these knowledge mapping ideas. Max, then at the University of Birmingham, and his research team were awarded a substantial ESRC grant by the UK government to investigate the evolution of intellectual leadership and the mapping of associated knowledge assets in the ATLAS collaboration at CERN. Subsequently, the mapping tools were also applied in a project with a large US-based aerospace company, and two popular HBR Blog articles were published (Ihrig, Boisot, and MacMillan 2011a, b). The next step should have been to refine an approach that maps the cultural and institutional structures that facilitate or impede the operation of different knowledge development strategies, but this will now unfortunately have to be done without Max.

Simulating evolution of knowledge assets in the *I-Space*

A map gives you a static picture of a particular environment or situation. Would it not be even more powerful to also have capacity for dynamic representation that allows one to explore how knowledge develops over time? This was the idea behind creating simulation software to model the dynamics of the *I-Space*; and it became a reality with *SimISpace* and *SimISpace2*.

Max's goal was to have a simulation environment developed that implements the main features of the *I-Space* as a conceptual framework. Together with MacMillan at Wharton, and with the help of some partners from Korea, particularly Kyeong Han from Soongsil University, a first prototype was created and successfully applied in research that studied different intellectual property rights regimes (Boisot, MacMillan, and Han 2007). Agustí Canals used this software for his dissertation and further developed it, modelling the spatial dimension of knowledge flows at ESADE and later at the Open University of Catalonia (Canals, Boisot, and MacMillan 2008).

Max wanted to expand the simulation approach and create software that serves as a generalized knowledge management engine that, through a user-friendly graphical interface, could be applied to a wide range of knowledge-related applications. This was the start of *SimISpace2*, an agent-based simulation package designed to simulate strategic knowledge management processes, in particular knowledge flows and knowledge-based agent interactions (Ihrig and Abrahams 2007). What followed was a multi-year effort building and testing a very complex piece of software that was finally successfully developed and applied by Ihrig in his dissertation on knowledge-based opportunity recognition strategies (Ihrig 2010; Ihrig, MacMillan, Zu Knyphausen-Aufseß, and Boisot 2010; Ihrig 2012).

SimISpace2 allows one to study the effects of individual strategic knowledge management actions and to carry out macro level explorations of knowledge processes (Ihrig 2013). It thus enables a user to go beyond static conceptual models and dynamically analyze a given agent's knowledge-related opportunities and threats from a strategic perspective. Its particular appeal is that a platform has been developed that allows users to design simulations using a graphical user interface to choose from a large number of design parameters rather than have to program their simulation models with computer code. From 2007 to 2009, together with a large international defense contractor, Max and the *I-Space Institute* team applied *SimISpace2* in two classified US Department of Defense (DoD) projects. In 2011, the Finnish Funding Agency for Technology and Innovation awarded a major research grant that will allow the team to apply *SimISpace2* in the context of open innovation. *I-Space Institute* will continue to leverage this simulation software to support research, policy analysis, and training activities. For the first time one can create virtual experiments around the *I-Space*. This will allow users to explore performance outcomes and knowledge development profiles resulting from specified strategies in the information economy. As such, it helps us in our efforts to do the results-oriented research about which Max was so passionate.

Conclusion

The fundamental question for participants in the information economy is how do you manage *knowledge* assets as opposed to *physical* assets? The *I-Space* is a unique conceptual framework that helps us understand the dynamics of a knowledge-based economy and its implications for both competitive and collaborative organizational strategies. With the tools that emerged from Max's research, decision makers can start managing their knowledge assets strategically.

Max's passing has been a great shock to all of us. We owe it to him to memorialize him by perpetuating his work and spread and further develop his ideas. This is what we intend to do with both, the *Strategic and Entrepreneurial Management of Knowledge* (SEM-K) Initiative at Wharton and *I-Space Institute*. In our last year with him, he was fired up about the following research

The Strategic Management of Knowledge

topics—as usual manifold and profound: *1.)* mapping the strategic knowledge assets of parties to a *merger* or *acquisition* and simulating its success or failure under different strategic knowledge development scenarios; *2.)* designing *science, technology and innovation policies* for countries, regions, or cities aiming to attract intellectual capital, and exploring micro and macro effects; *3.)* evaluating an organization's portfolio of knowledge assets and identifying appropriate intra- and inter-firm *technology transfer strategies*; *4.)* formulating the firm's strategic approach to *open innovation*; and *5.)* studying an organization's *knowledge creation* processes (e.g. in the healthcare, software and electronics industries) and the *cognitive arms races* in which it may be engaged.

We want to conclude this chapter not with an ending, but in the spirit of keeping Max ever with us, to propose a beginning. If you have any of these topics close to your heart and would like to advance Max's abruptly and tragically truncated research agenda, get in touch and let us know how you think we might move that particular passion of Max forward.

Part V
Knowledge in Big Science

8

Generating Knowledge in a Connected World: The Case of the ATLAS Experiment at CERN*

Max Boisot

Introduction

The spatial challenges posed by the dynamics of globalization together with the availability of new information and communication technologies (ICTs) have fostered the development of virtual collaboration. In many industries—automobile, aerospace, pharmaceuticals, heavy engineering, etc.—scientific and technological teams now collaborate transnationally. In companies like Ford, Boeing, etc. the design and development of new products is carried out through international networks. Face-to-face interaction can be maintained in the absence of physical co-presence through video-conferencing or Skype. Furthermore the ease of communicating through email actually reduces the need for frequent face-to-face interaction.

Driven by organizational authority systems, however, much of this activity remains of a top-down, hierarchical nature. Although the proportion of bottom-up activity has increased, it has not displaced the top-down bias in the governance structures of firms and the formal processes that give them effect. Yet recent developments are challenging the organizational assumptions that underpin such structures and processes. How, for example, do people ever get to collaborate in distributed, non-hierarchical networks such as Linux (Raymond, 1999)? How is network coordination actually achieved?

---

* Originally published as Max Boisot (2011). "Generating Knowledge in a Connected World: The Case of the ATLAS Experiment at CERN." *Management Learning*, 42 (4): 447–57. Reprinted with kind permission of SAGE Publications Ltd.

How does trust evolve to the point where it can substitute for hierarchical control? Finally, what level of task complexity are such networks capable of managing in this distributed fashion?

Such questions invite a deeper look at the nature of organizational coordination, that is, at the different ways that knowledge flows and gets integrated in space and time across formal and informal organizational and national boundaries. In what follows, we first offer a theoretical perspective on the above questions and then illustrate it with a look at the way that the ATLAS experiment at CERN—one of the four experiments that are using the Large Hadron Collider (LHC)—is organized and managed. The ATLAS Collaboration—the team of physicists responsible for the experiment—consists of a culturally heterogeneous and loosely coupled population of agents, each operating in a different institutional setting. We shall use our theoretical perspective to interpret some of the issues raised by this kind of big science experiment and discuss their implications for a broader class of organizations. We shall then offer a brief conclusion.

A conceptual framework: The *I-Space*

Managerial coordination requires that information-bearing data flows through communication channels between centers of authority and centers of task execution. Information is then extracted from the data to construct representations of situations that either match or fail to match prior expectations. If the essence of coordination is to bring situations, intentions and behaviors into alignment, the essence of *managerial* coordination is to do so through the agency of others (Barnard 1938). This requires communication—information flows—between human agents, the effectiveness of which depends in part on the way that information is structured. We explore this dependency by drawing on a conceptual framework, the Information-Space or *I-Space*, that relates the speed and extent of information flows within a population of agents to the possibilities for information structuring (Boisot 1995a, 1998). The structuring of information consists of two interrelated activities:

1. *Codification*—the creation of categories to which different phenomena can be assigned. The clarity with which categories can be created varies, and to that extent codification is a matter of degree. Also, discernible differences between phenomena can be simple, involving simple attributes such as color, weight, smell, size, etc. or they can be complex and involved multiple correlated attributes—e.g. does this person qualify for unemployment benefits? Does the candidate meet the requirements of our job description? Can this patient be considered cured?

2. *Abstraction*—Minimizing the number of categories to which a given phenomenon need be assigned. People's eligibility for unemployment benefits, for example, might be determined by a single variable: their income. A concrete representation of phenomena draws on a large number of categories; an abstract representation draws on a few.

Taken together, codification and abstraction minimize the amount of data processing required to categorize and respond to phenomena, and speed up data transmission. Thus, as illustrated in Figure 8.1, codified and abstract information will diffuse through a population of agents faster and more extensively per unit of time than information that is uncodified and concrete.

Managerial coordination requires that a diversity of information flows be integrated to make available unified representations of relevant phenomena to given agents. To achieve integration, the network of communication channels between different agents must be structured so as to ensure that information flows as intended. The structures of these networks will reflect the possibilities offered by the information environment in which coordination takes place. An information environment characterized by high degrees of codification, abstraction, and diffusibility, for example, will deliver impersonal networks where agents do not have to know each other in order to interact: *markets,* where the diffusion of information is uncontrolled; *bureaucracies,* where it is subject to some degree of central control. On the other hand, an information environment characterized by low degrees of codification, abstraction—and hence diffusibility—will deliver highly personalized networks in which trust and shared values are essential: *clans,* where the information is diffused face-to-face within a group of limited size; *fiefs,*

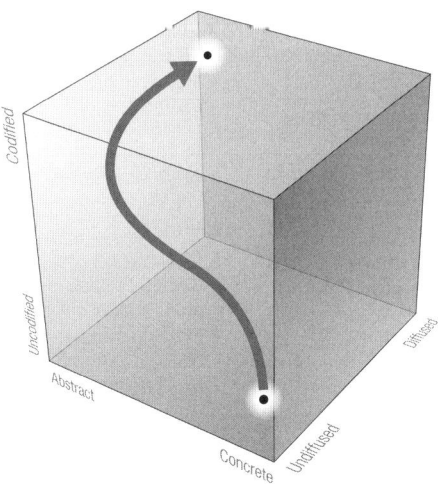

Figure 8.1. The Information-Space (*I-Space*)

where undiffused information remains confined within a single head to become a source of personal power.

Over time, where interactions are recurrent, the four types of interaction network identified above—others are, of course, possible—become sources of cultural values and practices and may even get institutionalized. We locate them in the different information environments of the *I-Space* as shown in Figure 8.2 and briefly outline their key attributes in Table 8.1.

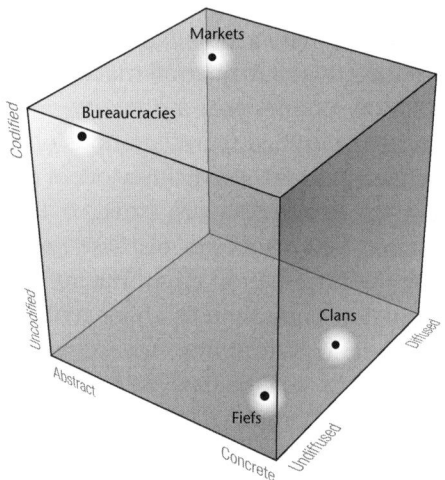

Figure 8.2. Institutions and cultures in the *I-Space*

Table 8.1. Cultures in the *I-Space*.

STRUCTURED INFORMATION	***Bureaucracies*** • Information diffusion limited and under central control • Relationships impersonal and hierarchical • Submission to super-ordinate goals • Hierarchical coordination • No necessity to share values and beliefs	***Markets*** • Information widely diffused, no control • Relationships impersonal and competitive • No super-ordinate goals—each one for himself • Horizontal coordination through self-regulation • No necesity to share values and beliefs
UNSTRUCTURED INFORMATION	***Fiefs*** • Information diffusion limited by lack of structure to face-to-face relationship • Relationships personal and hierarchical (feudal/chairsmatic) • Submission to super-ordinate goals • Hierarchical coordination • Necessity to share values and beliefs	***Clans*** • Information is party diffused but still limited by lack of structure to face-to-face relationships • Relationships personal but non-hierarchical • Goals are shared through a process of negotiation • Horizontal coordination through negotiation • Necessity to share values and beliefs
	UNDIFFUSED INFORMATION	DIFFUSED INFORMATION

Generating Knowledge in a Connected World

The information environments that characterize the different regions of the *I-Space* vary in their complexity. We distinguish between two types of complexity:

1. *Cognitive complexity*—associated with the amount of data processing that a given categorization task requires. Since more data processing implies more complexity, cognitive complexity increases as one moves into the lower-front regions of the *I-Space* where information is both uncodified and concrete.

2. *Relational complexity*—associated with the number of agents participating in a given interaction. The further to the right along the diffusion dimension of the *I-Space* social interactions take place, the more agents they will involve so that relational complexity increases as one moves to the right in the *I-Space*.

The interplay of cognitive and relational complexity delivers three regimes in the *I-Space*—the *ordered*, the *complex*, and the *chaotic*—located as indicated in Figure 8.3. As can be seen, bureaucracies are order-generating structures, whereas clans sit close to what complexity theorists call "the edge of chaos" (Bak 1996; Kauffman 1993).

Finally, new information and communication technologies (ICTs) increase both data processing and data transmission capacities. How might they affect the development of interaction networks? We identify two effects:

1. The *diffusion effect*—at all levels of codification and abstraction, the new ICTs can process and transmit more data to more people per unit of time

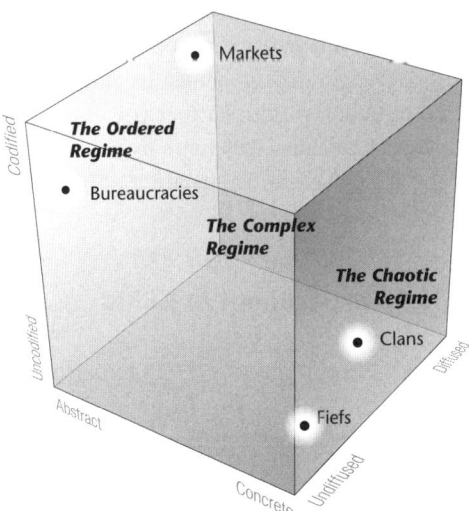

Figure 8.3. Ordered, complex, and chaotic regimes in the *I-Space*

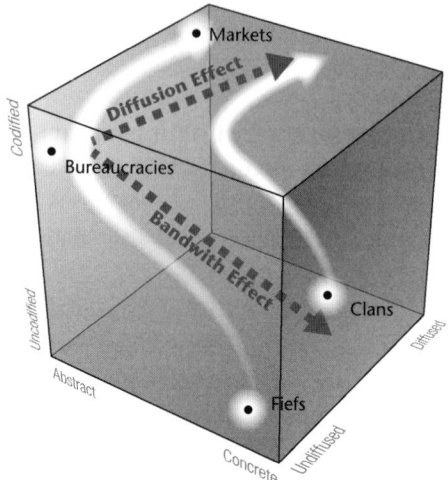

Figure 8.4. The impact of ICTs in the *I-Space*

than hitherto. We can describe this as a shift to the right in the diffusion curve. In Figure 8.4, the effect is indicated by the right-pointing arrow that is parallel to the diffusion dimension of the *I-Space*.

2. The *bandwidth effect*—a given target population in the *I-Space* can now be reached at a lower level of codification and abstraction than hitherto. Interactions at a distance that thirty years ago used to take place by telex now take place through videoconferencing. We depict this with the downward-pointing arrow in Figure 8.4.

As indicated by Figure 8.4, if by dint of the size of the population that can now be reached with the new ICTs, the diffusion effect favors market processes, the bandwidth effect, by re-personalizing communications, favors clan-like processes. How might these developments affect the challenge of coordination? In the next two sections we address this issue by briefly examining a complex big science project: the ATLAS experiment at CERN.

The case of the ATLAS experiment at CERN

ATLAS is one of four high-energy physics (HEP) experiments being conducted at CERN, the host laboratory, using the Large Hadron Collider (LHC). The LHC is designed to collide two counter-rotating beams of protons or heavy ions at an energy of 7 Teravolts (TeV) per beam. Protons are accelerated to within a tiny fraction of the speed of light and then made to collide with each other. Physicists then use detectors to get information about short-lived particles—the product of proton-to-proton collisions—whose paths are too short to detect. To do this they look at the particles' decay products which exist long enough to be detected. The proton beams move around the LHC ring inside a continuous vacuum guided by magnets.

The LHC is located in a circular tunnel, 27 km in circumference, that straddles the Swiss and French borders on the outskirts of Geneva and is buried between 50 and 175 m underground. The detector/accelerator system acts like a giant microscope, so powerful that it can make fundamental particle activity visible to us within the tiny atomic nucleus. Four detectors—ATLAS, CMS, ALICE, and LHCb—each with its own distinctive design and each conceived to carry out different experiments, are positioned at different points on the circumference of the LHC. The ATLAS experiment uses a multi-component detector, housed in an eight-storey underground cavern, to test different aspects of an event. Each of its components identifies different particle types and then measure their energies and momenta. When an event is detected, individual particles can be singled out from the multitudes for analysis. After each detected event, thousands of computers collect and interpret the vast quantity of data generated by the detector—the volume of data generated would fill up 100,000 CDs per second—and present the information extracted from these data to the physicist.

The performance of an accelerator/detector system is set by the rate at which collisions can be engineered, the sensitivity with which collisions can be detected, and recorded, and the capacity to process collision data. We can represent these three performance requirements on a spidergraph as shown in Figure 8.5. At the centre of the spidergraph, performance requirements are minimal—anyone, so to speak, can achieve them. As one moves toward the

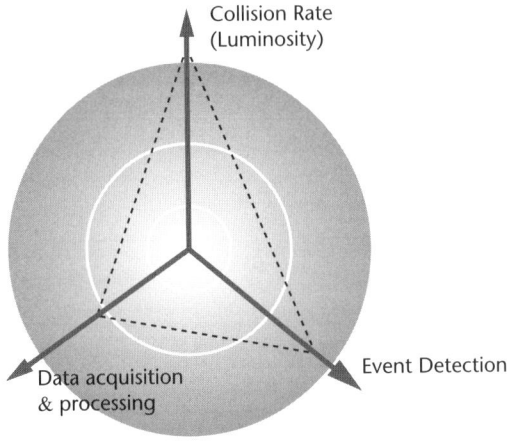

Figure 8.5. The ATLAS performance spidergraph

tip of any one performance dimension however, one enters unexplored territory where no one has yet ventured. Here much of the relevant knowledge has not yet been codified and, being embedded in the concrete, idiosyncratic behavior of specific pieces of equipment, measuring instruments and machinery, it resists summary abstract representations. Furthermore, as one approaches the tip of different performance dimensions, they begin to interact in unpredictable ways. An increase in the collision rate for example—the beam's *luminosity*—necessarily entails a requirement for an improvement in detection abilities. Improved detection, in turn, calls for greater data-processing capacities.

The ATLAS experiment, along with the other three, will explore the basic forces that have shaped our universe since its creation and that will determine its fate. It aims to understand the origins of mass—thought to be imparted to other particles by the elusive Higgs boson—the dimensionality of space, and microscopic black holes. It also seeks evidence for dark matter candidates in the universe. The detector is one of the most complex scientific instruments ever built, and the ATLAS Collaboration—the multinational team of scientists and engineers that developed the detector and will run the experiments—is one of the largest collaborative efforts ever attempted in the physical sciences. It involves the coordination of over 3000 physicists, working in 174 universities and laboratories, and spread across over 38 countries.

As indicated in Figure 8.6, the ATLAS Collaboration is organized around both the components and the need for integrating these. Each component is the responsibility of a team of physicists and engineers. The team will

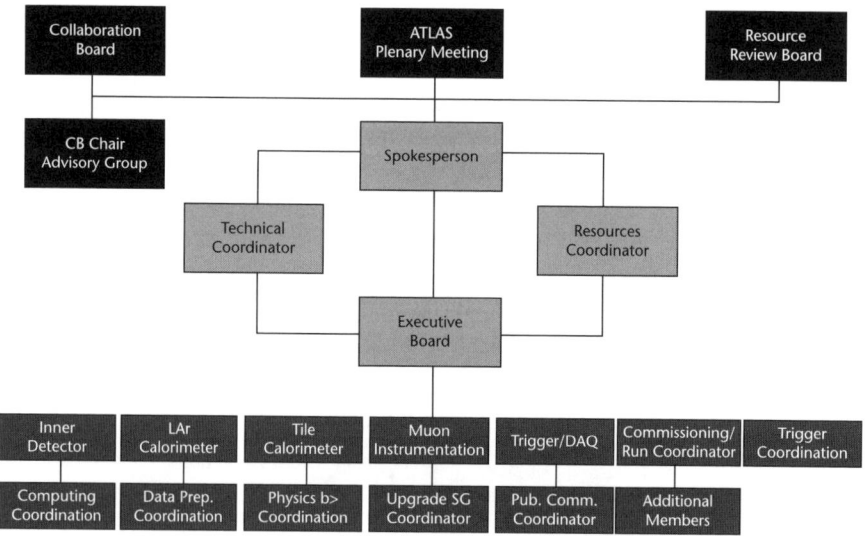

Figure 8.6. The organization of the ATLAS collaboration

typically have several hundred members, spread across the research institutes of many countries. The interactions between different—and sometimes conflicting—performance requirements call for trade-offs and often negotiations between the ATLAS teams responsible for the performance of the different components that make up the detector. Although the Collaboration has a project management team, it manages with a light touch with little formal managerial authority to draw upon. The glue that binds participating institutions together is not contracts but Memoranda of Understanding. Team members are paid for by their respective participating institutions and do not readily "take orders" from other members of the Collaboration. Indeed, the Collaboration's project leader is called a "spokesperson" and is considered a *primus inter pares* (a first among equals). Coordination is therefore mostly a bottom-up, consensus-driven affair, achieved by numerous face-to face meetings within and between the different teams, with many participants who cannot be physically present taking part virtually.

The ATLAS collaboration in the *I-Space*

The ATLAS Collaboration is a large global network undertaking what is perhaps the most complex and sophisticated big science project ever conceived. How might we characterize the network in *I-Space* terms? Where in the Space should we locate it? It draws on plenty of codified, abstract knowledge, but it does so in the context of tasks and performance requirements that have never been encountered before. Operating with highly intricate physical equipment at the scientific frontier, the *critical* knowledge it draws on is both uncodified and concrete, thus placing it in the lower regions of the *I-Space*. Yet being too loosely coupled to qualify as a clan, it is best thought of as what Mintzberg, following Alvin Toffler (1970) labels an *adhocracy*, an organizational configuration that enables sophisticated innovation and that is able to fuse networks of experts drawn from different disciplines into smoothly functioning ad hoc project teams (Mintzberg 1979). According to Mintzberg, no one in an adhocracy is in a position to monopolize the power to innovate. As he puts it: "Decision-making power is distributed among managers and nonmanagers at all the levels of the hierarchy, according to the nature of the different decisions to be made" (Mintzberg 1979, 436).

We view adhocracies as loosely coupled networks operating to the right of clans in the *I-Space*. If clans sit close to the "edge of chaos," however, adhocracies sit even closer. Chaos, in this context does not refer so much to *disorganization* as to the absence of codified and abstract structures that can serve a priori as a basis for organized action. Whatever structures guide action, emerge gradually from the interactions of the players themselves and remain provisional and subject to change—the outcome of what Mintzberg and Walters (1985) describe as *emergent strategies*. Yet if the ATLAS Collaboration is an adhocracy operating close to or in the chaotic regime in the *I-Space*, how has it managed to deliver one of the most complex pieces of machinery ever built? What is the nature of the coordination that can achieve this? The matrix structure of a typical NASA project leads to much more tightly coupled operations than those of the ATLAS Collaboration. How, then, does the latter manage to deliver?

We hypothesize that the detector itself, acting as a *boundary object* (Carlile 2002), provides the loosely coupled network that is ATLAS with much of the raw materials required for effective coordination. A boundary object acts as a common reference point that allows different actors to coordinate their actions without interacting directly with each other. One can best understand the role of a boundary object by briefly examining two options for the regulation of traffic intersections. One option is to use an authority-based system like traffic lights. A red light transmits an order to stop, a green light, an order to proceed. An alternative option is to use a roundabout in which the physical configuration of the roads themselves allows individual drivers to proceed at their own pace, making their own decision. In effect, a roundabout constitutes a boundary object that helps a multitude of individuals, each with a different destination, to coordinate their actions in a way that keeps traffic flowing. A set of traffic lights works most efficiently for a simple intersection of two roads. The large roundabout at the Place de l'Etoile in Paris, by contrast, can handle six intersecting roads and could probably handle more. Both the traffic lights and roundabouts can be thought of as boundary objects; but not only can roundabouts handle more complexity in a decentralized fashion than can traffic lights, their ability to coordinate is entirely self-contained whereas traffic lights depend on an external authority structure for their proper functioning.

As a boundary object, the ATLAS detector gradually moved up the *I-Space* toward higher levels of codification as it gained in definition. Through ever more detailed simulations and empirical tests, it also moved from being a highly abstract entity to being a concrete physical reality. Its coordinating role as a boundary object would today place it in the vicinity of the region labeled "bureaucracies" in the *I-Space*, but, as indicated in Figure 8.7, closer to the concrete end of the abstraction dimension. There it acts as a generator of order. No boundary object, however, could coordinate an adhocracy of the size and complexity of the ATLAS Collaboration unaided. We therefore hypothesize that two further conditions must be met:

1. The *maintenance of clan values*—The coherence that the ATLAS detector has been able to achieve in the course of its evolution draws upon deeply

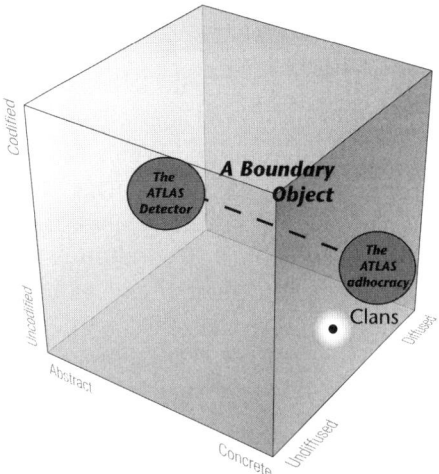

Figure 8.7. Adhocracies and boundary objects

held values, motivations and beliefs, tacitly shared by all members of the collaboration throughout the project. These ensure that the orientation of the different participants in the collaboration towards the detector as a boundary object will be compatible.

2. *The potential of the new ICTs must be fully exploited*—If shared values and beliefs provide the motivation to bind the adhocracy together, the new ICTs provide the connectivity that makes it possible to do so and to achieve organizational coherence across a wide variety of cultures and institutions that are geographically dispersed. The shift in the diffusion curve brought about by the new ICTs and depicted in Figure 8.4 allows clan values to extend to, and be maintained in larger populations than physical presence can achieve on its own. Face-to-face interactions can now be sustained at a distance through what we have called the bandwidth effect. Thus whereas in earlier times an adhocracy as large and geographically dispersed as the ATLAS Collaboration would have quickly degenerated into chaos—as implied by Figure 8.3—the global connectivity made achievable with the new ICTs allow this complex heterogeneous network to hang together in a coherent and productive fashion and to do so over decades.

To summarize, we believe that the adhocracy that is the ATLAS Collaboration is held together first by a common focus on the ATLAS detector acting as a coordinator of the collaboration's members; second, by the shared values and beliefs characteristic of clans that maintain the focus; and finally, by the enabling role played by the new ICTs in maintaining the necessary global connectivity between the collaboration's members.

Conclusion

Does big science, as practiced by the ATLAS Collaboration have something to teach commercial organizations? Could a commercial firm ever manage a project of such complexity and duration? We cannot answer this question. At the frontiers of science, many of the managerial principles by which commercial organizations operate lose their purchase. But the idea that, under the right cultural and technological conditions—ones in which values, beliefs and motivations are deeply shared, and global connectivity can be maintained—a large, complex, physical object could take over some of the more challenging tasks of coordinating a global network merits deep reflection and further research. Three avenues for such research suggest themselves: (1) What might be a minimal specification for a boundary object? (2) What might be the maximum size and geographical spread of the adhocracies that different types of boundary object could help coordinate? (3) How complex are the tasks that different boundary objects could help to coordinate?

9

Knowledge in Big Science

Agustí Canals

Introduction

The keystone of Max Boisot's thought is the *I-Space*. It is the result of many years of reflection on the nature of information processing actions performed by knowledgeable agents and on its implication for organization. Its purpose is to provide a theoretical framework that facilitates our understanding of the creation and transfer of knowledge in all sorts of organizations.

Boisot's interest in organizational problems started when he was complementing his original training in architecture with a MSc in Urban Planning at the MIT, but it was during his PhD at Imperial College on technology transfer that he got more and more interested in the problems of creation and diffusion of knowledge (Boisot 1981). Not happy with the prevalent theoretical ideas, after some years of interdisciplinary study and eclectic readings he gradually developed his own theoretical model and published the book *I-Space: A Framework for Learning in Organizations, Institutions and Culture* (Boisot 1995a). Further developed in *Knowledge Assets: Securing Competitive Advantage in the Information Economy* (Boisot 1998), the *I-Space* framework has been used to analyze knowledge and information flows in a varied number of organizational settings. But perhaps one of the areas where it has shown more potential is the study of big science, where the creation and transfer of knowledge are the most important *raisons d'être*.

Knowledge and science

Max Boisot had always shown a vivid interest in natural sciences. In fact, he sometimes claimed that, had it not been for his "inability" to deal with mathematics, he could well have been a physicist or other sort of natural scientist. In spite of this supposed limitation, he often resorted to scientific fields like physics, biology or cognitive science as sources of insights that allowed him to develop his own theories. For instance, Shannon's information theory (Shannon 1948; Shannon and Weaver 1963) and the concepts of discrimination and association in learning (Hahn and Chater 1998; James 1890) were two of the fundamental inputs he used in developing the underpinnings of the *I-Space* (Boisot 1995a; 1998).

But the natural sciences were not only used as a source of concepts and ideas for Boisot's theoretical developments. He also used the scientific discovery process as a model for any process of knowledge acquisition by individuals or organizations.

Science is mainly about creating new knowledge and diffusing it. The scientists' mission is to produce reliable pieces of new knowledge that make it easier to understand the world. In that process, new knowledge is created through the combination of older knowledge and new data coming from the observation of the world, often through designed experiments. In the development of his *I-Space* theory, Max found in the philosophy and epistemology of science interesting insights that he used to think about knowledge-related processes in more general environments. Specifically, he developed an interesting distinction between the concepts of data, information, and knowledge based on Popper's evolutionary epistemology (Popper 1959; 1979).

The role of natural science in Boisot's thinking became even more important when, in 2008, we had the opportunity to start studying the ATLAS experiment. A significant part of Boisot's research in the last years of his life was devoted to the study of the organizational and strategic aspects of this big science project. He could not find a better testbed of his ideas on information and knowledge and their role in complex social systems than the ATLAS Collaboration. After all, science has been historically the first social system that specialized in turning data into information useful to generate knowledge.

In this section, we will review some of these ideas and their application to the understanding of big science projects like ATLAS. First, we will look at some fundamental questions about the nature of knowledge and its differentiation from the concepts of data and information. From his original insights on these issues, Boisot derived interesting implications for organizations and the economic view of knowledge assets. Second, we will review Boisot's published research on big science, represented mainly by the article *Generating Knowledge in a Connected World: The Case of the ATLAS Experiment at CERN* (Boisot 2011), reproduced in this book, and the book *Collisions and Collaboration* (Boisot, Nordberg, Yami, and Nicquevert 2011). Finally, we will overview some of the ideas on which Boisot was working in the last months of his research about big science and some possible avenues for further research.

The agent-in-the-world

A theoretical framework like *I-Space* that attempted to explain the way in which information flows contribute to the transfer and creation of knowledge within social systems necessarily had to rely on a clear conceptual distinction between the terms data, information and knowledge. Boisot spent a lot of time searching for a coherent system of interrelated definitions of the three concepts.

The economics literature was not of much help in that objective. Economists often consider information as something that is independent of the information processor and its internal characteristics and stands apart from it. Knowledge is sometimes conflated with information (Hirshleifer and Riley 1992) or information with data (Shapiro and Varian 1999). At most, knowledge is considered to be a "stock" that is incremented by information, but the tacit assumption is that both are "things" that are independent of the information processing agent.

In the knowledge management literature one may find some conceptual distinctions between the terms data, information, and management; but they are often unclear and difficult to sustain under the light of cognitive sciences. For instance, some scholars claim that data, information and knowledge follow a sequential order, one being the raw material of the other, but it is not clear when one turns into the other. Others, like Nonaka and Takeuchi (1995) use the classical definition of knowledge as "justified true belief" and information as "belief neutral data," which does not seem to allow a clear discrimination between the three concepts.

Based on the evolutionary epistemology view triggered by the works of Karl Popper (Campbell 1987; Popper 1979), Boisot proposed in *Knowledge Assets* (Boisot 1998) a model that clearly distinguished data, information, and knowledge and provided a way to conceptualize the relationship between the three. That model was further developed in an article we published some years after (Boisot and Canals 2004).

While data are treated as originating in "discernible differences in physical states-of-the-world," information is "an extraction from data that, by modifying the relevant probability distributions, has a capacity to perform useful work on an agent's knowledge base," which is formed by a set of expectations (Boisot and Canals 2004, 46). The relationships between the three concepts are depicted in Figure 9.1. Each of them constitutes a different type of economic good, possessing a specific kind of utility. The utility of data resides on their capacity to carry information about the physical world, while that of

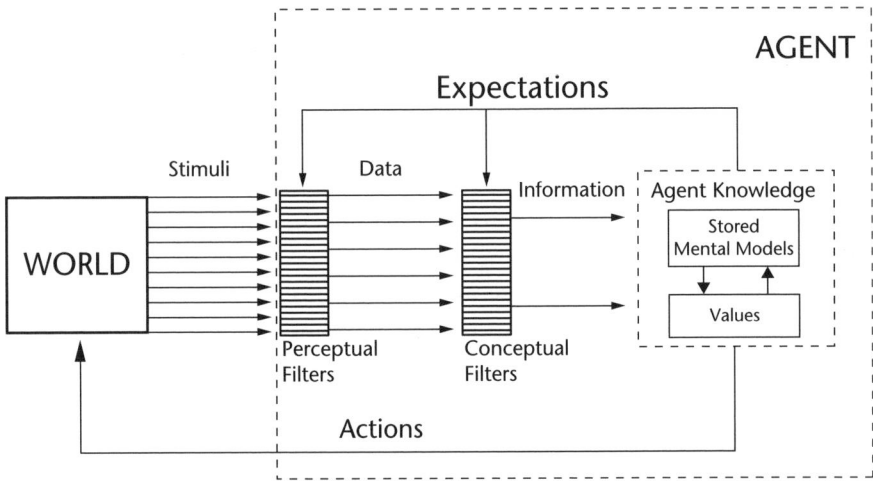

Figure 9.1. The agent-in-the-world (Boisot and Canals 2004)

information consists of being able to modify an expectation or a state of knowledge. On its turn, knowledge allows an agent to act in adaptive ways upon the physical world.

Karl Popper was often a source of inspiration for Boisot, as exemplified above. In spite of that, one cannot qualify his philosophical position as neo-positivist. From an ontological point of view, he was indeed an objectivist, since he considered that reality existed independently of consciousness. He used to refer to Karl Popper's expression "but reality kicks back" (Popper 1988, 116) when confronted with extreme social constructivist positions. However, from an epistemological point of view he did not believe in the ability of the human mind to comprehend our world thoroughly. His position was closer to that of the critical realism of Roy Bhaskar (1975).[1]

Information is subjective and physical

One of the main ideas behind the model introduced above is the need to consider the nature of data as well as that of information. For that, Max turned to physics and engineering. Two influences were especially relevant: Shannon's theory of information (Shannon 1948; Shannon and Weaver 1963) and the physics of information (Feynman 1996; Leff and Rex 1990; Zurek 1990).

Shannon's theory of information originates in the engineering tradition and concerns itself essentially with the technical problems of information

---

[1] Private conversations.

transmission from a sender to a receiver. A message consists of a number of symbols taken from a symbolic repertoire that is simultaneously known by both sender and receiver. Then, the amount of information that a channel will be able to transmit will depend on the size of the repertoire of symbols as well as the degree of noise in the channel that influences its reliability (Shannon 1948; Shannon and Weaver 1963). But if one wants to analyze social situations, the technical problem of information transmission is only one part of the equation. The content and meaning of the message need also to be considered. And then it becomes clear that in social settings symbolic codes are not always completely shared by sender and receiver and that differences in their respective contexts may lead to different interpretation of the symbols in the message. Thus, if information consists, following the definition above, of what has the capacity of modifying the knowledge of an agent, it is possible that data are transmitted from a technical point of view but they do not contain information for the receiver because she does not master the code in which the message has been prepared. And, therefore, what is information for one individual may be just noise for another, depending on their respective previous knowledge (Boisot and Canals 2004).

We act often as if information were something related to the mind and, therefore, somehow detached from the physical world. But the physics of information tells us that information relies always on a physical substrate and, therefore "information is physical" (Landauer and Hey 1999); and everything physical is information (Lloyd 2000). That means that there will be "physical limits to our access to data and hence to our ability to reliably extract information from data" (Boisot and Canals 2004, 57).

Thus, for Boisot, on the one hand knowledge may be modified by information but, at the same time, it is needed to extract information from data. On the other hand, the fact that information relies on its physical substrate makes it subject to physical limitations. These two ideas, which inspire Boisot's model of the agent-in-the-world, are particularly appropriate to big science experiments, where the aim is to obtain from matter the relevant information to increase scientific knowledge. Perhaps it is because of this that Max devoted such an amount of time and effort in his last years in studying one of the most relevant big science initiatives: the ATLAS experiment at CERN.

Big science

In September 2008, Max Boisot organized a two-day workshop in Sitges, a beautiful Catalan city on the Mediterranean coast south of Barcelona where he had established his residence some years before. That workshop congregated a group of different researchers who had been investigating different aspects of the ATLAS Collaboration, the organization in charge of building and operating the ATLAS detector at CERN. The objective of the meeting, conceived by Max and Markus Nordberg, the Resources Coordinator of ATLAS, was to share the results obtained by the different lines of research represented there and try to develop a common thread that could integrate them into a book.

The idea went back to some months before when Max and Markus had met and started to talk about the possibilities that ATLAS could offer for interesting research in the fields of organization and strategy. Although he is a physicist, Markus holds also a PhD in Economics and Business Administration, and he was perfectly aware of how interesting ATLAS could be as a subject of study for management scholars due to its singular characteristics. The book, finally published in 2011 under the title of *Collisions and Collaboration* (Boisot, Nordberg, et al. 2011), was the first project in a series of fruitful collaborations giving rise to a period of enthusiastic research about big science organizations that Max continued until his death in 2011. Here we will review some of the ideas developed during this research.

Big science may be defined as "large-scale scientific research consisting of projects funded usually by a national government or group of governments."[2] The term appeared in the 1960s when, scientific progress in some areas could not be achieved any more by small groups of scientists working in independent labs. As scientific knowledge became deeper, advancing it required bigger and more sophisticated machines and laboratories, which in turn required larger budgets and increases in staff. The former could only be provided by national governments or groups of governments and the latter usually called for the collaboration of different scientific institutions. The first big science projects appeared in the fields of physics (like the particle experiments at the Lawrence Berkeley National Laboratory or at CERN) and astronomy (with the construction of large telescopes). Towards the end of the 20th century, also life sciences had to resort to big science for challenges like the Human Genome Project.

ATLAS is one of the paradigmatic examples of big science. It is one of the four detectors that are gathering data from the collision events produced in the Large Hadron Collider (LHC), a particle accelerator built at CERN in a circular tunnel of 27 km straddling the Swiss-French border next to Geneva. When two beams of protons moving along the LHC at nearly the speed of light in opposite directions collide, they can reproduce conditions similar to the ones of the very first instants of the universe. Because of that, in these collisions it is possible to produce particles that are not present anywhere else in the observable universe. By analyzing the particles produced there, high

---

[2] Merriam-Webster dictionary.

Knowledge in Big Science

energy physicists can know more about the fundamental properties of the physical world. For instance, finding the *Higgs boson* particle signifies the validation of the so-called Standard Model of particle physics and, consequently, of the mechanism by which particles acquire mass proposed by the Scottish physicist Peter Higgs. But many other relevant findings like supersymmetric particles, new dimensions, magnetic monopoles or mini black holes are also possible.

ATLAS and CMS, its sister experiment, are general purpose detectors whose mission is to capture data on any particle that is produced in the proton-proton collisions. They are complemented at LHC by two smaller detectors, ALICE and LHCb, tailored to gather more specific data. The ATLAS detector is 45 meters in length and 25 meters in diameter; it weighs 7000 tons. It is one of the most complex machines ever built. It is designed to capture one billion collision events a second. For that, it has to take about 40 million snapshots a second, each with a resolution of about 100 megapixels. As it would be impossible to store all that information, the detector needs to incorporate a mechanism that automatically selects from those snapshots only about 200 every second—the ones that might be relevant to find new physical phenomena—and store them so that they are available for further offline analysis.

For an intellectual interested in all aspects of human activity like Max Boisot, a physics experiment like ATLAS was of course extremely interesting in its own right. But its characteristics and organization made it also extremely useful as a test bed of his ideas on information and knowledge flows. The purpose of the experiment was to produce new scientific knowledge that would allow a better understanding of our own world. That required the combination of cutting-edge knowledge coming from high-energy physics, but also from computer science, electronics, materials science or engineering. Moreover, from an organizational point of view it was an extremely complex project carried out by a collaboration of more than 3000 scientists with different backgrounds, coming from about 175 institutions and 38 countries, whose knowledge had to be integrated in order to attain the objectives. Studying ATLAS would allow Boisot to apply his ideas to a really knowledge-intensive organization and, hopefully, to obtain insights interesting for other big science experiments and perhaps for other kinds of organizations.

Studying the ATLAS collaboration

The importance of knowledge creation and transfer processes in big science had already been pointed out, among others, by the historian of physics Peter Galison and the sociologist Karin Knorr-Cetina. Galison coined the term *trading zone* to describe how different groups of physicists and engineers coming from different paradigms learn to interact and integrate their knowledge in order to build big science experiments (Galison 1997). Knorr-Cetina described how science produces knowledge through a set of specific sociological mechanisms and structures that she called *epistemic cultures*, which are different for each field of research. One of the epistemic cultures she studied was the high-energy physics community in the 1980s. She did that by looking at the big science experiments at CERN that lead to the discovery of the W and Z bosons (Knorr-Cetina 1999). Building on these ideas and other studies of the sociology of science such as those by Andrew Pickering (1984) and Sharon Traweek (1988), and with the application of his own theoretical developments, Max Boisot set up an ambitious research program to better understand information and knowledge flows in big science organizations.

One of the first results of this program was the article published in the journal *Management Learning* (Boisot 2011), reproduced in this book. In it, Boisot introduces some of the ideas on the organizational characteristics of the ATLAS Collaboration that are further developed in the book *Collisions and Collaboration* and in other works during his last year of life.

In *Knowledge Assets* (Boisot 1998), he had proposed four different archetypical models of institutional cultures attending to the preferential way to deal with information processing: bureaucracies, markets, fiefs, and clans. Those informational cultures populate different parts of the *I-Space* (see Figure 9.2).

While bureaucracies and markets deal principally with abstract and codified knowledge, fiefs and clans operate mainly in the lower part of the *I-Space* and, therefore, rely primarily on more concrete and less codified knowledge. What distinguishes bureaucracies from markets is the degree of diffusion of information. In the former, it is restricted to a small number of individuals occupying key hierarchical positions, while in the latter it is publicly available. Something similar occurs in the lower part of the *I-Space*. In fiefs, there is a single individual that has access to all information, what gives him control of knowledge and, therefore, power. In clans, knowledge is more distributed, but always within the boundaries of the clan members. The distinctive features of these four cultural and institutional structures are identified in Figure 9.3.

Boisot sees the ATLAS Collaboration as something similar to a clan-like structure bounded by common values and beliefs where power is distributed, as opposite to the more bureaucratic nature of CERN. However, the size and complexity of ATLAS goes beyond a typical clan, and therefore he proposes to characterize it as an *adhocracy* (Mintzberg 1979), a loosely coupled network operating close to the "edge of chaos" and, therefore, capable of dealing with complexity by absorbing uncertainty. As a coordinating mechanism for this adhocracy, he proposes the role of the ATLAS detector itself as a boundary object (Carlile 2002; Star and Griesemer 1989). The detector acts as "a common reference point that allows different actors to coordinate their actions without

Knowledge in Big Science

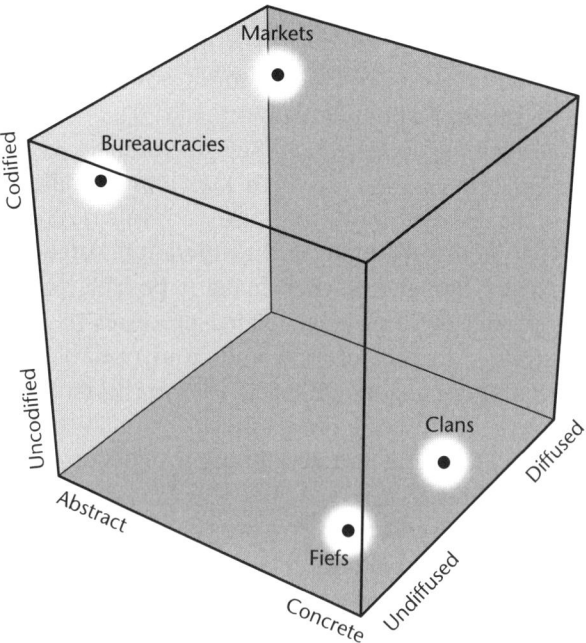

Figure 9.2. Institutions and cultures in the *I-Space*

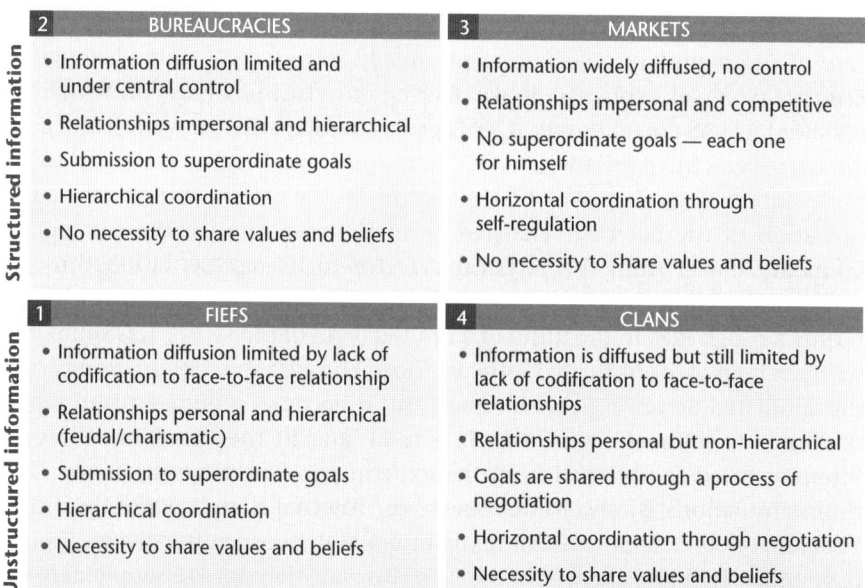

Figure 9.3. Cultures and institutional structures

interacting directly with each other" by facilitating knowledge transfer between the different groups involved. Finally, he stresses the decisive role of ICTs together with clan values in making it possible to achieve coordination, even in presence of a boundary object.

The book *Collisions and Collaboration* (Boisot, Nordberg, et al. 2011) constitutes a very interesting exercise in which Max and his different co-authors integrate a set of diverse contributions to the study of ATLAS as an example of a big science experiment. By looking at the different research works under the lenses of the *I-Space* framework, they make it possible to understand the important role played by knowledge-related processes in all aspects of big science, from strategy to organization and from operations to leadership, including interesting discussions on e-Science infrastructures and the future of high energy physics. The book proves the utility of Boisot's *I-Space* conceptual framework for provoking and developing insights on the most complex organizational problems.

ATLAS was also the object of study in a project on the strategic management of knowledge and leadership in big science projects. One of the more interesting results of this project were a set of maps of the relevant knowledge assets possessed by the ATLAS Collaboration in the *I-Space* (see Chapter 7).

During the last months of his research activity, Max Boisot directed his work towards the development of a couple of ideas also related to the study of ATLAS, that gave rise to two working papers presented in academic conferences. The first of these papers further explored the application to the ATLAS case of the boundary object concept already introduced in his *Management Learning* paper, as explained above. During our visits to CERN—in which we reviewed ATLAS documentation, engaged in participant observation and conducted several interviews with ATLAS scientists—we became gradually aware of the interesting role played by simulations in the design, construction, and operation of the detector. That led us to the extension of the concept of boundary object from the physical detector to its representation through simulations. From the beginning of the design phase of a detector, when it is only a rough idea in the mind of a limited team of physicists, it is simulated with the help of sophisticated software tools. Through the construction phase, the simulated detector grows in detail and it becomes a quite faithful representation of the real object, which is used later in the operation phase to interpret the data obtained from the experiment. Our proposition was that those simulations, by absorbing some of the internal complexity of the different parts of the detector, facilitate the interaction between the diverse groups of scientists building and operating it. In this way, they act as a supplementary evolving boundary object that contributes to the coordination of the collaboration (Canals, Boisot, Ihrig, Nordberg, and Mabey 2011). This kind of coordination mechanism could become quite relevant in open innovation settings (Chesbrough 2006).

The second paper presents an argument that uses the case of ATLAS as an example to develop some ideas on the nature of knowledge (Boisot, Canals, Ihrig, and Nordberg 2011). In economics, particularly in theories of endogenous technical change and associated growth theories (Aghion and Howitt 1998; Romer 1990), knowledge is taken to be non-rival and partially excludable because of learning and spillover dynamics. By analyzing the data acquisition process in the ATLAS experiment through Boisot's theoretical frameworks, we concluded that certain kinds of knowledge are in fact rivalrous. Although access to data may be in theory free to everyone, in fact access to relevant information and, therefore, to new knowledge is restricted to those that possess the previous knowledge needed to interpret that information adequately. With reference to the resource-based view of the firm (Barney 1991; Helfat et al. 2007; Wernerfelt 1984), it is precisely this rivalrous kind of knowledge that forms the basis of an organization's core competences and its competitive advantage. But surprisingly endogenous growth theory does not seem to consider this, reflecting a limited view of the nature of the knowledge that underpins competitive behavior.

Conclusion

The four short years that Max Boisot dedicated to the study of big science through the analysis of the ATLAS experiment produced extremely fruitful results. Using the *I-Space* framework and its associated theoretical ideas together with his wit and talent, Boisot was able to develop a great number of deep insights on the nature of the knowledge-related processes in this activity, as he had done previously with firms and other institutions.

The ideas we have sketched here are only the ones he had time to develop. But he had started to work on several other insights. Some of them are already presented in *Collisions and Collaboration*, while others emerged in several work discussions at CERN. Together they constituted what may be described as a program of research on knowledge and big science. The following are some of the main avenues of inquiry within this program:

- Development of further insights on the nature of the processes of knowledge creation and transfer derived from the study of scientific experiments.
- The strategic management of knowledge in big scientific institutions and collaborations: identification and mapping of relevant knowledge assets (see Chapter 7).

- Characterization of the distinctive features of institutional culture in modern scientific institutions.
- Study of the mechanisms of knowledge integration in big scientific collaborations characterized by a large degree of diversity between their members.
- Identification of adequate mechanisms to foster innovation derived from the knowledge produced in big basic research experiments and the possible application of open innovation schemes.
- Scientific governance structures and their adaptation to a situation of restricted budgets and an increasing demand for a higher return from science activity to society (Boisot and Nordberg 2011).
- Adaptation of strategic thinking to situations with a high degree of uncertainty, e.g. with the use of real options thinking (see Chapter 16, by Markus Nordberg).
- Organizational and personal learning in big science collaborations (Bressan and Boisot 2011).
- Distinctive characteristics of leadership in scientific enterprises (Liyanage and Boisot 2011).
- The effects on science of the development of ICTs: e-science (Hoffmann, Nordberg, and Boisot 2011).

Unfortunately Max Boisot will not be able to complete this ambitious program, but his ideas will continue to serve as inspiration for those that had the pleasure to know him and for others that will come. Trying to follow some of his insights will be our way of honoring his memory.

Part VI
Innovations in Education

10

Chinese Boxes and Learning Cubes: Action Learning in a Cross-Cultural Context*

Max Boisot and Michel Fiol

Introduction

Any learning situation involves in some degree the acquisition of knowledge or its utilization; learning to learn can then be viewed as the ability to devise strategies for the acquisition of knowledge that are appropriate to the circumstances in which such learning is likely to be applied. Various learning strategies have sometimes been given their own labels—i.e. deutero learning (Bateson 1980) or double-loop learning (Argyris and Schön 1978)—in the examples cited, each implying a certain detachment, a certain ability to remove oneself from the immediacy of the learning situation in order to perceive the larger pattern to which one must ultimately respond.

Yet learning to learn is a costly, time-consuming activity that is quite uncertain and risky in its outcome. Few formal training programs can afford to develop learning strategies that have such long incubation periods and offer so little in the way of a tangible output. Not only do they often require considerable adaptation to the learning styles of individual participants and a consequent loss of standardization, but the sensitivities and skills they require of the trainer tend to put them out of reach of most time-harassed practitioners. For many of them, learning to learn is either what we do unconsciously every waking moment—like Mr. Jourdain with prose, we have always had learning strategies but simply did not know it—or it is a counsel of perfection. In either case, it is the learner's not the trainer's, problem.

* Originally published as Max Boisot and Michel Fiol (1987). "Chinese Boxes and Learning Cubes: Action Learning in a Cross-Cultural Context." *Journal of Management Development*, 6 (2): 8–18. Reprinted with kind permission of Emerald Insight.

Is it? Action learning probably comes closest to seeing the process as one in which the learner and the trainer share responsibility for developing a suitable strategy. To put the matter in pseudo-Husserlian terms, *learning-in-the-world* draws from a broader repertoire than *learning-about-the-world* and involves learning how to make a strategic selection and combination of repertoire elements. We may all, as learners, have a strategy, but it is not necessarily a good one, and although sooner or later we have to make our own choices, just like grown-ups, in the early phases we may need to be guided towards those strategies that work best for us.

As an educational philosophy, action learning can be distinguished from others by the extent to which it addresses concrete real world problems, gives autonomy (not independence) to the learner and promotes learning through peer group interaction. We might represent these three characteristics of action learning as the end points of three dimensions that make up *the Learning Cube*, an analytical framework that allows a strategic analysis of diverse learning situations.

The Learning Cube is a simple diagnostic tool that has been developed by the authors to analyze and evaluate a training program in the People's Republic of China (PRC) that they have both been involved in: the China-EEC Management Programme (CEMP). As a tool, the cube is still a "blunt instrument" and has not yet been operationalized. It needs more refinement and testing before it can be used with any confidence on a wider scale. Yet its conceptual foundations need to be presented and discussed now, in the early phases of its development. After all, the higher you want to build, the deeper you must first dig.

In this paper, therefore, we shall first present the Learning Cube in outline form. Next we shall briefly describe the main features of the CEMP. In the third section we shall try to interpret the CEMP in strategic learning terms by a non-rigorous and informal application of the Learning Cube. Finally, we shall conclude the paper with a discussion of possible improvements to the CEMP suggested by our analysis.

The Learning Cube

If action learning occupies the end points of three dimensions, what are the dimensions? Taking them in turn, they are:

> *The Abstraction-Concreteness Dimension (ACD)*
> Abstraction involves the ability to simplify one's representation of the world by a judicious selection of its most relevant characteristics; such modeling is purposive in the sense that the selection is guided by what one wants from the world.

Concreteness, by contrast, calls for an ability to evoke the world in all its particulars, to acknowledge and embrace its richness. The move from abstraction to concreteness, then, essentially describes a process of "filling-in."

The Direction-Autonomy Dimension (DAD)
Directed learning implies a willingness to submit to knowledge-based authority in the acquisition and use of knowledge; autonomous learning on the other hand is achieved when one has the knowledge and confidence to act as one's own authority.

The Individual-Group Dimension (IGD)
Individual learning takes place when learning objectives can be achieved without social interaction; group learning, conversely, requires some form of interaction with peers or teachers in the learning process.

These three dimensions make up the Learning Cube shown in Figure 10.1. It should be clear from our brief description that a learner rarely occupies a fixed point along any of these dimensions but that he moves dynamically along them at a speed and within a range dictated by such features of his learning situation as his own preferred learning style, the prevailing educational philosophy, the resources available, and so on. The vertexes of our cube describe identifiable learning situations that give our model empirical reference (see Figure 10.2). Briefly, they are:

Vertex A—Directed/Abstract/Individual
Example: A learner working his way through textbook exercises at home, where he submits either to the authority of the text itself or of an absent teacher.

Vertex B—Directed/Abstract/Collective
Example: A team of two or three students carrying out a laboratory experiment under an instructor's supervision.

Vertex C—Autonomous/Abstract/Individual
Example: A learner solving a mathematical problem heuristically at home.

Vertex D—Directed/Concrete/Individual
Example: A learner ploughing his way through a personal computer user's manual at home.

Vertex E—Autonomous/Abstract/Collective
Example: A group of learners solving together a mathematical problem heuristically without an instructor's supervision.

Vertex F—Directed/Concrete/Collective
Example: Supervised cabin crew training for airline stewards and hostesses.

Vertex G—Autonomous/Concrete/Individual
Example: The individual lathe operator "watching Nelly" as part of an on-the-job training program.

Vertex H—Autonomous/Concrete/Collective
Example: An action learning "Set," addressing a real world problem within an enterprise.

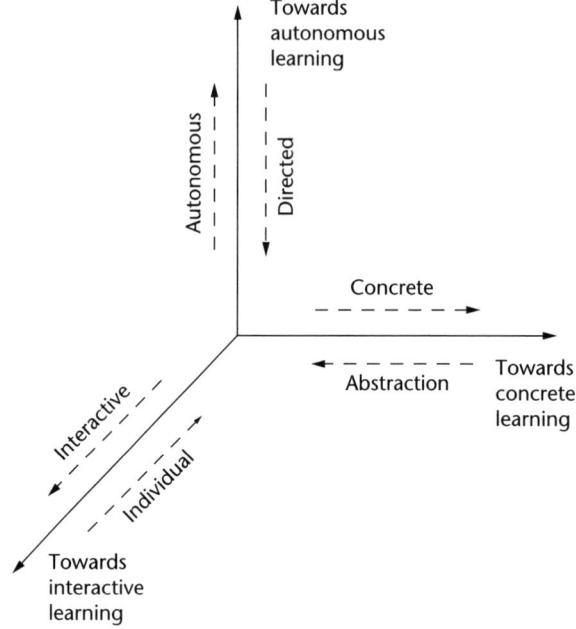

Figure 10.1. The three dimensions of learning

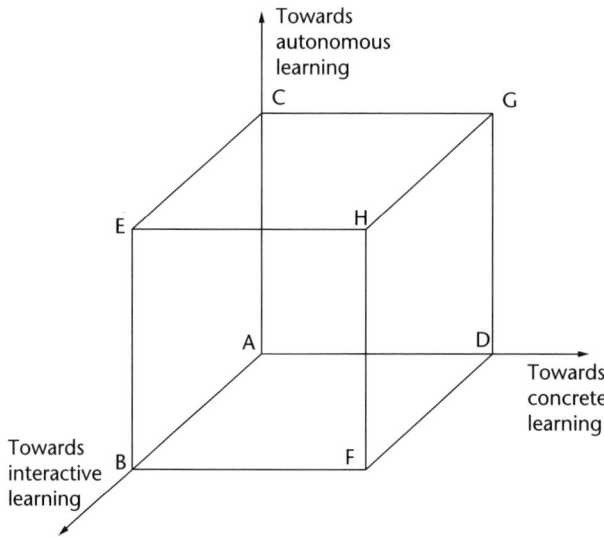

Figure 10.2. The Learning Cube

Although educational philosophies may push towards one region of the cube rather than another, it is the individual learner's existing stock of skills with respect to what he is required to learn that ultimately constrains the final choices. Thus if learning consists of developing a repertoire of responses appropriate to a variety of situations we are led to the following simple propositions:

Proposition 1: Effective learning consists of filling the Learning Cube rather than occupying a single position within it.

Proposition 2: Developing a learning strategy consists of specifying a path in the learning space through which the cube can be filled.

Thus learning to learn presupposes that gaps in the Learning Cube can be identified in such a way that a learning path can be specified. The approach is eclectic and not wedded to any given "one best way" of learning; it is contingent on the profile of the learner and the specifics of the situation that calls for a learning response. In practice, however, the Learning Cube may appear to promise more than can be delivered. Available strategies—i.e. paths—are not necessarily feasible ones.

One particularly important constraint that we now wish to explore is that imposed by culture. To what extent, we may ask, do culturally determined educational values bias the choice of strategy so as to favor certain regions of the Learning Cube at the expense of others?

Since the Learning Cube remains a conceptual rather than an operational tool, we can only hint at an answer here. Yet an action learning management training program in the People's Republic of China offers a fruitful field of investigation. As we shall presently see, the dominant value system in Chinese education favors learning strategies that are confined to a region around Vertex A of the cube. The CEMP if anything has a vertex H philosophy, but one tempered by an awareness of the filling that first had to be done in other parts of the cube. How are such divergences reconciled in practice?

The China-EEC Management Programme (CEMP)

Since the program has already been described in Boisot (1986a), it will only be recapitulated here in a summary form.

The system reforms that have been in progress in China since 1979 have brought home to the leadership the urgent need for extensive management training in state-owned and collective enterprises. In October 1984 the Central Committee of the Chinese Communist Party introduced a number of enterprise reforms designed to give the market mechanism greater scope in regulating the performance of Chinese industry. Industrial enterprises would have more freedom to set their own prices and determine their own output and they would be responsible for their own profits and losses. As an incentive to better performance they would be allowed to retain a part of their profits and distribute it as bonuses to the workforce. In order to concentrate the minds of the laggards within the industrial sector, a bankruptcy law would be introduced that would allow firms to perish as well as prosper. This law, today, is alive and kicking and has just claimed as its first victim an ammunition factory in the city of Shenyang.

In 1985, fiscal reforms were introduced that would establish a more arm's length relationship between the industrial sector and the state, and this year the need to create some kind of a free labor market—at least for qualified people—is currently under discussion among policy makers. Clearly, the way in which Chinese enterprises are managed will have to change if the reforms are to succeed. But how? What kind of managers are effectively going to be needed in a system that ideologically speaking is neither fish nor fowl, that is, neither wholly centrally planned, nor wholly market driven? To what configuration of values should they respond and what skills should they possess? No affirmative answers to these questions could be given either by the Chinese leaders themselves or, for that matter, by anyone else. The scope and extent of the reforms were simply too great to allow pat answers.

In a characteristically pragmatic way, the Chinese leaders, working through the State Economic Commission (SEC), decided to seek out foreign help in developing a Chinese managerial model appropriate to their circumstances and invited certain countries to co-sponsor the creation of National Management Training Centers in which different foreign approaches to management training and development would be tried out. The SEC would then choose that approach which best suited the country's requirements. According to this scheme, American management would be taught in the city of Dalian, Japanese management in Tianjin, Canadian management in Chengdu, and European management in Beijing. In each case management would be taught as it is taught "back home" and the adaptation to local circumstances would be carried out by the Chinese themselves.

Such an approach to the transfer of management skills typifies the Chinese approach to the transfer of technology in general. It can be best understood with the help of a diagram (Figure 10.3). On the left hand side of the diagram a set of skills is developed in a foreign context. The Chinese wish to receive these skills without recreating the context which they regard as alien to their culture. Yet the skills being transferred to the right hand side of the diagram may be likened to the transplanting of an organ that will suffer rejection unless the host culture—in this case the Chinese context—undergoes a number of adjustments that will ensure a good match. How should this adjustment be carried out? The Chinese view is that theirs is an opaque

Chinese Boxes and Learning Cubes

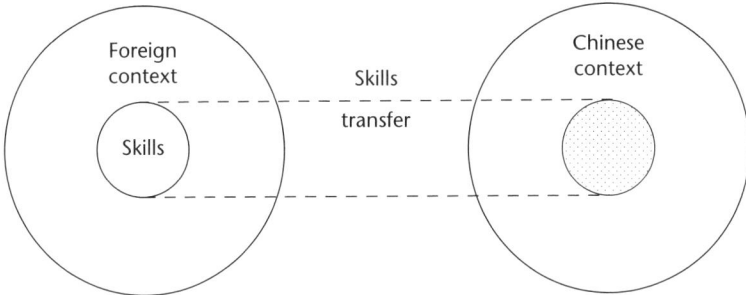

Figure 10.3. The traditional Chinese view of technology transfer

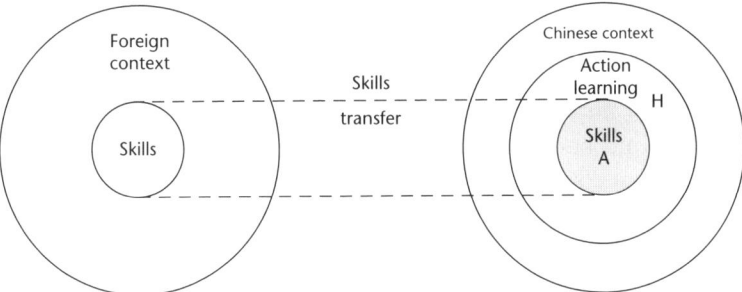

Figure 10.4. The CEMP approach to technology transfer

culture, generally inaccessible to foreigners and that only they understand their context enough to carry out the necessary adjustments. So what was the SEC asking for? Two sequential management training programs, the first being run for 35 managers, the second for 70, each leading to an MBA. The programs were to teach management as it was taught in Europe. They would be preceded by a six months intensive English course and would be followed by a six months in-company training period in Europe. However, an alternative view of the transfer process might be that, like fish swimming in water, the Chinese are not always going to see in what part of their culture adjustments will be called for, so that some foreign involvement in the adjustment process would be needed. Such was the view on which the CEMP proposal was developed, with action learning mediating between a set of management skills from which a selection would have to be made, and a cultural context in which those skills actually selected would have to be integrated. The approach is described schematically in Figure 10.4.

The CEMP, then, financed by the EEC Commission and working as far as possible within the constraints imposed by its future Chinese partners, offered in response a project-based approach that would work as follows:

175

(1) Students would be placed in teams of five or six, and each team would be appointed as consultant to a Beijing-based state owned enterprise for the duration of the MBA. Half their MBA credits would come from projects carried out within these enterprises and the other half would come from conventional classroom work.

(2) In the first year of their two-year MBA course—this excludes both the language and the in-company training periods—they would only carry out descriptive work inside their enterprises, mapping out their production, financial, marketing, and human resource systems, using Western-based analytical tools presented in class. In the second year they would act as consultants to the firm, addressing one or more key problems faced by the enterprise acting on the knowledge they acquired in the first year.

(3) Western case studies and conventional course texts would be used sparingly and cautiously, particularly where they presupposed a background knowledge of the Western business environment—i.e. of the foreign context. An additional reason for exercising care in the use of Western teaching material had to do with the limited language skills of the students. Merely by imposing a conventional MBA reading load on students with limited reading skills, one could almost guarantee that the more conventional classroom component of the course would quickly swallow up the time available for the project component.

The proposed approach was designed to ensure that the teaching would not take place in a vacuum and that the process of adapting the material to the requirements of the Chinese economic environment would become a constituent part of the learning experience itself. It was important not to have participants casting overboard their expensively acquired Western educational baggage—3.5 million ECUs over five years was the budgeted cost of CEMP—at the first sign of bad weather when they returned to their enterprises at the end of the course.

The Chinese response to the approach outlined above can only be described as caution tempered by anxiety. For the SEC the risks of failure were perceived to be considerable in an aid project that had a high political profile. For the students, reared on a diet of rote learning and over-predictable curricula, the prospects of having to work in such an unstructured and interdependent situation—they would be getting group grades for their project work—was a source of many misgivings. Finally, for the targeted enterprises themselves, when they were finally approached, the idea of giving detailed company data to outsiders was bad enough; making it available to foreigners was quite unheard of. Nevertheless after a certain amount of cajoling and persuasion, the SEC decided to give the approach a try, and subsequently applied to the

State Council—the PRC's highest governing body—for permission to open up Chinese industrial enterprises to foreign gaze. Six state-owned enterprises were "instructed" to accept the CEMP's student teams and the program kicked off with six months of language training (run by the Language Learning Centre of the Manchester Business School) in September 1984.

The CEMP is now entering its third year of operation; the first MBA program is now drawing to a close and a provisional assessment—obviously subject to revision—is now possible.

— The students started off with a strong bias towards theory and abstract concepts. The projects were therefore initially perceived to be a troublesome distraction from the "real" learning task and the playing down of book learning and examinations caused some perplexity.

— Yet the enterprises, by proving far more co-operative than could have been hoped for—some are now asking to have a team of students from the second MBA program—gradually built up the status of the enterprise projects. As students gained confidence in their work they started to take initiatives such as carrying out their own market surveys on behalf of enterprises or addressing specific issues at the firm's request. In doing this some of them have become aware that they have acquired something more than the mechanical ability to apply a management technique.

— The continued bias towards "armchair theorizing" has pushed some of the students' teams towards over-ambitious and impractical consultancy projects in their second year. The scaling down of expectations and settling for more modest and realistic projects have been a source of frustration to those who did not expect to find the real world so messy and refractory to the elegant application of technique.

— Students are still finding it difficult to work effectively in groups. There is a tendency to break down project work into individual work packages that are then reassembled in an additive fashion, with little group evaluation, discussion or co-ordination. But most groups are learning fast—under the pressure of grades, of course!

A Learning Cube interpretation of CEMP

An intuitive application of the Learning Cube shows Chinese students starting their course with a strong vertex "A" orientation as evidenced by a strong preference for abstract learning, clear authoritative direction from a teacher, and independent work in which they could shine as individuals. Taken in isolation, such an orientation might prove sufficient for the acquisition of certain types of Western management skills but would prove of little value in learning how to apply and adapt them. What the economic reforms called for was a learning style that could cope with complex and rapidly changing real world problems (concrete), was willing to take risks and learn from mistakes (autonomy) and was willing to accept interdependencies (group learning). In other words, in order to absorb disembodied Western management techniques, China needed managers trained at "H."

Yet "H" could not form a point of departure for management training in the PRC given that in the field of management the rest of the Learning Cube was almost empty. In Western countries, for example, action learning programs are only effective when they can build on a prior knowledge base acquired elsewhere. The CEMP's learning strategy, therefore, would have to be one that created a diagonal path from "A" to "H" and built up both regions in an iterative fashion.

The key problem for such a strategy, of course, is that while a pedagogical investment in "A" is compatible with traditional Chinese educational values, the investment in "H" is not, so that the path from the former to the latter has to be constructed with care. Moving along the path involves much more than broadening one's learning repertoire; it calls for a change in a number of core cultural values that will prove much more painful in China than in Western countries where the cultural context for such a move is more supportive from the outset. Nevertheless, the move is essential, for in the next 20 years it will be the learning skills acquired at "H" that will determine whether Chinese managers can absorb and adapt Western technology and management skills located at "A."

Conclusion

Does the foregoing discussion suggest improvements in the way that the CEMP goes about achieving its strategic learning objectives? Three come to mind.

— Use the six months period of the English language course to promote "H"-type learning in a non-threatening way, i.e. no grades given. This is directly under CEMP's control and quite feasible. It will be tried out with the second MBA intake.

— Release further resources for the continuing development of "H"-type learning, such as time, teachers, etc. by capitalizing on the students' already highly developed "A"-type learning skills. Some of CEMP's current classroom teaching, for example, could be packaged in such a way as to encourage more self-study, possibly using a distance learning

format. Classroom activities could then be reoriented towards more "H"-type work. Discussions are currently under way with the SEC to explore this possibility.
— Create incentives that make "H"-type learning more rewarding. Unfortunately, this last suggestion is, for the most part, quite outside the CEMP's control. Indeed, it presupposes the very cultural changes that "H"-type learning is designed to bring about.

To conclude, the Learning Cube is still the work of amateur carpenters rather than joiners, but as a conceptual framework it has allowed the authors to gain a better idea of where they were coming from and where they were heading for in a complex cross-cultural situation.

11

Innovations in Education

Dana Kaminstein and John Child

No one who knew Max Boisot even briefly could doubt that they were in the company of a master-teacher, a person whose life revolved around learning and diffusing knowledge, an educator in the deep sense of the term (Chen 2012; Dornfeld 2012). Our purpose in this chapter is to examine Max's writings on education and his educational practices to identify the ways in which they were innovative.

Although Max wrote little about his educational ideas and philosophy, he impacted dozens of colleagues and hundreds of students in often profound and long-lasting ways. In order to supplement Max's writing on education we have interviewed a number of colleagues and former students.[1] In addition, the authors of this chapter both worked closely with Max on different continents. John Child followed Max as Dean of the CEMI (originally CEMP) Program in China and co-authored some seminal papers with him (Boisot and Child 1988; Boisot and Child 1996a, b; Boisot and Child 1999). Dana Kaminstein first worked with Max on a leadership development program in South Africa, numerous short leadership development programs at Wharton Executive Education and then on the design and implementation of a Global Learning Journey run by Wharton Executive Education.

Max was an innovator in the full sense of the term. He tackled complex theoretical tasks, and always tried to put theories to the test via practice. During our interviews, the term "visionary" was used a number of times in reference to Max. In this chapter we will examine Max's largely uncodified educational philosophy and practice to see what aspects of it can be categorized as innovative. We believe that by examining Max's writing about education and his educational philosophy and practice we can:

---

[1] Chen (2012), Dornfeld (2012), Lu (2012), Mabey (2012), MacMillan (2012).

1) Continue to build the bridge between theory and practice that was so important to Max.
2) Provide some increased and preliminary codification of Max's nascent educational ideas, so that they can be more widely diffused.
3) Discuss some of Max's educational practices that may help the field of management education attune its philosophy and practice more precisely to the needs of the executives, managers and students it is eager to reach and impact.

We define management education innovations as those that provide new approaches, frames, methods, and technologies to the practice of management education. Management education innovations can be divided into the following categories:

1) philosophical innovations
2) design innovations
3) methodological/instructional innovations
4) technological innovations
5) innovations related to the transfer of knowledge
6) innovations related to the reception of knowledge.

In the educational literature a number of these categories would be subsumed under the more general heading of "pedagogy" (i.e. philosophical, design, methodological, instructional, and technological). Actually, the more appropriate term to use would be Andragogy as this refers to the art and science of teaching adults (Knowles, Holton, and Swanson 1973/1998). We have chosen to examine these categories, as they help to illustrate the range of management education innovations that Max Boisot developed directly or indirectly.

Innovations in management education philosophy

Max's conception of the *I-Space* provides a number of clear philosophical innovations for management education. These philosophical innovations are perhaps most obvious in "Crossing Epistemological Boundaries: Managerial and Entrepreneurial Approaches to Knowledge Management" (Boisot and MacMillan 2007). Epistemology focuses on the nature and justification of knowledge (Audi 1995). Boisot and MacMillan were concerned with "what constitutes valid knowledge for who and under what circumstances. Epistemology provides the basis for action and thus serves as a foundation for the institutionalization of practice" (2007, 52). In this essay Boisot and MacMillan are particularly concerned with understanding what type of knowledge would be most meaningful and relevant to managers, as opposed to entrepreneurs.

The *I-Space* is a philosophical innovation for management education because it provides a basis on which to make thoughtful and hypothetically based decisions about what type of knowledge is most relevant to what type of management student in what contextual circumstances. Applying the *I-Space* enabled Max to distinguish three types of knowledge according to their level of codification and ease of sharing (diffusion), as shown in Figure 11.1. These types of knowledge are experiential, narrative and abstract symbolic. One of the key tenets of Max's educational philosophy is that students should be encouraged to move back and forth between these levels of knowledge. This enables them to combine conceptual abstraction with concrete experience—preferably their own, but also that provided by case studies—so that they can appreciate the practical value of applying good theory to specific situations and equally the need always to theorize reflectively about their own experience.

By way of illustration, take the MBA program that Max helped to design and initiate in China in 1984 (Child and Chen 2009). This was the first MBA program to be offered in China and it still exists, albeit in modified form, having migrated to the newly founded CEIBS in 1994 (Child and Chen 2009, 29). Other Western educational programs that were coming to China at that time chose to stick with traditional methods of instruction, which was mostly in lecture format (Boisot and Fiol 1987—current volume; Child and Chen 2009, 30–1; Chen 2012). In contrast, the MBA program that Max helped to design emphasized project work by the MBA students, a deep form of action learning (Child and Chen 2009, 30). At first glance, action learning seems like the wrong educational method in the wrong circumstance because it did not rely on educational methods that were familiar to Chinese students (Boisot

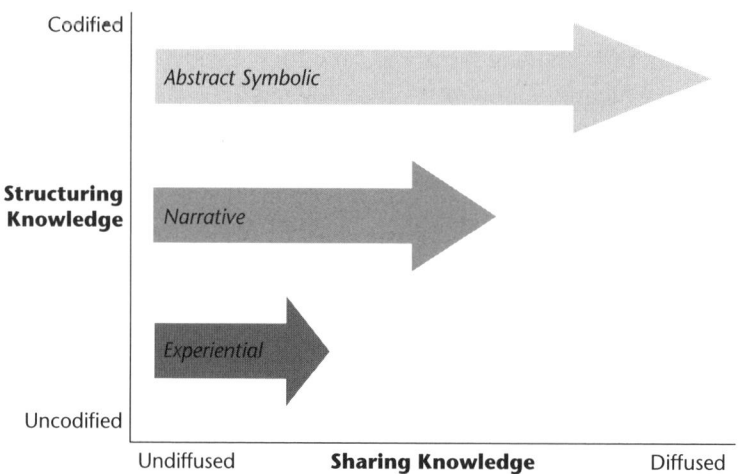

Figure 11.1. Types of knowledge identified by the *I-Space*

and Fiol 1987—current volume). However, the *I-Space* (or as Max called it at that time, "the C-Space") (Boisot 1987b) provided Max with a way of understanding educational needs that was grounded in a sophisticated and more complex understanding of the Chinese context (Boisot and Fiol 1987—current volume).

First, the *I-Space* helped Max plot the current state of Chinese managerial education (Boisot 2007, 153). In 1984 Chinese managerial education was in the lower left-hand side of the *I-Space* (relatively uncodified and undiffused). Although Western management education was quite codified by 1984, imposing Western management education on China in a wholesale fashion was likely to ignore the important and crucial distinctions between Chinese firms and Western firms, and the economic environment in which they existed. The article in this volume, "Chinese Boxes and Learning Cubes: Action Learning in a Cross Cultural Context" by Boisot and Fiol (originally published in 1987) represents an early formulation of hypotheses about what learning approach would work best with Chinese MBA students in the mid-1980s. It is clear that this early paper presaged an innovative way of understanding the Chinese context, in order to help Chinese students move toward a learning style that could "cope with complex and rapidly changing real work problems (concrete), was willing to take risks and learn from mistakes (autonomy) and was willing to accept interdependencies (group learning)" (Boisot and Fiol 1987, 17—current volume).

The *I-Space* gave Max crucial theoretical information. The problem was how to move Chinese management education up the ladder of codification without losing important contextual and cultural features (Boisot 2007, 157). Although not immediately obvious, Max argued that the answer was to use action learning (Boisot and Fiol 1987—current volume). Action learning would help MBA students, using management practices and tools, to codify aspects of state-owned enterprises, thus contributing to developing understanding of both individual firms and how they operate within the Chinese bureaucratic structure (Child and Chen 2009, 32–3). There were, of course, other alternatives to this process of increasing codification, but those such as deploying dozens of faculty members and/or consultants to examine and assess a range of Chinese state-owned enterprises would have taken an extraordinary amount of time and money. Even if these costs could have been surmounted, there were not enough trained faculty or consultants in China who could have done this work.

Using action learning accomplished a number of goals simultaneously. It gave the graduate students practical experience with assessing and diagnosing organizations, applying the concepts and theories they were learning in the classroom and proposing and implementing ways to improve efficiency in state-owned enterprises (Boisot and Fiol 1987—current volume; Child and Chen 2009, 30–2). Interestingly enough, as the students helped to codify knowledge about the individual firms they were working with, they also diffused the knowledge they were acquiring in the classroom in their diagnostic and consulting work with the state-owned enterprise. Here the *I-Space* not only gave Max a framework from which to begin to solve the issue of lack of codification, but it also suggested the impact (diffusion) that the knowledge gained by the management students would have on the larger system.

According to a recent history of the program (Child and Chen 2009) and two of those we interviewed (Chen 2012; Lu 2012), there was resistance to using action learning as a main focus of the MBA program (Child and Chen 2009, 33–4). The opposition came in a number of forms. First, some government officials were worried that Western faculty would gain private knowledge about Chinese state-owned enterprises by supervising and evaluating the student projects (Boisot and Fiol 1987—current volume). This was a predictable response from an *I-Space* perspective, as China was very much in the bureaucratic quadrant of the *I-Space* at that time, with a strong desire to not diffuse its firm-related and economic knowledge.

There was also some opposition from the students. Some students wanted to study Western cases and experience, as they believed they could learn more than by studying a Chinese state-owned enterprise (Child and Chen 2009, 33–4). Was this perhaps a desire by the Chinese students to have more easily digestible (because it was more highly codified) information and knowledge from Western cases? Did it also reflect the then traditional Chinese mode of rote learning? Max and others recognized that although studying Western cases might make the learning more acceptable to the students in the short run, it would work against them in the long run. They would be applying codified knowledge to Chinese circumstances that was very different from the circumstances (Western economies and firms) from which the information and knowledge was derived (Child and Chen 2009).

There was also concern about whether they could get enough state-owned enterprises to open their doors to a team of MBA students who would be scrutinizing their operations. Again, this reaction was predictable as noted above, by locating the Chinese state-owned enterprises on the *I-Space*. It is likely that most state-owned enterprises did not want knowledge of their firm to be diffused beyond a very small audience of mostly insiders.

One can imagine that in 1984 there would have been a strong temptation to design a management education program based on traditional methods of learning in China. China was just opening up to the West, and commonsense might have dictated that when introducing Western management tools and concepts it would be wise to stick with instructional methods that Chinese students were comfortable with. However, Max realized that using a largely lecture format for an MBA program would not help codify the current management practices in China; it would not help students to come to grips with how to apply Western concepts and tools to Chinese firms; and this passive form of learning would not actively engage students in grappling with the ideas and concepts the faculty was presenting (Boisot and Fiol 1987—current volume).

Despite some initial resistance to action learning via project work, as the *I-Space* predicted, it was the right learning methodology for that time in Chinese management education history. Students came to see the value of the action learning work, and one interviewee noted that this type of learning was intellectually challenging as well as helping him to understand the management concepts he was learning in class in a practical and applied way (Lu 2012). State-owned enterprises also found the students' work to be valuable to them, with some enterprises saying that the work done by the students was better than that of the consultants they hired (Chen 2012; Lu 2012).

These examples of how the *I-Space* provides a basis for understanding and determining what managerial educational methods and processes are appropriate illustrates that the *I-Space* is a tool that can help determine what "constitutes valid knowledge for who under what circumstances" (Boisot and MacMillan 2007, 52). In this sense, the *I-Space* is an epistemological tool that has innovative managerial educational uses.

Innovations in managerial educational design

There are at least three other examples of innovative educational designs that Max Boisot developed. One was a program for Chinese entrepreneurs, which was not successful. The second was a Global Learning Journey that Max designed for three cohorts of executives from Dubai, which was very successful. The third concerns his proposal for the management of PhD programs.

In 2002, Max Boisot and Ian MacMillan came up with the idea of training Chinese entrepreneurs via a virtual classroom format (MacMillan 2012). In part, this idea came out of the work that Max and Ian MacMillan had done on the epistemological differences between managers and entrepreneurs. Once again, the *I-Space* provided some of the epistemology behind this innovative design. Like the state of management understanding in China in 1984, the state of entrepreneurial understanding in China in 2002 was relatively uncodified. To merely impose Western entrepreneurial understanding on Chinese entrepreneurs would have been misleading to them, would not have valued their own entrepreneurial experience, and would have succumbed once again to a passive learning format. Instead, Boisot and MacMillan envisioned gathering a group of Chinese entrepreneurs together in a classroom in China with the instructors brought into the classroom via the Internet. This innovative format solved a number of issues. One, it greatly reduced expenses.

The format meant that Western faculty did not have to travel to China to conduct these classes, and so entrepreneurs could obtain this educational experience at a much lower cost. Secondly, by having the Chinese entrepreneurs gather together in a classroom, the format could include face-to-face discussions, exchange of ideas, and reports on projects. This format captures the engagement involved when entrepreneurs/students meet face-to-face, while capitalizing on the use of a range of Western faculty without extensive time and travel expenses. Unfortunately, the program did not get off the ground, not because of the design, but because at that time the Internet connection with China was unreliable and the class kept losing contact with the instructors during sessions. Not surprisingly, the entrepreneurs' patience for an unreliable Internet connection and fuzzy or lost instructors quickly waned.

Wharton Executive Education asked Max to design and implement a Global Learning Journey for a group of executives from Dubai. Max worked with three cohorts of Dubai executives between 2006 and 2008. The design involved a day of pre-work at Wharton several months before the journey, in which Max oriented the cohort to the upcoming trip and briefed them on some issues related to the city-states (Singapore and Hong Kong) that they would be visiting. The actual learning journey lasted approximately seven days, with about three days in each city-state, and a day for travel from one city to the other. Sub-groups of the cohort were working simultaneously on action learning projects, and during the Global Learning Journey they worked in their action learning teams. In both Singapore and Hong Kong the executives visited firms and state agencies, and heard talks by government officials. Max gave each team questions that he wanted them to answer from their visits. After the visits each day, the group would assemble and report out about their visits, and Max would pull together themes from the visits that he wanted the participants to understand and examine more fully. Several months after the Global Learning Journey, the cohort reconvened at Wharton, and each team would report out about some of their key learnings from the experience. Max would help them integrate these learnings with the themes of the whole learning program.

Some of the logic of the Global Learning Journey was to take the Dubai executives out of their familiar milieu and culture and to expose them to other city-states that had some similarities with Dubai, but with a longer history. Max wanted to give the executives a chance to learn about the development cycles that city-states go through, as a way to help prepare the Dubai executives for dealing with some of the trends and uncertainties that their future held. In addition, he was particularly keen to have the Dubai executives understand more about how culture influences organizational design and performance, and to emphasize that culture has a great impact on economic development. He thought this could best be accomplished by giving these executives concentrated first-hand experience in two city-states other than their own.

Although many of the Dubai executives on the programs had traveled extensively, this was an educational experience and they were not on this trip as tourists. Accordingly, Max designed the whole experience and a number of specific exercises to highlight the learning he wanted the participants to encounter. As an example, on one evening in each city-state he gave the participants the assignment of being anthropologists, and they were sent forth with a series of cultural questions that they needed to answer and report back on the next day.

The design of both of these educational endeavors was innovative in a number of respects. The design of the classes with Chinese entrepreneurs attempted to exploit the positive aspects of recent communication technology (i.e. instructors being beamed via the Internet), in combination with bringing together groups of Chinese entrepreneurs who could learn from each other's experiences. Entrepreneurial knowledge from the West could be communicated to Chinese entrepreneurs while they acted as a filter to see what knowledge fitted their own circumstances and which needed to be modified. Had the experience worked, it would likely have increased the codification of Chinese entrepreneurial knowledge, and each successive class could have then diffused the knowledge to future groups and to a larger audience of entrepreneurs and managers.

Although the authors have heard of other global learning journeys, the design Max developed was unique. It involved: 1) helping participants investigate two other cultures and how each culture influences economic and social development of a city state, and 2) exposing participants to firms in other cultures at different stages of economic development. The other global learning journeys that the authors have heard about focus more on exposing executives to social issues in developing countries, to potential new markets (e.g. at the bottom of the pyramid—Prahalad 2005), or to giving executives a personally transformative experience.

These two innovative designs built on Max's understanding about the importance of context and culture. The *I-Space* helped to design educational experiences that would have moved knowledge to greater codification and diffusion. In the successful design, executives from Dubai learned about city-states whose knowledge of economic development was more advanced (codified), and they had the opportunity to bring these new understandings back to their organizations and city-state (hence absorbing and diffusing the knowledge they had gained).

The third innovation was one that Max proposed to the Birmingham Business School for its PhD program. Max discerned that there are two distinct aspects to the running of the doctoral learning and research process. The first is "program management", focused on making sure that students fulfill the formal requirements of the program and also keep up to speed. Program management can proceed on a codified basis and one person or office can apply the relevant codified procedures on a universalistic basis, "diffused" to all students on the program. Indeed, it can benefit from the availability of codified project management software. The other aspect of running a doctoral program is to provide students with academic guidance and stimulation. By contrast, this aspect is particularistic and concerned with facilitating the creation of new uncodified knowledge rather than with applying known techniques (cf. March 1991). It is also heavily dependent on the 'chemistry' between student and supervisor. Max noted that this contrast is why academic supervisors often make poor program managers. Because a suitable supervisor for a student's chosen topic might be located outside of the home university, and because students might also benefit from the combined support of several supervisors, Max envisaged that with the facilitation of modern ICTs, such as Skype, a bespoke network of supervisors could be appointed for each student. Whereas the program management aspect of the doctoral program would operate in the bureaucratic segment of the *I-Space*, the academic supervisory aspect would operate much less formally on a fief-like basis. If several students shared areas of interest and supervisors, they could form a community of practice operating like a small clan.

Methodological/instructional innovations in management education

We discuss two examples of Max's teaching methods/instructional style that were innovative. The first was the way in which Max combined consulting (providing deep knowledge about a company) with executive education or leadership development. The second example is Max's personal style, which although idiosyncratic in some ways, has aspects that others might be able to adopt to good effect.

It is now more commonplace to see instructors combining knowledge about a company with the teaching of more general managerial topics like finance, strategy, and organizational change. Some of this has come about as the demand for more customized (bespoke) programs has increased. However, as usual, Max was ahead of his time as he began combining consultative knowledge with his teaching in executive education or leadership development programs as early as 1998. In 1998 Kaminstein asked Max to teach for two days on the subject of strategy to a parastatal in South Africa. Max agreed to teach on the program only if he could do comprehensive background pre-work about the organization. Accordingly, he examined strategy documents from the company, interviewed key executives in the parastatal, and developed a number of hypotheses about the current state of the company's strategy beforehand. I (Kaminstein) remember detailed and spirited discussions with Max about where the company was headed, ways in which the current strategy was misguided, and plans for his two days of teaching.

Max undertook this teaching assignment as much as a consultant as he did as a teacher. He did not see his role as just giving the senior executives who were attending the program some general concepts about strategy, or reviewing recent developments in the field of strategy; instead he was determined to help them to think through their current strategy, its limitations and its strengths. He was troubled by what he viewed as a mismatch between the company's strategy and the current thrust of economic development in South Africa—as defined by the government—and the core competences and resources of the company.

The way he defined his role (i.e. consultant-instructor) was unusual at the time, and reflected an expanded definition of educator in a leadership development program. It was not just his personal investment and concern for this organization that motivated this combination of roles, but we would argue that it was his understanding of knowledge and how it gets transmitted and received. Max understood that general concepts, even compelling ones, were less likely to change people's understanding, much less their behaviors, unless they could apply it to their own circumstances. Furthermore, if you could illustrate that the bus the participants were driving was about to crash into a wall, you could not only gain people's attention, but you could also fulfill a mission of making knowledge relevant to people's immediate circumstances.

The second instructional innovation had to do with Max's teaching style. During the program described above in South Africa, Max spoke for a full two days. He rarely broke the group into subgroups for discussion, and there were only a few breaks. Max did not lecture, but rather his style was conversational. Max also used this conversational style when he introduced DBA students to the research process. What is amazing is that he employed this style in two four-day modules. From morning to evening for four days at a stretch he kept DBA students engaged in learning about the research process (Mabey 2012).

While listening to Max in front of a classroom one could easily imagine sitting in Max's living room. What made this conversation style work, and what made it so engaging, was a combination of Max's educational philosophy and his personal style. For Max education was a very broad endeavor, and involved making connections between different disciplines and ideas. Because Max was so well read, he could bring in articles and books from a wide range of fields and relate them to the matter at hand. In this sense, his intellectual understanding was very wide and also deep. However, Max was not pretentious or arrogant about his knowledge, so he engaged with students, managers, and executives as fellow travelers on a learning journey of great excitement (Dornfeld 2012; Lu 2012). Underlying his keen intellect and vast knowledge, we believe, was a curiosity and an excitement about learning that was infectious. Every encounter, every class, every meal was a chance to learn, to discover and to share that learning with others. In addition, several of those we interviewed remarked on Max's sense of humor. We can both attest to the fact that conversations with Max were never dull, and often included humorous observations or asides.

Is a conversational teaching style really innovative? Although this style may be rare, it is certainly not unique. Nevertheless, we argue that Max's teaching style was innovative because of its unusual combination of attributes: it was intellectually rigorous without being stuffy, it was thought-provoking—sometimes challenging—without being confrontational, it was wide-ranging without being unfocused, it was open to new ideas without being wishy-washy, it was erudite without being arrogant, it was deeply engaging without being sheer entertainment, and it was inspiring without playing on people's emotions. One of the people we interviewed (Mabey 2012) described Max's teaching style with great detail and passion, and yet thought that it was a style that would be difficult if not impossible to imitate. Although we would agree that no one could clone Max's teaching style, it does seem to us that there are some innovative aspects that we might want to emulate.

Although some of his style had to do with his unique background and personality, some of it appears to have grown out of his understanding about knowledge (Boisot and Li 2007a). His development of the Social Learning Cycle helped him to more deeply understand the process by which we absorb new learning (Boisot 2002, 74). The first step of the social learning cycle is scanning. In the educational enterprise this has to do with assessing what the audience you are addressing needs to learn. Max did this with the leaders in the parastatal in South Africa and also with the DBA students at the University of Birmingham. The second step of the social learning cycle is problem solving. What are the problems or dilemmas that the leaders in South Africa or the DBA students are likely to encounter? The third step in the social learning cycle is abstraction. How can one take the concepts and codify them in ways that the executives or students can understand? The fourth step in the social learning cycle is diffusion. How best to share this codified knowledge with this particular group? The fifth step is absorption. This is where Max used his conversational style, filled with broad knowledge and examples from his experience, to help the executives/students to absorb what he was presenting. The sixth step is impacting. This step is more apparent in the action learning used in the CEMI program. However, Max also engaged executives/students in thought experiments that enabled the codified information he was presenting to be absorbed more fully. Viewing Max's teaching style through the lens of the social learning cycle indicates that it was more than personal teaching charisma. Using the social learning cycle as a guide to one's instructional method is innovative, as it breaks down the teaching process in steps that are related to the needs of the learner. One might even say that the social learning cycle helps the teacher/instructor to become more learner-centric and less focused on his or her own style.

Technological managerial educational innovations

By technological educational innovations we mean new methods, processes, and devices that change how learning is diffused, delivered or absorbed. Max Boisot and Ian MacMillan (MacMillan 2012), as discussed above, attempted to use a recent technological development (the Internet) to teach entrepreneurism to Chinese entrepreneurs. Although this indicates Max's vision, as Ian MacMillan told us "he was ahead of his time." Since the technology was slow and often crashed, the program was called off while it was still in its first iteration. One can only imagine how different the results would have been if the technology were as developed as it is today—or even a few years later.

The Global Learning Journey is certainly a new learning process. It was innovative in a number of respects: 1) it was a cross-cultural learning experience, 2) participants had the opportunity to compare and contrast the organizations they worked for with organizations in two city-states, 3) participants learned about the ways in which economic and social development impact organizations and the broader marketplace, and 4) participants had the opportunity to reflect on their learnings individually, in small groups, and in the whole group.

The *I-Space* is most certainly a technological innovation, as well as an epistemological innovation. Recent work (Boisot, MacMillan, and Han 2007) indicates that computer simulations using the *I-Space* may not only increase our knowledge about the future trajectory of knowledge in firms and how two or more firms fit in terms of their knowledge capabilities and interests, but it may also be an educational tool. Martin Ihrig (2012) is continuing this work.

Innovations in transferring managerial knowledge

There is an extensive literature on the transfer of learning, ranging from a bestselling book (Heath and Heath 2007/2008) to studies by developmental psychologists that document in great detail the transfer of learning process (Lobato 2006; Longenecker 2004; Wagner 2006). Max was very interested in the issue of knowledge transfer. Both the *I-Space* and the Social Learning Cycle (*SLC*) helped to predict and understand how knowledge was transferred (Boisot and Li 2007a; Boisot and Li 2007b; Boisot, MacMillan, and Han 2007).

The *I-Space* makes the assumption that until knowledge is codified, it is very difficult to transfer to another agent or agents (Boisot and Li 2007b). In addition, the *I-Space* predicts under what circumstances transfer happens more slowly/narrowly, as opposed to more quickly/broadly.

Max had a sense of the complexity involved in the transfer of knowledge. "[I]n reality it is never knowledge as such that flows between agents, but data. Some measure of resonance can be achieved between the knowledge states of two agents that are sharing the same data—we call this 'getting on the same wavelength'" (Boisot 2002, 68). Sadly, Max did not pursue this aspect of the Social Learning Cycle (*SLC*) or the *I-Space* in detail. However, contrary to the position that some teachers or educators take ("I teach; it is the students' responsibility to learn"), Max understood that learning and knowledge transfer was a two-way boulevard. This is apparent in his educational philosophy, the way he designed programs and learning experiences, and in his teaching style.

The fact that both the *I-Space* and the Social Learning Cycle are concerned with diffusion and absorption indicates just how central Max understood the aspect of knowledge or learning transfer to be. The *I-Space* can help to predict *when* certain types of knowledge are more likely to be transferred effectively, under *what* contextual circumstances this transfer is more likely to happen and *how* this transfer can be most effective.

The way Max designed programs (two of the examples given above are especially illustrative: the CEMI program in China and the Global Learning Journey), confirms that knowledge transfer was central to the educational endeavor. Max understood that without active engagement of the learner in the knowledge acquisition process, new knowledge was likely to be quickly forgotten. By using action learning and live case studies, Max not only insured the involvement of students and executives, but also gave them a chance to apply what they were learning in the classroom. In addition, Max often used questions to stimulate the conversation and learning (Lu 2012). Although this was counter-intuitive in China in 1984, it became one avenue that enabled the students to start to think critically about their system and other systems, which was especially important as they were just emerging from a very authoritarian regime.

Lastly, Max's teaching style was designed to facilitate the transfer of learning and knowledge. In part because of Max's wide range of knowledge of many different disciplines, he was able to make connections, use examples from a variety of fields, and integrate ideas across disciplines. Research indicates that these ways of presenting knowledge facilitate its transfer (Lobato 2006; Longenecker 2004).

We believe that the further development of the *I-Space* in relation to the transfer of knowledge in learning settings would be very fruitful. Potentially the *I-Space* has a lot of predictive power in management education and could facilitate more effective transfer of knowledge and learning by providing a basis from which to match educational philosophy, design and teaching methods with particular students'/executives' needs.

Innovations in the reception of managerial knowledge

This is an area that Max did not focus on to a great degree, although the fifth and sixth stages of the Social Learning Cycle (absorption and impact) are related to receiving knowledge. An agent, student or executive's ability to receive new learning or knowledge depends on a complex set of factors (Boisot and Canals 2004), and it overlaps substantially with the research and work on transfer of knowledge or learning. In addition, it also involves the content of knowledge, something that Max noted the *I-Space* does not address (Boisot, MacMillan, and Han 2007, 182).

Although not an innovation, albeit rare, preparing material, planning the instructional methods you use and identifying the teaching style you will employ, depending on the audience you are teaching, is a foundational aspect of preparing the learner to receive the knowledge or learning you are sending (Boisot and Li 2007b, 130). Max was always thorough and diligent in this regard. He traveled to Singapore and Hong Kong before the Global Learning Journey, and wrote an extended case study for participants on that program. Before teaching in the program in South Africa, he did some in-depth analysis of the parastatal's strategy. No doubt there are many other examples as well.

How an agent, student, or executive receives and absorbs new knowledge or learning is another issue that we believe could benefit from further explication of the Social Learning Cycle and more direct application of the *I-Space* to learning environments (Boisot 2007, 152, 155).

Conclusion

Because Max Boisot understood the great importance of linking good theory with practice, he has left a legacy of some very innovative approaches to the transfer of knowledge and learning. The *I-Space* and the Social Learning Cycle represent theoretical innovations that can help us to understand what type of knowledge or learning is most effectively used in different cultural and historical circumstances. They have predictive power, as illustrated most clearly by the paper reprinted in this volume and the innovative and successful approach taken to the design and development of the CEMI program in China. Through his writing and practice, Max left us with innovative approaches to the design of managerial educational programs, an understanding of the types of instructional practices that can be most effective, and guidelines for when to employ them. His work on transferring knowledge and the absorption of knowledge gives us a strong basis on which to better understand these processes. For those of us who worked or studied with Max the excitement he exuded about learning and knowledge will remain long into the future. And perhaps his excitement about learning is his greatest legacy of all—he demonstrated that learning matters and is to be approached always with robust enthusiasm and engagement.

Part VII
Concluding Reflections

12

The *I-Space* as a Key to History and to Culture

Gordon Redding

This brief reflection acknowledges two contributions to thinking, each of them transformational and radical, and each of them the result of facing a massive issue and grappling with it using a new form of intellectual implement. They are also inter-laced. The first contribution has been about how societies evolve historically, either towards "success" or relative failure, with a special interest in the fascinating recent trajectory of China along that path. This is the stuff of economic history but that discipline always benefits from the incursion of occasional foxes among its hedgehogs and here we celebrate the ultimate fox in our fields. The second contribution is on culture, the permanent unseen force so manifestly powerful but so highly resistant to being grappled with and tied down into the larger frameworks and assigned a respected role. From Adam Smith's "invisible hand," to David Landes' (1998, 516) "culture makes all the difference" in economic history, and Douglass North's (2005, viii) acknowledgement of culture and "the way its scaffolding constrains the players," centuries of scholarship show a consistent search for guidelines to this mystery.

The studying of history

Max Boisot noticed, when he was coming to terms with China during an almost pioneering period of living there, that the long-established puzzle known as "the Needham question" could be answered in terms of the societal handling of knowledge. Five hundred years ago in China the retention of knowledge by the governing bureaucracy, and so the lack of its diffusion, was a major determinant of the slowing down of scientific progress compared to the surge then beginning in Europe. What has been happening in the past half century in China is similarly explicable in terms of how knowledge is acquired and diffused. Allowing that history is never properly explained in terms of single causes, it is nevertheless valuable to seize on the *I-Space* as a leading illumination of the emergence of what we see today in Mainland China, and what happened earlier. This is far more accessible history than most, and so makes sense to more people.

The relevance and the feel of immediacy of such a perspective is further enhanced by the current surrounding drama of the revolution in information and telecommunications. This historically sudden and vertiginously steep upward curve has shot many societies in decades rather than centuries into worlds almost beyond their comprehension. The average manager, lacking a driving logic of explanation, will deal with it on his or her own terms and make workable sense of an immediately surrounding environment, but the typical larger picture available to executives remains fuzzy and only loosely integrated. Surprise has become normal. Given the central role of information-handling in recent industrial and societal transformations, it is not at all surprising that an information-centered theory would have the right to assume centre-stage, and be capable of yielding well-justified applause. I was teaching about the evolution of China and the *I-Space* recently to a group of globally active specialists in the information industry, and they reported that the scales had fallen from their eyes. So many "a-ha" moments were recorded that they proposed organizing to have a BBC film series made on it. That meeting happened to be in Valencia, just down the Spanish coast from Max's house in Sitges, where John Child and I had joined him a couple of years earlier for the ultimate joyful weekend of intellectual indulgence to write the piece I was presenting (Boisot, Child, and Redding 2011). So my satisfaction at the feedback was muted by nostalgia and by humility over my role as messenger. But at least there were grounds for celebration that here was something the recipients of which were crying out to see diffused.

The main reason why the *I-Space* makes such a good framework for history is that it captures something that efficiently represents a great deal else. Like all great theory it seizes the essence of matters. It enters the field of meaning, i.e. the organizing of sense-making, in a way that is clearly delineated. That is where it started; with an author capable of excitement over mathematics, but familiar with the European civilizational classics—not an unusual combination in the Enlightenment, but rare nowadays—exploring *meaning,* guided by Mary Douglas at Imperial College, and soon living on the slopes of Mount Fuji to immerse himself in an alternative frame.

One of the pleasures of using the *I-Space* is its capacity to handle the historical trajectory of a society, or enterprise, or any collective social body. The most insightful paper on China has always for me been Boisot and Child

(1988) in which the then startling statement was made that China's problem was not too much bureaucracy but not enough of the right type. With that the revered accomplishment of China as the first "modern" society (Fukuyama 2011) could be seen as a historic phenomenon. China's current state bureaucracy, when seen as something that might diffuse meaning, was now revealed as a relative failure. It had become a device for tight control and has essentially remained so. Independent intellectual professionalism within it is of limited nature. As it choked science in the Ming, it now chokes entrepreneurship, and as Marie-Claire Bergere (2007, 20) has observed, in now stifling a *bourgeoisie* it is trying to produce a form of capitalism without capitalists. There are many ways of explaining such phenomena, but few as revealing as the workings of codification, abstraction, and diffusion.

From its earliest appearance, the *I-Space* was used to analyze historical shifts. In Boisot (1983) the earlier work of Dore (1973) in studying two factories—British and Japanese—was analyzed through a new lens, so as to throw light on the convergence hypothesis (Kerr et al. 1960), and its amendment by Dore, the latter being sensitive to the different ways in which societies get along with the job of coordinating economic action. This revised reading by Boisot took the role of communications as central to the development of culture, and produced a very revealing set of insights:

> We see both firms investing in the lower left-hand quadrant but whereas the British firm's investment matures in the lower right-hand quadrant of the diagram as its codified firm-specific know-how diffuses, that of the Japanese firm matures in the top left-hand quadrant as its codified firm-specific knowledge gets embedded in a matrix of uncodified firm-specific knowledge. Most of English Electric's know-how eventually becomes available to the world under institutional arrangements designed to make it so. Conversely, most of Hitachi's knowledge will remain within the firm with the blessing of Japanese society. The first dynamic will lead to a horizontal integration of knowledge across firm boundaries but a greater differentiation of knowledge within the firm by hierarchical level. The second dynamic integrates knowledge more efficiently within the firm but is likely to produce a far more pronounced differentiation between firms and, hence, a vertical segmentation of industrial society. (Boisot 1983, 187)

Here we have an analysis that covers managerial action, organizational structure and communications, corporate culture, national culture, political economy, industrial structure, organizational behavior, and managerial ideology. It is also set against a changing societal story and may be anticipated to evolve internally as a pattern of reactions and configurations. In that evolution the organization will somehow absorb learning. The subsequent history of major Japanese success and then relative decline suggests that the dynamic nature of these complex processes will leave the patterns of stable configurations as temporary. The need for analysis capable of handling such shifting complexity is clear.

The 1983 date of this work is noteworthy. It is a very early statement of the *I-Space* framework, and that theory was never fundamentally altered, except for the later folding in of the third dimension of abstraction. Instead the work of a lifetime of scholarship saw it enriched in application across a huge swathe of situations, and a consequent enriching of its relevance and inner workings.

The processes of cultural influence

In Boisot (1986b) a challenge was made to international business theory. International business was for a long time in a somewhat critical condition as a discipline (Toyne and Nigh 1997; Child 1981, 2000), from which it has since hardly escaped because it has lacked the ability to handle "context" (Kogut 2003, Redding 2005). It was in need of a unified theory to replace the longstanding eclectic approach established by Dunning (1988) and acknowledged by him since (2003) as requiring additional injections. Boisot's proposal was to place markets and hierarchies in cultural perspective. His underlying proposition was that with priority of explanation given to market environment and technology, it had been possible to explain the *facts* of internationalization, but not yet to account for the varying *patterns,* in other words: why do firms settle in some markets rather than others? He contended that "cultural variables might be interposed in the Strategy-Structure couplet" (1986b, 139) and not be treated as "washed away in the process of industrialization." He argued that some cultures converge and others do not. In contending then that much organization theory and industrial sociology needed re-thinking, he saw an organization's transactional preferences as rooted in culture. This would require a reformulation of the rationality postulates drawn on by institutional economics and their replacement with a broader and more complex set.

Starting at an organizational level of analysis of the kind seen above for the British/Japanese factory comparison, the surrounding context of knowledge codification and diffusion was added so as to produce a theory of convergent and non-convergent cultures. This includes the possibility of historical change as the knowledge cycle might proceed.

The level of analysis is here organizational but with close attention paid to the environment relationship. It is not a long step from that to theorizing about ideal types of organization across a societal space. This would be the topic of many of our conversations over decades in Hong Kong and elsewhere.

I wrote down something Max said once, with his typical verbal elegance (as we sat on his balcony he, John and I). It was: "Everything that makes microeconomics tractable empties the firm of its specificity. We should start with the specificity." As we then discussed the matter a number of issues flowed from this starting point: similarity is the wrong default assumption; the question is not when do we converge, but what out of the total converges, how, and to what extent?; although IT brings new connections, the rules of engagement remain culturally fixed; dominant meanings shared between two opposites will be determined by who has the power. Chineseness is not so much visible *en bloc* but exists in the configurations of parts.

A related discussion picked up the issue of evolution: Darwin's puzzle was the absence of blended inheritance; Mendel saw genetics as maintaining distinctiveness; complexity theory stressed the role of configurations of components which then limited adjustments at the boundary; a country in the *I-Space* is a scatter not a point.

In an early statement of a culturally based view of the large firm, and the relevance of the markets and hierarchies dichotomy, Boisot (1986b, 157) stated that "the codification and diffusion of knowledge are the key dimensions through which the cultural order is expressed and transmitted both within and between firms." He also proposed a releasing of the longstanding debate in organization theory between structure and process, seeing each of these as "products of the articulation and flow of knowledge in social aggregates that yield a variety of transactional preferences and strategies." In this richer view, the organizational rationality of internal transactions, and the economic rationality of external ones, share a common parentage: that of the surrounding context of meaning.

His warning at that time was that economists working instinctively to build up the normative status of the market space—so visible in the eventual dominance of policy-making by the Washington Consensus (Williamson 1989)—may be blind to the no-less-economic rationality of other transactional forms. The "varieties of capitalism" literature (Hall and Soskice 2001, Whitley 1999) and within it the express attention to alternative rationalities (Guillen 2001, Redding 2005), as well as more generally the emergence of socio-economics as an integrated field, pay tribute to such insight.

As to culture *per se*, Boisot was clear at the outset that it was best seen as a set of interrelated but distinguishable provinces of meaning. In describing the connection between organizational culture and external culture he saw the two as "interrelated sets of transactional configurations that exhibit dynamic stability as they evolve through time" (1986b, 157). Cultural convergence then becomes one of a number of transactional outcomes of that evolution. It is however severely qualified: some parts of organizations inhabit regions of the space where absorption of alternatives is easier and more likely, and this might induce partial convergence; convergence driven by technology will depend on the stage reached by the driver in the knowledge cycle; it will also be affected by the organizational articulation of such knowledge in the wider culture space. By such means did ISO 9000 become legitimate, but it took time.

If shared meaning illuminates the economics of information-sharing then we have a key insight into the workings of culture in the economy. As already noted, the extra idea of discrete provinces of meaning was always implicit in Max's work. It had its roots in earlier work in which he was deeply immersed, such as that of Schutz (1972), Bourdieu (1977), and Luhmann (1985/2003).

When one accepts the notion of such "semantic fields" and applies it to the social world, and especially the world of organizations designed to coordinate and control economic action, then the meaning spaces are defined by the action for which such spaces act as envelopes. At the most obvious level an organization is such a space, but so too might be a division inside it such as "the boardroom" or the "shop floor." Equally so above it there might be a space definable by an industry, or a sector, or a type of organization. As long as meanings are shared inside the envelopes and are distinct, then those meanings can be said to interact with the behavior in the spaces. Thus culture is enacted in nested boxes, available for analysis at all levels. Clearly the most commonly analyzed is that of the society, as its actions normally include so much of the standardizing of meaning through institutions, including language, law, education, religion, hierarchy, and the norms governing order of the kind analyzed empirically by Leung and Bond (2004) as social axioms.

In the 2011 paper John Child and I had the pleasure of joining Max in working through this notion for the case of China, and seeing the three main sub-systems of that economy reflect their embeddedness in different regions of the *I-Space*. I like to think that, as Max wrote a quarter of a century earlier, by concentrating on the sharing of information about information, we had been—like Moliere's Monsieur Jourdain and his speaking prose—talking culture all along.

13

The Three Phases of Max Boisot's Theorizing

John-Christopher Spender

It is too bad Max never got to read Manuel DeLanda's *Philosophy and Simulation* (DeLanda 2011). It would have given him much pleasure and encouragement. An architect also, DeLanda theorized the "self-organizing" systems that intrigued Max throughout his academic life. The pair would have had a great time had they met—vast scholarship, well-travelled with several languages and cultures to hand, deeply concerned with the real-world impact of theorizing. Self-organizing systems, labeled so by Prigogine—who later regretted it and wanted to rename them "self-contained"—are those wherein management plays a relatively minor facilitating role. We discover that in the real world many things—passengers streaming off a train or water eddying around a pillar—have a capacity to organize themselves—under which circumstances managers, entrepreneurs, or strategists can do little to architect their order. Note the aesthetics of self-containment stand against American individualism, especially the command and control notions that dominate management teaching.

DeLanda argued the universe's fundamental elements "flow" continuously between their allowed states. Though we may have some hand in "river management," what will be will be, and flow from source to sea and atmosphere and back again, however we choose. The self-contained system theorist's challenge is to find the analytic level that reveals this flow. Most systems thinkers deny growth as in, for instance, LSE's Phillips model of the economy as a closed hydraulic system. This certainly flowed but flushed the concept of growth. Rather than follow the systems fashion dominating English language economics, Max and DeLanda both looked elsewhere, to biology especially—because it embraces growth as part of a larger cycle of contained flow. But biological models have not fared well as attempts to incorporate flow and growth into English language economics (e.g. Daly 1968; Penrose 1952).

Being Anglo-French Max knew of and drew on an alternative French tradition. Lavoisier's "conservation of mass" principle essentially created the science of chemistry by focusing at the level of the material's molecular mass, the attribute of theoretical importance rather than its color, humor or cultural significance. The next step into science was to move to yet another level and define energy as the mass-less component that flowed—leading to the "conservation of energy" principle and the first Law of Thermodynamics. Carnot extended this to the Second Law of Thermodynamics, that energy flows lead to increases in entropy as energy moves from being more available to being less available. Leveraging from Shannon and Weaver's theory of information, Max linked all this to the flow and transformation of information within social entities, an insight going back to his time at MIT. The result would be the *I-Space*, but its first incarnation was the C-D (codification-diffusion) framework presented in his 1982 "Keio Economic Studies" article (Boisot 1982). He eventually associated four types of information with four types of governance (Boisot 1986b).

Reaching well beyond power-based sociology or institutional theory, the C-D and *I-Space* frameworks suggested a complex economics of information, an information-based approach to political economy. It was an astonishingly bold step that opened up an entirely new way of analyzing organizations and economics. This economics of information or socio-informatics project was the spine to Max's theorizing, as his 2007 "Cognitive Edge" blog entries and his last papers confirm. His fundamental assumption was that the two-dimensional matrix and, later, the three-dimensional box, were "self-contained" in energy terms. Then the flow around the Social Learning Cycle (*SLC*) in *Knowledge Assets* (Boisot 1998, 58) "worked" because the unit of information flowing could not be at all places in the cycle at the same time—it is trading-off the contrasting energy natures and values of the different types of information itemized in the Keio paper. There was a corresponding change in entropy as information moved around the cycle because in the real world, as opposed to the abstractions of neoclassical or "Newtonian economics," generating, transforming, codifying and deploying information is entropy-raising work.

Max's socio-informatics has wide application, especially to managing the social, economic and organization impact of technological innovation—his PhD topic (Boisot 1981). Neoclassical economics has not been able to theorize information because it does not conform to its axiom of scarcity. Neoclassical goods must be rivalrous—if I sell you an apple, I no longer have it when you do. But information is non-rivalrous. When I tell you how to manufacture synthetic rubber, you gain the information but I have no less of it. How best, then, to theorize the economics of information? Neoclassical economics can only proceed by transforming information into a neoclassical good by, for instance, patenting or copyrighting it. This elides the capacity of information to act as a tool and, skillfully applied, generate a stream of economic value—as encapsulated in the Chinese proverb "give a man a fish and you feed him for a day, teach him to fish and you feed him for a lifetime." Neoclassical economics likewise denies an economics of generating information or learning. In contrast, the C-D matrix and *I-Space* work because the modes and consequences of information containment differ as one type of knowledge flows into another. Being contained, the *SLC* repeats endlessly, seeking the dynamic equilibrium implied by Zipf's principle of least effort.

Many biological, physical and thermodynamic instances of self-containment arise without human intervention. While these interested Max, his emphasis was elsewhere, on the lived world. The analysis is socio-informatic when the interacting processes of information generation, containment and application are problematic matters over which people have some influence. The differences between the costs and values of information in its various possible states are the socio-economy's dynamic. Thus driven, Max's socio-informatics is about entropy-raising work and learning, nothing to do with the mathematical games marginalist economics offers. Organizing, people's attempts to deal with the economic impact of different types of socio-information, was what should be analyzed, not organizations or their direction—topics that Max sometimes dismissed as both intractable and irrelevant. He sought the analytic level at which the information flows would be self-contained and, finding Ashby's notions of requisite variety appealing, agreed with Maturana that what most management researchers call "organizations" cannot be autopoietic and self-contained. Thus organizations were not the appropriate objects of theoretical attention, in spite of a legal and economic system that presents private-sector firms as entities of great import. Rather, our institutional arrangements needed to be analyzed in terms of their impact on the persisting social entity's *SLC*.

These intuitions gave Max a special vantage point from which to critique Williamson's "markets and hierarchies." Written from beyond the bounds of neoclassical economics, the Keio paper was a penetrating attack on Williamson's presumption that hierarchy—"fiat" or management control—was the organizing mode of last resort (Boisot 1982). Uncertainty rendered this mode of governance irrelevant in the lived world. As Mary Douglas's student, Max was inclined to give culture-based stability better odds. Drawing on Mauss's work on "gift-economies," and Bernstein's studies of culture and the formative impact of language, he saw "federation" as a more economically relevant mode of stability. Williamson's "micro-foundational" presumptions put the analysis at the wrong level, ensuring nothing useful to real society could emerge from "transactions cost economics." The Keio paper rephrased Max's PhD, a critique of international trade theory for presuming fixed factors of production while ignoring the link between non-rivalrous-ness and economic growth (Boisot 1981). At the same time Max politely implied Williamson's appeal to markets was no more than dogmatic belief in an "invisible hand," relocating the flow into an abstraction far from socio-economic life.

In 1981 Max was teaching in Japan, researching technology transfer in the South East Asian chemicals industry for his PhD, a long association with Eastern thought and society that began at INSEAD's Euro-Asia Center in 1979. At the time many economists and management theorists were studying the managerial and technological performance of the Japanese economy. The topic prompted Max towards the second phase of his academic career as he applied the C-D framework to broader questions of technology's impact on societies. Drawing again on his PhD, he concluded that one society's institutions may promote technology creation and diffusion while another's might promote their absorption and adaptation. The result was a masterly exploration of socio-economic and public policy that outshined today's pallid discussions of budget balancing between exploration and exploitation (Boisot 1982, 1986b). Inevitably the analysis was extended as Max went to China to set up the China/EEC program, spend time in Beijing, and work directly with Chinese bureaucrats. A long series of papers on innovation policy in various countries at a macro level resulted, often written with John Child, Gordon Redding, Marshall Meyer, Sheila Puffer, or others. These buttressed his ongoing writing and information management consulting work at the corporate level.

Max's underlying project burst back into full view in 1994 with an astonishing paper energized by recent publications that (a) further explored biologists' increasing interest in informatics, post genetics, and (b) found common cause with his critique of neoclassical economics (Boisot 1994). This precipitated the third phase of his work. His paper began: "The second half of the twentieth century will be remembered as the period in which information came to replace energy as the central fact of life in post-industrial societies." Information, he implied, will have more impact on how we live than energy; so innovations in information generation, distribution and application will have more impact than the energy innovations that led to the Industrial Revolution. Here Max returned to theorizing socio-economic growth, noting "innovation is precisely what in the neoclassical paradigm, given its orientation towards static equilibrium, has been unable to explain" (Boisot 1994, 237). Few of today's innovation authors appreciate this failure, sticking doggedly to the growth-denying Newtonian framework. Again Max drew on the French tradition, citing Maupertius's "principle of least action." Even though Google Scholar indicates his 1994 paper has been cited only once, it sketched a post-Newtonian economics that also built on the biological and evolutionary writings of Salthe and Eldredge. Sadly Max seemed unaware of Ekelund's work on the French engineers' impact on neoclassical economics, especially Jules Dupuit's and Alfred Marshall's relative contributions to marginalism; the first presuming containment and boundaries, the second advancing into boundary-less mathematical abstraction (Ekelund 1968; Ekelund and Hébert 1999). Aside from connecting to the French tradition, this would have helped Max better target the position he was attacking. These developments also paralleled the US Scientific Management movement that transformed management into a data-intensive activity. Data, Max argued, must be understood within an interrelated self-contained triad—data, space-time, and energy. Today's profligate use of energy to cope with our space-time activity is unsustainable. We might learn better practices by seeing how past re-conceptualizations of data enabled humankind to move forward into novel social arrangements or modes of governance, something more obvious today as we stagger under the social, political and economic impact of "total surveillance" and "social media."

In an equally under-cited 1999 article with Benita Cox, Max anticipated much of today's socio-informatics (Boisot and Cox 1999). It turned on another version of the contained—uncontained disjunction between Dupuit and Marshall—explored with Donald Hebb's (and Thorndike's) notions of neurological level self-organization; a level of self-organization more easily simulated. Computer scientists call this "connectionism," the notion that repeated execution can induce adaptive networks of elementary units towards unanticipated but contextually contingent order that reveals the level at which the order arises. The "connectionists" battle with "computationalists," contrasting "bottom-up" connectionist processes against static "top-down" computation, noting the crucial element missing from most discussions of network adaptive-ness is that it requires a memory lying outside the computation. Memory's inputs enable connections to adjust and order to emerge. Observing and remembering are orthogonal to the computation, opening up the logical space in which to catch time's passing and accumulated experience. Top-down computing executes unchanging routines, offering no metaphor for lived time or learning. It is time-free, the way neoclassical markets clear. Real world processes turn on learning and are time-full, like all socio-economic actions under uncertainty. The authors wrote of "a computational machine's conditional readiness to change and learn," recalling Grey Walter's "turtles" for which bounding and self-containment were axiomatic. As autopoietic theory presumes, self-containment is a prerequisite to self-organization and memory's finiteness is a metaphor for this. The authors also noted a distinction between uncertainty reduction and its absorption, the first *a priori*, the second experiential. Connectionist machines learn in human ways and so can merge with how we live our lives. So the authors anticipated an era of socio-computing as humans and machines participated and learned collaboratively while social order emerged.

Working with Ian MacMillan and colleagues at Wharton, Max probed emerging order further with Sim-*I-Space* and set up the *I-Space* Institute (Boisot, Eun, Han, and MacMillan 2005). He was also energized by working with the biologist Jack Cohen (Boisot and Cohen 2000), on the new literature of complexity theory and "emergence" with Mike Lissack and Bill McKelvey (this volume), and the simulations of self-organization coming out of the Santa Fe Institute.

Then came ATLAS—a heaven-sent opportunity to work with Markus Nordberg (this volume) and his colleagues on the earlier distinction between "uncertainty reduction" and "uncertainty absorption," vital to the LHC's architecture. Our schooling leads us to ignore the energy issues around data-collection in say, anthropology, materials research, or chemistry lab experiments. Experimentation and observation seem independent. The Industrial Age evolved as we discovered how to harness energy to our projects, to create it and apply it—the shift from Lavoisier to Carnot. Experiments that sometimes went disastrously wrong as energy flowed into the wrong place, observation and experiment intertwine. The LHC lies at an extreme here, requiring enormous energy to generate its nuclei splitting events and collect the data, energy enough to dim lights across the entire Geneva region. At these energy levels experimentation and data-collection merge and we sense the boundaries to what can be known in the physical realm.

But Max's intuitions about the interplay of data, space-time, and energy in the post-Industrial Age pointed to new notions of value in the socio-economic realm. Cracking the enemy's codes can save thousands of lives, bullets and bombs. Beyond the Industrial Age framework, information's socio-economic value can be realized in very different ways. Financial trading, especially high-speed trading, turns on miniscule nuggets of information, sometimes passed illegally between individuals—a butterfly triggering thunderstorms (Ormerod 2000). Behind the flows stand questions about our "surveillance-intensive" societies. How does information flow relate to personal freedom and social order—questions that take us back to Max's socio-informatic distinctions between market, hierarchy and federation? Can we theorize these as Boisotian socio-informatic phenomena and get behind the Newtonian concepts of individuals or social institutions with gravity-like power and discover the self-contained relations or patterns of order that individuals struggle to influence? The sciences of fractals and small-world phenomena, that also occur at the neurological level, show the potential for a huge Boisotian program (Watts and Strogatz 1998). But to make this work the analysis has to be at the level of the information flow and deterministic Newtonian "machine" or "causal mechanism" metaphors have to be left far behind.

To summarize, Max was fortunate to intuit a question of fundamental theoretical and social significance while young. The intellectual challenges of expressing, exploring, expanding, and testing it sustained his seemingly boundless academic enthusiasm and appetite throughout his life. He pointed us towards a post-Newtonian discourse in which our attempts to organize in situations that are partially self-organizing is radically reframed, throwing up insights that bear directly on the most portentous aspects of our socio-economy. Sadly he did not live long enough to do more than sketch this socio-informatic theory, but unquestionably he left us with a rich socially-relevant project that found common cause with Manuel DeLanda and the socio-economic theorists that really matter.

14

Writing with Max Boisot

Marshall Meyer

It was a lot of fun writing with Max. He was an original, saw the world unconventionally, and transformed routine research into an intellectual adventure.

Our joint adventure was an article titled, "Which Way Through the Open Door: Reflections on the Internationalization of Chinese Firms" (Boisot and Meyer 2008). The article published in *Management and Organization Review* was much shorter than the original. Frankly, it was creamed in a protracted review process, but MOR's editors thought it sufficiently intriguing to merit publication somewhat shortened. "Which Way..." appears to have been moderately successful. Google Scholar counts 79 citations. It is the third most cited article MOR has published since SSCI began counting in 2008. And a condensed version of the article, in English and Chinese, is the lead article in the inaugural issue of a new publication targeting executives, *Chinese Management Insights*.

"Which Way..." made three related arguments, all heterodox. The first, simplified, was as follows: the weak go out. Much of received internationalization theory, of course, claims that the strong oligopolistic firms go abroad while the weak languish at home. We disagreed, at least for China. The second argument concerned domestic versus international barriers to trade. Received theory argues that domestic barriers are insignificant in comparison with international barriers. Here we also took exception with respect to China, citing as evidence a small literature on domestic border effects or protectionism in China. The third coined the term "institutional arbitrage" to suggest that Chinese outward investment may be neither market- or resource-seeking but rather institution-seeking: Chinese firms "go out" in search of stable platforms from which to do business at home.

Since writing "Which Way..." more than five years ago, I've rethought these arguments. Among the topics I'll cover are strength versus weakness since size may not be an indicator of strength in China, domestic trade barriers or border effects within China, and the institutional props undergirding and sometimes undermining Chinese firms both at home and abroad.

Size and strength

The standard argument is that strong firms "go out." In the international management literature, strength may arise from size and market power, but it also may arise from unique knowledge or intellectual property that cannot safely be licensed or otherwise transferred to firms abroad. China presents an interesting case because size and strength do not necessarily correspond; indeed they may be inverse. The larger firms, most of which are state enterprises, may look strong but often aren't. The weakness or smallness of putatively large companies has multiple sources. Chief among them is the challenge of operating as a unified firm in an economy characterized by cellularity and localism, where national economic integration remains incomplete. The sources of localism include a disinclination to trust strangers and hence to build national firms, the policy of administrative decentralization where much of the control of the national economy was delegated to provincial and municipal governments following the Cultural Revolution, and identification of the workforce with the local branch of the company rather than the larger firm. Localism is manifest in fragmented markets, fragmented logistics, and perhaps most importantly the prevalence of a parent-subsidiary system where parent firms lack full control of subsidiaries.
To elaborate briefly:

1. Distrust of strangers. The idea of a corporation apart from persons and the government still does not occupy a central place in the Chinese cultural firmament. China was late to adopt a company law, and when it did, in 1904, few investors appeared because shareholding was understood as a personal rather than an impersonal transaction: "The idea that members of the public would be invited to join one's business and share in its control and profits was indeed repugnant...the notion that one's money be put into the pocket of some strangers for them to run a business was just as unthinkable" (Li 1974, 205, quoted by Kirby 1995, 50).

2. Administrative decentralization. The policy of administrative decentralization, implemented shortly after the Cultural Revolution, shifted much of the control of the Chinese economy to local governments—the centralized Soviet model simply proved unworkable in a country as vast as China. Governmental administration was also

delegated to provinces and municipalities. Among other functions, tax collection remains decentralized to localities; businesses pay taxes based on their place of registration regardless of where they do business. Local authorities will prefer locally registered entities to businesses from "foreign" regions; this preference, further, is exacerbated to the extent of local government ownership of locally registered entities. Worse, profits earned by a regional subsidiary cannot be offset by losses incurred subsidiaries registered from other regions—profits in Guangzhou are not offset by losses in Gansu. This creates disincentives for specialization; the result is firms that look big but whose regional units duplicate each other and do not realize scale economies.

3. Legacy state ownership. Legacy state ownership also contributes to local solidarity and resistance to central coordination of large firms. These are driven by the definition of state ownership enshrined in the Chinese Constitution, ownership by "the whole people," which promotes a sense of psychological if not of actual equity ownership among the workforce. Chinese workers remain attached to a local factory or facility rather than to the larger firm and identify with their peers but not the larger company; consolidation of smaller into larger units is experienced as a loss and provokes resistance, especially in legacy industries like shipping and steel.

4. Market fragmentation. The fragmentation of Chinese retailing is fairly staggering: in 2009, the largest 50 retailers accounted for only five percent of total retail sales (Stores 2010), while in 2010 the largest 100 retailers accounted for 11 percent of sales (My Decker Capital 2011, 9). The Chinese logistics industry is similarly fragmented: there are several thousand national logistics operators in China compared to fewer than 100 in the U.S., and logistics costs run from 18 to 21 percent of Chinese GDP compared to 8 or 9 percent in the U.S. (Supply Chain Digest 2011).

5. Weak parental control. Typically, Chinese parent firms do not have 100 percent ownership and control of regional subsidiaries; rather, fractional control is retained by local interests (Meyer and Lu 2005). The airline industry is illustrative: while it is the stated policy of the central government to consolidate the airlines into three large carriers (Air China, Eastern, and Southern), the policy is pursued by absorbing regional carriers into local subsidiaries of the big three rather than full integration of regional airlines into the national carriers.

Let's take this discussion back to my collaboration with Max. The initial premise, from received internationalization theory, was that large firms "go out;" like others, we assumed size and strength to correspond. We then asked whether this premise held for China since we suspected it did not. Here I'm taking a slightly different tack by asking whether size and strength, which theories from Edith Penrose to evolutionary economics treat as synonymous, correspond closely in China. My suspicion is that they do not because (1) given the dispersion of power in China, the larger the firm the greater the compromises to central coordination and control; and hence (2) the barriers to *acting* like a large firm are somewhat higher than in the West. Somewhat differently: in China firms that are large statistically (in terms of sales or profits or people) may not be so operationally (in terms of their capacity to act in a concerted and coordinated manner). Hence, size and strength are not necessarily correlated in China and the correlation between size and "going out" may be weak, nonexistent, or possibly inverse in China.

Push: do barriers to domestic commerce push Chinese firms out?

Max and I did a lot of thinking about the impact of domestic barriers to commerce on the inclination of Chinese firm to "go out." Our intuition was that these barriers are higher than in other countries and hence that the usual correlations between physical distance and transaction costs did not hold in China. Based on a series of studies available at the time, we argued that the costs of doing business internally often exceeded the costs of doing business internationally and that modern information and communication technologies, ICTs, have widened this gap. Since the publication of "Which Way...," however, I've done some further thinking and informal research, and I've also tried to track new research bearing on domestic trade barriers.

First the thinking: it is not obvious why any market-seeking—as distinct from resource-seeking, knowledge-seeking, and institution-seeking—Chinese firm would want to "go out" given the rush of Western firms into China. After all, Chinese markets have experienced some of the fastest growth rates in the world, and growth is expected to accelerate as China's middle class develops. Max and I were forced to argue that, somehow, domestic transaction costs made it advantageous for domestic firms, especially small domestic firms, to go abroad while advantaging large foreign firms in China. We cited then-current research on domestic trade barriers in support of the argument.

Next, my informal research: In 2007, I stood by a toll gate on route 312 just east of Turpin in Xinjiang Province. Even though we had already written "Which Way...," I didn't realize the significance of what I saw: many trucks from distant provinces, especially Anhui, Henan, Jiangsu, and Jilin, despite discriminatory tolls favoring local truckers. I then observed roadside restaurants just beyond the toll barrier. The restaurants served regional cuisine, e.g. Anhui, Jilin, and truckers uniformly pulled up to the restaurant serving home-town (or home-province) food. This was more than a matter of palate since the restaurants, which were plain, also served as dispatch centers for return loads. Thus, a driver from Anhui would pull into the Anhui restaurant to connect with the Anhui network in Turpin or in Urumqi, three hours distant, and eventually a return load to Anhui. I finally observed a dispatch center operated by the Xinjiang government several kilometers ahead on route 312. It was empty. The truckers ignored it. Here is what I should have learned but didn't: transaction costs in logistics were high not so much due to discriminatory tolls as to the absence of a national dispatch system coordinating trucks more efficiently.

Three years later I interviewed a team charged with rethinking rural distribution for a flagship Chinese company. Their description of the Chinese countryside was reminiscent of anthropological work done fifty years ago (Skinner 1964; 1965a; 1965b). Markets remained periodic, that is, coordinated by calendar rather than demand, and distribution followed an inefficient hub-and-spoke system. Thus, town-level merchants would travel to county-level distribution centers for a day every two weeks to replenish their stocks, and trucks would be dispatched from the distribution center to town-level outlets once goods were available. The cost of this system was enormous: merchants spent two days a month ordering goods, trucks ran half-empty between distribution centers and the town-level outlets and empty on the way back, and inventories piled up both at distribution centers and in the town-level outlets. The solution involved computerized ordering and reconfiguring from a hub-and-spoke to a circular system for delivery to town-level outlets. These operational changes followed from fundamental changes in the firm's management and a substantial investment in technology. Moreover, the cost-effectiveness of the circular distribution system depended on a high density of outlets. I do not know how rapidly this model will diffuse given the huge investment needed to support it.

Now my reading: looking back, I think Max's basic intuition was right: many Chinese firms "go out" because of high transaction costs or nearly insuperable obstacles to doing business at home. However, I think we made a couple of errors. First, we focused too much on barriers to inter-provincial trade like discriminatory tolls and tariffs. The original work on domestic border effects by Poncet (2003; 2005) and Young (2000) has since been revisited, e.g. Bai et al. (2004) have shown that these barriers abated somewhat beginning around 1990, and Holz (2009) seems to have discredited Young's work by showing that the Young's methodology applied to the U.S. would lead to the inference that domestic trade barriers in the U.S. are higher than China's. It also looks like we did not pay enough attention to urban-rural differences and especially to the challenges unique to rural distribution and distribution in remote Chinese provinces consistent with growing rural-urban income disparities (Xu 2011). I now think the following model more apt than

"Which Way....": China's urban markets, principally those on the East coast, were ripe for colonization by foreign firms because of their wealth and the cachet of foreign brands to their residents. This left domestic firms with the choice between penetrating rural markets and markets in remote provinces, both difficult, and positioning themselves as low-cost producers in overseas markets. The latter seems to have been the easier path, although this may change. Hence, the two-way flow traffic through China's open door has been propelled by (1) the preference of affluent urban residents for foreign brands, (2) the traditional barriers to doing business in rural and interior regions of China, and (3) the opportunity for Chinese brands to enter overseas markets as low-cost producers.

Pull: will opportunities for institutional arbitrage pull firms out of China?

We now need to add pull factors to the discussion, especially the tug of Western institutions on Chinese firms. The term institutional arbitrage was provoked by Max. Institutional arbitrage is the borrowing of overseas institutions in order to operate more effectively in China. Since institutions are not readily transportable and the firm's legal registration is, institutional arbitrage can take place by moving the domicile of the firm outside of China (typically to Hong Kong, sometimes the British West Indies or the Cayman Islands) and then operating in China as a foreign-invested enterprise. Institutional arbitrage also occurs, though perhaps to a lesser extent, when a Chinese firm lists its shares overseas but remains domiciled in China. Both options have been formalized in Hong Kong where "Red chips" are Chinese companies domiciled in Hong Kong while "H-share" companies are Chinese-domiciled firms listed in Hong Kong. Our conception of institutional arbitrage involved moving something out of the home country (in these examples, registration and listing of the company). Max believed that institutional arbitrage was propelled by the liability of foreignness faced by Chinese firms operating outside their home provinces: since a Hubei company operating in Shanghai is effectively a foreigner, a denizen but not a full citizen, could it be any less disadvantageous to operate outside of China and enjoy the benefit of overseas institutions?

The answers to this question today are less clear than when we wrote "Which Way...." Think first of the tangible benefits of shifting institutional allegiance to Hong Kong or the U.S. Five years ago, among other benefits were favorable tax rates *within China*, access to Western capital markets, and ease of repatriating capital. The first of these benefits has vanished and the second is at risk. Preferential earned income tax rates for foreign firms have been rescinded. (Foreign firms, however, may still file consolidated income tax returns.) The welcome mat is no longer out for Chinese firms seeking to list in the U.S. or Canada. In the first half of 2012, only one Chinese firm listed in the U.S. while 19 Chinese firms were delisted from American exchanges. The immediate cause of most delistings is suspected or actual accounting fraud. The larger issue, however, is conflicting Chinese and U.S. accounting regulations. Under current Chinese rules, Chinese companies must use Chinese-registered auditors that are forbidden from sharing their working papers with foreign entities. In direct conflict with these rules, the U.S. Public Company Accounting Oversight Board will not register an auditor whose working papers are not available for inspection by the Securities and Exchange Commission, effectively barring Chinese companies from the U.S. exchanges. So far, neither side has budged. Until the RMB becomes fully convertible, it remain easier for investors to repatriate capital from overseas- than from Chinese-registered firms because the former are not subject to Chinese controls on capital accounts.

Still, some of the less tangible benefits of institutional arbitrage remain. In particular, moving a company's registration, assets, or listing outside of China is a form of diversification and a partial buffer from uncertainties of the Chinese economy and Chinese politics. "Going out" may also carry a certain cachet and signal strength: operating on four continents rather than in four rural counties of Wuhan, signals that you are a strong, sound company even if China-based. Thus, while institutional arbitrage is somewhat less attractive than five years ago, some advantages remain.

This leads to a subtle difference between institutional arbitrage and institutional borrowing, the latter meaning "integrating with someone else's system both abroad and at home" (Steinfeld 2010, 69). The difference is in the level at which the phenomenon operates: institutional borrowing occurs between countries and their economic and political systems while firms seeking to substitute more attractive for less attractive institutions engage in institutional arbitrage. Thus, while countries can converge or diverge with respect to their institutional roadmaps, firms choose to stay at home or "go out" in pursuit of different or better institutions. In a sense, the two processes are mirror images of one other: to the extent there is institutional borrowing, institutional arbitrage becomes less advantageous and will be less frequent. At the same time, certain institutional blockages can also render institutional arbitrage less attractive. An example of the latter is China's rethinking of the legality of variable interest entities, financial structures used to channel foreign capital to telecom, and internet firms like Baidu where Chinese law forbids direct foreign investment.

"Which Way...." was very firm-centric. We missed the interplay between institutional borrowing and institutional arbitrage and thus the overarching yet obvious proposition: the more borrowing, the fewer the arbitrage opportunities. My guess is that Max would argue with the view that borrowing will lead to interdependence if not convergence of China with the West. The colloquy would have been interesting and illuminating to all of us.

A final word

Max was a rare intellectual force. His bandwidth was immense. An article was an occasion for a year-long conversation and an extended friendship. His writing was elegant and ironic. And he was a kind person. Max will be deeply missed.

15

Remembering Max Boisot: Recollections of a Gifted Intellect at Work

Ron Sanchez

Like a few other exceptionally lucky people, I was privileged to work with Max Boisot as a colleague and to know him as a friend. During the 15 or so years that I knew Max, I became increasingly aware that I was enjoying the great good fortune to be exchanging ideas with one of the most gifted intellects to think and write about organization and management in our generation. In this personal retrospective on Max Boisot, I try to elaborate certain "qualities of thought" that I believe distinguished Max's way of seeing and thinking about the world.

I have always had two simple criteria for selecting the people I would like to work with as colleagues and, if possible, to build friendships with: First, do you have anything interesting going on upstairs? Second, are you a nice person? As I am sure everyone who ever met Max Boisot knew well, Max met both criteria to an extraordinary degree.

The Max Boisot that I knew and can never forget was a gentleman in the classic mold: always considerate, unfailingly courteous, and endlessly charming. Max inevitably raised the good spirits of any group of people he happened to join just as much as his presence would inevitably raise any group's average IQ. But here I will leave the profoundly nice person that Max was to our individual memories and will instead focus on the qualities of thought that I believe distinguished Max's keen intellect as I came to experience it through our collaborations. To do so, I briefly describe the all-too-short period of 15 years during which Max and I collaborated, and then I draw on that experience to comment on Max's amazing intellect. I conclude with some final comments on Max's Information-Space Model, which I believe will be an enduring contribution to our understanding of organizations.

Our work together

I was privileged to spend many days and evenings talking with Max over a period of years beginning in the mid-1990s—at his home in Sitges, at my home in Oregon, in hotel lobbies and dining rooms in London, Singapore, and Copenhagen, and at conference venues around the world. As anyone who has spent more than a few minutes with Max would know, beginning a conversation with Max meant that you'd better get ready for a high speed ride through an astounding range of ideas, all emanating in rapid succession from Max's amazing erudition, piercing intelligence, passion for ideas, love of conversation, and visible delight in producing an inevitably well-turned phrase.

I first met Max in 1996 at the Third International Conference on Competence-Based Management in Gent, Belgium. As one of the conference organizers and a reviewer of submitted papers, I was drawn to an innovative paper on knowledge management that Max and co-authors Dorothy Griffiths and Veronica Moles submitted to the conference.[1] The paper was an application of Max's early "Culture-Space" model,[2] which was a precursor to Max's now-famous Information-Space Model of organizational learning. At the time I was also working on a model of organizational learning, one that I call the Five Learning Cycles Model (Sanchez 2001, 2005), and it was immediately apparent on reading Max's and his colleague's paper that we shared a number of ideas about the nature and interactions of individual and collective cognitive processes involved in organizational learning. I contacted Max before the conference and sent him a draft of a paper elaborating my model. He replied with insightful comments that convinced me that he had actually taken the time to read my paper carefully, and we agreed to meet at the conference for a chat.

A few minutes into our first conversation at the conference, I began to understand that Max was not your garden-variety academic—as rich and varied as the academic garden may be. For one thing, Max seemed to have read every book of significance written in the last 100 years, as well as most of the significant books before that. For another, he seemed to have some amazing insights into how the intellectual currents in a number of fields of science and philosophy were beginning to converge in ways that suggested exciting possibilities for fundamentally new perspectives on economic activities and organization. I quickly came to the conclusion that Max Boisot was a person with an extraordinary lot going on upstairs.

---

[1] The paper was subsequently published in the Strategic Management Society book series as "The Dilemma of Competence: Differentiation versus Integration in the Pursuit of Learning" by Max Boisot, Dorothy Griffiths, and Veronica Moles, pp. 65–82 in *Strategic Learning and Knowledge Management*, Ron Sanchez and Aimé Heene, editors, Chichester: John Wiley and Sons, 1997.

[2] See, for example, Max Boisot (1986b). "Markets and Hierarchies in Cultural Perspective." *Organization Studies*, 7 (2): 135–58.

After an hour or so, Max and I began to sense some promising complementarities between his encyclopedic knowledge of concepts and theories from many fields and my interest in developing more systemic perspectives, inclusive concepts, and integrated theories about economic and organizational phenomena. Max suggested, and I was delighted to agree, that we should find an interesting opportunity for collaboration. Although we could not yet clearly define just what we might collaborate on, we agreed to exchange some ideas and to get together for more extended conversations in the near future. I recall feeling very good about the prospect of working with Max, but I only realized later how great my good fortune was that day to have become another node in the global network of people with whom Max would share his enthusiasm for ideas.

Between 1997 and 2002, Max and I met for a number of extended conversations. Our first conversation was a veritable "moveable feast" of ideas that wandered through the lobby and dining rooms of a central London hotel over a two-day period. During this extended conversation, Max and I became quite animated by various juxtapositions of ideas—and by a host of resulting "What if?" possibilities for new theory. For me personally, our first extended conversation was one of the most stimulating intellectual experiences of my life, though in retrospect I can well imagine that it was just another day at the office for Max.

An outcome of our first extended conversation was our recognition that we were both attracted to some fairly fundamental concepts and theories that were relevant to, but not yet connected within, economic and organizational theory. We decided that it would be great fun to try to draw those disconnected concepts and theories together in roughing out nothing less than a new, integrated theoretical perspective on economic organizing.

Our subsequent conversations took place at various places around the world where we could manage to make our paths cross, and also as Max and I exchanged visits to my home in Oregon, USA, and to Max's home in Sitges, Spain. Each meeting spawned conversations that lasted several days and roamed widely. Of course, the visit to Max's home was as invigorating physically as it was intellectually. As some other friends of Max know well, Max would really hit his stride intellectually while climbing the streets, walking the beaches, and then visiting the cafes of his beloved Sitges.

During this period of extended conversations, no matter what subject we started with, we would always be drawn to and marvel at the systemic interconnectedness of everything—at the implicit as well as explicit ways in which organization somehow happens, whether intended or emergent, whether natural or human. Max's way of seeing the world seemed innately to lead him to "see the system in everything,"—to grasp the many forms of the systemic interrelatedness of people, ideas, and the physical world that both enables and constrains all forms of organization.

By early 2002, Max and I agreed that our various conversations appeared to be converging towards an interesting new perspective on economic organizing, and that perhaps the time had come to do the first draft of a paper. Max volunteered to "put something together," and a few weeks later Max emailed me a 60-page tour de force of juxtaposed ideas imported from half a dozen major fields of inquiry. The draft had only three headings—Introduction, Our Main Argument, and Concluding Comments—each about 20 pages in length. As I read through the draft, I began to realize why there were no subheadings: Max had woven such a novel and compelling tapestry of juxtaposed ideas that decomposing his discussion into smaller chunks with subheadings would be highly problematic.

I nonetheless added some further ideas to the draft, and we then had an 80-page document. It then fell to me to wield Occam's razor to reduce our draft down to the essential set of concepts and relationships necessary to compose a coherent theoretical argument. We eventually managed to reduce our paper to about 45 pages, but only at the cost of deleting a dozen or so fascinating but ultimately tangentially related ideas that of course Max had largely provided—and that we both agreed would really take a future book to elaborate adequately. Not having the opportunity now to write that book with Max is a terrible personal loss that I cannot even begin to describe.

By 2004 our pared-down paper was titled "Organization as a Nexus of Rules: Emergence in the Evolution of Systems of Exchange" (Boisot and Sanchez 2010). The paper develops "a combined systems, evolutionary, cognitive, and game-theoretic perspective on [economic] organizing." The paper seeks to contribute to economic organization theory not by adding to the existing explanations as to *why* economic activities become organized, but rather by presenting a theory that explains *how* economic activities become organized. In essence, the paper seeks to explain the essential cognitive processes of trial-and-error rule making and routine generation through which economic actors seek to create Pareto-preferable systems of exchange, and which result both in specific instances of economic organizing like individual firms and in more aggregated systems of economic organizing like markets.

Needless to say, our paper incorporates Max's Information-Space Model. The theory of organizing advanced in our paper is not derived from Max's Information-Space Model in any basic sense, but the model served very well as a conceptual framework for integrating and illustrating the systems, evolutionary, cognitive, and game-theoretic perspectives we elaborate in the paper.

To round out the story of our paper, I suppose I need to add that Max and I first thought to communicate our new "Nexus of Rules" theory of economic organizing as widely as possible by submitting the paper to the leading journals in management, economics, and organization that claim that their mission is the development and advancement of theory. Without exception, our paper was rejected at these journals by reviewers who said, in one form or another, that their field was already familiar with each of the individual theories we had invoked and undertaken to integrate—*and thus that there was nothing new in the paper!* As one rejection followed another, Max and I began to realize that the reviewers at the major management, economics, and organization journals—and the editors to whom we sometimes appealed—simply did not perceive any intellectual value-added in achieving a conceptually coherent and logically consistent integration of systems theory, evolutionary theory, cognitive theory, and game theory in explaining how economic organization happens.

Of course, it is possible that the reviewers were right and that our effort to develop an integrative theory of economic organizing adds little or nothing to existing theory. But it may also be possible that the string of rejections our paper received from leading journals in three fields were symptomatic of the state of intellectual processes in academia, many if not most of which have become so compartmentalized and disconnected that very few academics now recognize any value to be derived from integrating theories to provide a more complete representation and explanation of economic and organizational phenomena. If that is so, then perhaps we all need to be concerned that the institutional incentives and processes now driving the compartmentalization of and resulting disconnects among ideas in academia are making it increasingly difficult, if not impossible, for those rare, boundary-less, system thinkers like Max Boisot to contribute the fruits of their expansive thought to our increasingly disconnected, incremental, and empirical academic discourse.

In any event, Max and I continued to believe that we had done something of value, and so we decided just to be patient and to continue to submit our paper until we found some reviewers and editors who would recognize what we considered to be the value-added of our effort. I am happy to say that in 2010 the paper was accepted and published—virtually as submitted—by *Management Revue,* whose editor described the paper as "explosive in its theoretical implications." Max and I agreed that the editor's characterization of our paper more than compensated for all the rejections we received during our paper's six-year pilgrimage through most of academia's leading journals.

Certain qualities of thought

I will now try to suggest some distinctive qualities of Max Boisot's amazing mind and thought that were evident in the intellectual process that I was privileged to sustain with Max—and that I believe are evident in the many other works he undertook alone and with others. All the qualities of thought that I mention below were integral elements of the "systemic view of everything" that Max always brought to every conversation.

Breadth of perspectives

While there is no doubt that much may be gained by pushing a single theoretical perspective to its logical limits, that particular form of intellectual effort was clearly not Max's preferred style of thought. Max's perspective on the many topics we discussed was invariably kaleidoscopic, not microscopic, and Max would inevitably suggest at least three or four major perspectives through which any issue or question could be addressed. Perhaps this distinctive quality of thought also reflected Max's training in architecture and urban studies and his fascination with economic history—fields that admit the influence of multiple factors and forces in shaping the evolution of events and systems, rather than seeking a single theoretical explanation for complex, multifaceted phenomena.

At the same time, Max had an uncanny ability to quickly grasp the fundamental implications of any given theoretical perspective for virtually any issue at hand. While some who look widely see only the surface, Max could think broadly and understand deeply at the same time. Certainly one of the most remarkable qualities of Max's thought therefore was not just that he was capable of engaging a multitude of interesting problems in economics and organization through a broad spectrum of theoretical perspectives, but that he was also capable of achieving remarkable clarity and depth in viewing each issue through the many sharply focused theoretical lenses he could bring to bear on virtually any issue.

New conceptualizations based on novel representations

Given his almost reflexive tendency to view economic and organizational issues from multiple theoretical perspectives, it is no surprise that Max was able to reframe some key aspects of economic and organizational phenomena in novel ways by adopting representational schema that incorporate multiple aspects of human cognition and behavior—something that single-theory lenses necessarily fail to capture. Most notably, I think Max found a particularly welcoming and fertile home for his thought process in his conceptualization of organizational phenomena as driven by economic *agents*, a representation that is flexible enough to embrace insights into human decision-making and behavior from fields as diverse as psychology, cognition, organization behavior, and behavioral economics—all of which were domains in which Max could reason with remarkable facility and powerful effect.

I think it is no accident then that what I regard as Max's crowning achievement, the Information-Space Model, takes as its focus and unit of analysis the cognitive processes of agents interacting in an organizational setting. Through the conceptual portal of agents, Max was able to introduce a theoretically diverse and thus more conceptually complete representation of the multiple aspects of human behavior that ultimately drive organizational behaviors and resulting organizational phenomena. In a fundamental sense, the representation of economic actors as agents provided Max with a conceptual vehicle for introducing multiple theoretical perspectives into his Information Space Model of organizations, and then for applying the model in a diverse set of projects underway at his untimely death.

Rigorous categorizations and hierarchical classifications

Given the multiplicity of theoretical perspectives within which Max could work with skill and grace, it should be no surprise that Max was extremely adept at categorizing the conceptual representations used in various theories. Max seemed to have an innate drive—coupled with an extraordinary ability—to construct hierarchical classification systems for ideas that helped greatly to make clear the commonalities (the basis of vertical relationships) and differences (the basis of horizontal distinctions) in the conceptual representations invoked in various economic and organizational theories.

I recall vividly that several times during our extended conversations, Max would get quite animated and say to me, "Oh, no! Now you are conflating [something] with [something else]!" Only an extended discussion of definitions of terms would ultimately resolve whether some Representation or Concept X was actually being confused or equated with another Representation or Concept Y. Working with Max, at least in the extended process of writing our paper, was thus often like an elaborate exercise in making verbal Venn diagrams to clarify the differences and commonalities in the fundamental representations and conceptualizations invoked in various theories. This exercise was of course essential to identify the commonalities, possible complementarities, and fundamental incommensurabilities among the many theories we discussed.

In this regard, Max was one of the few people I know in the academic profession who regarded clear conceptual definitions as an absolute prerequisite to correctly understanding the meanings and interrelationships of ideas in general and of economic and organization theories in particular. In our conversations we willingly spent as many hours as we needed to clarify our respective understandings of critical concepts in various theories—an investment of time and effort that both Max and I regarded as essential to building an intellectual foundation for mutual understanding in our subsequent work together. Perhaps more than any other of our interactions, these extended conversations about fundamental representations and conceptual meanings were the source of the profound intellectual respect and admiration that I came to have for Max.

Some comments on the Information-Space Model

Although Max published many papers and books that contributed in many ways to our understanding of organizations and institutions, perhaps his most significant and enduring contribution may prove to be his masterful Information-Space Model of organizational learning. In crafting a model that insightfully interrelates individual and collective learning processes in organizations, Max not only accomplished a remarkable intellectual feat, but also created a model that can demonstrably be applied to improve the management of learning processes in real organizations. I believe that Max took deep personal pride in the Information-Space Model as perhaps his most significant brainchild, and I know he was deeply gratified to witness the growing acceptance of his model in academic research and its increasing use in management practice.

I should also mention a more personal perspective on Max's Information-Space Model that I have only come to realize as I reflected at length on the process of working with Max on our 2010 paper. I have now come to realize that Max's Information-Space Model describes very well the process that Max and I went through together—as an organization of two, as it were—in trying to create a base of shared cognitions that would enable us to learn from each other and to work productively together. In fundamental respects, the processes of sense-making that Max explained so well in his model—the process of inferential reasoning from the concrete and particular to the abstract and general, followed by the deductive derivation and codification of rules and routines for achieving coordinated action—describe very well our own efforts to connect cognitively and "make sense" together in articulating the processes through which economic organizing happens.

I think it is safe to say that Max has made an enduring contribution to our understanding of organizations. For the Information-Space Model perhaps first and foremost, but certainly also for his many other insightful contributions to our understanding of human organization in many forms, I have no doubt that Max Boisot will be remembered and appreciated not just by the people who were fortunate enough to know him personally, but also by future generations of scholars for whom the breadth and depth of insights generated by his extraordinary intellect will be both a beacon and an inspiration.

16

I-Space and the Value of Basic Research

Markus Nordberg

Introduction

How to capture the value of the process generated by basic research, for example, that of experimental particle physics? This question has been of great interest to government agencies funding basic research, and to industry, policymakers, sociologists and economists for decades. In the specific case of particle physics, it has been approached from several angles, ranging from studying the nature and structure of scientific and R&D collaboration (Knorr Cetina 1999; Tuertscher 2008), contractual benefits to suppliers (Hähnle 1997; Bianchi-Streit et al. 1984, 1988; Autio et al. 1996, 2003; Nordberg and Verbeke 2000; Liyanage et al. 2006; Vuola 2006), looking at innovation strategies (Santalainen 2006; Yami et al. 2010), and exploring the larger relationship between fundamental physics and society (Lederman 1984, Kay and Llewellyn Smith 1985). Despite these contributions, the nature and flow of scientific knowledge such as from particle physics to societal use in its many facets has, so far, not been addressed in terms of one consistent framework.

Max Boisot's conceptual framework of the Information-Space or *I-Space* (Boisot 1998) offered the potential and insights for us at CERN—and more specifically, the ATLAS Collaboration Management—to obtain a holistic view of the full value experimental particle physics research could offer society in the longer run. We were looking for a new angle to the story, to understand ourselves better; also to understand which elements in the scientific process have the potential of generating value for society, and how to categorize and capture this scientific knowledge. We were very pleased when Max agreed to help us, co-chairing two workshops in 2007 and 2008 to go through much of the material referred to above. This work resulted in Max's last book, *Collisions and Collaboration* (Boisot et al. 2011). In the following sections, I shall rely heavily on this work and use it as a basis for raising future research questions that Max's important contribution has triggered related to the value of basic research, using CERN's ATLAS project as a case example.

The relevance of *I-Space* and Social Learning Cycle for particle physics

While scientific knowledge is generally considered to be reliable in nature (Ziman 1968), it emerges from a process under conditions of uncertainty and complexity. For this reason, it is generally perceived to have potential value. The process of scientific research transforms data from an uncodified and concrete state into a codified and abstract state. It can be described as a process of "learning by doing". It then diffuses into society, and over time having been absorbed and further elaborated by individuals, turns back into uncodified knowledge, having gone through a full social learning cycle [SLC] (Boisot, 1998). In Chapter 6 of *Collisions and Collaboration*, this cycle is summarized to six distinctive steps or stages as follows:

1. *Scanning*—A scientific experiment such as ATLAS produces new data, resulting from particle collisions generated by the Large Hadron Collider (LHC) accelerator at the center of the ATLAS detector. These data—and thus possible new physics discoveries—are commonly available to the research community which is a small sub-set of the entire population of the society. Example: the recent observation of the much-sought Higgs-particle seems to have some puzzling properties that may extend the current framework and scope within particle physics.

2. *Codification*—A movement up in the level of codification where fuzzy insights are gradually clarified and articulated as categorically relevant information is extracted from noisy data. New knowledge is created as it gets diffused, involving few members of the population. Example: all ATLAS physics results are published and made available to the scientific community for scrutiny and continuous tests. This requires documenting the methodology and allowing independent verification of the presented results. Some aspects of the published results may be of interest to scientists in other fields. For instance, the physics Higgs mechanism originated from, solid state physics (phase transitions). The experimental results from ATLAS and the other experiments might feed back into future solid state physics theories.

3. *Abstraction*—Different categories that underpin an insight gradually get correlated with each other. When this happens, one category can then represent another leading to a reduction in the total number of categories

required to generate a compact and parsimonious representation of the insight. Example: as the full implications of the Higgs—and other expected—observations in ATLAS get digested, understood and recorded (i.e. published) over time, particle physics theories will be able to integrate more accurately past discoveries and insights into models with higher level of abstractions and explanatory and predictive power. This process is similar to what Mendeleev did while extrapolating from individual observations of properties of elements in the periodic table of elements, followed by the quark model of Gell-Mann and others and integrated further into the current Standard Model of matter. As the total number of categories reduce in these models, the interdependency between the increasing number of parameters increases.

4. *Diffusion*—The size of the population that has access to given items of data, increases, irrespective of whether these have been wrought into meaningful patterns or not. Example: ATLAS makes all its findings and tools available, in the public domain. Although it is unlikely this material will find its way into every living room, it is nevertheless possible that it will inspire, or diffuse somewhere else with no direct relationship with particle physics.

5. *Absorption*—A movement over time where codified data is gradually internalized and assimilated to pre-extant implicit models and value systems. When data gets so internalized it acquires a taken-for-granted quality that makes it more difficult to challenge. Example: the observations of the Higgs particle is expected to consolidate the Standard Model which, over time, could become the basis of ideas and insights which assumes the Standard Model as given, without needing to build up the argumentation from scratch. These insights do not necessarily need to remain in the domain of physics.

6. *Impacting*—A movement away from the abstract and towards the concrete in which abstract knowledge is tested out in concrete applications. Such applications, by contextualizing the knowledge and adapting it to the requirements of specific situations, will increase the number of real-world categories that now have to be dealt with. Example: it is too early to quote such examples resulting from ATLAS, but the history of physics has many examples. Newton's theories of motion, gravitation and light had significant impact on developments made in maritime navigation, electro-magnetism and ballistics.

The insight that the *I-Space* framework provides here is that basic research facing complexity and a high degree of uncertainty, such as experimental particle physics, is designed to *absorb uncertainty* by scanning in a phase of

I-Space where new ideas and inventions can be extracted from the new data generated by scientific experiments. That is, there is a relationship between the design of scientific apparatus and the data it produces: they feed each other. As the level of sophistication of the experiment increases, new and novel technologies need to be deployed. But the technical hurdles that are encountered cannot all be anticipated beforehand—for example, ATLAS has over 10 million functional elements—which means that some of them have to be solved as the problems appear, perhaps adopting several parallel routes and then selecting the most effective one. This process of finding novel solutions while keeping "all options open" is characteristic to the scanning phase in the *I-Space*. This scanning phase is in sharp contrast with the later phases of the *I-Space* related to diffusion and impacting, where industrial companies operate within the market place and where knowledge is in codified and abstract form, distributing it as part of their value-creation process. Established business management practices prevail in this region and are designed and optimized to *reduce uncertainty*.

Boisot et al. (2011) thus suggest applying different types of management models for different phases in the *I-Space*. In the former region, the goal is to maintain the maximum flexibility in the research strategy and problem solving process as long as possible. In the latter region, management structures are geared to optimize production efficiency by reducing associated risks. These fundamental differences imply important policy implications for conducting basic research as well as managing industrial innovation processes as discussed in Boisot et al. (2011). They are closely related with the question of how to create and assess value.

The paradox of value

According to the *I-Space*, every step in an *SLC* enhances society's overall stock of knowledge and hence adds value. As the scientific process involves capital investments and human effort, the value of knowledge acquired by moving through the different phases of an *SLC* must be large enough to offset the costs incurred. But how to assess its value? The classical economic view holds that value is created through utility and scarcity (Walras 1954). In the context of fundamental research this implies stable, reliable knowledge which is then protected and sold—the first part (creating knowledge) is trivial but the latter (hoarding it) is in clear contrast with what have been the fundamental principles of open science for centuries (David 2004). The basic research community is animated by the spirit of the gift (Hagstrom 1965) and broadly favors information sharing through peer-reviewed journals. It thus is in favor of speeding up general technology adaptation but against protecting the related knowledge. So how can science then capture value if it speeds up the *SLC* but then erodes it by giving it away to society as a free gift?

Knowledge, absorption of uncertainty and options thinking

The key insight that Max's *I-Space* offers to solve this value riddle related to basic research is to treat it as a generator of options, and society as executing these options (Boisot et al. 2011). Options offer the right, but not the obligation, to defer a choice to some specified point in the future. By managing options in an inventive manner, upsides can be captured and downsides avoided when considering large and irreversible investments (Sanchez 1993), which are typical for big basic research projects. The basic questions to ask are then: how many options are feasible for possible future selection and what factors determine it? Who creates them? Which options to keep, which to drop and when? What are the costs and benefits of doing so? Who can exercise the options and how?

In a separate paper, McGrath and Boisot (2005) suggested that adequately resourced organizations dealing with complexity and high degrees of uncertainty use their internal coordination processes that link together rules and routines, under strategic guidance, to build up connections or interactions between the elements of identified but limited resources. These resources contain within them latent potential, also called "shadow options" (Bowman and Hurry 1993). The complexes of interactive options could then expand in emergent, adaptive ways. It is the responsibility of the manager—the agent of selection—to recognize the opportunity to exercise options. One of the key arguments in the paper is that the generated option value or eventual payoff would not be linear if interconnectivity is achieved between the created options, i.e. not simply by adding them up—and in the case of basic research, the impact of scientific discoveries has proven to follow a distribution of a power law (Boisot et al. 2011). This would make the potential payoff significantly higher than the arithmetic sum of individual option values. Thus scientific research projects, while also seeking funding and approval, need to put effort toward structuring interconnected resources and assets into work packages or deliverables that maintain maximum flexibility so as to favor emergent outcomes or solutions within an agreed delivery schedule.

Unfinished business and future research

Our purpose was, together with Max, to test the above ideas and further generalize his ideas of extending (non-linear) options theory to the *I-Space* framework. Alas, this did not happen. However, he did lay out his thoughts in the summer of 2011 on how this work could proceed. His key idea was to focus more on the concept of "adjacent possible" (Kauffman 2000) which refers to states of the world that have not happened yet but which can be reached through inventive research strategies and processes, thus transforming states of possibilities to those of probabilities and being able to work down the path from exploration to exploitation (March 1991). The research model applicable to basic research, for example ATLAS, needs to take into account that front-line research requires highly technical and performing equipment where the rate of technical development is high and where the related level of asset specificity is high. That is, the pieces of apparatus are "out of this world" in terms of their capabilities, and the resources made available are very specific and hard to deploy elsewhere—they are not standard products. Scientific instruments such as ATLAS are, in fact, prototypes never to be re-built in (large) quantities but which instead give rise to second-generation, order-of-magnitude more powerful instruments of future research projects. If one uses the well-established notion of Research and Development (R&D) as a point of reference, the emphasis is more on the "R" rather than on the "D" part.

Another important feature to capture in an options-based model is that basic research is typically longer term in nature and is designed to maintain flexibility in terms of creating and maintaining multiple, parallel research paths for as long as possible. This has important implications for the way such research projects are run and managed. It requires a collaborative, bottom-up, consensus-driven management style. It may include a relaxed approach to protecting intellectual property so as to maximize an environment of open innovation (Chesbrough, 2003), with potential consequences for value creation for potential industrial partners.

A third and related challenge is to address the question of probability distributions related to the decision-making process and value creation. The classical Black and Scholes model (Black and Scholes 1973) applies log normal distributions to address future uncertainty. But experience has cruelly proven that conditions of high uncertainty do not necessarily follow a log normal distribution (Taleb 2007; Knight 1921). Although the use of options theory could therefore be questionable in this context, options *thinking* might nevertheless apply. In particular, the question of volatility and how to interpret it, while addressing the states of "adjacent possible," needs to be given careful consideration. The latter requires taking into account the behavior models, both assumed and possible, of the actors, including the scientists, funding agencies and industry. In terms of designing a research model, the following components need to be addressed:

I-Space and the Value of Basic Research

1. Laying out the basic assumptions concerning the nature and classification of available, bounded resources or assets (tangible/intangible) of the research organization in *I-Space*; their life-cycle and inter-dependence; time-dependency; required level of interconnectivity and complexity; value; probability distributions: availability and access to new, future information.
2. Definition of "adjacent possible" as a (value) state that can be operated upon and altered through scientific assets such as those available at CERN.
3. Definition of downstream decision points which can generate new opportunities or strategic choices, or where the option needs to be "dropped."
4. Definition of the actors/agents; their inter-relationships; relationships with resources and assets; behavioral (economic) models; time-dependencies.
5. Definition and description of the key parameters (resource; option; value; expiry time or milestone event).
6. Modeling and simulation of selected actors/agents using e.g. an agent-based model, optimizing the generated option value for CERN-projects such as ATLAS.

All these components above build on one another. Specifying each of them will require additional research. Max's guidance in progressing further is sorely missed.

Conclusion

The *I-Space* framework developed by Max Boisot offers a new and powerful framework to address the question of the value of basic research. It allows us to analyze the value-creation process in terms of the social learning cycle in a novel way. Regrettably, the work launched by Max remains incomplete and merits further effort. I have proposed some guidelines, based on Max's recent work and informal discussions.

17

Boisot and the God Particle

Marzio Nessi

Trying to portray an eclectic personality like Max Boisot is simply an impossible task. Every one of us, who came across him one way or another, has been fascinated by his curiosity, his common sense and his way of jumping into any problematics that captured his interest.

Our community of scientists at CERN in Geneva, which is bravely trying to understand how nature works in its deepest aspects, had attracted Max's interest since the mid-1990s. We try in fact to answer questions which most people in society do not even manage to formulate. This is an enormous challenge, but also a huge privilege.

The project is ATLAS at the LHC, the Large Hadron Collider. At first sight we look a bit disorganized, with no formal hierarchical chain of command and an enormous plan in front of us. We are scattered across the planet, coming from about 200 universities and national research laboratories located in 38 nations—a variety of cultural, linguistic and ethnic differences. In July 2012 we presented our research on the Higgs particle, the famous "God particle" which is responsible for our being composed of mass and not just pure energy. This is a fundamental building block of nature, which is at the basis of everything, in a manner nature's physical DNA, captured in its most intimate secrets. It seems we were right in looking for it, and we are presently scoring very high. It was a challenging piece of information for Max, which unfortunately he did not manage to follow up to the end.

One can imagine Max's reaction facing such a fertile and unexplored ground. He was intrigued by the way we create new knowledge. Max was interested in the Higgs discovery as a "proof of concept." Its discovery closes many doors to interpretation or possibilities, as much as it consolidates the present Standard Model, but at the same time it opens up a new alley of options in other fields of science, because it suggests a new way of looking at things, and it can inspire a new way of thinking.

It probably represents the most abstract level of thinking that mankind has reached up to now. The Higgs mechanism is a fundamental one, which breaks a basic symmetry in nature in order to allow different basic components of our Universe to acquire or not acquire mass, a necessary step to allow for the existence of atoms, stars and galaxies. It was postulated in the mid-1960s, borrowing the idea from other fields of science, like solid state physics. It took us more than 40 years to prove it: an incredible adventure in science and technology, at the edge of science fiction.

I would say that over the past five to six years, Max was like a therapist to us: we would be telling him how we work, how we organize ourselves, how we relate to each other, and what our deepest motivations are. He would listen to us, ask many questions, and make us think. We came to understand that there is some kind of logic and some common behavior in the way we operate. Nothing is random, as we initially thought. There was more logic in the way we were organizing ourselves than we could ever imagine.

Basic research is typically a longer-term endeavor and it is designed to remain flexible in terms of creating and maintaining, as long as possible, multiple and parallel paths. This implies a truly collaborative behavior, a bottom-up approach, and a consensus-driven management style.

All this is not exactly what you learn in today's business schools, and we thought that this was our weakness. Instead, Max taught us that this was indeed our strength, possibly the only way of dealing with very complex problems, of working down the path from exploration to exploitation.

Big science is intrinsically complex, since it does not depend on individuals or leaders, but rather relies increasingly on an incredibly extended network of individuals, organizations and institutions. In ATLAS we count 3000 to 4000 scientists working together for almost two decades. We share resources, we all sign together the scientific publications we produce. No secrets, pure democracy at all levels.

The kind of leadership needed to not only get such a show on the road, but also keep it going for many years (35–40 years in our case), is not vested in a few individuals. We are three managers in ATLAS today, but we do not control people nor the process. We just do our best to coordinate the activities, to keep the project focused and to keep basic responsibilities under control. This seems to work rather well.

I think Max was fascinated by this way of going forward. He saw a value for society in all this, a new way of proceeding in dealing with extreme complexity. At the same time, he was puzzled while observing us. How does a scientific collaboration as large as ATLAS generate and sustain creative and constructive interactions among thousands of researchers from diverse cultures, traditions and habits?

There is no obvious answer to this; it is all based on a long tradition, a habit strongly permeating the scientific community since its beginnings in the first half of the last century. The whole of CERN was built in the 1950s around this concept. The collaboration's rules and mechanisms grew over time and in size. The delivery of the World-Wide Web protocol by CERN to humanity in the early 1990s, best summarizes the spirit behind it all.

Maybe the answer is a simple one, and it is sufficient to look at nature: do bees care about their queen? Max introduced us to terms such as Adhocracy. He told us that we act as a clan, and that we profit from our power of self-organization. He told us that we are working on a cliff, very close to chaos, and from that comes our productivity and capability to innovate.

We did not always agree with his analysis, in particular when he pushed to the extreme his views on the self-organizational capability of the collaboration. Thinking that we can run such a complex process, with nobody having a full overview, is possibly too much. Maybe the real leadership is just hidden and not obviously visible. If only I could, I would now challenge him on the difference between authority and responsibility. Authority is easy and often relates to the ego inside each one of us. Responsibility is a more serious step to take, it roots deeply in our personality, it reflects best our deepest values in life. It is on the concept of responsibility that most of our society and ethics are based.

When we saw Max for the last time, at the 2011 EGOS conference in Gothenburg, he wanted to go further and address the next big question: what is the value of all this for society? We understood that our value is in the "R" of R&D. Scientific instruments like ATLAS are in fact prototypes, which will never be rebuilt again. They will evolve, however, towards second-generation, one order of magnitude more powerful instruments of future research projects. Real quantum jumps, new paradigms for our society, which face ever-increasing complexity. These are real bridges between fundamental questions and society. We do not know how far all this will take us. Time will teach us how to best use the scientific and technical progress we make. Exactly in the same way, at the beginning of the last century, the discovery of quantum mechanics and general relativity created the basis of today's world, in terms of technology, of quality and life expectation. One hundred years ago nobody understood how a microchip or a GPS would work. But the knowledge was set right then. We just profit from it now. Nowadays we seek medical help and we use antimatter to be diagnosed. Very few people realize how far we have gone.

Max introduced us to his *I-Space* concept, which to me, as a physicist, looks like the cycle of Carnot in thermodynamics. One expands, one concentrates, one opens and closes possibilities, one increases entropy, one nails down options. Max spoke of steps like: Scanning, Codification, Abstraction, Diffusion, Absorption, Impacting. Different management styles apply to each step. And this is exactly how it happened in our case.

Going more deeply, the next question was how to capture the value of the process generated by basic research. He taught us the concept of intensive research, which goes into fundamental laws, in contrast to extensive research, which goes into explaining the phenomena in terms of known fundamental laws. Public opinion hardly makes any distinction between the two.

Today, intensive research is under attack. It is difficult to explain it to the public, which has a hard time understanding it and does not look favorably at the large costs it generates. Nevertheless, extensive research needs fundamental laws to continue existing. Applied research needs the underlying research it applies.

This is the fundamental value of innovation—the key to progress, the boost to the economy and to a better quality of life. Why sell products in a market economy? It is much better to sell knowledge. Today's economy thrives on the creation, diffusion, internalization and application of new knowledge. The knowledge generated by intensive research itself has no great value or consideration. It has become a public good.

All of this puzzled Max. His passing is a real loss. We were just starting to move into new territory. The discovery of the Higgs particle, I am sure, would have triggered his imagination.

We miss him. We miss his fantastic common sense, his unique way of making a synthesis of what he observed. Exactly the way we act in our research field.

Thank you, Max.

18

Conclusion and Outlook

John Child and Martin Ihrig

There are two remarkable attributes of Max Boisot's work that the contributions to this book and its selection of his writings clearly identify. The first is that his thinking rests on the premise that information and knowledge are the most fundamental attributes of human collective existence. They are the essence of communication and are crucial to survival and prosperity in our environment. The second attribute is that Boisot applied this apparently simple insight to create new understanding of an extremely wide spectrum of social phenomena. As this book has shown, these range from managerial work to national business systems, from the emergence of human organization to the contemporary challenge of organizing in complex environments, and from the abstraction of high theory to modes of learning which enable practitioners to experience its relevance. It was the centrality and simple elegance of his underlying premise that facilitated such a wide range of applications. Boisot's structuring of his key insight, through the *I-Space* framework, into the underlying dimensions of information greatly assisted its dissemination. Although this facilitation of knowledge dissemination through its structuring is precisely what Boisot's framework would predict, one should not discount the unrelenting effort that he put into expounding his approach.

This concluding chapter has two aims. The first is to provide an integrated and summary overview of the areas in which Boisot forged new understanding. Brevity is in order because this is ground already covered by previous chapters. The second aim is to suggest how we might constructively take Boisot's work forward in terms of further research and debate. This requires that we consider some of its limitations as well as its underlying strengths.

Summary overview

Information and knowledge are absolutely central to Boisot's *I-Space* framework. For Boisot, "information is something immaterial that is extracted from data and that modifies an agent's disposition to act. Such a disposition constitutes an agent's knowledge base so that knowledge is a possession of individual agents" (Boisot 1998, 154). Knowledge is derived through a process of consolidating data into information, which is then interpreted with reference to a situation that is meaningful to an agent (actor). In other words, knowledge is a validated platform for an agent to take action. A particular body of knowledge, with its associated interpretations, is typically shared among groups of agents, in their capacity as members of the same organization, occupation, network, village, country or other social unit. This is the basis of their common culture and their occupancy of the same "semantic space."

In this book, we have recorded most of the issues to which Boisot applied the *I-Space* and its forerunner, the *C-Space*. The extensive compass of the issues he addressed, and the publication of his writings in journals from different disciplines, presents a challenge to appreciating the underlying unity of his work around his core framework. This is why we have attempted in this book to collect the main areas in which Boisot forged new understanding and to clarify the power of his analytical framework to illuminate such a wide range of major concerns in the study of organization and management.

A fundamental requirement for Boisot was to conceptualize knowledge in relation to the associated notions of data and information. This conceptual clarification, as several of our contributors have noted, was long overdue. Boisot's view of knowledge as comprising a set of expectations that guide action has profound implications. For, insofar as these expectations are cognitively and normatively shared, it identifies knowledge as a cultural construct. It places at the center of inquiry questions concerning the extent that the same knowledge is socially shared, and the role of knowledge structuring in facilitating this sharing. Variations along these dimensions identify the singularity of cultural systems by locating them in different segments of the *I-Space*.

Boisot focused on the form of information rather than on its content. Form was expressed in terms of the three dimensions of the *I-Space*: codified-uncodified; abstract-concrete; diffused-undiffused. This may appear at first sight to be somewhat stylized, but Boisot regarded the *I-Space* as providing the key insight into how social and organizational systems are governed, and how well adapted they are to the conditions of their environments. The four segments of the *I-Space*: bureaucracy, market, fief and clan distinguish broad options for the governance of transactions. At the same time, they also identify different forms of knowledge asset that a society or an organization might possess ranging from the tacit to the explicit, and the private to the public. However, reflecting the aphorism that "an organization always possesses more knowledge than it knows," it is typically the case that not all available knowledge assets are recognized. The strategic importance of knowledge coupled with its frequent underutilization places a premium on its management, both in terms of ensuring that the full variety of relevant information is recognized and accessed, and that it is integrated into a viable platform for action.

Boisot maintained that three knowledge management conditions are required for organizations and societies to realize their full potential. First, the different repositories of available knowledge that are critical to an organization's operations need to be identified and mapped. Second, the balance between structured and unstructured knowledge, and the degree of formality with which it is communicated, need to be adjusted to the complexity and variability of the environment in which the organization or society has to make its way. Thus the variety of information within an organization needs to match the variety of the environment and of threats and opportunities emanating from it. This insight gives rise to the "law of requisite complexity." It also raises the question whether an attempt to reduce complexity through retaining existing informational structures is likely to succeed as against the alternative of the "complex regime" which is receptive to a range of different forms and sources of new information. The former approach is only likely to succeed in simple and stable environments, or in circumstances where the leaders of an organization have the power to impose their preferred conditions upon the environment (Child and Rodrigues 2011). Boisot did not, however, develop this latter possibility. His view was that, in the face of the increasing informational complexity that characterizes the contemporary organizational environment, optimization involves learning how to manage a complex regime close to, but not over, the edge of chaos. This would be particularly true for the organization seeking to develop through innovation. The third requirement for organizations to realize their full potential is that their managers need to have sufficient overall understanding of the organization's different knowledge domains to be able to switch between them as conditions require and to integrate them. Integration involves both the bringing together of complementary knowledge sets, and the constructive conversion of knowledge between tacit and explicit forms as in the social learning cycle.

As an example of a highly complex large organization that is operating close to the edge of chaos towards the lower right-hand corner of the *I-Space*, the ATLAS project at CERN assumed major significance for Boisot. Its primarily bottom-up loosely coupled network, which effectively draws together the knowledge contributions of over 3000 diverse scientists scattered around the world, indicates the presence of a super-clan model of organizing, close to

Mintzberg's model of an adhocracy (Mintzberg 1979). Not only does this offer an apparently effective model for the organization of big science; it also suggests a way forward in society as a whole towards a less hierarchical and more open model of organization that can provide greater innovation, commitment and satisfaction—and less opportunity for self-serving leadership. As Canals notes in his chapter, Boisot's analysis of the ATLAS project developed insights that offer a program of research for many years to come.

There is general agreement among those who had direct experience of Boisot as an educator that his pedagogical style also followed a comparable model of non-hierarchical open discourse. It reflected his deep belief that the transfer of knowledge requires not just communication but also absorption. Absorption means internalization, ideally though blending theory with personal experience. Here Boisot's educational philosophy was informed by his view that there are three types of knowledge which reflect a progression of codification and diffusion (ease of sharing) in the *I-Space*. In the non-codified zone there is experiential knowledge that comes from people's individual senses—what they can see, hear, feel, smell, or touch. This kind of knowledge can be difficult to convey to others and hence to diffuse. Open to greater codification and sharing, there is narrative knowledge as conveyed in description. At the codified level, there is abstract symbolic knowledge which can arise from narrative through the process of classification. Abstract symbolic knowledge can be expressed in a standardized, stable and durable form that is amenable to wide diffusion among a large population of other people. Boisot was keenly aware of the need to move back and forth between these levels of knowledge so as to combine concrete experience and conceptual abstraction in order to help students fully appreciate the practicality of applying good theory to specific situations and the need always to theorize reflectively about their own experience.

Looking to the future

Boisot's work amply satisfied the oft-cited criterion for truly creative scholarship, namely that it should raise more questions for further inquiry than it answers. Many paths of discovery remain to be travelled in terms of further specifying and testing the core *I-Space* framework, particularly in applying it to a range of policy issues. The contributors to this book were all working with Boisot in one capacity or another, many on lines of research that they intend to continue or that they would like to encourage others to pick up and run with.

Even some of the fundamentals of Boisot's work remain open to further reflection and investigation. For example, he regarded knowledge as the consolidation of information in a way that stabilized an agent's expectations about his or her social relationships and identity. There are several ways in which such stabilization can be achieved, and Boisot recognized that these could range from highly codified contracts backed by legal codes, to quasi-codified normative systems such as corporate cultures, and to the uncodified realm of trust. There is still much work to be done into the personal and contextual conditions that impact on these bases for stabilizing expectations with reference to how they are selected, how they may combine and the consequences they have. It was also one of Boisot's fundamental assumptions that information has the potential to become a knowledge asset. But we still do not know enough about the conditions that assist this process. For instance, does an agent's prior knowledge assist him or her to record and interpret information more adequately so as to transform it into an asset? Does experience in drawing upon knowledge assets give rise to a further capability, which is making good use of knowledge and which we often call "wisdom" (Bierly, Kessler and Christensen 2000)?

There is also a need for further investigation into the process of knowledge creation and transfer. There are types of organization in which knowledge creation still remains somewhat of a mystery, including those in the "knowledge" sectors themselves such as health sciences and software development. The process of knowledge transfer between organizations often fails to meet expectations, especially in mergers, acquisitions and joint ventures, and we need to achieve a better understanding of the reasons for this—for instance, whether the presence between organizations of different semantic spaces in the *I-Space* is a factor. Although the *I-Space* assumes that the codification of information assists its diffusion, it is common experience that the presence of multiple coding schemes within or between organizations can create cognitive, and maybe emotional, barriers to information sharing. It is with an awareness of challenges such as these, some of which Boisot himself articulated in the last year of his life, that the *I-Space* Institute and his colleagues at the Wharton School aim to continue to push forward the frontiers of knowledge research along the lines that Ihrig and MacMillan set out in the conclusion to their chapter.

Other significant issues in the strategic management of knowledge remain open to investigation with the benefit of the *I-Space* and *SLC* models. For example, the long-standing recognition that organizations embody paradoxes based on intrinsic contradictions (Cameron and Quinn 1988) raises questions such as how multiple activities within a single organization or even within an individual role can be managed effectively when these are at different stages of the *SLC*. The need to combine a variety of positions within the *I-Space* presents a significant practical challenge that requires further investigation—for example, how in medical practice to combine codified prescriptions with creative diagnoses unfettered by prior codification. The former can provide high reliability; the latter can enable a creative response to unusual combinations of idiosyncratic patient conditions. Another avenue for research concerns the relationship between cognitive and relational complexity (Boisot and Child 1999). Thus, whereas high relational complexity (extensive networking) may help to cope with high cognitive complexity by permitting its absorption and keeping options open, one can ask whether the reverse is equally true. Are different capabilities required to manage cognitive and relational complexity?

Boisot's work on big science is also likely to continue in the hands of his collaborators in the CERN project. Productive though this work already was, it had hardly taken off in the light of the many significant issues that it raised and which Canals lists in his chapter. There is the promise here of learning a great deal more about how society can achieve a better return from its investment in scientific activity.

Avenues of future inquiry also arise from certain issues that are related to Boisot's work, which either he did not explore to their limits, or which amount to gaps in his thinking. Culture provides an example of the former. Boisot was always keenly aware of culture, coming as he did from a multicultural background. He was very interested in how the material forces of economic and technological development (especially ICTs) might modify the effects of cultural configurations within the *I-Space*. However, he gave rather less attention to questions concerning the substantive content of cultures. Such questions would include the degree to which cultural values and practices are malleable rather than firmly embedded and whether they can be suppressed through the ideological manipulations of non-democratic regimes. Can ideologies be sufficiently influential as to lead to reinterpretations of traditional cultural codes? Here the experiences under communist regimes of Maoist China and contemporary North Korea would provide instructive case studies. We see many examples of where ideology, serving political ends, can apparently influence what is accepted as valid knowledge. This process is also present in the gentler regimes of democratic societies, and in the attempts of corporations to inculcate managerially-inspired "corporate cultures" and images of social responsibility. An important question is whether such attempts at cultural indoctrination are lasting or merely skin deep, and whether specific contextual and historical conditions affect this. Reference to the *I-Space* may help provide an answer, suggesting that people living in societies with less codified, more implicit, systems of social norms are likely to be more resistant to internalizing ideological precepts that are highly codified in formulaic slogans—i.e. conveyed in an alien form.

Boisot's analysis of institutional or organizational arrangements in terms of different configurations of informational dimensions, meant that he was, at least implicitly, regarding them as cultural products. This may account for the way that he tended to omit another factor that influences the shaping of institutions and organizations, namely power and interest. This is a surprising limitation because Boisot was well versed in political studies and in the "old" institutionalism that took power into account (e.g. Selznick 1949). This neglect is significant because even though Boisot's analysis of large-scale cooperative systems like CERN may offer an exciting alternative to traditional hierarchical organization outside the realm of big science, it would be naïve to assume that this alternative will readily be accepted by those who currently enjoy the favorable returns of a high hierarchical position.

This limited attention to power is also surprising in view of the old adage that "information is power." As Boisot elegantly explained in his 1995 and 1998 books, information is superseding physical energy in economic activity. This means that increasingly it is information which creates value. Its accumulation and hoarding therefore become a source of economic power. Information also bolsters organizational power both because it is the means through which those in control can monitor what is going on and because, as we just noted in the case of ideology, it is the bearer of ideas around which collective action can be mobilized and behavior socially legitimized. To take an example: while Boisot was correct in his technical appraisal that ICTs enable a greater diffusion of information at a given or lower level of structuring, he did not address the question of whether governing authorities would permit this to happen. The relevance of this question is not confined to authoritarian regimes like China's. We are seeing many instances in the Western democracies of governments attempting to limit the information that is available to their electors through the media, including IT-based social media channels. Their attempt to suppress Wikileaks is merely a prominent example of a general trend.

Power is also relevant when considering how organizations can cope with external complexity. This is not simply a technical challenge of matching internal variety and information processing capability to that of the relevant outside world, vital though that is. For relations between organizations and external parties may be subject to negotiation in ways that can permit some "reduction" of external complexity. It largely depends on the power that organizational leaders have over external parties like government agencies, and which they may be able to enhance through the effective mobilization of support (Child and Rodrigues 2011). The incorporation of power and interest into future explorations of information and knowledge is therefore necessary and it offers a means to build on Boisot's work in order to address issues of great significance to all of us.

We conclude this book in anticipation of all the significant future research that will be based on Max Boisot's work. The various chapters clearly demonstrate how Max applied his core insights into the central role of knowledge to create a new understanding of many fundamental issues in organization and management. Though there are still further doors to unlock, he has left us with the keys to do so. Through the ideas he helped seed, he will live forever.

Bibliography

1. Writings by Max Boisot

Boisot, M. (1981). "A Framework for Analysing the Diffusion of Technical Knowledge: The Chemical Industry in South East Asia." Unpublished PhD thesis, Imperial College, London.

Boisot, M. (1982). "The Codification and Diffusion of Knowledge in the Transactional Strategy of Firms." *Keio Economic Studies*, 19 (1).

Boisot, M. (1983). "Convergence Revisited: The Codification and Diffusion of Knowledge in a British and Japanese Firm." *Journal of Management Studies*, 20 (2): 159–190.

Boisot, M. (1986a). "Action Learning with Chinese Characteristics: The China-EEC Management Programme." *Management Education and Development*, 17 (2): 128–36.

Boisot, M. (1986b). "Markets and Hierarchies in a Cultural Perspective." *Organization Studies*, 7 (2): 135–158.

Boisot, M. (1987a). "Industrial Feudalism and Enterprise Reform — Could the Chinese Use Some More Bureaucracy?" In M. Warner (ed.), *Management Reforms in China*, London: Frances Pinter, 217–237.

Boisot, M. (1987b). *Information and Organizations: The Manager as Anthropologist*. London: Fontana/Collins.

Boisot, M. (1994). "Information, Economics, and Evolution: What Scope for a Ménage à Trois?" *World Futures: The Journal of General Evolution*, 41(4): 227–256.

Boisot, M. (1995a). *Information Space: A Framework for Learning in Organizations, Institutions and Culture*. London: Routledge.

Boisot, M. (1995b). "Is your Firm a Creative Destroyer—Competitive Learning and Knowledge Flows in the Technological Strategies of Firms." *Research Policy*, 24 (4): 489–506.

Boisot, M. (1998). *Knowledge Assets: Securing Competitive Advantage in the Information Economy*. Oxford: Oxford University Press.

Boisot, M. (2002). "The Creation and Sharing of Knowledge." In C. W. Choo and N. Bontis (eds), *The Strategic Management of Intellectual Capital and Organizational Knowledge*, Oxford: Oxford University Press, 65–77.

Boisot, M. (2007). "Moving to the Edge of Chaos: Bureaucracy, IT, and the Challenge of Complexity." In M. Boisot, I. C. MacMillan, and K. S. Han (eds), *Explorations in Information Space: Knowledge, Agents, and Organization*, Oxford: Oxford University Press, 147–170.

Boisot, M. (2011). "Generating Knowledge in a Connected World: The Case of the ATLAS Experiment at CERN." *Management Learning*, 42 (4): 447–457.

Bibliography

Boisot, M. and Canals, A. (2004). "Data, Information and Knowledge: Have We Got It Right?" *Journal of Evolutionary Economics*, 14 (1): 43–67.

Boisot, M. and Child, J. (1988). "The Iron Law of Fiefs: Bureaucratic Failure and the Problem of Governance in the Chinese Economic Reforms." *Administrative Science Quarterly*, 33: 507–527.

Boisot, M. and Child, J. (1996a). "From Fiefs to Clans and Network Capitalism: Explaining China's Emerging Economic Order." *Administrative Science Quarterly*, 41 (4): 600–628.

Boisot, M. and Child, J. (1996b). "The Institutional Nature of China's Emerging Economic Order." In D. Brown and R. Porter (eds), *Management Issues in China: Volume I Domestic Enterprises*, London: Routledge, 35–58.

Boisot, M. and Child, J. (1999). "Organizations as Adaptive Systems in Complex Environments: The Case of China." *Organization Science*, 10 (3): 237–252.

Boisot, M. and Child, J. (2007). "China and the New Economy: A Case of Convergence?" In A. Corallo, G. Passiante and A. Prencipe (eds), *The Digital Business Ecosystem*, Cheltenham: Edward Elgar.

Boisot, M. and Cohen, J. (2000). "Shall I Compare Thee to an Organization?" *Emergence*, 2 (4): 113–35.

Boisot, M. and Fiol, M. (1987). "Chinese Boxes and Learning Cubes: Action Learning in a Cross-Cultural Context." *Journal of Management Development*, 6 (2): 8–18.

Boisot, M. and Griffiths, D. (1999). "Possession is Nine-Tenths of the Law: Managing a Firm's Knowledge Base in a Regime of Weak Appropriability." *International Journal of Technology Management*, 17 (6): 662–676.

Boisot, M. and Li, Y. (2007a). "Codification, Abstraction, and Firm Differences: A Cognitive Information-Based Perspective." In M. Boisot, I. C. MacMillan, and K. S. Han (eds), *Explorations in Information Space: Knowledge, Agents, and Organization*, Oxford: Oxford University Press, 77–108.

Boisot, M. and Li, Y. (2007b). "Organizational versus Market Knowledge: From Concrete Embodiment to Abstract Representation." In M. Boisot, I. C. MacMillan, and K. S. Han (eds), *Explorations in Information Space: Knowledge, Agents, and Organization*, Oxford: Oxford University Press, 109–146.

Boisot, M. and Lu, X. (2007). "Competing and Collaborating in Networks: Is Organizing Just a Game?" In M. Gibbert and T. Durand (eds), *Strategic Networks: Learning to Compete*, Malden, Mass: Blackwell Publishing, 151–69.

Boisot, M. and MacMillan, I. C. (2004). "Crossing Epistemological Boundaries: Managerial and Entrepreneurial Approaches to Knowledge Management." *Long Range Planning*, 37 (6): 505.

Boisot, M. and MacMillan, I. C. (2007). "Crossing Epistemological Boundaries: Managerial and Entrepreneurial Approaches to Knowledge Management." In M. Boisot, I. C. MacMillan, and K. S. Han (eds), *Explorations in Information Space: Knowledge, Agents, and Organization*, Oxford: Oxford University Press, 48–76.

Boisot, M. and McKelvey, B. (2005a). "Counter-Terrorism as Global Neighborhood Watch." Presented at the Department of Justice Conference on Neighborhood Watch, August 23, Los Angeles.

Boisot, M. and McKelvey, B. (2005b). "Counter-Terrorism as Global Neighborhood Watch: A Socio/Computational Approach for Getting Patterns from Dots." Presented at the 47th Annual Conference of the International Military Testing Association, November 8, Singapore.

Boisot, M. and McKelvey, B. (2006a). "Speeding up Strategic Foresight in a Dangerous, Complex World: A Complexity Approach." In G. Suder (ed.), *Corporate Strategies Under International Terrorism and Adversity*, Cheltenham, UK: Edward Elgar, 20–37.

Boisot, M. and McKelvey, B. (2006b). "A Socio/Computational Method for Staying Ahead of Terrorist and Other Adversities." In G. Suder (ed.), *Corporate Strategies Under International Terrorism and Adversity*, Cheltenham, UK: Edward Elgar, 38–55.

Boisot, M. and McKelvey, B. (2007). "Extreme Events, Power Laws, and Adaptation: Towards an Econophysics of Organization." *Best Paper Proceedings*, Academy of Management Conference, August, Philadelphia, PA.

Boisot, M. and McKelvey, B. (2010). "Integrating Modernist and Postmodernist Perspectives on Organizations: A Complexity Science Bridge." *Academy of Management Review*, 35 (3): 415–433.

Boisot, M. and McKelvey, B. (2011a). "Ashby's Law of Requisite Variety: A Complexity Perspective." In P. Allen, S. Maguire, and B. McKelvey (eds), *Handbook of Complexity and Management*, London: Sage, 279–98.

Boisot, M. and McKelvey, B. (2011b). "Connectivity, Extremes, and Adaptation: A Power-Law Perspective of Organizational Effectiveness." *Journal of Management Inquiry*, 20 (2): 119–133.

Boisot, M. and Meyer, M. W. (2008). "Which Way Through the Open Door? Reflections on the Internationalization of Chinese Firms." *Management and Organization Review*, 4 (3): 349–365.

Boisot, M. and Nordberg, M. (2011). "ATLAS and the Future of High-Energy Physics." In M. Boisot, M. Nordberg, S. Yami, and B. Nicquevert (eds), *Collisions and Collaboration: The Organization of Learning in the ATLAS Experiment at the LHC*, Oxford: Oxford University Press, 268–288.

Boisot, M. and Sanchez, R. (2010). "Organization as a Nexus of Rules: Emergence in the Evolution of Systems of Exchange." *Management Revue*, 21 (4): 378–405.

Boisot, M. and Xing, G. L. (1992). "The Nature of Managerial Work in the Chinese Enterprise Reforms: A Study of Six Directors." *Organization Studies*, 13 (2): 161–184.

Boisot, M., Child, J., and Redding, G. (2011). "Working the System: Towards a Theory of Cultural and Institutional Competence." *International Studies of Management and Organization*, 41 (1): 62–95.

Boisot, M., Griffiths, D., and Moles, V. (1997). "The Dilemma of Competence: Differentiation versus Integration in the Pursuit of Learning." In R. Sanchez and A. Heene (eds), *Strategic Learning and Knowledge Management*, Chichester: Wiley, 65–82.

Boisot, M., MacMillan, I. C., and Han, K. S. (2007). "Property Rights and Information Flows: A Simulation Approach." *Journal of Evolutionary Economics*, 17 (1): 63.

Boisot, M., MacMillan, I. C., and Han, K. S. (2008). *Explorations in Information Space: Knowledge, Agents, and Organization*: New York: Oxford University Press.

Bibliography

Boisot, M., Canals, A., Ihrig, M., and Nordberg, M. (2011). "Knowledge as Public Good? The Case of the ATLAS Experiment at the LHC." Paper presented at the 2011 SMS Conference, Miami, USA.

Boisot, M., Eun, S. H., Han, K. S., and MacMillan, I. C. (2005). "Sim *I-Space*: An Agent-Based Modelling Approach to Knowledge Management Processes." In S. O. Kimbrough and D. J Wu (ed.), *Formal Modelling in Electronic Commerce, International Handbooks on Information System*, Berlin: Springer-Verlag, 247–294.

Boisot, M., Nordberg, M., Yami, S., and Nicquevert, B. (eds) (2011). *Collisions and Collaboration: The Organization of Learning in the ATLAS Experiment at the LHC*. Oxford: Oxford University Press.

Bressan, B. and Boisot, M. (2011). "The Individual in the ATLAS Collaboration: A Learning Perspective." In M. Boisot, M. Nordberg, S. Yami, and B. Nicquevert (eds), *Collisions And Collaboration: The Organization of Learning in the ATLAS Experiment at the LHC*, Oxford: Oxford University Press, 201–225.

Canals, A., Boisot, M., and MacMillan, I. (2008). "The Spatial Dimension of Knowledge Flows: A Simulation Approach." *Cambridge Journal of Regions, Economy and Society*, 1 (2): 175–204.

Canals, A., Boisot, M., Ihrig, M., Nordberg, M., and Mabey, C. (2011). "The 'Intangible Hand' in a Knowledge-Based Organization: The Case of the ATLAS Experiment at the LHC." Paper presented at the EGOS 2011 Colloquium, Gothenburg, Sweden.

Griffiths, D., Boisot, M., and Moles, V. (1998). "Strategies for Managing Knowledge Assets: A Tale of Two Companies." *Technovation*, 18 (8–9): 529–539.

Hoffmann, H., Nordberg, M., and Boisot, M. (2011). "ATLAS and E-Science." In M. Boisot, M. Nordberg, S. Yami, and B. Nicquevert (eds), *Collisions and Collaboration: The Organization of Learning in the ATLAS Experiment at the LHC*, Oxford, UK: Oxford University Press, 247–267.

Ihrig, M., Boisot, M., and MacMillan, I. (2011a). "Are you Wasting Money on Useless Knowledge Management?" *HBR Blog Network*: Harvard Business Review.

Ihrig, M., Boisot, M., and MacMillan, I. (2011b). "Forget IP. Mine Strategic Knowledge Instead." *HBR Blog Network*: Harvard Business Review.

Ihrig, M., MacMillan, I., Zu Knyphausen-Aufseß, D., and Boisot, M. (2010). "Knowledge-Based Opportunity Recognition Strategies: A Simulation Approach." Paper presented at the Strategic Management Society Conference, Rome, Italy.

Liyanage, S. and Boisot, M. (2011). "Leadership in the ATLAS Collaboration." In M. Boisot, M. Nordberg, S. Yami, and B. Nicquevert (eds), *Collisions and Collaboration: The Organization of Learning in the ATLAS Experiment at the LHC*, Oxford: Oxford University Press, 226–246.

McGrath, R. G. and Boisot M. (2005). "Options Complexes: Going Beyond Real Options Reasoning." *ECO*, 7: 2–13.

McKelvey, B. and Boisot, M. (2003). "Redefining Strategic Foresight: 'Fast' and 'Far' Sight via Complexity Science." *INSEAD Conference on Expanding Perspectives on Strategy Processes*. Fontainebleau, France.

McKelvey, B. and Boisot, M. (2009). "Redefining Strategic Foresight: 'Fast' and 'Far' Sight via Complexity Science." In L. A. Costanzo, and R. B. MacKay (eds), *Handbook of Research on Strategy and Foresight*, Cheltenham, UK: Edward Elgar, 15–47.

Bibliography

2. Other references

Adamic, L. A. and Huberman, B. A. (2002). "Zipf's Law and the Internet." *Glottometrics*, 3: 143–50.

Aghion, P. and Howitt, P. (1998). *Endogenous Growth Theory*. Cambridge, MA: The MIT Press.

Albert, L., Jeong, H., and Barabási, A.-L. (2000). "Attack and Error Tolerance of Complex Networks." *Nature*, 406: 378–82.

Aliseda, A. (2006). *Abductive Reasoning: Logical Investigations into Discovery and Explanation*. Dordrecht, The Netherlands: Springer.

Allen, P. M. (2001). "A Complex Systems Approach to Learning, Adaptive Networks." *International Journal of Innovation Management*, 5: 149–80.

Allen, P., Maguire, S., and McKelvey, B. (2011). *The SAGE Handbook of Complexity and Management*. London: Sage.

Anderson, C. (2006). *The Long Tail*. London: Random House Business Books.

Anderson, P. (1974). *Lineages of the Absolutist State*. London: Verso.

Andriani, P. and McKelvey, B (2007). "Beyond Gaussian Averages: Redirecting Organization Science Toward Extreme Events and Power Laws." *Journal of International Business Studies*, 38 (7): 1212–30.

Andriani, P. and McKelvey, B. (2009). "From Gaussian to Paretian Thinking: Causes and Implications of Power Laws in Organizations." *Organization Science*, 20 (6): 1053–71.

Andriani, P. and McKelvey, B. (2011a). "From Skew Distributions to Power Law Science." In P. Allen, S. Maguire, and B. McKelvey (eds), *Handbook of Complexity and Management*, London: Sage, 254–73.

Andriani, P. and B. McKelvey (2011b). "Managing in a Pareto World Calls for New Thinking." *M@n@gement*, 14 (2): 89–117.

Andriani, P. and McKelvey, B. (2011c). "Using Scale-Free Processes to Explain Punctuated-Change in Management-Relevant Phenomena." *International Journal of Complexity in Leadership & Management*, 1 (3): 211–51.

Anthony, M. and Bartlett, P. L. (1999). *Neural Network Learning: Theoretical Foundations*. New York: Cambridge University Press.

Anthony, R. (1965). *Planning and Control Systems*. Cambridge, MA: Harvard University Press.

Aoki, M. (1984). *The Economic Analysis of the Japanese Firm*. Amsterdam: North-Holland.

Aoki, M. (1990). "Toward an Economic Model of the Japanese Firm." *Journal of Economic Literature*, 28: 1–27.

Argote, L. (1999). *Organizational Learning: Creating, Retaining and Transferring Knowledge*, Norwell, MA: Kluwer.

Argyris, C. (1957). *Personality and Organization*. New York: Harper.

Argyris, C. and Schön, D. A. (1978). *Organizational Learning: A Theory of Action Perspective*, Reading, MA: Addison-Wesley Publishing Co.

Arrow, K. (1984). "Information and Economic Behaviour." In *The Economics of Information: Collected Papers of Kenneth J. Arrow*, Cambridge, MA: Belknap Press, 136–152.

Arthur, B. (1994). *Increasing Returns and Path Dependence in the Economy*. Ann Arbor, MI: University of Michigan Press.

Bibliography

Arthur, W. B. (1990). "Positive Feedback in the Economy." *Scientific American*, 262: 92–9.

Ashby, W. R. (1956). *An Introduction to Cybernetics*. London: Chapman and Hall.

Ashby, W. R. (1962). "Principles of the Self-Organizing System." In H. von Foerster and G.W. Zopf (eds), *Principles of Self-Organization*, New York: Pergamon, 255–78.

Audi, R. (1995). *The Cambridge Dictionary of Philosophy*. Cambridge: Cambridge University Press.

Auerbach, F. (1913). "Das Gesetz der Bevolkerungskoncentration." *Petermanns Geographische Mitteilungen*, 59: 74–6.

Autio, E., Bianchi-Streit, M., and Hameri, A.-P. (2003). *Technology Transfer and Technological Learning Through CERN's Procurement Activity*. Geneva: CERN Scientific Information Service.

Autio, E., Hameri, A.-P., and Nordberg, M. (1996). "A Framework of Motivations for Industry–Big Science Collaboration: A Case Study." *Journal of Engineering and Technology Management*, 13 (3–4): 301–14.

Axtell, R. L. (2001). "Zipf Distribution of U.S. Firm Sizes." *Science*, 293: 1818–20.

Axtell, R. L. (2008). "Nonexistence of a Typical Firm in the U.S. Economy: Extremely Heavy Tails in Firm Size and Growth." Presented at Organization Science Winter Conference, The Resort at Squaw Creek, CA, Feb. 8.

Ayres, R. (1994). *Information, Entropy and Progress: A New Evolutionary Paradigm*. Woodbury, NY: AIP Press.

Bai, C.-E., Du, Y., Tao, Z., and Tong, S. Y. (2004). "Local Protectionism and Regional Specialization: Evidence from China's Industries." *Journal of International Economics*, 63 (2): 397–417.

Bak, P. (1996). *How Nature Works: The Science of Self-Organized Criticality*. New York: Copernicus.

Balazs, E. (1968). *La Bureaucracie Céleste: Recherches Sur L'économie Et La Société De La Chine Traditionelle*. Paris: Gallimard.

Ball, P. (2004). *Critical Mass: How One Thing Leads to Another*. London: Arrow Books.

Barabási, A.-L. (2002). *Linked: The New Science of Networks*. Cambridge, MA: Perseus.

Barabási, A.-L. and Albert, R. (1999). "Emergence of Scaling in Random Networks." *Science*, 286 (5439): 509–12.

Barnard, C. (1938) *The Functions of the Executive*. Cambridge, MA: Harvard University Press.

Barney, J. B. (1991). "Firm Resources and Sustained Competitive Advantage." *Journal of Management*, 17: 99–120.

Barney, J.B. and Zhang, S. (2009). "The Future of Chinese Management Research: A Theory of Chinese Management versus a Chinese Theory of Management." *Management and Organization Review*, 5 (1): 15–28.

Barro, R. J., and Jin, T. (2011). "On the Size Distribution of Macroeconomic Disasters." *Econometrica*, 79 (5): 1567–89.

Bateson, G. (1972). *Steps Towards an Ecology of Mind: Collected Essays in Anthropology, Psychiatry, Evolution and Epistemology*. St. Albans, Herts: Paladin.

Bateson, G. (1980). *Mind and Nature: A Necessary Unity*. London: Fontana/Collins.

Battiston, S. and Catanzaro, M. (2004). "Statistical Properties of Corporate Board and Director Networks." *European Physical Journal B*, 38 (2): 345–52.

Batty, M. (2005). *Cities and Complexity*. Cambridge, MA: MIT Press.

Baum, J. A. C. and McKelvey, B. (2006). "Analysis of Extremes in Management Studies." In D. J. Ketchen, and D. D. Bergh (eds), *Research Methods in Strategy and Management*, Vol. 3. Oxford, UK: Elsevier, 123–197.

Benacerraf, P. and Putnam, H. (eds) (1964). *Philosophy of Mathematics: Selected Readings*. Cambridge, UK: Cambridge University Press.

Bénard, H. (1901). "Les Tourbillons Cellulaires dans une Nappe Liquide Transportant de la Chaleur par Convection en Régime Permanent." *Annales de Chimie et de Physique*, 23: 62–144.

Benbya, H. and McKelvey, B. (2006). "Using Coevolutionary and Complexity Theories to Improve IS Alignment: A Multi-level Approach." *Journal of Information Technology*, 21: 284–298.

Benbya, H. and McKelvey, B. (2011a). "Applying Critical Realism to IT Phenomena: An Ontological, Epistemological, and Methodological Perspective." Working paper, UCLA Anderson School of Management, Los Angeles, CA.

Benbya, H. and McKelvey, B. (2011b). "Using Power-Law Science to Enhance Knowledge for Practical Relevance." *Best Paper Proceedings*, Academy of Management Annual Meeting, San Antonio, TX.

Benbya, H. and McKelvey, B. (2012). "Using Power-Law Science to Enhance Knowledge for Practical Relevance." Working paper, GSCM-Montpellier Business School, France.

Bennis, W. and O'Toole, J. (2000). "Don't Hire the Wrong CEO." *Harvard Business Review*, 78 (May–June): 170–76.

Berg, M. (1994). *The Age of Manufactures 1700–1820: Industry, Innovation and Work in Britain*. London: Routledge.

Bergere, M-C. (2007). *Capitalisme et Capitalistes en Chine: Des Origines a nos jours, XIXe–XXIe siècle*. Paris, Perrin.

Berle, A. A. and Gardiner, C. M. Jr. (1932). *The Modern Corporation and Private Property*. New York: Harcourt, Brace & World.

Bhaskar, R. (1975). *A Realist Theory of Science*. London: Leeds Books [2nd edn. published by Verso (London) 1997].

Bianchi-Streit, M., Blackburne, N., Budde, R., Reitz, H., Sagnell, B., Schmied, H., and Schorr, B. (1984). "Economic Utility Resulting from CERN Contracts (second utility)." CERN Yellow Report CERN 84/14.

Bianchi-Streit, M., Blackburne, N., Budde, R., Reitz H., Sagnell, B., Schmied, H., and Schorr, B. (1988). "Quantification of CERN's Economic Spin-off." *Czechoslovak Journal of Physics*, 36 (1): 23–29.

Bierly, P. E. III, Kessler, E. H., and Christensen, E. W. (2000). "Organizational Learning, Knowledge and Wisdom." *Journal of Organizational Change Management*, 13 (6): 595–618.

Biggart, N. W. and Hamilton, G. G. (1992). "On the Limits of a Firm-Based Theory to Explain Business Networks: The Western Bias of Neoclassical Economics." In N. Nohria and R. G. Eccles (eds), *Networks and Organizations: Structure, Form, and Action*, Boston: Harvard Business School Press, 471–490.

Black, F. and Scholes, M. (1973). "The Pricing of Options and Corporate Liabilities." Journal of Political Economy, 81 (3): 637–654.

Bibliography

Blau, P. M. (1955). *The Dynamics of Bureaucracy*. Chicago: University of Chicago Press.

Bolton, P. (1995). "Privatization and the Separation of Ownership and Control: Lessons from Chinese Enterprise Reform." *Economics of Transition*, 3: 1–12.

Bond, M. H., and Hwang, K. (1986). "The Social Psychology of Chinese People." In M. H. Bond (ed.), *The Psychology of the Chinese People*, Hong Kong: Oxford University Press, 213–266.

Borys, B. and Jemison, D. B. (1989). "Hybrid Arrangements as Strategic Alliances: Theoretical Issues in Organizational Combinations." *Academy of Management Review*, 14: 234–249.

Bourdieu, P. (1977). *Outline of a Theory of Practice*. Cambridge, Cambridge University Press.

Bowman, E. H., Hurry, D. (1993). "Strategy Through the Option Lens: An Integrated View of Resource Investments and the Incremental-Choice Process." *Academy of Management Review*, 18: 760–782.

Boyd, R. and Richerson, P. J. (1985). *Culture and the Evolutionary Process*. Chicago: The University of Chicago Press.

Braudel, F. (1979). *Civilisation Matérielle, Économie Et Capitalisme, XVe–XVIIIe Siècle*, 3 vols. Paris: Armand Colin.

Bressan, B. (2005). *CERN Technology Transfers to Industry and Society*. CERN TT Group.

Brock, W. A. (2000). "Some Santa Fe Scenery." In D. Colander (ed.), *The Complexity Vision and the Teaching of Economics*, Cheltenham, UK: Edward Elgar, 29–49.

Bruun, O. (1993). *Business and Bureaucracy in a Chinese City*. Berkeley: Institute of East Asian Studies, University of California.

Brynjolfsson, E., Hu, Y., and Smith, M. D. (2006). "From Niches to Riches: The Anatomy of the Long Tail." *Sloan Management Review*, 47 (4): 67–71.

Butler, R. J. (1983). "Control Through Markets, Hierarchies, and Communes: A Transactional Approach to Organizational Analysis." In A. Francis, J. Turk, and P. Willman (eds), *Power, Efficiency and Institutions: A Critical Appraisal of the "Markets and Hierarchies Paradigm"*, London: Heinemann, 137–158.

Butterfield, H. (1931). *The Whig Interpretation of History*. Middlesex: Penguin.

Byrd, W. A. (1991a). *The Market Mechanism and Economic Reforms in China*. Armonk, NY: M.E. Sharpe.

Byrd, W. A. (1991b). "Contractual Responsibility Systems in Chinese State-Owned Industry: A Preliminary Assessment." In N. Campbell, S. R. F. Plasschaert, and D. H. Brown (eds), *The Changing Nature of Management in China. Advances in Chinese Industrial Studies*, 2: 7–35. Greenwich, CT: JAI Press.

Cameron, K. S. and Quinn, R. E. (1988). "Organizational Paradox and Transformation." In R. Quinn and K. Cameron (eds), *Paradox and Transformation: Toward a Theory of Change in Organization and Management*, Cambridge, MA: Ballinger, 1–18.

Campbell, D. T. (1975). "'Degrees of Freedom' and the Case Study." *Comparative Political Studies*, 8: 178–93.

Campbell, D. T. (1987). "Evolutionary Epistemology." In G. Radnitzky and W. W. Bartley Iii (eds), *Evolutionary Epistemology, Racionality, and the Sociology of Knowledge*, La Salle, IL: Open Court, 47–89.

Carlile, P. R. (2002). "A Pragmatic View of Knowledge and Boundaries: Boundary Objects in New Product Development." *Organization Science,* 13 (4): 442–455.

Carver, A. (1996). "Open and Secret Regulations in China and their Implication for Foreign Investment." In J. Child and Y. Lu (eds), *Management Issues for China in the 1990s: International Enterprises,* London: Routledge, 11–29.

CEA (The Chinese Economic Association in the UK). (1993). Seminar on "Overheating and the Chinese Economy." London School of Economics, September.

CERN Yellow Report CERN 84/14.

Chaitin, G. J. (1974). "Information-Theoretic Computational Complexity." *IEEE Transactions on Information Theory,* 20: 10–5.

Chakrabarti, B. K., Chakraborti, A., and Chatterjee, A. (eds) (2006). *Econophysics and Sociophysics: Trends and Perspectives.* Weinheim, Germany: WILEY-VCH.

Chandler, A. (1962) *Strategy and Structure: Chapters in the History of the American Industrial Enterprise.* Cambridge, MA: MIT Press.

Chandler, A. D. (1977) *The Visible Hand: The Managerial Revolution in American Business.* Cambridge, MA: Belknap Press.

Chatterjee, A. and Chakrabarti, B. K. (2006). *Econophysics of Stock and Other Markets.* Berlin: Springer-Verlag Italia.

Chen D. (1995). *Chinese Firms between Hierarchy and Market: The Contract Management Responsibility System in China.* London: Macmillan.

Chen, D. (2012, April 20). Skype Interview conducted by John Child.

Chesbrough, H. W. (2003). *Open Innovation: The New Imperative for Creating and Profiting from Technology.* Boston, MA: Harvard Business School Press.

Chesbrough, H. W. (2006). *Open Business Models: How to Thrive in the New Innovation Landscape.* Boston, MA.: Harvard Business School Press.

Child, J. (1981). "Culture, Contingency and Capitalism in the Cross-national Study of Organizations." In L. L. Cummings and B. M. Staw (eds), *Research in Organizational Behaviour,* 13: 303–356. Greenwich CN, JAI Press.

Child, J. (1994) *Management in China During the Age of Reform.* Cambridge: Cambridge University Press.

Child, J. (2000). "Theorizing about Organization Cross-nationally." In J. L. C. Cheng and R. B. Peterson (eds), *Advances in International Comparative Management,* 13: 27–75. Stamford CN, JAI Press.

Child, J. and Chen, D. (2009). "The China-Europe Management Institute: A Pioneer Of Management Education In China." In M. Warner and K. Goodall (eds), *Management Training and Development in China: Educating Managers in a Globalized Economy,* London: Routledge, 29–49.

Child, J. and Rodrigues, S. B. (2011). "How Organizations Engage with External Complexity: A Political Action Perspective." *Organization Studies,* 32 (6): 803–824.

Child, J. and Yuan Lu. (1996). "Institutional Constraints on Economic Reform: The Case of Investment Decisions in China." *Organization Science,* 7: 60–77.

Chmiel, A. M., Sienkiewicz, J., Suchecki, K., and Holyst, J. A. (2007). "Networks of Companies and Branches in Poland." *Physica A,* 383 (1): 134–138.

Christensen, C. (1997). *The Innovator's Dilemma.* Boston, MA: Harvard Business School Press.

Bibliography

Chu, D., Strand, R., and Jelland, R. F. (2003). "Theories of Complexity." *Complexity*, 8 (3): 19–30.

Churchland, P. M. (1989). *A Neurocomputational Perspective: The Nature of Mind and the Structure of Science*. Cambridge, MA: MIT Press.

Clark, A. (1997). *Being There*. Cambridge, MA: MIT Press.

Coble, P. M. (1980). *The Shanghai Capitalists and the Nationalist Government, 1927–1937*. Cambridge, MA: Council on East Asian Studies, Harvard University.

Cohen, M. L. (1993). "Cultural and Political Inventions in Modern China: The Case of the Chinese 'Peasant'." *Daedalus*, 122: 151–170.

Colander, D. (2006). *Post Walrasian Macroeconomics: Beyond the Dynamic Stochastic General Equilibrium Model*. Cambridge, UK: Cambridge University Press.

Cook, P. and Kirkpartick, C. (eds) (1988). *Privatization in Less Developed Countries*. New York: Harvester.

Corning, P. (2003). *Nature's Magic: Synergy in Evolution and the Fate of Humankind*. Cambridge: Cambridge University Press.

Crawford, G. C. (2012). "Emerging Scalability and Extreme Outcomes in New Ventures: Power-Law Analyses in Three Studies." *Best Paper Proceedings*, Academy of Management Annual Meeting, Boston, MA.

Crozier, M. (1964). *Le Phénonème Bureaucratique*. Paris: Seuil.

D'Aveni, R. A. (1994). *Hypercompetition: Managing the Dynamics of Strategic Maneuvering*, New York: Free Press.

Dalton, M. (1959). *Men Who Manage*. New York: Wiley.

Daly, H. (1968). "On Economics as a Life Science." *Journal of Political Economy*, 76 (3): 392–406.

Davenport, T. H. and Probst, G. (2002). *Knowledge Management Case Book: Siemens Best Practises* (2nd ed.) Erlangen, New York: Publicis Corporate Pub., Wiley.

David, P. A. (2004). "Can 'Open Science' be Protected from the Evolving Regime of Intellectual Property Rights Protection." *Journal of Theoretical and Institutional Economics*, 160: 1–26.

De Vany, A. (2004). *Hollywood Economics*. New York: Routledge.

DeLanda, M. (2011). *Philosophy and Simulation: The Emergence of Synthetic Reason*. London: Continuum.

Dewey, J. (1998). *The Essential Dewey*. Bloomington: Indiana University Press.

Dilthey, W. (1883/1988). *Introduction to the Human Sciences*. London: Harvester Wheatsheaf.

Dore, R. (1973). *British Factory – Japanese Factory*. London: George Allen and Unwin.

Dornfeld, B. (2012, April 30). In person interview conducted by Dana Kaminstein.

Douglas, M. (1973). *Natural Symbols: Explorations in Cosmology*. Middlesex: Penguin.

Dretske, F. (1981). *Knowledge and Flow of Information*. Cambridge, MA: MIT Press.

Dunning, J. H. (1988). "The Eclectic Paradigm of International Production: A Restatement and Some Possible Extensions." *Journal of International Business Studies*, 19 (1): 1–31.

Dunning, J. H. (ed.). (2003). *Making Globalization Good: The Moral Challenges of Global Capitalism*. Oxford: Oxford University Press.

Durkheim, E. (1933). *The Division of Labor in Society*. New York: Free Press.

EBRD (European Bank for Reconstruction and Development). (1993). *Annual Economic Outlook*. London: EBRD.
Edvinsson, L. (1997) *Intellectual Capital: the Proven Way to Establish Your Company's Real Values by Measuring its Hidden Brainpower*. New York: HarperBusiness.
Eisenhardt, K. M. (1989). "Making Fast Strategic Decisions in High-velocity Environments." *Academy of Management Journal*, 32: 543–576.
Ekelund, R. B. (1968). "Jules Dupuit and the Early Theory of Marginal Cost Pricing." *Journal of Political Economy*, 76 (3): 462–471.
Ekelund, R. B. and Hébert, R. F. (1999). *Secret Origins of Modern Microeconomics: Dupuit and the Engineers*. Chicago, IL: University of Chicago Press.
Elias, N. (1939). *The Civilizing Process, Vol. 2: State Formation and Civilization*. Oxford: Basil Blackwell.
Escoffier, N. and McKelvey, B. (2013). "Using 'Crowd-Wisdom Strategy' to Reduce Market Failure: Proof-of-Concept from the Movie Industry." In R. DeFillippi and P. Wikstrom (eds), *Business Innovation and Disruption in Creative Industries*.
Faure, D. (1994). "China and Capitalism: Business Enterprise in Modern China." Annual Workshop in Social History and Cultural Anthropology, 1993, Occasional Paper no. 1, Division of Humanities, Hong Kong University of Science and Technology.
Ferber J. (1999). *Multi-Agent Systems: An Introduction to Distributed Artificial Intelligence*. London: Addison Wesley/Pearson.
Feyerabend, P. K. (1975). *Against Method*. London: New Left Books.
Feynman, R. P. (1996). *Feynman Lectures On Computation*. Reading, MA: Addison-Wesley.
Fine, C. H. (1998). *Clock Speed: Winning Industry Control in the Age of Temporary Advantage*. Reading, MA: Perseus.
Fischer, S. (1993). "Socialist Economy Reform: Lessons of the First Three Years." American Economic Association, Papers and Proceedings, 83 (May): 390–395.
Foss, N. and Knudsen, C. (eds) (1996). *Towards a Competence Theory of the Firm. Studies in Business Organization and Networks, 2*. New York: Routledge.
Foucault. M. (1969). *L'archéologie du Savoir*. Paris: Gallimard.
Foucault, M. (1972). *Histoire de la Folie à L'Age Classique*. Paris: Editions Gallimard.
Friedman, M. (1953). *Essays in Positive Economics*. Chicago: University of Chicago Press.
Fujiwara, Y., (2004). "Zipf Law in Firms Bankruptcy." *Physica A*, 333: 219–30.
Fujiwara, Y., Di Guilme, C., Aoyama, H., Gallegati, M., and Suoma, W. (2004). "Do Pareto-Zipf Laws Hold True? An Analysis with European Firms." *Physica A*, 335 (1–2): 197–216.
Fukuyama, F. (2011). *The Origins of Political Order: From Pre-Human Times to the French Revolution*. London: Profile Books.
Gabaix, X. (2009). "Power Laws in Economics and Finance." *Annual Review of Economics*, 1: 255–93.
Galbraith, J. R. (1973). *Designing Complex Organizations*. Reading, MA: Addison-Wesley.
Galison, P. (1997). *Image and Logic*. Chicago, IL.: The University of Chicago Press.
Gay, B. and Dousset, B. (2005). 'Innovation and Network Structural Dynamics Study of the Alliance Network of a Major Sector of the Biotechnology Industry'. *Research Policy*, 34: 1457–1475.

Bibliography

Gell-Mann, M. (1988). "The Concept of the Institute." In D. Pines (ed.), *Emerging Synthesis in Science*, Boston, MA: Addison-Wesley, 1–15.

Gell-Mann, M. (2002). "What is Complexity?" In A. Q. Curzio and M. Fortis (eds), *Complexity and Industrial Clusters*, Heidelberg, Germany: Physica-Verlag, 13–24.

Gellner, E. (1981). *Muslim Society*. Cambridge: Cambridge University Press.

Gerlach, M. L. and Lincoln, J. R. (1992). "The Organization of Business Networks in the United States and Japan." In N. Nohria and R. G. Eccles (eds) *Networks and Organizations: Structure, Form, and Action*, Boston: Harvard Business School Press, 491–520.

Gernet, J. (1982). *A History of Chinese Civilization*. Cambridge: Cambridge University Press.

Gerow, A. and Keane, M. T. (2011). "Mining the Web for the 'Voice of the Herd' to Track Stock Market Bubbles." *Proceedings of the 22nd International Joint Conference on Artificial Intelligence*. Barcelona, Spain.

Gilbert, N. and Troitzsch, K. G. (1999). *Simulation for the Social Scientist*. Buckingham, UK: Open University Press.

Glaser, P. (2012). "Inequality in an Increasing Returns World." In B. McKelvey and J. Bragin (eds), *Power-law Distribution in the Business World*. London: Routledge, 410–423.

Gleick, J. (1987). *Chaos: Making a New Science*. New York: Penguin.

Glymour, C. (1980). *Theory and Evidence*, Princeton, NJ: Princeton University Press.

Gong, Y. (1992). "Dialogue on the Socialist Market Economy." *Beijing Review*, Oct 26–Nov 1: 34–38.

Goody, J. (1987). *The Interface between the Written and the Oral*. Cambridge: Cambridge University Press.

Goto, A. (1982). "Business Groups in a Market Economy." *European Economic Review*, 19: 53–70.

Gouldner, A. W. (1954). *Patterns of Industrial Bureaucracy*. Glencoe, IL: Free Press.

Gran, T. (1994). *The State in the Modernization Process: The Case of Norway, 1850–1970*. Oslo: Ad Notam Gyldendal.

Granovetter, M. (1985). "Economic Action and Social Structure: The Problem of Embeddedness." *American Journal of Sociology*, 91: 481–510.

Greene, W. H. (2002). *Econometric Analysis* (5th ed.). Prentice-Hall, Englewood Cliffs, NJ.

Greene, W. H. (2011). *Econometric Analysis* (7th ed.). Englewood Cliffs, NJ: Prentice-Hall.

Gregory, R. L. (1981). *Mind in Science*. Middlesex, UK: Penguin Books.

Grünwald, P., Myung, I., and Pitt, M. (2005). *Advances in Minimum Description Length*. Cambridge, MA: MIT Press.

Guastello, S. J. (1995). *Chaos, Catastrophe, and Human Affairs*. Mahwah, NJ: Lawrence Erlbaum.

Guillen, M. F. (2001). *The Limits of Convergence*. Princeton NJ, Princeton University Press.

Habermas, J. (1970). *Towards a Rational Society*. London: Heinemann.

Habermas, J. (1972). *Knowledge and Human Interests*. London: Heinemann.

Hage, J. (1965). "An Axiomatic Theory of Organizations." *Administrative Science Quarterly*, 10: 289–320.

Hagstrom, W. (1965). *The Scientific Community*. New York: Basic Books.

Bibliography

Hahn, U. and Chater, N. (1998). "Similarity and Rules: Distinct? Exhaustive? Empirically Distinguishable?" In S. A. Sloman and L. J. Rips (eds), *Similarity and Symbols in Human Thinking*. Cambridge, MA.: MIT Press.

Hähnle, M. (1997). "R&D Collaboration between CERN and Industrial Companies. Organisational and Spatial Aspects." Dissertation, Vienna University of Economy and Business Administration.

Haken, H. (1977). *Synergetics, an Introduction*. Berlin: Springer-Verlag.

Hall, E. T. (1976). *Beyond Culture*. Garden City, NY: Doubleday.

Hall, P. A. and Soskice, D. (eds) (2001). *Varieties of Capitalism: The Institutional Foundations of Comparative Advantage*. Oxford: Oxford University Press.

Hamel, G. and Prahalad, C. K. (1994). *Competing for the Future*. Boston, MA: Harvard Business School Press.

Hamilton, G. G. and Biggart, N. W. (1988). "Market, Culture, and Authority: A Comparative Analysis of Management and Organization in the Far East." *American Journal of Sociology*, 94, Supplement: S52–S94.

Harris, S. (2005). "Groups of Concerned Citizens have Reduced Street Crime. Can They Do the Same for Terrorism?" *Government Executive: Government's Business Magazine*, 37 (10): 24–25.

Hastings, C. (1993). *The New Organization: Growing the Culture of Organizational Networking*. London: McGraw-Hill.

Hayek, F. (1945). "The Use of Knowledge in Society." *American Economic Review*, 35 (4): 519–530.

Heath, C. and Heath, D. (2007/2008). *Made to Stick: Why Some Ideas Survive and Others Die*. New York: Random House.

Helfat, C. E., Finkelstein, S., Mitchell, W., Peteraf, M. A., Singh, H., Teece, D. J., and Winter, S. G. (2007). *Dynamic Capabilities: Understanding Strategic Change in Organizations*. Malden, MA: Blackwell.

Hirshleifer, J. and Riley, J. J. (1992). *The Analytics Of Uncertainty and Information*. Cambridge, UK: Cambridge University Press.

Hoffman, M. (1996). *Das Problem der Zukunft im Rahmen holistischer Ethiken*. Im Ausgang von Platon und Peirce. In NaturStöcke, Zur Kulturgeschichte der Natur. H. W. Ingensiep and R. Hoppe-Sailer, (eds), Ostfildern: (3rd ed.), 17–41.

Holland, J. H. (1975). *Adaptation in Natural and Artificial Systems*. Cambridge, MA: MIT Press.

Holland, J. H. (1988). "The Global Economy as an Adaptive System." In P. W. Anderson, K. J. Arrow, and D. Pines (eds), *The Economy as an Evolving Complex System*, Proceedings of the Santa Fe Institute, Vol. V. Reading, MA: Addison-Wesley, 117–124.

Holland, J. H. (1995). *Hidden Order*. Cambridge, MA: Perseus Books.

Holland, J. H. (1998). *Emergence: From Chaos to Order*. Cambridge, MA: Perseus Books.

Holland, J. H. (2002). "Complex Adaptive Systems and Spontaneous Emergence." In A. Q. Curzio and M. Fortis, (eds), *Complexity and Industrial Clusters*, Heidelberg, Germany: Physica-Verlag, 24–34.

Holz, C. (2009). "No Razor's Edge: Reexamining Alwyn Young's Evidence for Increasing Inter Provincial Trade Barriers in China." *Review of Economics and Statistics*, 91 (3): 599–616.

Bibliography

Hussain, A. (1990). "The Chinese Enterprise Reforms." *Development Economics Research Program*, London School of Economics, CP No. 5, June.

Hussain, A. (1992). "The Chinese Economic Reforms in Retrospect and Prospect." *Development Economics Research Program*, London School of Economics, CP No. 24, August.

Iannaccone, P. M. and Khokha, M. (1995). *Fractal Geometry in Biological Systems: An Analytical Approach*. New York: CRC Press.

Ihrig, M. (2010). *Investigating Entrepreneurial Strategies Via Simulation*. Paper presented at the European Conference on Modelling and Simulation, Kuala Lumpur, Malaysia.

Ihrig, M. (2012). "Simulating Entrepreneurial Opportunity Recognition Processes: An Agent-Based and Knowledge-Driven Approach." In A. Byrski, Z. Oplatková, M. Carvalho, and M. Kisiel-Dorohinicki (eds), *Advances in Intelligent Modelling and Simulation, SCI 416*, 27–54, Heidelberg: Springer.

Ihrig, M. (2013). *SimISpace2: a simulation platform for exploring strategic knowledge management processes, Transactions on Computational Collective Intelligence* (Springer), Issue 10, Vol. LNCS 7776, March 2013.

Ihrig, M. and Abrahams, A. S. (2007). "Breaking New Ground in Simulating Knowledge Management Processes: SimISpace2." Paper presented at the 21st European Conference on Modelling and Simulation (ECMS 2007), Prague.

Ishikawa, A. (2006). "Pareto Index Induced from the Scale of Companies." *Physica A*, 363 (2): 367–376.

James, W. (1890). *Principles of Psychology* (Vol. II). New York: Henry.

James, W. (1907). *Pragmatism: A New Name for Some Old Ways of Thinking, Popular Lectures on Philosophy* (1st ed.). London; New York: Longmans, Green.

Janis, I. L. (1972). *Victims of Groupthink*. Boston, MA: Houghton Mifflin.

Janis, I. L. (1982). *Groupthink: Psychological Studies of Policy Decisions and Fiascos*. Boston: Houghton Mifflin.

Jiang, C. (1993). "China Embarks on the Road to a Socialist Market Economy." *China Scholars Abroad*, 1: 7–8.

Jiang, X. (1992). "The Evolution of Property Rights in China: A Long-Run Analysis with Special Reference to the Hefeng Textile Mill." Unpublished PhD thesis, University of Cambridge.

Johnson, N. L. (2000). "A Developmental View into Evolving Systems: Roles of Diversity, Non-selection, Self-organization, Symbiosis." *Artificial Life VII*: Proceedings of the Seventh International Conference on Artificial Life. Vol. 7, pp. 317–326. MIT Press.

Kang, S. H. and Yoon, S.-M. (2007). "Long Memory Properties in Return and Volatility: Evidence from the Korean Stock Market." *Physica A*, 385: 591–00.

Kanter, R. M. (1983). *The Change Masters*. London: Allen & Unwin.

Kaplan, A. (1964). *The Conduct of Inquiry*. San Francisco, CA: Chandler.

Kaplan, D. (2000). *Structural Equation Modeling: Foundations and Extensions*. Thousand Oaks, CA: Sage.

Kauffman, S. A. (1969). "Metabolic Stability and Epigenesis in Randomly Constructed Nets." *Journal of Theoretical Biology*, 22: 437–67.

Kauffman, S. A. (1993). *The Origins of Order*. Oxford: Oxford University Press.

Kauffman, S.A. (2000). *Investigations*. New York: Oxford University Press.

Kay, J. A. and Llewellyn Smith, C. H. (1985). "Science Policy and Public Spending." *Fiscal Studies*, 6 (3): 14–23.

Kelso, J. A. S. and Engstrøm, D. A. (2006). *The Complementary Nature*. Cambridge, MA: MIT Press.

Kerr, C., Dunlop, J. T., Harbison, F. H., and Myers, C. A. (1960). *Industrialism and Industrial Man*. Cambridge, MA: Harvard University Press.

Kirby, W. (1995). "China Unincorporated: Company Law and Business Enterprise in Twentieth-Century China." *Journal of Asian Studies*, 55 (1): 43–63.

Kirchgaessner, S. and Kelleher, E. (2005). "UK Bombs Drive Insurance Debate." *Financial Times Europe* (Mon., July 11) 5.

Klein, G. (1998). *Sources of Power: How People Make Decisions*. Cambridge, MA: MIT Press.

Knight, F. H. (1921). *Risk, Uncertainty and Profit*. Chicago: University of Chicago Press.

Knorr-Cetina, K. (1999). *Epistemic Cultures: How the Sciences Make Knowledge*. Cambridge, MA.: Harvard University Press.

Knowles, M. S., Holton, E. F. and Swanson, R. A. (1973/1998). *The Adult Learner: The Definitive Classic in Adult Education and Human Resource Development* (5th ed.). Woburn, MA: Butterworth-Heinemann.

Kogut, B. (2000). "The Network as Knowledge: Generative Rules and the Emergence of Structure." *Strategic Management Journal*, 21 (March):405–425.

Kogut, B. (2003). "Context in International Business Theory." Opening address, JIBS First Annual Conference on Emerging Research Frontiers. Duke University. 21 June.

Kraus, W. (1991). *Private Business in China: Revival between Ideology and Pragmatism*. London: Hurt.

Krober, A.L. and Kluckhohn, C. (1952). *Culture: A Critical Review of Concepts and Definitions*. Cambridge, MA: Peabody Museum of American Archaeology and Ethnology.

Krugman, P. (1996). *The Self-Organizing Economy*. Malden, MA: Blackwell.

Kuhn, T. S. (1962). *The Structure of Scientific Revolutions*, Chicago, IL: University of Chicago Press.

Kumar, K. (1978). *Prophecy and Progress*. Harmondsworth: Penguin.

Lakatos, I. (1976). *Proofs and Refutations: The Logic of Mathematical Discovery*, J. Worrall and E. Zahar (eds) Cambridge, UK: Cambridge University Press.

Lakatos, I. (1978). *The Methodology of Scientific Research Programmes: Philosophical Papers Vol. 1*, Cambridge, UK: Cambridge Univ. Press.

Landauer, R. & Hey, A. J. G. (1999). *Information is Inevitably Physical* (pp. 77–92). Cambridge, MA: Perseus.

Landes, D. (1969). *The Unbound Prometheus: Technological Change and Industrial Development in Western Europe from 1750 to the Present*. Cambridge: Cambridge University Press.

Landes, D. S. (1998). *The Wealth and Poverty of Nations*. New York, Norton.

Latour, B. and Woolgar, S. (1986). *Laboratory Life: The Construction of Scientific Facts*. Princeton, NJ: Princeton University Press.

Lawrence, S. and Giles, C. L. (1998). "Searching the World Wide Web." *Science*, 280 (5360): 98–00.

Lawson, T. (1997). *Economics & Reality*. New York: Routledge.

Bibliography

Ledermann, L. M. (1984). "The Value of Fundamental Science." *Scientific American*, 25: 34–41.

Lee, Y., Amaral, L. A. N., Canning, D., Meyer, M., and Stanley, H. E. (1998). "Universal Features in the Growth Dynamics of Complex Organizations." *Physical Review Letters*, 81: 3275–78.

Leff, H. S. and Rex, A. F. (1990). *Maxwell's Demon: Entropy, Information, Computing.* Bristol, UK.: Adam Hilger.

Leonard-Barton, D. (1995). *Wellsprings of Knowledge.* Boston, MA: Harvard Business School Press.

Lettvin, J. Y., Maturana, H. R., McCulloch, W. S., and Pitts, W. H. (1959). "What the Frog's Eye Tells the Frog's Brain." *Proceedings of the IRE*, 47 (11): 1940–59.

Leung K. and Bond, M. (2004). "Social Axioms: A Model for Social Beliefs in Multicultural Perspective." *Advances in Experimental Social Psychology*, 36: 119–197.

Lewin, K. (1951). *Field Theory in Social Science.* New York: Harper.

Li, C. (1974). "The Kung-ssu-lii of 1904 and the Modernization of Chinese Company Law." *Zhengda faxue pinglun [Chengchi University Legal Review]*, 11:163–209.

Lichtenstein, B. B. (2000). "Self-Organized Transitions." *Academy of Management Executive*, 14: 1–14.

Lieberman, M. and Dhawan (2005). "Assessing the Resource Base of Japanese and U. S. Auto Producers: A Stochastic Frontier Production Function Approach." *Management Science*, 51 (7): 1060–75.

Liyanage, S., Wink, R., and Nordberg, M. (2006). *Managing Path-Breaking Innovations: CERN-ATLAS, Airbus, and Stem-Cell Research.* Westport, CT: Praeger.

Lloyd, S. (2000). "Ultimate Physical Limits to Computation." *Nature,* 406 (31), 1047–1054.

Lobato, J. (2006). "Alternative Perspectives on the Transfer of Learning: History, Issues, and Challenges for Future Research." *The Journal of Learning Sciences*, 15 (4): 431–449.

Longenecker, C. O. (2004). "Maximizing Transfer of Learning from Management Education Programs." *Development and Learning in Organizations*, 18 (4): 4–6.

Longo, G., Montevil, M., and Kauffman, S. (2012b). "No Entailing Laws, but Enablement in the Evolution of the Biosphere." In *Proceedings Of The Fourteenth International Conference On Genetic And Evolutionary Computation Conference Companion*, pp. 1379–1392. doi -> 10.1145/2330784/2330946.

Lorenz, E. N. (1972). "Predictability: Does the Flap of a Butterfly's Wings in Brazil Set off a Tornado in Texas?" Paper presented at the 1972 meeting of the American Association for the Advancement of Science. Washington, DC.

Lu, Y. (2012, April 25). Telephone Interview conducted by John Child.

Lu, Y., and Child, J. (1996). "Decentralization of Decision Making in China's State Enterprises." In D. Brown and M. Easterby-Smith (eds), *Management Issues for China in the 1990s: Domestic Enterprises,* London: Routledge, 61–84.

Luhmann N. (1985). *A Sociological Theory of Law,* (transl. K. A. Ziegert 2003). Oxford: Oxford University Press.

Mabey, C. (2012, April 24). In person interview conducted by John Child.

MacMillan, I. (2012, May 4). In person interview conducted by Dana Kaminstein.

Bibliography

Maguire, S., McKelvey, B., Mirabeau, L., and Öztas, N. (2006). "Complexity Science and Organizational Studies." In S. R. Clegg, C. Hardy, T. Lawrence, and W. Nord (eds), *Handbook of Organizational Studies* (2nd ed.) Thousand Oaks, CA: Sage, 165–214.

Main, I. (1997). "Earthquakes—Long Odds on Prediction." *Nature* 385: 19–20.

Mainzer, K. (2004). *Thinking in Complexity*. New York: Springer-Verlag; [5th ed. published in 2007].

Mandelbrot, B. (1983). *The Fractal Geometry of Nature* (2nd ed.). New York: Freeman.

Mann, S. (1987). *Local Merchants and the Chinese Bureaucracy, 1750–1950*. Stanford, CA: Stanford University Press.

Mantegna, R. N., Stanley, H. E. (2000). *An Introduction to Econophysics*. Cambridge, UK: Cambridge Univ. Press.

March, J. G. (1991). "Exploration and Exploitation in Organizational Learning." *Organization Science*, 2: 71–87.

March, J. G. and Simon, H. A. (1958). *Organizations*. New York: Wiley.

March, J. G., Sproull, L. S., and Tamuz, M. (1991). "Learning from Samples of One or Fewer." *Organization Science*, 2: 1–13.

Marion, R. and Uhl-Bien, M. (2001). "Leadership in Complex Organizations." *Leadership Quarterly*, 12: 389–418.

McCauley, J. L. (2004). *Dynamics of Markets: Econophysics and Finance*. Cambridge, UK: Cambridge University Press.

McKelvey, B. (1997). "Quasi-Natural Organization Science." *Organization Science*, 8: 351–380.

McKelvey, B. (1998). "'Good' Science from Postmodernist Ontology: Realism, Complexity Theory, and Emergent Dissipative Structures." Keynote Address at the 1st Annual Winter Sun-Break Conference on Non-Linearity & Organization, January, New Mexico State University, Las Cruces, NM.

McKelvey, B. (2001). "Energizing Order-Creating Networks of Distributed Intelligence." *International Journal of Innovation Management*, 5: 181–12.

McKelvey, B. (2004). "'Simple rules' for Improving Corporate IQ: Basic Lessons from Complexity Science." In P. Andriani and G. Passiante (eds), *Complexity Theory and the Management of Networks*, London: Imperial College Press, 39–52.

McKelvey, B. (2008). "Emergent Strategy via Complexity Leadership: Using Complexity Science & Adaptive Tension to Build Distributed Intelligence." In M. Uhl-Bien and R. Marion (eds), *Complexity and Leadership, Vol. I: Conceptual Foundations*. Charlotte, NC: Information Age Publishing, 225–268.

McKelvey, B. (2010). "Complexity Leadership: The Secret of Jack Welch's Success." *International Journal of Complexity in Leadership & Management*, 1 (1): 4–36.

McKelvey, B. (Forthcoming). "Fixing the UK's Economy." In J. McGlade, M. Strathern, and K. Richardson (eds), *Complexity in Human and Natural Systems*. Litchfield Park, AZ: ISCE Publishing.

McKelvey, B. and Andriani, P. (2005). "Why Gaussian Statistics are Mostly Wrong for Strategic Organization." *Strategic Organization*, 3: 219–229.

McKelvey, B. and Andriani, P. (2010). "Avoiding Extreme Risk Before it Occurs: Scalability Lessons from Complexity Science." *Risk Management: An International Journal*, 12 (1): 54–82.

Bibliography

McKelvey, B. and Salmador Sanchez, M. P. (2011). "Explaining the 2007 Bank Liquidity Crisis: Lessons from Complexity Science & Econophysics." Working paper, UCLA Anderson School of Management, Los Angeles, CA.

McKelvey, B., Lichtenstein, B. B., and Andriani, P. (2013). "When Organizations and Ecosystems Interact: Toward a Law of Requisite Fractality in Firms." *International Journal of Complexity In Leadership & Management*, 2 (1): 104–136.

Merali, J. and McKelvey, B. (2006). "Using Complexity Science to Effect a Paradigm Shift in Information Systems for the 21st Century." *Journal of Information Technology*, 21 (4): 211–215.

Meyer, M. and Lu, X. (2005). "Managing Indefinite Boundaries: The Strategy and Structure of a Chinese Firm." *Management and Organization Review*, 1: 57–86.

Miles, R., Snow, C., Matthews, J. A., and Miles, G. (1999). "Cellular-network Organizations." in W. E. Halal and K. B. Taylor (eds), *Twenty-First Century Economics: Perspectives of Socioeconomics for a Changing World*, New York: Macmillan, 155–73.

Miles, R. E. and Snow, C. C. (1994). *Fit, Failure and the Hall of Fame*. New York: Free Press.

Miller, J. G. (1978). *Living Systems*. McGraw-Hill, New York.

Miller, J. H. and Page, S. E. (2007). *Complex Adaptive Systems: An Introduction to Computational Models of Social Life*. Princeton, NJ: Princeton University Press.

Mintzberg, H. (1979). *The Structuring of Organizations: A Synthesis of the Research*. Englewood Cliffs, NJ: Prentice-Hall.

Mintzberg, H. and Walters, J. (1985). "Of Strategies, Deliberate and Emergent." *Strategic Management Journal*, 6 (3): 257–272.

Mirowski, P. (1989). *More Heat Than Light*. Cambridge University Press: Cambridge, UK.

Mislove, A., Marcon, M., Gummadi, K.P., Druschel, P., and Bhattacharjee, B. (2007). Measurement and analysis of online networks. *7th ACM SIGCIMM Conference on Internet Measurement*, IMC'07. San Diego, CA, USA.

Mitchell, M. (1996). *An Introduction to Genetic Algorithms*. Cambridge, MA: MIT Press.

Mitchell, M. (2009). *Complexity: A Guided Tour*. New York: Oxford University Press.

Morin, E. (1992). *Method: Toward a Study of Humankind*. Peter Lang, New York.

Moss, S. (2002). "Policy Analysis from First Principles." *Proceedings of the National Academy of Sciences*, 99 (Suppl. 3): 7267–74.

My Decker Capital. (2011). China retail sector—macro trends. <http://www.mydeckercapital.com/Documents/20110130%20MDC%20China%20Retail%20Sector%20-%20Macro%20Trends.pdf>, accessed 12 August 2012.

Naughton, B. (1987). "The Decline of Central Control over Investment in Post-Mao China." In D. M. Lampton (eds), *Policy Implementation in Post-Mao China*, Berkeley, CA: University of California Press, 51–80.

Nee, V. (1992), "Organizational Dynamics of Market Transition: Hybrid Forms, Property Rights, and Mixed Economy in China." *Administrative Science Quarterly*, 37 (1): 1–27.

Newman, M. E. J. (2005). "Power Laws, Pareto Distributions and Zipf's Law." *Contemporary Physics*, 46: 323–51.

Newman, M. E. J., Barabási, A.-L., and Watts, D. J. (eds) (2006). *The Structure and Dynamics of Networks*. Princeton, NJ: Princeton University Press.

Bibliography

Nicolis, G. and Prigogine (1989). *Exploring Complexity: An Introduction.* New York: Freeman.

Nohria, N. and R. G. Eccles (eds) (1992). *Networks and Organizations: Structure, Form and Action.* Boston: Harvard Business School Press.

Nonaka, I. and Takeuchi, H. (1995) *The Knowledge Creating Company: How Japanese Companies Create the Dynamics of Innovation.* New York: Oxford University Press.

Nordberg, M. and Verbeke, A. (1999). *Strategic Management of High Technology Contracts: The Case of CERN.* Oxford: Pergamon Press.

North, D. C. (2005). *Understanding the Process of Economic Change.* Princeton, NJ: Princeton University Press.

North, D. C. and Thomas, R. P. (1973) *The Rise of the Western World.* Cambridge: Cambridge University Press.

North, M. J. and Macal, C. M. (2007). *Managing Business Complexity: Discovering Strategic Solutions with Agent-Based Modeling and Simulation.* New York: Oxford University Press.

O'Boyle, E., Jr. and Aguinis, H. (2012). "The Best and the Rest: Revisiting the Norm of Normality of Individual Performance." *Personnel Psychology*, 65: 79–119.

Ormerod, P. (1994). *The Death of Economics.* New York: Wiley.

Ormerod, P. (1998). *Butterfly Economics: A New General Theory of Social and Economic Behavior.* New York: Pantheon.

Ormerod, P. and Mounfield, C. (2001). "Power Law Distribution of the Duration and Magnitude of Recessions in Capitalist Economies Breakdown of Scaling." *Physica A*, 293: 573–82.

Ouchi, W. G. (1980). "Markets, Bureaucracies and Clans." *Administrative Science Quarterly*, 25 (1): 129–141.

Page, S. E. (2007). *The Difference: How the Power of Diversity Creates Better Groups, Firms, Schools, and Societies.* Princeton, NJ: Princeton University Press.

Pareto, V. (1897). *Cours d'Economie Politique.* Paris: Rouge.

Park, J.W., Moral, B., and Madhavan, R. (2010). "Riding the Wave: Self-Organized Criticality in Merger and Acquisition Waves." *Best Paper Proceedings*, Academy of Management Annual Meeting, Montreal, CA.

Peirce, C. S. (1931–1935) *Collected Papers of Charles Sanders Peirce* (Volumes I–VI, ed. by C. Hartshorne and P. Weiß, (Volumes VII–VIII, ed. by A. W. Burks, 1958). Cambridge, MA: Harvard University Press.

Peirce, C. S. (1935). *Collected Papers.* Vol. 5 (C. Hartshorne and P. Weiß eds). Cambridge, MA: Harvard University Press.

Peirce, C. S. (1992). *The Essential Peirce: Selected Philosophical Writings.* Bloomington: Indiana University Press.

Penrose, Edith T. (1952). "Biological Analogies in the Theory of the Firm—I." *American Economic Review*, 42, 804–819.

Perrow, C. (1984). *Normal Accidents.* Princeton, NJ: Princeton University Press.

Peters, T. (1992). *Liberation Management.* New York: Knopf.

Piaget, J. (1967). *Biologie et Connaissance: Essai surles Relations entre les Regulations Organiques et les Processus Cognitifs.* Paris: Gallimard.

Bibliography

Pickering, A. (1984). *Constructing Quarks: A Sociological History Of Particle Physics.* Chicago, IL.: The University of Chicago Press.

Plotkin, H. (1993). *Darwin Machines and the Nature of Knowledge.* Cambridge, MA: Harvard University Press.

Podobnik, B., Fu, D., Jagric, T., Grosse, I., and Stanley, H. E. (2006). "Fractionally Integrated Process for Transition Economics." *Physica A*, 362 (2): 465–70.

Polanyi, M. (1958) *Personal Knowledge: Towards a Post-critical Philosophy.* London: Routledge and Kegan Paul.

Poncet, S. (2003). "Measuring Chinese Domestic and International Integration." *China Economic Review*, 14: 1–21.

Poncet, S. (2005). "A Fragmented China: Measures and Determinants of Chinese Domestic Market Disintegration." *Review Of International Economics*, 13 (3): 409–430.

Poole, M. S., Van de Ven, A. H., Dooley, K., and Holmes, M. E. (2000). *Organizational Change and Innovation Processes: Theory and Methods for Research.* New York: Oxford University Press.

Popper, K. R. (1935). *Logik der Forschung.* Springer Verlag, Vienna. [Reprinted as *The Logic of Scientific Discovery*, New York: Harper and Row, 1959.]

Popper, K. R. (1959). *The Logic of Scientific Discovery.* London: Routledge.

Popper, K.R. (1972) *Objective Knowledge: An Evolutionary Approach.* Oxford: Clarendon Press.

Popper, K. R. (1988). *The Open Universe: An Argument for Indeterminism* (Vol. 2). London: Routledge.

Porter, M. E. (1990). *The Competitive Advantages of Nations.* New York: Free Press.

Porter, M. E. (1996). "What is Strategy?" *Harvard Business Review*, 74 (6): 61–78.

Portes, A. (1994). "The Informal Economy and its Paradoxes." In N. J. Smelser and R. Swedberg (eds) *The Handbook of Economic Sociology*, Princeton, NJ: Princeton University Press, 426–449.

Potter, P. B. (1995) "Foreign Investment Law in the People's Republic of China: Dilemmas of State Control." *China Quarterly*, 141: 155–185.

Powell, W. W. and DiMaggio, P. J. (1991). *The New Institutionalism in Organizational Analysis.* Chicago: University of Chicago Press.

Powell, W. W. and Smith-Doerr, L. (1994). "Networks and Economic Life." In N. J. Smelser and R. Swedberg (eds), *The Handbook of Economic Sociology*. Princeton, NJ: Princeton University Press, 368–402.

Prahalad, C. K. (2005). *The Fortune at the Bottom of the Pyramid: Eradicating Poverty Through Profits.* Upper Saddle River, NJ: Wharton School Publishing.

Prahalad, C.K. and Hamel G. (1990). "The Core Competence of the Corporation." *Harvard Business Review*, 68 (3):79–91.

Prietula, M. J., Carley, K. M., and Gasser, L. (eds) (1998). *Simulating Organizations.* Cambridge, MA: MIT Press.

Prigogine, I. (1955). *An Introduction to Thermodynamics of Irreversible Processes.* Springfield, IL: Thomas.

Prigogine, I. (1980). *From Being to Becoming.* San Francisco, CA: W. H Freeman.

Prigogine, I. and Stengers, I. (1984). *Order Out of Chaos: Man's New Dialogue with Nature.* New York: Bantam.

Bibliography

Prusak, L. (1996). "The Knowledge Advantage." *Strategy and Leadership*, 24: 6–8.

Pye, L. W. (1995). "Factions and the Politics of Guanxi: Paradoxes in Chinese Administrative and Political Behavior." *China Journal*, 34: 35–53.

Qian, Y. and Xu, C. (1993). "Why China's Economic Reforms Differ: The M-Form Hierarchy and Entry/Expansion of the Non-State Sector." *Economics of Transition*, 1: 135–170.

Ravasz, E. and Barabási, A.-L. (2003). "Hierarchical Organization in Complex Networks,' *Physical Review E*, 67: 026112.

Rawski, T. G. and Li, L. M. (eds) (1992) *Chinese History in Economic Perspective*. Berkeley: University of California Press.

Raymond, E. (1999) *The Cathedral and the Bazaar: Musings on Linux and Open Source by an Accidental Revolutionary*. Beijing: O'Reilly.

Redding, G. (2005). "The Thick Description and Comparison of Societal Systems of Capitalism." *Journal of International Business Studies*, 36: 123–155.

Redding, G. and Witt, M.A. (2007). *The Future of Chinese Capitalism*. Oxford: Oxford University Press.

Redding, S. G. (1990). *The Spirit of Chinese Capitalism*. Berlin: De Gruyter.

Richardson, G. B. (1972). "The Organization Of Industry." *Economic Journal*, 82: 883–896.

Romer, P. M. (1990). "Endogenous Technical Change." *The Journal of Political Economy*, 98 (5 Part 2), S71–S102.

Rosenberg, N. and Mowery, D. C. (1989). *Technology and the Pursuit of Economic Growth*. Cambridge: Cambridge University Press.

Saito, Y. U., Watanabe, T., Iwamura, M., (2007). "Do Larger Firms Have More Interfirm Relationships?" *Physica A*, 383 (1): 158–163.

Sanchez, R. (1993). "Strategic Flexibility, Firm Organization, and Managerial Work in Dynamic Markets: A Strategic Options Perspective." *Advances in Strategic Management*, 9: 251–91.

Sanchez, R. (2001). "Managing Knowledge into Competence: The Five Learning Cycles of the Competent Organization." In R. Sanchez (ed.) *Knowledge Management and Organizational Competence*. Oxford: Oxford University Press.

Sanchez, R. (2005). "Knowledge Management and Organizational Learning: Fundamental Concepts for Theory and Practice." In B. Renzl, K. Matzler, and H. Hinterhuber (eds), *The Future of Knowledge Management*, London: Palgrave Macmillan, 29–61.

Sansom, G. (1931). *Japan: A Short Cultural History*. London: Barrie and Jenkins.

Santalainen, T. (2006). *Strategic Thinking*. Helsinki: Talentum.

Santiago, A. and Benito, R. M. (2008). "Connectivity Degrees in the Threshold Preferential Attachment Model." *Physica A*, 387: 2365–2376.

Schumpeter, J. (1934/1959). *The Theory of Economic Development*. Boston, MA: Harvard University Press (republished by Oxford University Press 1978).

Schutz, A. (1972). *The Phenomenology of the Social World*. London: Heinemann.

Selznick, P. (1949). *TVA and the Grass Roots*. Berkeley: University of California Press.

Shannon, C. E. (1948). "The Mathematical Theory of Communication." *Bell System Technical Journal*, 27, 379–423, 623–656.

Bibliography

Shannon, C. E. and Weaver, W. (1963). *The Mathematical Theory of Communication.* Urbana: University of Illinois Press.

Shapin, S. and Shaffer, S. (1985). *Leviathan and the Air Pump: Hobbes, Boyle, and the Experimental Life.* Princeton, NJ: Princeton University Press.

Shapiro, C. and Varian, H. (1999). *Information Rules: A Strategic Guide to the Network Economy.* Boston: Harvard Business School Press.

Sheffi, Y. (2005). *The Resilient Enterprise.* Cambridge, MA: The MIT Press.

Simon, H. A. (1962). "The Architecture of Complexity." *Proceedings of the American Philosophical Society,* 106: 467–482.

Simon, H.A. (1982) *Models of Bounded Rationality.* 2 vols. Cambridge, MA: MIT Press.

Simon, H. A. (1986). "Rationality in Psychology and Economics." In R. M. Hogarth and M. W. Reder (eds), *Rational Choice: The Contrast between Economics and Psychology.* Chicago, IL: University of Chicago Press.

Simon, H. A. (1999). "Coping with Complexity." In Groupe de Recherche sur l'Adaptation la Systémique et la Complexité Economique (GRASCE) (eds), Entre systémique et complexité chemin faisant... Mélange en hommage à Jean-Louis Le Moigne, Paris: Presses Universitaires de France, 233–240.

Sinha, S., Chatterjee, A., Chakraborti, A., and Chakrabarti, B. K. (2011). *Econophysics: An Introduction.* Weinheim, Germany: Wiley-VCH.

Sipser, M. (1997). *Introduction to the Theory of Computation.* Boston: PWS Publishing Co.

Siu, H. F. (1989) *Agents and Victims in South China.* New Haven, CT: Yale University Press.

Skinner, G. W. (1964) "Marketing and Social Structure in Rural China: Part I." *Journal of Asian Studies,* 24 (1), 3–43.

Skinner, G. W. (1965a). "Marketing and Social Structure in Rural China: Part II." *Journal of Asian Studies,* 24 (2): 195–228.

Skinner, G. W. (1965b). "Marketing and Social Structure in Rural China: Part III." *Journal of Asian Studies,* 24 (3): 363–99.

Slywotsky, A. (1996). *Value Migration.* Boston, MA: Harvard Business School Press.

Snijders, T. A. B. and Bosker, R. (1999). *Multilevel Analysis: An Introduction of Basic and Advanced Multilevel Modeling.* Thousand Oaks, CA: Sage.

Snowden, D. (2011). *Max Boisot 1943–2011.* <http://www.cognitive-edge.com/blog/entry/3272/max-boisot-1943-2011/>.

Solé, R. V., Alonso, D., Bascompte, J., and Manrubia, S. (2001). "On the Fractal Nature of Ecological and Macroevolutionary Dynamics." *Fractals,* 9: 1–16.

Solinger, D. J. (1989). "Urban Reform and Relational Contracting in Post-Mao China: An Interpretation of the Transition from Plan to Market." *Studies in Comparative Communism,* 23: 171–185.

Solinger, D. J. (1993). *China's Transition from Socialism: Statist Legacies and Market Reforms, 1980–1990.* Armonk, NY: M.E. Sharpe.

Song, D.-M., Jiang, Z.-Q., and Zhou W.-X. (2009). "Statistical Properties of World Investment Networks." *Physica A,* 388 (12): 2450–2460.

Sornette, D. (2002). "Predictability of Catastrophic Events." *Proceedings of the National Academy of Sciences,* 99 (Suppl. 1): 2522–29.

Sornette, D. (2003). *Why Stock Markets Crash: Critical Events in Complex Financial Systems*. Princeton, NJ: Princeton University Press.

Sornette, D. and Zhou, W.-X. (2006). "Predictability of Large Future Changes in Major Financial Indices." *International Journal of Forecasting*, 22: 153–68.

Souma, W., Aoyama, H., Fujiwara, Y., Ikeda, Y., Iyetomi, H., and Kaizoji, T. (2006). "Correlation in Business Networks." *Physica A*, 370 (1): 151–5.

Sprat, T. (1662). *A History of the Royal Society*.

Stacey, R. D. (1995). "The Science of Complexity: An Alternative Perspective for Strategic Change Processes." *Strategic Management Journal*, 16: 477–95.

Stanley, M. H. R., Amaral, L. A. N., Buldyrev, S. V., Havlin, S., Leschhorn, H., Maass, P., Salinger, M. A., and Stanley, H. E. (1996). "Scaling Behavior in the Growth of Companies." *Nature*, 379: 804–6.

Star, S. L. and Griesemer, J. R. (1989). Institutional Ecology, "'Translations' and Boundary Objects: Amateurs and Professionals in Berkeley's Museum of Vertebrate Zoology 1907–39." *Social Studies of Science*, 19 (4), 387–420.

Starbuck, W. H. (1965). "Mathematics and Organization Theory." In J. G. March, (ed.), *Handbook of Organizations*. Rand-McNally, Chicago, IL, 335–386.

Starbuck, W. H. (n.d.). "Learning from Extreme Cases." <http://www.pages.stern.nyu.edu/~wstarbuc/>.

Staw, B. M., Sandelands, L. E., and Dutton, J. E. (1981). "Threat-Rigidity Effects in Organizational Behavior: A Multilevel Analysis." *Administrative Science Quarterly*, 26: 501–24.

Steinfeld, E. (2010). *Playing Our Game: Why China's Economic Rise Doesn't Threaten the West*. New York: Oxford University Press.

Stores (2010). "Despite Growth, China Remains Fragmented Retail Market." <http://www.stores.org/despite-growth>, accessed 12 August 2012.

Su, S. (1994). "The Dynamics of Market-Oriented Growth of Chinese Firms in Post-Maoist China: An Institutional Approach." Unpublished Ph.D. thesis, Cornell University.

Suder, G. G. S. (ed.) (2006). *Corporate Strategies Under International Terrorism and Adversity*, Cheltenham, UK: Edward Elgar, 38–55.

Supply Chain Digest (2011). "State of the Logistics Union 2011." <http://www.scdigest.com/assets/FirstThoughts/11-06-16.php?cid=4641>, accessed 12 August 2012.

Surowiecki, J. (2004). *The Wisdom of Crowds*. Doubleday, New York.

Taleb, N. (2007). *The Black Swan. The Impact of the Highly Improbable*. London: Penguin Books.

Thagard, P. (2006). *Hot Cognition*. Cambridge, MA: The MIT Press.

Thaler, R. (1992). *The Winner's Curse*. Princeton, NJ: Princeton University Press.

The Economist. (1994a). "China's Communists: The Road from Tiananmen." 4 June: 23–25.

The Economist. (1994b). "Democracy and Growth." 27 August: 17–19.

The Economist. (1995a). "A Survey of China." 18 March: Supplement: 1–26.

The Economist. (1995b). "Emerging Market Indicators." 7 May: 136.

The Economist (2007). "The Nimble Sumo." 384 (August 4): 57.

Thelen, E. and Smith, L. (1994). *A Dynamic Systems Approach to the Development of Cognition and Action*. Cambridge, MA: MIT Press.

Bibliography

Toffler, A. (1970) *Future Shock*. New York: Bantam Books.

Tönnies, F. (1955). *Community and Society [Gemeinschaft und Gesellschaft]*. London: Routledge.

Toyne, B. and Nigh, D. (eds) (1997). *International Business: an Emerging Vision*. Columbia SC: University of South Carolina Press.

Traweek, S. (1988). *Beamtimes and Lifetimes: The World of High Energy Physicists*. Cambridge, MA.: Harvard University Press.

Tu, W. (1993). "Introduction: Cultural perspectives." In Special Issue on China in Transformation, *Daedalus*, 122: vii–xxiii.

Tuertscher, P. (2008). "The Emergence of Architecture in Modular Systems: Coordination across Boundaries at ATLAS, CERN." Thesis No. 3578. University of St. Gallen.

Uhl-Bien, M., Marion, R., and McKelvey, B. (2007). "Complex Leadership: Shifting Leadership from the Industrial Age to the Knowledge Era." *Leadership Quarterly*, 18: 298–18.

Ungar, J. and Chan, A. (1995). "China, Corporatism, and the East Asian Model." *Australian Journal of Chinese Affairs*, 33: 29–53.

Vasconcelos, G. L. (2004). "A Guided Walk Down Wall Street: An Introduction to Econophysics." *Brazillian Journal of Physics*, 34 (3): 1039–65.

Vaughan, D. (1996). *The Challenger Launch Decision*. Chicago, IL: The University of Chicago Press.

Vermeij, G. (2004). *Nature: An Economic History*. Princeton, NJ: Princeton University Press.

Vuola, O. (2006). "Innovation and New Business through Mutually Beneficial Collaboration and Proactive Procurement." Dissertation, HEC Lausanne.

Wagner, J. F. (2006). "Transfer in Pieces." *Cognition and Instruction*, 24 (1): 1–71.

Walras, L. (1954). *Elements of Pure Economics*. Homewood, IL: Richard D. Irwin.

Wang, S. (1993). "Basic framework and advanced pattern of the economic systems of the socialist market economy." *China's Economic Structure Reform*, 1: 16–18.

Wank, D. L. (1995). "Private Business, Bureaucracy, and Political Alliance in a Chinese City." *Australian Journal of Chinese Affairs*, 33: 55–71.

Wasserman, S. and Faust, K. (1994). *Social Network Analysis*. New York: Cambridge University Press.

Watts, D. J. (2003). *Six Degrees: The Science of a Connected Age*. New York: Norton.

Watts, D. J. and Strogatz, S. H. (1998). "Collective Dynamics of 'Small-World' Networks." *Nature*, 393 (6684): 440–42.

Weber, M. (1964). *The Theory of Social and Economic Organization*. Trans., A. M. Henderson and T. Parsons. New York: Free Press.

Weick, K. (1995) *Sensemaking in Organizations*. Thousand Oaks, CA: Sage.

Weick, K. E. (1979). *The Social Psychology of Organizing*. Reading, MA: Addison-Wesley.

Weick, K. E. (1993). "The Collapse of Sensemaking in Organizations: The Mann Gulch Disaster." *Administrative Science Quarterly*, 38: 628–652.

Weick, K. E. and Sutcliffe, K. M. (2001). *Managing the Unexpected*. San Francisco, CA: Jossey-Bass.

Weick, K. E., Sutcliffe, K. M., and Obstfeld, D. (1999). "Organizing for High Reliability: Processes of Collective Mindfulness." *Research in Organizational Behavior*, 21: 81–123.

Bibliography

Weitzman, M. L. and Xu, C. (1993). "Chinese Township Village Enterprises as Vaguely Defined Cooperatives." *Development Economics Research Program*, London School of Economics, CP no. 26, September.

Wernerfelt, B. (1984). "A Resource-Based View of the Firm." *Strategic Management Journal*, 5 (2): 171–180.

West, B. J. and Deering, B. (1995). *The Lure of Modern Science: Fractal Thinking*. Singapore: World Scientific.

White, H. C. (1963). *An Anatomy of Kinship: Mathematical Models for Structures of Cumulated Roles*. Englewood Cliffs, NJ: Prentice-Hall.

Whitley, R. (1999). *Divergent Capitalisms*. Oxford, Oxford University Press.

Whitley, R. D. (1991). "The Social Construction of Business Systems in East Asia." *Organization Studies*, 12: 1–28.

Whitley, R. D. (1992). *Business Systems in East Asia: Firms, Markets and Societies*. London: Sage.

Whitley, R. D. (1994) "Dominant Forms of Economic Organization in Market Economies." *Organization Studies*, 15: 153–182.

Wiener, N. (1948). *Cybernetics*. Cambridge, MA: MIT Press.

Williamson, J. (1989). "What Washington Means by Policy Reforms." In J. Williamson (ed.), *Latin American Readjustment: How Much Has Happened?* Washington DC, Institute for International Economics.

Williamson, O. (1975). *Markets and Hierarchies: Analysis and Antitrust Implications*. New York: Free Press.

Williamson, O. (1985). *The Economic Institutions of Capitalism*. New York: Free Press.

Wong, R. B. and Perdue, P. C. (1992). "Grain Markets and Food Supplies in Eighteenth-Century Hunan." In T. G. Rawski and L. M. Li (eds), *Chinese History in Economic Perspective*, Berkeley: University of California Press, 126–144.

World Bank (1985). *China: Long-Term Issues and Options*. Baltimore, MD: Johns Hopkins University Press.

Xu, C. (2011). "The Fundamental Institutions of China's Reforms and Development." *Journal of Economic Literature*, 49: 1076–1151.

Yami, S., Castaldo, S., Dagnino, G. B. and Le Roy, F. (eds) (2010). *Competition: Winning Strategies for the 21st Century*. Cheltenham: Edward Elgar.

Yin, R. K. (1989). *Case Study Research: Design and Methods*. London: Sage.

Young, A. (2000). "The Razor's Edge: Distortions and Incremental Reform in the People's Republic of China." *Quarterly Journal of Economics*, 115 (4): 1091–1135.

Ziman, J. (1968). *Public Knowledge: The Social Dimension of Science*. Cambridge: Cambridge University Press.

Zipf, G. K. (1929) "Relative Frequency as a Determinant of Phonetic Change." *Harvard Studies in Classical Philology*, 40: 1–95.

Zipf, G. K. (1949). *Human Behavior and the Principle of Least Effort*. New York: Hafner.

Zucker, L. G. (1986). "Production of Trust: Institutional Sources of Economic Structure, 1840–1920." In L. L. Cummings and B. M. Staw (eds), *Research in Organizational Behavior*, 8: 53–111. Greenwich, CT: JAI Press.

Zurek, W. H. (1990). *Complexity, Entropy and the Physics of Information*. Reading, MA: Perseus.

Index

Page numbers in *italics* refer to illustrations.

abduction 82
  scalable 82–3
abductive reasoning 82
absorption of knowledge 11, 122–3, 244
  ATLAS project analysis 231
abstraction 10, 25, 114–15, 145, 170
  ATLAS project analysis 230–1
  Chinese bias against 25
  knowledge diffusibility and 121, *122*
abstract symbolic knowledge 183, *183*, 244
action learning, China 170, 183–6
  resistance to 185–6
  see also learning; management education
adaptive systems 74–5
adaptive tension 64, 79, 85, 101
  maximum adaptive capability 65
additive-independent data points 69–70
adhocracies 151–3, *153*, 162, 244
  see also ATLAS Collaboration, CERN, Geneva
adjacent possible 234, *235*
advertising 113
agents 70, 113, 226–7
  knowledge diffusion 121
Allen, P. M. 94
alliances, China 34, 38–9, 41, 45
  joint ventures 38, 45
Alstom 135
Anderson, C. 84
Anderson, Philip 65
andragogy 182
Andriani, P. 67, 85
anticipation 103
AOL–Time-Warner merger 135
Arthur, Brian 65
articulation 121
Ashby, Ross 14, 63, 71–3, 93, 97
  Law of Requisite Variety 14, 63, 71–83, 93
Ashby Space 14, 72, *73*, 94, 103–4
  information processing in 79–83
  ontological regimes 76–9, *76*, 94–5
ATLAS Collaboration, CERN, Geneva 10, 15, 137, 148–54, 160–6, 210
  detector as a boundary object 152–3, *153*, 162–4
  future research 233–5
  ICT role 153, 164
  I-Space analysis 151–3, 229, 230–2
  organization 149–50, *150*, 237–40, 243–4
  performance spidergraph 149–50, *149*
  shared values and beliefs 152–3, 162, 164
  simulations 164–5
atomism 62, 101
attention 121
authority 239
autonomous learning 171
Axtell, R. L. 68–9, 87

Bak, Per 65, 89, 90
bandwidth effect 148
basic research 238
  value of 229, 232–5, 239–40
  see also science
Bateson, G. 113
beliefs 133–4
  shared values and beliefs 152–3, 162, 164
Bergere, Marie-Claire 201
Berle, A. A. 38
Bhaskar, Roy 158
Biggart, N. W. 46
big science 15, 155, 156–7, 159–61, 238, 244
  see also ATLAS Collaboration, CERN, Geneva
Birmingham Business School 8
  PhD program management 188–9
Bolton, P. 38
Boltzmann, Ludwig 65
boundary objects 152–3, *153*, 162–4
BP 135, 136
Bruun, O. 28, 41–2
bureaucratic cultures 6, 24, 50, 145, 162
  Chinese experience 24, 26, 199–200, 201
  European experience 23–4
  position in the *I-Space* 6, *146*, 162
butterfly events 63, 66, 77, 79
butterfly-levers 87–8
Byrd, W. A. 33

Index

C-Space 3–4, 21, 50, 130
    Chinese modernization analysis 21–9, 46, 50, 57
    development 7
Californian earthquakes 88
Canals, Agustí 133, 137
capabilities 117
Carnot, N. 206
centralization, China 40
centrifugal business system 33
CERN, Geneva 162
    see also ATLAS Collaboration
chaos 151
    edge of 65, 151, 243
chaos theory 64–5
chaotic regime 76, 77, 94–5, 147, *147*
Chen, D. 37
China 12–13, 199–200, 208
    Boisot's experience in 7–8
    business systems 13, 29–33, *30*, 55
    capitalism form 35–9
    collectively owned enterprise 30–1, 37–8
    convergence towards a market order 54–5, 201
    domestic transaction costs 56–7, 216–18
    economic order 19–21, 29–48, 52–3
    economic reform 26–7, 49–51, 56
    entrepreneur training program 186–7, 188
    globalization impact 54, 57
    government role 39–43
    growth 26–8
    ICT impact 54–5, 58
    institutional arbitrage 218–20
    internationalization of firms 56–7, 214–18
    management education 173–7, 183–8
    managerial work 56
    market arrangements 33–5
    market fragmentation 215
    marketized firms 30, 31–2
    modernization compared to Europe 21–48, *44*, 51–2
    network capitalism 13, 44, 46–7, 51, 53
    non-marketized firms 30, 31
    non-state sector 28, 29
    power 58
China-EEC Management Programme (CEMP) 7, 170, 173–9
    innovations in management education 183–8
    Learning Cube interpretation 177–8
China-Europe International Business School (CEIBS), Shanghai 7
Chinese Management Centre, Hong Kong University 8
Christensen, C. 86
city size 67
clan cultures 6, 21, 50, 145, 162
    China 34, 44, 45
    coordinating role of clan values 152–3
    position in the I-Space 6, *146*, 162
    see also ATLAS Collaboration, CERN, Geneva
codification 10, 21–3, *22*, 53, 115, 144
    ATLAS project analysis 230
    Chinese experience 25, 28, 43–4, 53, 184–5
    C-Space 21, *22*, 50
    European modernization experience 23–4, 47
    knowledge diffusibility and 121, *122*
codification-diffusion (C-D) framework 3–4, 206
    see also C-Space
cognitive complexity 147, 246
cognitive inertia 81–2
Cohen, Jack 210
Cohen, M. L. 35
collaboration 10
    virtual collaboration 143
    see also ATLAS Collaboration, CERN, Geneva
collectively owned enterprise, China 30–1, 37–8
Columbia space shuttle disaster 97
communication 144–5, 201, 241
    see also information and communication technologies (ICTs)
compartmentalization 225
competences 117
complex adaptive system (CAS) 136
complexity 63, 94, 147, 243
    bridge between Modernism and Postmodernism 100–4
    Chinese approach 53
    cognitive complexity 147, 246
    emergent complexity 95, 97
    organizational complexity 13–14, 102
    relational complexity 147, 246
complexity science 64–9, *64*
complex regime 76, 77, 83, 147, *147*
conceptual definitions 227
concreteness 171
connectionism 209–10
connectivity 63, 85–7, 101
    ICT role 153
conservation of energy principle 206
Contract Responsibility System (CRS), China 37
convergence hypothesis 54–5, 201, 203
conversational teaching style 190–2
coordination
    big science projects 156–7, 163–4
    managerial 87, 144–5
    organizational 144
copyrights 126
corruption, China 28, 42
counter-terrorism efforts 96–9
Courtaulds 136
Cox, Benita 209
culture 6, 50, 246–7

Index

convergence 203
  epistemic 162
  in the *I-Space* 6, *6*
  processes of cultural influence 202–4
  see also C-Space
cybernetics 72

data 113–14, 157, 209, 242
  flow 121
  see also information
data overload 111, 118
data processing 79–83, *81*
decentralization 23
  Chinese experience 24, 26, 32, 40–1, 44, 51–2, 214–15
  European experience 21
deep simplicity 67, 86
Defence Science and Technology Laboratories, UK Ministry of Defence 135
degrees of freedom 94
DeLanda, Manuel 205
Deutsch Post 135
diffusion of knowledge 11, 21, *22*
  ATLAS project analysis 231
  C-Space 21, *22*, 50
  ICT effects 147–8
directed learning 171
disaster avoidance 97–9
discourse 10
dissipative structures 64
Douglas, Mary 200, 207
Drucker, Peter 3
Dunning, J. H. 202
Dupuit, Jules 209

economic organization 224–5
  China 19–21, 29–48, 52–3
economic reform, China 26–7, 49–51, 56
economic value 5
  see also value
econophysics 63, 64–9, 90–1, 99–100
edge of chaos 65, 243
  adhocracies 151
edge of order 64
education 15–16, 181–2
  Chinese entrepreneur training program 186–7, 188
  Global Learning Journey, Dubai executives 187–8, 192
  see also learning; management education
Edvinsson, L. 116
Ekelund, R. B. 208–9
emergence 65–6, 89, 210
emergent complexity 95, 97
emergent scalability dynamics 88–90
emergent strategies 152
encyclopedias 109

Enron collapse 97
entrepreneurial behaviors 90
entrepreneurs 86
  Chinese entrepreneur training program 186–7, 188
  firm as entrepreneur 116
epistemic cultures 162
epistemology 182
ESADE Business School, University of Ramon Llull, Barcelona 8
Escoffier, N. 88
Euro-Arab Management School, Granada 8
Euro-Asia Centre, INSEAD 7, 8
European modernization compared to China 21–9
evolution 203
experiential knowledge 183, *183*, 244
explanatory power 67
extreme outcomes 61–4, 99–100, 102
  Ashby's *Law of Requisite Variety* 71–83
  complexity science 64–9
  Gaussian perspective 69–70
  organization science implications 69–71, 83–90
  Paretian 70–1

farsight 95–6
fastsight 95, 96
Faure, D. 37, 39
fief-based cultures 6, 21, 50–1, 145–6, 162
  iron law of fiefs 24, 28, 51
  position in the *I-Space* 6, *146*, 162
Fine, C. H. 97
firm
  as entrepreneur 116
  knowledge-based theory (KBT) 131–2
  resource-based view (RBV) 131–2
  size 68–9, 87
First Law of Thermodynamics 206
Five Learning Cycles Model 222
flow 206
  data 121
  information 206–7, 210
foresight 95
forgetting *see* unlearning
fractals 66–7, 210

Galison, Peter 161–2
Gaussian ontology 62, 69–70
Gell-Mann, Murray 63, 65, 67, 72, 76–7, 86
Gellner, E. 42
globalization 54, 57, 92
  intellectual property protection issues 134
Global Learning Journey, Dubai executives 187–8, 192
governance 127
government role, China 39–43
  local government legitimacy 42

277

Index

Greene, W. H. 65, 83
Griffiths, Dorothy 7, 136
group knowledge 115–17
group learning 171
growth
    China 26–8
    firms 68–9

Habermas, J. 23
Hage, J. 63
Hahn, Kurt 7
Hall, E. T. 23
Hamilton, G. G. 46
Han, Kyeong 137
Hayek, Frierich 98
headless chicken strategy 74, 78, *78*
Hebb, Donald 209
hierarchies *see* markets and hierarchies continuum
Higgs particle 150, 161, 230, 237
history, study of 199–202
Holland, John 65, 66
Hong Kong 218
Hong Kong University Business School 8
H-share companies, Hong Kong 218
hybrid firms, China 38–9

I-Space 4–6, *4*, 113, 130, 134–5, 144–8, *145*, 155, 228, 242–3
    ATLAS collaboration analysis 151–3, 229, 230–2
    Chinese business system analysis 13, 54
    cultures in 6, *6*
    examples of use 135
    future research 244–6
    history study 199–202
    ICT impact 147–8, *148*
    innovative nature of 182–6, 192
    institutional positions 6, *6*, 145–6, *146*, 162, *163*
    knowledge evolution 10
    knowledge transfer 193–4
    knowledge types 183, *183*
    mapping knowledge assets 136–7
    simulating knowledge asset evolution 137–8
I-Space Institute 11, 15, 130, 138, 210
idiographic science 62
Ihrig, Martin 15
imagination 119
impacting 122–3
    ATLAS project analysis 231
Imperial College, London 8
independent thought 119
individual learning 171
information 113–14, 157–9, 208, 242
    in big science 161–2
    complexity 147
    flow 206–7, 210
    physics of 159
    Shannon's information theory 156, 158–9
    structuring of 144–5
    value 124
    see also data; knowledge
information and communication technologies (ICTs) 52, 111, 147–8
    bandwidth effect 148
    China 54–5, 58
    diffusion effect 147–8
    impact in the *I-Space* 147–8, *148*
    knowledge diffusion 121
    role in big science projects 153, 164
information overload 111, 118
information processing 79–83, *81*
Information Space *see* I-Space
innovation 208
    in management education 186–94
    value of 240
institutional arbitrage, China 218–20
institutional order 22–3
institutions 6
    in the *C-Space* 22
    in the *I-Space* 6, *6*, 145–6, *146*, 162, *163*
intellectual capital 116–17
intellectual property rights 126, 134
intelligent systems 74–5, 88
interdependency 101
International Futures Forum 9
internationalization 202, 213
    China 56–7, 214–18
internet use, China 58
    see also information and communication technologies (ICTs)
interorganizational relations
    in Asian capitalism 46
    China 25, 32, 48
    see also networking
iron law of fiefs 24, 28, 51

Japan 25, 201, 208
Judge Institute of Management Studies, University of Cambridge 8

Kaminstein, South Africa 189–91
Kauffman, Stuart 65
Kluckhohn, C. 50
Knorr-Cetina, Karin 161–2
knowledge 112, 113–17, 133, 157–8, 242–3
    absorption 11, 122–3, 231, 244
    acquisition *see* learning
    articulation 121
    in big science 161–2
    creation 116, 156, 245
    diffusion 11, 21, *22*, 50, 121, 147–8, 231
    discarding (unlearning) 118, 120, 128

future research 244–7
generation 119–20
group knowledge 115–17
impacting 122–3, 231
integration 243
internalization 122–3
knowing as a social phenomenon 112
power issues 112–13
rivalrous knowledge 165
sharing 121
social knowing 120–1
state interest in 110
structure 4–6, *4*
tacit knowledge 115, 117, 120–1, 134
technological versus scientific knowledge 110
transfer 192–4, 245
types of 183, *183*
see also information; *I-Space*; knowledge assets; knowledge management
knowledge assets 133–4
  mapping in the *I-Space* 136–7
  paradox of value 125–7, *126*, 232–3
  simulating evolution of in the *I-Space* 137–8
  strategic knowledge assets 133–4
  tacit knowledge 135
knowledge-based theory (KBT) of the firm 131–2
knowledge management 109–13, 117, 243
  demand-pull approach 133
  governance 127
  historical background 109–11
  outstanding issues 112–13
  paradox of value 125–7, *126*
  product-push approach 132
  recent interest in 111–12
  strategic management 14–15, 130–3
  see also strategy
Kroeber, A. L. 50

Landes, David 199
language 101
Large Hadron Collider (LHC), CERN 144, 148–9, 160, 210, 230, 237
  see also ATLAS Collaboration, CERN, Geneva
Lavoisier, A. 206
Law of Excess Variety 94
Law of Large Numbers 65
Law of Requisite Complexity 14, 104, 243
  cognitive interpretation 72–5
Law of Requisite Variety 14, 63, 71–83, 93
learning 15–16, 118, 169–70
  abstraction-concreteness dimension (ACD) 170–1, *172*
  action learning 170, 183–6
  cultural constraints 173
  direction-autonomy dimension (DAD) 171, *172*

individual-group dimension (IGD) 171, *172*
knowledge transfer 192–4
opportunities 119
social learning 118
strategies 169
unlearning 118, 120, 128
see also education; Social Learning Cycle (*SLC*)
Learning Cube 170–3, *172*
  application to China-EEC Management Programme (CEMP) 177–9
least-effort theory 90
lever point phenomena 66
Lewin, K. 62–3
life-world 75
Li, L. M. 35
localism, China 214
locality 124–5

Ma & Pa stores 83–4
McDonalds 87
McGrath, R. G. 233
MacMillan, Ian 15, 133, 192, 210
Madhavan, R. 89
management education
  China 173–7, 183–8
  design innovations 186–9
  knowledge reception innovations 194
  knowledge transfer innovations 192–4
  methodological/instructional innovations 189–92
  philosophical innovations 182–6
  technological innovations 192
management inquiry 103
management training, China 173–7
managerial behaviors 90
managerial work
  China 56
  coordination 87, 144–5
Mantegna, R. N. 66
mapping knowledge assets 136–7
March, J. G. 97
marginalism 209
market cultures 6, 50, 145, 162
  Chinese market arrangements 33–5, 39
  position in the *I-Space* 6, *146*, 162
  socially distributed processing 98
market fragmentation, China 215
markets and hierarchies continuum 20–1, 43–4, 50, 207
Marshall, Alfred 209
Marxism-Leninism 24–5
maximum adaptive capability 65
meaning 200
melting zone 65
message 159
Meyer, M. W. 56–7

279

Index

mindfulness 89
Mintzberg, H. 151, 152
modernism 100–1
modernization 23–5, 43–4, 51
   China versus Europe 21–48, *44*, 51–2
Moles, Veronica 136
Moral, B. 89

narrative knowledge 183, *183*, 244
NASA Columbia space shuttle disaster 97
nation-state 39–40, 43
Nee, V. 20, 30–2, 52
neoclassical economics 206–7
network capitalism, China 13, 44, 46–7, 51, 53
networking 11, 45–7, 53, 128
   China 34–5, 44–6, 53
   network coordination 143–4
   social networks 96
neuronal activation patterns 114
Nexus of Rules theory of economic organizing 224–5
Nonaka, I. 157
nonlinearities 66
Nordberg, Markus 160, 210
Nordberg, Max 160
normal distribution 69–70, 101
North, D. C. 35
North, Douglass 199
Norway effect 66

options 233
ordered regime *76*, 77, 83, 147, *147*
organizational complexity 13–14, 109
organizational coordination 144
organization science 69–71, 83–90, 91–2

Page, S. E. 88
paradox of value 125–7, *126*, 232–3
Paretian ontology 62, 82–3
   butterfly-levers 87–8
   connectivity 85–7
   organization science implications 83–90
Pareto-adaptive strategy 80
Pareto distribution 67, *68*, 70–1, 91, 101–2, *101*, *102*
Pareto, V. 66
Park, J. W. 89
patents 126
pattern recognition/processing 80–1, *81*, 94, 95–6, 119
pedagogy 182
Peirce, C. S. 82
People's Republic of China (PRC) *see* China
Perdue, P. C. 35
Perrow, C. 61
personal relationships in transacting
   China 24–6, 32–4, 41–2, 51

Europe 23
perspectives, breadth of 226
Peters, T. 47
phase transition 64, 89
physics of information 159
Pickering, Andrew 162
PL (power law) distributions 67–71, *68*, 82–3, 101–2, *101*, *102*
Polanyi, Michael 117
Popper, Karl R. 156, 157, 158
positivism 100
postmodernism 100–4
power 57–8, 247
   China 58
   knowledge as source of 112–13
power-law science 85
   see also PL (power law) distributions
Prigogine, Ilya 64, 205
principle of least effort 90
probability distribution 69
problem-solving 10
property rights 24, 35–6
   China 29, 36–9, 44–5
   group property rights 116
   intellectual property 126, 134

quasi-capitalism, China 39

Rawski, T. G. 35
Red chip companies, Hong Kong 218
Redding, S. Gordon 45–6, 54–5
reductionism 67, 82
reductionist regularities 76
regularities 62
relational complexity 147, 246
relational transacting, China 24–6, 32–4, 41–2, 51
research and development (R&D) 110
   see also basic research
resource-based view (RBV) of the firm 131–2
responsibility 239
Richardson, G. B. 34
robustness techniques 102
routinizing strategy 74, 80

scalability 66, 84–5
   emergent scalability dynamics 88–90
scalable abduction 82–3
scale-free regularities 77, 82, 89
scale-free theories (SFTs) 67, *68*
scanning 10
   ATLAS project analysis 230
schema 63, 72–3
schema development 76–9
   information processing 79–83
   limit to schema-building capacity 76
Schumpeter, J. 27, 86
science 155–7, 230

Index

big science 15, 156–7, 159–61, 238, 244
  knowledge creation 156
  see also basic research
science of the unique 85
Second Law of Thermodynamics 206
segmented society 42
self-organization 65, 205, 210, 239
  neurological 209
self-organized criticality (SOC) 89–90
September 11 World Trade Center attack 97, 98
SFTs *see* scale-free theories (SFTs)
shadow options 233
Shannon's information theory 156, 158–9, 206
shared values and beliefs 152–3, 162, 164
Siemens 135
silo effects 98
SimISpace 137, 210
SimISpace2 137–8
Simon, H. A. 89, 97
Skinner, G. W. 35
SLC *see* Social Learning Cycle (*SLC*)
Smith, Adam 199
Snider Entrepreneurial Research Center, Wharton School, University of Pennsylvania 8, 11, 15, 129
social knowing 120–1
social learning 118
Social Learning Cycle (*SLC*) 5, *5*, 9–11, 123, *123*, 130
  absorption 11
  application to education 16
  ATLAS collaboration analysis 230–2
  diffusion 11
  information flow 206–7
  phases of *124*
  problem-solving 10
  scanning 10
socially distributed processing 98
social networks 96
socio-informatics 206–7
Solinger, D. J. 32, 33–4, 36–7
South Africa, teaching program 189–91
Soviet Union 24, 50
Standard Model of particle physics 161, 231, 237–8
Stanley, Eugene 65, 66, 68
Stanley, M. H. R. 84
Starbuck, W. H. 63
state 39–40, 43, 45
  government role, China 39–43
state-owned enterprises, China 30, 31, 37, 42, 215
strategic foresight 95
strategy 127–8, 129
  emergent strategies 152
  knowledge-based strategy 133–5
  strategic knowledge management 14–15, 130–3

structural capital 116
Surowiecki, J. 88
Su, S. 38–9

tacit knowledge 115, 117, 120–1
  as strategic knowledge asset 134
Takeuchi, H. 157
teaching style 190–2
Templeton College, University of Oxford 8
terrorism surveillance 96–9
Tesco Fresh & Easy stores 84
Thomas, R. P. 35
Toffler, Alvin 151
township-village enterprises (TVEs), China 31, 37–8, 42
trading zone 161–2
Training Centre for Economic Cadres of the State Economic Commission, Beijing 7
transactional coverage 23
Traweek, Sharon 162
Tu, W. 41, 43

uncertainty management 232, 233–5
Universitat Oberta de Catalunya, Barcelona 8
unlearning 118, 120, 128

value 125
  basic research 229, 233–5, 239–40
  knowledge goods 124, 125–8
  maximum value in the *I-Space* 125, *126*
  paradox of 125–7, *126*, 232–3
  utility and scarcity relationship 125
varieties of capitalism 203
variety 80, 94
Vaughan, D. 61
virtual collaboration 143
volatility 234

Walmart 83–4
Walter, Grey 209
Wank, D. L. 41
Waters, J. 152
Weick, K. E. 87, 89, 91
Weitzman, M. L. 37
Whitley, R. D. 29, 31–3
Williamson, O. 20–1, 23, 34, 50–1, 97, 207–8
Wong, R. B. 35
World Trade Center attack 97, 98

Xi'an Jiaotong University Management School, China 8
Xing, Guo Liang 56
Xu, C. 37

Yin, R. K. 83

Zipf, G. F. 90